Political theory as we knc
theory from political tl
modern era. But its own ir.
of the nineteenth century has left it still entrammelled in the suspicions
and inhibitions from which it has wanted to break free. The author con-
tends that to pass beyond suspicion and totalised criticism of politics and
to achieve a positive reconstruction of political thought, theology must
reach back behind the modern tradition, achieving a fuller, less selective
reading of the Scriptures and learning from an older politico-theological
discourse which flourished in the patristic, medieval and Reformation
periods. Central to that discourse was a series of questions about authority,
generated by Jesus' proclamation of the Kingdom of God.

The desire of the nations

THE DESIRE OF THE NATIONS

Rediscovering the roots of political theology

OLIVER O'DONOVAN

Regius Professor of Moral and Pastoral Theology
University of Oxford, and Canon of Christ Church

PUBLISHED BY THE PRESS SYNDICATE OF THE UNIVERSITY OF CAMBRIDGE
The Pitt Building, Trumpington Street, Cambridge, United Kingdom

CAMBRIDGE UNIVERSITY PRESS
The Edinburgh Building, Cambridge CB2 2RU, UK
40 West 20th Street, New York, NY 10011–4211, USA
477 Williamstown Road, Port Melbourne, VIC 3207, Australia
Ruiz de Alarcón 13, 28014 Madrid, Spain
Dock House, The Waterfront, Cape Town 8001, South Africa

http://www.cambridge.org

First published 1996
First paperback edition 1999
Reprinted 2002, 2003

Printed in the United Kingdom at the University Press, Cambridge

A catalogue record for this book is available from the British Library

Library of Congress Cataloguing in Publication data
O'Donovan, Oliver.
The desire of the nations: rediscovering the roots of political theology /
Oliver O'Donovan.
    p.   cm.
Includes bibliographical references and index.
ISBN 0 521 49677 2
1. Christianity and politics. 2. Church and state. 3. Kingdom of
God. I. Title.
BR115.P7O36   1996
261.7–dc20   95–51131 CIP

ISBN 0 521 49677 2 hardback
ISBN 0 521 66516 7 paperback

Contents

Preface to the paperback edition

Saint Francis set out to discover the nakedness of Christ, and ended up the co-founder of scholastic theology. Scholastic theology, no doubt, rather than nakedness, was what his age demanded of him. I set out to discover the kingship of Christ, and ended up, as I am told, with a 'defence of Christendom'. Is this because a defence of Christendom is what our age insists that it must have? I can think of worse charges to bring against our age. But what matters is not to be *for* Christendom or *against* it – what earthly point could there be in either of these postures? – but to have such a sympathetic understanding of it that we profit from its achievements and avoid repeating its mistakes. The discussion of Christendom should be read, perhaps, not so much as a defence, but as a word of advice to its would-be critics.

The Desire of the Nations took shape as the first panel of a diptych: a historico-theological exploration of the themes surrounding the proclamation of God's kingship, preparing the way for a more deliberatively oriented exploration of the tasks of politics. I have called the two parts – contestably, perhaps, but serviceably – 'political theology' and 'political ethics'. If God grants me to complete the second, the relation of the two aspects of the enterprise will, I hope, be clearer to readers. I should stress, however, that they are not *separate* enterprises, but two moments in one train of thought. The passage from what God said to Abraham to what we are now to do about Iraq, is one which the intuition of faith may accomplish in a moment, and a preacher's exhortation in under twenty minutes. An intellectual account of it, however, can be the work of decades!

This book has met with generous interest. To all who have offered me their help by engaging with its argument, and to those who may yet do so, I would like to express my most grateful thanks. The lover of truth has no truer friend than an intelligent critic.

December 1998

Providentiae divinae circa res hominum non leve argumentum et philosophi et historici agnoscunt, in conservatione rerum publicarum.

Grotius, *De veritate religionis Christianae* 1.12.

Acknowledgments

A sabbatical term in 1986, the fruit of Oxford University's far-sighted policies towards its academic staff, was spent, as I recall, reading Hobbes's *Leviathan* very slowly; since when everything in the idea of this book has been altered except the author's excitement at discovering a Great Tradition of political theology, almost unknown to today's theologians. If Hobbes is not the best example of it – though surely Hobbes the theologian, too, deserves a rehabilitation – yet he marks the point at which the Tradition, as it were, abdicated, leaving the characteristic problems of modern political theory in its wake; and so he affords a point of view from which the contemporary value of the Tradition can be grasped afresh. The careful reader will notice that this book is only the first half of what was originally planned. To the 'political theology' a 'political ethics' demands to be added. That is not said by way of a promise, which the conditions of academic life and human mortality could hardly justify; but as an expression of hope that, if not through me then through someone more able, what is asked for may be given. If it is, then some loose ends, of which I am well aware, should be tied up, and particularly the bearing of my interpretation of political authority as power, right and tradition.

I am conscious of having many debts, conscious also that not all of them are obvious to my ungrateful memory. First, of course, to the Syndics of Cambridge University Press, and to Mr Rufus Black, of Magdalen College, Oxford, who has equipped the book with a bibliography and an index. It is hard to imagine that anything would have been accomplished without the rich library resources and technical support of Christ Church, where I am also fortunate to have a home. Successive generations of Oxford students have heard, and improved on, large portions of the book. Invitations from Fuller Theological Seminary, Pasadena, to give Payton Lectures in 1989, and from General Theological Seminary, New York, to give Paddock

Acknowledgments

Lectures in 1990, brought parts of chapter one and chapter seven respectively into focus. Then the University of Cambridge invited me to be Hulsean Lecturer in 1994, which allowed the whole argument to be layed out before an attentive and critical audience. My colleagues Professor H. G. M. Williamson of Christ Church and Professor C. C. Rowland of the Queen's College have educated me on matters where my biblical scholarship was too thin to support my ambitions to skate. A similar obligation was conferred by Dr J. C. D. Clark of All Souls' College, who piloted me through unfamiliar straits of modern history. My former colleague and lifelong friend the Very Revd N. T. Wright, Dean of Lichfield, contributed not only by commenting on drafts but by sharing his own pursuit of new readings of the Gospels which allow important matters to come into focus. None of these, I know, will feel the slightest resentment if I add that the most important intellectual influence comes from another source. I have been guided every step of the way by my wife, Joan Lockwood O'Donovan, whose own scholarly explorations opened up questions I never knew were there, and whose careful interpretative skills unravelled questions I never thought I could understand.

Prologue

Tu rex gloriae, Christe. It is striking how much *political* vocabulary the second stanza of the Te Deum contains:

> Thou art the king of glory, o Christ.
> Thou art the everlasting Son of the Father.
> When thou tookest upon thee to deliver man
> thou didst not abhor the Virgin's womb.
> When thou hadst overcome the sharpness of death,
> thou didst open the kingdom of heaven to all believers.
> We believe that thou shalt come to be our judge.
> We therefore pray thee, help thy servants,
> whom thou hast redeemed with thy precious blood.
> Make them to be numbered with thy saints
> in glory everlasting.

The words 'king', 'kingdom' and 'judge' leap to the eye; 'deliver', 'servants', 'numbered', 'saints' and 'glory' follow quickly behind. Other terms have acquired political resonances from their context: 'overcome', 'redeemed', even 'Son' and 'pray'. The general picture is a political one, quite clearly: there is a ruler; he has achieved a decisive public act of liberation; by that act he has founded and sustained a community. Yet it all belongs not within the usual sphere of earthly politics but in heaven. And at its centre is the breathtakingly unpolitical image of the Virgin's womb.

The question is, what does this paradoxical redeployment of political description, with a Virgin at its centre and heaven at its perimeter, intend to achieve? Is it meant to be the start of a new mode of political thinking? Or is it, on the contrary, a stratagem for overwhelming politics with religion, shrewdly converting the language of politics into a grand religious metaphor? When we call God 'King of kings and Lord of lords and only ruler of princes', does that place the public business of our human communities upon a surer foundation? Or does it cancel it out, turning the language of political power back against itself, so allowing us to conceive of a God above and beyond politics? The name 'political theology' is generally given to proposals of the first kind, which draw out an earthly political discourse from the political language of religious discourse. These proposals understand themselves as part of the 'postmodern' current in theology, in opposition to a traditional 'modernity' (Enlightenment and especially Kantian) to which the second line of interpretation belongs.

To avoid caricature, let us be clear that political theology (except in some ideal-type of civil religion, which may be thought of but as far as I know has never been espoused in Christendom) does not suppose a literal synonymity between the political vocabulary of salvation and the secular use of the same political terms. It postulates an analogy – not a rhetorical metaphor only, or a poetic image, but an analogy grounded in reality – between the acts of God and human acts, both of them taking place within the one public history which is the theatre of God's saving purposes and mankind's social undertakings. The Kingdom of God is not a mere kingdom, but it is a real kingdom. The point is not to reduce the semantic range of speech about God's acts to the limits of our commonplace political discussion – *that* would be reductionism indeed! – but to push back the horizon of commonplace politics and open it up to the activity of God. Earthly events of liberation, rule and community-foundation provide us with partial indications of what God is doing in human history; while, correspondingly, we must look to the horizon of God's redemptive purposes if we are to grasp the full meaning of political events that pass before our eyes. Theology needs more than scattered political images; it needs a full political conceptuality. And politics, for its part, needs a theological conceptuality. The two are concerned with the one history that finds its goal in Christ, 'the desire of the nations'.

Equally, the alternative to political theology (for which no convenient name exists, but which we may call 'modern', as a term of art) does not (except in some ideal-type of pietism which may be thought of but as far as I know has never been held) intend to banish politics from human discourse. It means simply to keep the types of discourse distinct, so that the one does not contaminate the other. Yet politics may, and indeed does, serve as a source of religious imagery, part of that broken glass whose reflections the soul transcends as it moves on and up towards the divine glory. And religion may and does shape politics through carefully guarded channels of influence that preserve a cordon sanitaire. Ethics, especially an ethics of interior motivation, provides a safe mediation, insulated against theocratic misunderstanding, by which religion may make politics more honest without presuming to make it more divine.

The renewed advocacy of political theology in our own time has had as its concern to break out of the cordon sanitaire. When that advocacy has been at its clearest, it has insisted that theology is political simply by responding to the dynamics of its own proper themes. Christ, salvation, the church, the Trinity: to speak about these has involved theologians in speaking of society, and has led them to formulate normative political ends. They have turned out to know something about the ends of politics, and perhaps about the means, too, without needing to be told. It is not a question of adapting to alien requirements or subscribing to external agenda, but of letting theology be true to its task and freeing it from a forced and unnatural detachment. Political theology tries to recover for faith in God, Christ and salvation what scepticism surrendered to mechanistic necessity. Theology must be political if it is to be evangelical. Rule out the political questions and you cut short the proclamation of God's saving power; you leave people enslaved where they ought to be set free from sin – their own sin and others'.

That is when the advocacy has been at its clearest. There may, of course, be some truth in the suspicion that political theology has gained a following among those who have grown tired of talking about God. Minds suffering from metaphysical exhaustion, weary with witnessing to the ultimate horizon in societies that exclude it from their interests, may welcome an opportunity to turn to a purely practical discipline. It did not need the political theology of the Southern hemisphere to suggest this to the theologians of the North; but it accounts, no doubt, for the ersatz character of some Northern writing under the influence of the Southern school. Still, it is not hard to see the difference between politics as an escape and politics as a serious theological concern. A theologian who begins with the political discourse of the Kingdom of God will prove bona fides by demonstrating how it illumines the topics that responsible theology attends to: repentance and forgiveness, the Incarnation, the sharing of the life of Godhead in the Spirit, justification and adoption, creation and the renewal of the world, the life of the Church and its ministry of word and sacrament. The Southern school of political theology – I use that term to include more than the Latin American Liberation Theology, though that is naturally central to these remarks – has proved its seriousness in this way, not least by bringing back into circulation theological themes for which liberal modernism had no use: judgment, original sin, demon-possession, for example.

The modern use of the term 'political theology' is generally held to begin with the *Politische Theologie* of Carl Schmitt (1922), which, reflecting the mood of the times in which it seemed possible to find some hope in German National Socialism, would seem to confirm the worst fears of liberal moderns and might have made the title unusable for ever after. The remarkable fact that it has proved not to be so invites some clarification as to how it can be used. It should not be restricted to programmes which, like the majority of contemporary essays, conceive theologico-political discourse as critical, even subversive, of other political discourses. Civil religion, too, counts as part of the genre, as well as those attempts, of which this is one, to combine critical and constructive elements. Nor should it be confined to programmes that make common cause with other critical political discourses, as the Latin Americans have made limited borrowings from Marxism. Programmes of an 'anabaptist' slant deserve to be reckoned in, such as that of Stanley Hauerwas, who finds the church's own native ecclesiology, properly deployed, to constitute 'a political community necessary for our salvation' (*After Christendom*, p. 26). The term is, however, overextended when it is embraced by an approach to theology which has no interest in political questions as such, but merely professes an ecclesial anti-foundationalism, the political content reduced to the banal reminder that theology must relate to some community of discourse.

But dated from the Medellin Conference the Southern school is hardly thirty years old. Political theology itself, by contrast, has many centuries behind it. To define a High Tradition the period 1100–1650 suggests itself: at one end the Gregorian Reforms bring the conflict between the papacy and secular rule to the centre of theological discussion; at the other the Moral Science of the early Enlightenment lifts political theory out of the purview of theology. But the High Tradition itself did not spring from nothing, but drew on thinkers and ideas of the patristic and Carolingian ages. Nor did the Enlightenment succeed in suppressing its impulses for long, as the first protests can be detected in the Christian socialists of the early to mid nineteenth century. But the relation of the contemporary political theology to the tradition can be summed up in a single bleak word: ignorance. The feeling of invigorating new departure is in considerable measure due to the loss of antecedents from view. Occasionally our contemporaries light on moments in the tradition and recognise their importance (Boff on St Francis, the *Kairos Document* on John of Salisbury, for example); but for the most part the tradition, with its wealth of suggestive theopolitical debate and analysis, has been occluded by the shadow of the modern period.

Why has the shadow been so dark and the eclipse so total? To understand the task faced by political theology today we need to make contact with the tradition again, but we need something further: to understand the causes of the eclipse, which will otherwise survive and subvert an attempt to overcome it. We begin, then, from the modern separation of politics and theology and the suspicions that produced it.

I.   *Beyond suspicion*

Ethics, politics and the practice of suspicion

Two persistent suspicions, antithetical but complementary, shaped the modern tradition of separating politics from theology.

The first is voiced in a famous pronouncement of Kant: 'I can actually think of a moral politician, i.e. one who so interprets the principles of political prudence that they can be coherent with morality, but I cannot think of a political moralist, i.e. one who forges a morality to suit a statesman's advantage' (*Perpetual Peace*, AA VIII.372). Kant meant, of course, that he *could* think of a statesman forging a pseudo-morality to his advantage, but couldn't think of anything *else* 'political morality' might mean! There is the decisive statement of a troubled motif that has recurred throughout the long tradition of Christian political reflection: distrust of a 'forged' morality – a mere 'legitimation', as our current idiom has it, for an arbitrary grip on power by given individuals or classes. Politicians are corruptors of moral discourse. Their moral sentiments are like bad coinage pumped into the currency, which can only lower its value and destroy it. This unmasking of political morality is what sets a distance between the Christian West and the Aristotelian conception of ethics as a subdivision of politics.

There are two sides to Kant's objection to the political moralist. In the first place it is a forgery, this morality which serves the convenience of the political order, when a true morality would dictate its terms to the politicians. This claim bears its theological ancestry on its face; there is a *true* morality to reckon with, not forged from within the political system but compelling it from above; and there is a *true* order which endures no matter who finds it inconvenient. In the second place, the political order itself should not be treated with too much solemnity, for it is, after all, only a 'statesman's advantage', a certain constellation of benefits and disbenefits of power which happens to suit one person rather than another. Politics is historically contingent, and therefore arbitrary. Only when subordinated to morality can its claims carry weight with us.

This second claim was of ancient Cynic origin, but long naturalised into Christian thought. When Augustine rhetorically denied the difference between kingdoms and 'large-scale criminal syndicates', he took his inspiration from a popular story about what a pirate said to Alexander: 'Because I use a small boat I am called a robber; because you use a large fleet you are called an emperor!' What raised this quip to the dignity of a political principle was the theological point of view. Augustine was in a position to belittle the political culture of antiquity; he could dismiss its achievements as 'the fragile splendour of a glass which one fears may shatter any moment'; he could do this without turning his back on society as the Cynics did, simply because he could point to a divine authority and a more lasting social order (*City of God* 4.3,4). Unmasking supposes a theological point of vantage, essentially an eschatological one. Christ has led captivity captive; he has disarmed the principalities and powers; the Kingdom of Heaven is at hand. When we claim to have seen through the appearances of political power, we act, as King Lear says (v.3), 'as if we were God's spies'.

So Kant disposes of the political moralist. But it is evident that the political moralist is one and the same as the political theologian. Kant's idea of morality, modelled on the thought of conscience as a form of divine revelation, makes it a surrogate for theology. So we may say that we can think of a theological politician, who interprets the principles of political prudence in a way coherent with God's will, but we cannot think of a political theologian, who forges a theology to suit a statesman's advantage. (Or, again, we can *think* of one all too easily, but not as a figure who commands authority.) Theological forgery came to the notice of the Christian church directly from its contest with the religious ideology of the Roman empire. The actual expression 'political theology' can, it has been suggested, be taken back to the *civile genus theologiae* of the Roman philosopher Marcus Varro, which Augustine dismissed as 'mendacious' (*City of God* 6.5; cf. Duncan Forrester, *Theology and Politics*, p. 57). 'Civil religion' is the title under which such forgeries are usually discussed today. More circumspectly, but with increasing conviction, Augustine seems to have found the same mendacious tendency in those historians of his time who made the conversion of Constantine and the dawning of the 'Christian epoch' an irreversible step in the unfolding of God's purposes. (On this development in Augustine's thought R. A. Markus's *Saeculum* is still the unchallenged authority.) But to the moralist of modernity, wielding the inner criticism of reflective consciousness rather than the public criticism of the church's theology, this critique is directed categorically against all postures which unite theological and political judgments. The suspicion has become total.

The second suspicion is apparently opposite: not the corruption of morality or theology by politicians, but the corruption of politics by theologians. This fear was voiced by advocates of the imperialist cause in the fourteenth century, based on a classicising account of political authority (uniting elements of Aristotle, Roman law and feudalism) which derived it from the will of the people. The anxiety was: could divine authority intervene in politics in any way without overwhelming the authority of political structures? Revelation seemed to pose a threat to political freedom. The experience of confronting Islam, and in later centuries of inter-confessional war in Christendom itself, no doubt made this anxiety worse; but, once again, it was an early-modern philosophical development that extended its scope beyond theocratic hierarchs to reject every kind of political morality or theology.

In the seventeenth century philosophy came to lose confidence in the objectivity of final causes. Political communities, even when created from below, had been believed to be ordained by Providence to serve the end of earthly perfection; but now there arose a tradition of explaining societies entirely by reference to efficient causes, focussing these in a notional compact whereby each individual citizen was supposed to have surrendered sovereignty over his own person in return for certain protections. Individual agents had their ends; but objective structures only had their origins. Moral purposes and goals, questions of human virtue and fulfilment, seemed intrusive, another form of theocratic temptation. The internalising of morality, then, led modernity once again to radicalise its suspicions.

In the popular imagination of late-modern liberalism these twin suspicions have broadened and fused together. It is no longer the statesman who stands alone, uniquely suspect. All of us have our political interests, especially class interests, so that all fine public sentiments may be unmasked, from whatever source. Principles of morality, though not denied all claims to truth, may never shape the deliberations of a self-ruling people which determines its will in response to certain recognised and universal pre-moral interests. They are relegated to the status of 'ideals'. The original incompatibility of the two reasons for separating politics and morality (or theology) has been left behind. We still occasionally see old-fashioned sideshows in which churchmen accuse statesmen of the blasphemous invocation of God's name – the Thatcher era in Britain, replete with atavistic moments, staged one or two of these – and others in which statesmen accuse churchmen of deploying 'the power of the crosier' – Ireland, forever resistant to fashion, continues to replay this popular medieval morality play. But what has really happened is that the division has become internalised. Each of us has a mind partitioned by a frontier, and accepts responsibility for policing it. It was said of Harold Wilson, preacher and politician, that he would go through the drafts of his speeches removing every echo of the biblical inflexions that came too naturally to him. That is the paradigm for late-modern liberal culture.

The Southern school is the most effective, though not the only, twentieth-century challenge to this late-modern liberal consensus on the separation of theology and politics. But in framing its challenge, it drew help from secondary currents within late-modernity itself. For epochs are characterised not by positions but by debates; it is the way they state their disagreements rather than their agreements that binds the thinkers of any age together. If the primary thesis of modernity has been the liberal one, there have been counter-theses which attempted to put together what liberal convention put asunder. Most notably, the idealist tradition, deriving through Hegel, has reasserted the old Aristotelian claim that morality is a subspecies of politics. This has been reconciled with the modern tradition of suspicion by way of a uniquely modern idea of history. The critical viewpoint was absorbed into the historical process. 'History' is the history of society, which embraces *both* the patterns of social order and of social right *and* the moments of unmasking in which these patterns are seen through and over-thrown. The Enlightenment consensus itself, with its attempt to establish a pure ethics (whether theological or rational) in the light of which all political dynamisms can be seen through, can itself be seen through. Criticism can be turned back upon the critic *ad infinitum.* For criticism, too, is the strategy of some actor within the socio-historical polyphony, the representative speech of some historical grouping. With this move the two strands of suspicion in the liberal tradition are safeguarded; but they are woven back into a greater harmony in which ethics and politics are one again. But the matrix is political, not ethical. For it is the *social* dynamisms of history that provide a context in which moral commitments become intelligible. The autonomous self-justifying character of politics is thus preserved; so is the critical role of moral thought. The philosopher is licensed to go on being sceptical of every claim to authority, but this no longer seems to imply a perpetual distance from the political process; rather, it seems to make a useful contribution to it.

But for this attempt to reintegrate politics and ethics modern idealism paid a fearfully high price. The historical processes of society, offered as the matrix which would unify them, do not, apparently, leave either of them intact. Ethics, on the one hand, is deprived of authority when it is made to serve merely a reactive critical function. It degenerates into little more than a rhetoric of scepticism. We can see this from the characteristic dilemma which besets the favourite causes of liberal idealism: how to claim moral licence for themselves without licensing their opposites. Each movement of social criticism draws in its train a counter-movement, and there is no ground in logic for paying more or less respect to the one than to the other. So Black consciousness, for example, requires (logically), invites (historically) and licenses (morally) a movement of White consciousness; feminism entails male chauvinism; homophilia entails homophobia, and so on. Our intuitions tell us that some of these movements are worth more than their shadows, but our intuitions are allowed no way of justifying themselves, and we are compelled, by the logic of historical dialectic, to give away whatever it is we think we may have gained. Each generation of God's spies has to settle for being spied upon by the next. No one can have the last word. There is, therefore, no end in sight to any issue of contention, except its replacement by some other more urgent one or its collapse from exhaustion. The law of historical process is contingency, and that gives us no space to object when our liberal arguments attract redneck free-riders.

On the other hand, social process, which is supposed to fill the place assigned to politics by Aristotle, is not the same thing as politics at all. The account of society that it yields we call (non-technically) 'sociology'; and though sociology was obviously a *classicising* movement of thought in its eighteenth-century origins, it was never a *classical* one. It could not recover the classical innocence which had once conceived as one object of study both the natural ordering of society and the art of government. It had to take into its system the critical deconstruction of the art of government; and that meant that the society in which it hoped to reunite politics and ethics was conceived headless, shorn of its decision-making capacities, an organism that blundered forward undirected save by the unconscious dynamics at work within it. Hence the recurrent charge that sociology was, in fact, anti-political. A politics that does not encompass the direction of society ceases to be a politics at all. But there is no room for direction in a society ruled by the imperative of universal suspicion.

All this goes some way towards explaining the difficulties faced by the renewed advocacy of political theology in our own time, and its vulnerability to the same charge of 'legitimation' that it has made against others. If in place of 'the statesman's advantage' it promotes the class-advantage of the poor, how, some influential critics have asked, does that improve matters? But, though this line of attack may find some targets, it fails to recognise the inspiration of the movement, which has been to take up the cause of the poor *as a theologically given mandate*. If the question of the poor is, quite specifically, the question of Latin Americans because it arises in their context, it is, at the same time, a question for everyone because it arises from scriptural warrants to which we must all attend. The true weakness lies not in taking up the cause of the poor in a preferential manner, but in partially concealing the theological warrants for doing so in order to conform to the historical dialectic of idealism. By relying on the deconstructive 'cui bono?' question to empower its rejection of liberal secularism, political theology found itself with an unsustainable combination of political affirmation and universal suspicion. It became tied in to the eternally inconclusive exchanges of historicism: allegations of sectional interest volleyed to and fro across the net, never to be ruled out of court, never to land beyond reach of return.

In a political theology that hopes to be constructive and to tell the truth, the 'cui bono?' question has a distinct but strictly limited usefulness. It alerts us to the fact that political theories are related to the actual political commitments of those who hold them. But it does not tell us whether those commitments are good or bad, generous or mean-spirited, true or false. It does not entitle us to think that no theory ever looks beyond the interests of its proponents. It is therefore useful as an interpretative tool, to test and prove the scope and integrity of any given theory, one's own or another's. What it cannot do is to provide that vision of reality which gives rise to theory in the first place. Once totalised, criticism merely evacuates itself of content and turns into a series of empty gestures. One cannot gain a truer understanding of the world by criticism alone, any more than one can make a dish of mince with a grinder and nothing to put through it. Totalised criticism is the modern form of intellectual innocence – not a harmless innocence, unhappily, for, by elevating suspicion to the dignity of a philosophical principle, it destroys trust and makes it impossible to learn.

We may put the same point theologically by replying to King Lear's invitation to 'take upon's the mystery of things as if we were God's spies' (v.3). God has no spies. He has prophets, and he commissions them to speak about society in words which rebuke the inauthentic speech of false prophets. But true prophets cannot speak *only* of the errors of false prophets. Their judgment consists precisely in what they have to say of God's purposes of renewal, his mercy towards even such weak and frangible societies as Israel and Judah, unstable communities on which the fate of souls depends. Christian theology must assume the prophet's task, and, accepting history as the matrix in which politics and ethics take form, affirm that it is the history of God's action, not sheer contingency but purpose. The prophet needs a point of view from which it is possible to criticise without criticism becoming a mere form, empty of substance. The prophet is not allowed the luxury of perpetual subversion. After Ahab, Elijah must anoint some Hazael, some Jehu.

Political concepts

The wisest advocates of political theology have understood that they must find a more objective point of reference for their work than the historical dialectic on which the strategy of unmasking depends. But where could that point be found? On the one hand they have often turned to look for a *knowledge won from action*: the act of 'transforming' the world would surely give a privileged viewpoint on the world, a thought which was once meant to be conveyed by the term 'praxis', now weakened by fashionable over-use. On the other hand they sometimes turned towards a *knowledge won from suffering*, making solidarity with the oppressed a primary category of epistemology. In fact neither of these turns could give political theology the commanding epistemological freedom it needed. The one steered it in a technological direction, opening it to the influence of the Western doctrine of progress, the worst possible platform from which to urge the cause of the marginalised classes. The other turned it towards the romantic and world-renouncing strands of European tradition, and cut its nerve for action. What it was striving for, and sometimes, but only sometimes, seemed to achieve, was a concept of knowledge gained in *obedient* action, an authentically Christian and prophetic concept (cf. John 7:17), for which late idealism found it difficult to make room because of the transcendent reference in the idea of obedience.

> A word of honour is due to Gustavo Guttiérez, who, in the course of a career devoted to clarifying the authentic shape that theology must take in his own cultural situation – and refusing to be the stooge of anyone else's agenda – has come to articulate this principle with perfect clarity: 'The ultimate criteria come from revealed truth, which we accept in faith, and not from praxis itself. It is meaningless – it would, among other things, be a tautology – to say that praxis is to be criticised "in the light of praxis". Moreover, to take such an approach would in any case be to cease doing properly theological work' (*The Truth Shall Make You Free*, p. 101). Meaningless, possibly – if one can describe the whole Promethean self-positing of mankind against God as meaningless, which is to

say that sin is meaningless – and tautological simply in the way that all founding axioms generate tautology to define their scope. But certainly untheological.

I will not, I hope, seem to cast doubt on the seriousness of this statement if I still look for an account of how the characteristic factitive and transformative language of Liberationist epistemology is to be understood in its light. Take, for example, one of Guttiérez's own earlier statements: 'Truth is something *verified*, something "made true". Knowledge of reality that leads to no modification of that reality is not verified, does not become true' (*The Power of the Poor in History*, p. 59). Would it have made any difference to the force of these words if he had written 'proved true' instead of 'made true', or 'action into reality' instead of 'modification of reality'? Perhaps not, since he can quote with approval a statement from *Laborem exercens* in which John Paul II explains 'verification' as 'checking' (*Truth*, p. 98). Guttiérez then went on (*Power*, p. 59): 'The praxis that transforms history is not a moment in the feeble incarnation of a limpid, well-articulated theory, but the matrix of authentic knowledge and the acid test of the validity of that knowledge.' Certainly, an acted 'incarnation' of a true theory, whether limpid or otherwise, might be said to be an acid test of the knowledge it claims; it might even be said to be a matrix of that knowledge, in that 'it is the place where [human beings] know the reality in which they find themselves and thereby know themselves as well'. But is it only rhetoric, this constant suggestion that praxis is rather more than the place and condition of *knowledge* of the world, but *determines* the world that is to be known? Does history need 'transforming', or only to be *acted into* with creaturely integrity? Is knowledge by which human beings 'recreate the world and shape themselves' really knowledge any more, or simply will?

Consider the familiar phrase: reflecting upon praxis. It suggests, but at the same time denies, the essential structure of good practical theology. It suggests, first, that action demands its own proper form of reasoning: 'practical reason' the tradition used to call it, 'deliberation' is perhaps a better term. It is reasoning ordered to action, reasoning that justifies doing something in particular. It suggests, secondly, that we need more than reasoning *towards* our actions, we need *reflection*, which is reasoning that reaches for an understanding of the world which comports with the action we venture there. Without it we cannot envisage our practical engagements clearly. It suggests, thirdly, that practical engagement is *prior in experience* to reflection, so that certain occasions of understanding are open to us only as we give ourselves to act. All three suggestions are true. But in the space between reflection and deliberation is a moment of transcendent criticism, a moment of obedience to God's word; and that is squeezed out by collapsing the two, the backward and the forward glance, into one moment, 'reflection upon praxis'. Our practical engagements now seem to yield us all the understanding we need. We have snatched a knowledge of the world that is *fait accompli*, stolen from God by getting in first. Our action becomes the predetermining matrix for whatever God may say to us, ensuring that we hear nothing from him but the echo of our own practical energies. And with that we are deprived of the freedom at the root of all freedoms, the freedom to repent.

The phrase arises from an argument within historicist idealism: does theoretical knowledge, which is by definition knowledge of history, arise retrospectively, as an aftermath, as Hegel's famous 'owl of Minerva' metaphor suggests? Or does it arise *mediis in rebus*, in the heat of the action, as Marx maintained? But behind that argument lay the Enlightenment contention, to which both sides subscribed, that practical reasoning begins on its own, apart from history. Ethics was a discipline of formal, underived principles of action, which could be applied indifferently to any sphere of human action – as Kant's 'moral politician' 'interpreted' his tasks 'to be consistent with morality'. But this was a defective account of moral reason in any sphere. For no deliberative question can be answered without a description of the situation to which it is put. The large moral disagreements all turn on competing descriptions. No doubt some personal sins may arise simply from insufficient application of formal moral principles such as 'impartiality', but the world-shaping, cultural sins have to do with bad descriptions: of sexual intercourse as a merely physical encounter; of deterrence as a threat that does not commit one to consequent action; of a foetus as a piece of maternal tissue; of justice as the will of the majority, and so on. Serious moral debate cannot avoid arbitrating questions of description and so enquiring into the structures of reality.

In the case of politics this enquiry is especially difficult; for political structures are historically fluid, not, as some other structures are, given in nature. A theologian may have much that is distinctive to say about sex, but will work from a core-description of the biological phenomena that in principle is common. In politics there is no such core-description. In Augustinian political theology it used to be said that only sociality itself was given in creation, all other political structures were given by divine providence. The phenomena themselves have changed, the tribe, the military empire, the nation kingdom and the bureaucratic state replacing each other in the course of history. And there are different discourses conducted about politics, which might as well belong to different universes: politics as power, politics as justice, politics as the extension of the home, politics as the construct of the market-place etc. Before political *ethics* can begin, then, there must be a work of descriptive theory, which will define the events and orders that are of *this* kind and not some other. Political theology – as a *theoretic* discipline, though not detached from experience and engagement – must precede political ethics.

But true concepts are an essential prerequisite for organised theory. We may be seduced into thinking that concepts are interchangeable, communicative forms, so that we may express what we have learned through one set of concepts quite as well through another. But this is not so. Concepts disclose the elementary structures of reality in relation to which we can begin to identify questions for theoretical development. Concepts must be – as their very name suggests – 'grasped'; and grasping true concepts is the achievement of that great army of non-intellectuals who have, as we say, common sense, who *think* without *theorising*. Only theorists could be so foolish as to think that it did not matter *which* concepts one grasped – apart, that is, from the morally immature. A class of sixteen-year-olds, told for the first time that what one calls a 'terrorist' another calls a 'freedom fighter', may miss the point so badly as to conclude there is no difference between the two; but that is the privilege of being sixteen. The mature adult knows it is because one and the same thing can *look different* that we need the two concepts of 'freedom fighter' and 'terrorist' to differentiate. Those two concepts are not interchangeable; if we did not have both, we could not frame the question that has to be put, nor understand why it might be difficult to reach an agreed answer. To grasp the opposed concepts of freedom and terror is to know something about the alternative shapes political experience may take, and about the scope of practical political decision.

Our search, then, is for true political concepts. But if the notion of a 'political theology' is not to be a chimera, they must be authorised, as any datum of theology must be, from Holy Scripture. Nothing assures us a priori that politico-theological concepts are to be found; the question of their existence must be put to Scripture itself. It may be, as some accounts have presumed, that the church in each age, lacking a political conceptuality that is native to it, simply deploys those current concepts which fit best its present tasks of worship, ministry and proclamation; in which case there is no political theology. For in any branch of theology concepts mediate between the reading of the scriptural text (the lector's task) and the construction of theory (the theologian's). Theory has to respond to the concepts found in Scripture, and its adequacy as theology will be measured by how well it has responded to them. Identifying concepts comes before constructing theory; but it comes after reading the text, for it is not a matter simply of emphasising key words in the text, 'judgment', 'love' or whatever, and even if key words may sometimes be used (as we shall use them) to identify the concepts, the words themselves are not the concepts but are like flags on a map which signal their presence. It is an *exegetical* task.

The Southern school has taken the search for scriptural concepts seriously; and though its stock of these sometimes appears rather small, they are undoubtedly foundational to its enterprise. They have, however, advocated a strategy of enriching them with other concepts borrowed from the social sciences. This strategy as such need cause no qualms; theology has often borrowed concepts from other disciplines of thought, and, indeed, the work of theory more or less demands it. The important question is how well its borrowings have been metabolised into the system of theological intelligibility. Some of the borrowings of the Southern school (the use of class-conflict analysis is an example) have remained painfully wedged in the oesophagus like an undigested bolus; others (dependency theory, for example) have helped the theological enterprise forward quite authentically.

The problem is that the choice of social-scientific guidance is a restrictive one, closing off the possibility of a fully political conceptuality. As we have observed, in speaking of 'society' late-moderns abstract from questions of government. This abstraction can serve as a useful ascetic preparation for political theory: it can correct the formalism to which theories of government are prone; it can remind us that society is a vital dynamism that controls its leaders as much as it is controlled by them. Yet the societies we actually inhabit are *politically formed*. They depend upon the art of government; they are interested in the very questions from which the study of society abstracts. We know this whenever we see a society slide into the abyss of sub-political disintegration, as we have seen happen in Somalia and Bosnia. The epithet 'social', however, forecloses the agenda against such questions, often narrowing it to economic matters which are only a fraction of what a living society cares about.

Building itself on an acephalous idea of society, dissolving government in deconstructive scepticism, lacking a point of view which can transcend given matrices of engagement, the Southern school has lacked a concept of *authority*. I say 'a' concept, because it would be inauthentic to make advance stipulations for what kind of concept of authority it might derive from reading Holy Scripture. But it is proper to say to theologians of the Southern school that, just as poverty was their issue first, but also ours, so authority is our issue first, but also theirs. Authority is the nuclear core, the all-present if unclarified source of rational energy that motivates the democratic bureaucratic organisations of the Northern hemisphere; but it is also a central theme of the pre-modern political theology, which sought to find criteria from the apostolic proclamation to test every claim to authority made by those who possessed, or wished to possess, power.

When raised, the question of authority has often been met by a massive deployment of suspicion on the part of contemporary political theologians. Some have rejected the idea outright: Dorothee Soelle, for example, is concerned with 'the conditions under which authority can be seen through, controlled and ultimately destroyed' (*Political Theology*, p. 67). But those who have taken this ground are fewer than those who have simply kept their silence, not knowing how to address the topic without abandoning the posture of totalised criticism and returning to 'legitimation'. Historical dialectic has made the category seem unusable, and the result is a *political* incoherence at the heart of contemporary politico-theological aspirations.

I take a pastoral example of this incoherence, the baptismal liturgy of the Episcopal Church of the USA, a liturgy which displays the same high level of creativity that is evident throughout that church's 1979 *Book of Common Prayer.* Its drafters hit upon the fine idea of including, together with the traditional affirmation of the Apostles' Creed, a brief moral catechesis requiring of each candidate a series of promises which outline the elements of Christian life in the world. The candidate promises to attend the worship of the church, to resist sin and to repent of it, to proclaim the good news of Jesus Christ, and to love every neighbour as him- or herself. The final question and answer address society and politics, and read: 'Will you strive for justice and peace among all people, and respect the dignity of every human being?' – 'I will with God's help.'

This brave attempt to instruct the Anglican faithful in their political duty identifies correctly both an active and a passive responsibility in respect of the political horizon of their lives: to 'strive' and to 'respect'. It identifies correctly both a social and an individual constituent to the common good: 'justice and peace' and 'the dignity of every human being'. What better formula could one devise for sketching political obligations on a thumbnail? One thing is lacking: there is no recognition that this 'striving' and 'respecting' must take place within a context of political institutions supposedly serving those very ends, and that our political service of the human community consistently involves us in relations with those institutions. We are offered a vision of political responsibility in a vacuum, whereas in life it is mediated through the exercise of, and through obligation to, structures of political authority: government, elected representation, law, policing, administration and so on.

Perhaps the only previous attempt to embody political catechesis in an Anglican liturgy was Cranmer's Catechism of 1549, in which the candidate acknowledged an obligation 'to honour and obey the King, and all that are put in authority under him: to submit myself to all my governors, teachers, spiritual pastors and masters: to order myself lowly and reverently to all my betters'.

It would be flogging a dead horse these days to expatiate on the inadequacies of this vision of political order as a pyramid of command and obedience reaching its summit and source in the monarch. But if the contrast between it and the modern formula shows what has been recovered since the heyday of authoritarian voluntarism, it also shows what, in the course of the recovery, has been forgotten. Nothing in modern democracy has changed the fact that political existence depends upon structures of command and obedience. If modern democracy has broadened the extent to which citizens find themselves sometimes commanding as well as obeying, and if it has developed expectations about the duty of those who command to consult first, one would expect to find these elements present in a more developed reference to political authority. But the whole problematic is strikingly absent.

This rejection has tended to restrict the immediate usefulness of political theology influenced by the Southern school to questions faced in the North. On the peculiar forms of necessity which constrain a daily commuter in a large Northern conurbation, a checkout assistant in a supermarket, or a democratic politician hoping for reselection by the party and the voters, political theology in its current forms sheds rather little light. The questions that confront the Northern democracies require detailed attention to the structures of authority which undergird their unruly democratic culture: can democracy avoid corruption by mass communications? Can individual liberty be protected from technological manipulation? Can civil rights be safeguarded without surrendering democratic control to arbitrarily appointed courts? Or stable market-conditions without surrendering control to arbitrarily appointed bankers? Can punishment be humane and still satisfy the social conscience? Can international justice be protected by threats of nuclear devastation? Can ethnic, cultural and linguistic communities assert their identities without oppressing individual freedoms? Can a democracy contain the urge to excessive consumption of natural resources? Can the handicapped, the elderly and the unborn be protected against the exercise of liberty demanded by the strong, the articulate and the middle-aged? Should the nation-state yield place to large, market-defined governmental conglomerates? These are the questions that political theology, in its self-conscious forms, is most notable for never addressing.

It is not to political theologians that we look for the beginnings of a treatment of these questions, but to the philosophically motivated 'modernity-critics', and especially to those who have concentrated on the philosophical character of technology (e.g. Jacques Ellul, George Grant) and of modern moral and political thought (Leo Strauss, Alasdair MacIntyre). Not, I am glad to say, that this collection of rather diverse thinkers has been without its own theological seriousness. If a new generation of political theologians nourished on the Southern school were to effect a meeting with this tradition, they might discover some welcome echoes of their own concerns.

A central thesis in what follows is that theology, by developing its account of the reign of God, may recover the ground traditionally held by the notion of authority. That notion has wasted away into unintelligibility, and with it the idea of political activity as kingly. The restoration of the lost theological horizon promises a point of purchase on the impasse of Northern political experience. To start from the reign of God is to follow the modern tradition to the extent of organising talk of politics within the category of history. But in placing political history within the history of God's reign, three elements are added, or restored, which free modern historicism from its always-disturbing suggestions of arbitrariness:

In the first place, the history of divine rule safeguards and redeems the goods of creation. Divine rule is not the *potentia absoluta* that underlies the bare fact of creation itself, but the *potentia ordinata* which works within the covenant that is established through creation. When we speak of divine rule, we speak of the fulfilment promised to all things worldly and human. To judge politics in the light of the divine rule is to be assured of its world-affirming and humane character.

> It was for this reason that I took, in *Resurrection and Moral Order*, the resurrection of Jesus as the foundation for Christian morality. Those who so mistook me as to find in this merely a cover for a return to a 'natural ethic' were, I think, failing to grapple with the central problematic of the book, how an *ethics* could be *evangelical*, which is to say proclamatory of the divine action. By rooting ethics in the resurrection I argued that it could only be grasped *within* the history of divine action. But that history is demonstrated precisely in its vindication of creation order as a basis for rational action. We must speak, therefore, of a *history* of creation order, and yet of a history of *creation order*, at once a proclamation rooted in the contingency of history and at the same time a vindication of reality which affords us an authority for doing something without equally affording an authority for doing the opposite. (See especially chapter 7 of that book, in which the connexions between its thesis and the thesis of this book become most apparent.)
>
> To that thesis we now add the connexion between history and politics; arguing that, as true ethics is grounded in *that* history because it is a history of the vindication of creation order, so it is also grounded in *that* politics, which is the politics of the divine rule. What follows can be seen as a retracing and elaboration of the work already done in *Resurrection and Moral Order*, with this

simple connexion between history and politics made more explicit. It goes back before the starting-point of that earlier book, so that the moment of resurrection does not appear like an isolated meteor from the sky but as the climax of a history of the divine rule; and it goes beyond the Pneumatological second part, dealing with the relations of freedom and authority, giving it a more church-historical development out of the traditions of Christendom.

In the second place, when the divine rule forms the ground for speaking of human political authority, we are forced to strip away the institutional fashions with which the Western (or Northern) tradition has clothed the idea of authority. A rather ruthless unclothing of that idea is necessary if it is to be further clothed. Instead of speaking primarily of the authority of *institutions*, we are forced to speak first of a human *act*, the 'political act' we may call it, which, performed by one or few on behalf of many, witnesses faithfully to the presence and future of what God has undertaken for all. The political act is the divinely authorised act. A political theology will seek to understand how and why God's rule confers authority upon such acts. It is not its goal to describe an ideal set of political institutions; for political institutions are anyway too fluid to assume an ideal form, since they are the work of Providence in the changing affairs of successive generations. The assimilation of the idea of authority to office and structure was a cardinal mistake which arose as Western politics turned its back on its theological horizons. Nevertheless, a truthful description of the political act, which will establish its conditions, purpose and mode of execution, will also shed light upon political institutions. It would be absurd if it did not; there can be no virtue in a theory which makes ordinary patterns of political relationship appear grotesque and unintelligible. Still, they cease to be the primary focus and become the explained, not the explanation. By opening up the horizon again, theology can restore to the idea of authority its proper depth as a moment of vocation. It can reorient the focus of political understanding to the innovative moment in which God calls on us to act not only on our own behalf but on behalf of others and in their name.

I learned the term 'political act' from the teacher from whom, one other person apart, I have learned most about the subjects dealt with in this book. To pay tribute I take the liberty of a self-quotation: 'For [Paul] Ramsey – and I do not think he misunderstood the sixteenth and seventeenth century just-war thinkers whose support he claimed – the form of the *act* was decisive for everything else in political theory. It bound together international and domestic, public and private, in one moral field; it laid the foundation for civil society and the authority of government; it drew justification from theologico-moral principle, and in turn provided justification for a diverse range of political responses to diverse situations. At once flexible and comprehensive, it allowed of no exceptions and inhibited no properly political judgments, and by its very flexibility it prevented the absolutizing of relative political values, however important. The political act was not bounded by institutions. At home in the city it could extend itself into open spaces across the boundaries erected by civilized institution-building. It was impossible for Ramsey to conceive politics as an island-kingdom, washed on all sides by the trackless ocean of a state of nature. The Lockean liberalism that conceived it that way had placed the abstract political institution at the core of political theory, in the place where political action belonged' ('Karl Barth and Ramsey's "Uses of Power"', p. 23).

In the third place, the history of divine rule is presented to us as a *revealed* history which takes form quite particularly as the history of Israel. Against this canonical history our understanding of general and universal history as a whole must be measured. The implications of this for political theology are extensive, and we shall explore them in the third section of this chapter.

Israel and the reading of the Scriptures

The excitement which accompanied the recovery of political theology in our time arose very evidently from the reading of the Bible. In Israel's political experience of Yhwh's rule there was, it seemed, a word which shed light and understanding on the practical situations of the present day. The question of how adequately the theologians articulated their indebtedness to Scripture is important, but secondary. The chief thing is that it was there. The adventure into political questioning was driven by the energy of biblical discovery.

That is why the Southern school remains important for theologians in other contexts, despite its inability to address the major practical questions of the North. There is a paradoxical truth about sameness and difference in Christian theology. Since no context is the same as any other, no one theological undertaking will exactly mirror another; and yet as each enterprise takes seriously its own authorisation in the Gospel of Jesus Christ, it will find that it is in a symbiotic relation to every other enterprise that does so. The Gospel is one Gospel, which has manifold implications for us as we believe and obey it. Theology is a manifold witness, which has a unified object on which it concentrates its witness. The 'political hermeneutic' is discovered and explored in a particular context of discipleship; yet it does not belong only to that context, nor is it the context that imposes it in the first place. It belongs to the Scriptures and is imposed by the exercise of reading the Scriptures.

The Scriptures in their entirety, that is, and not only certain texts within them. Older traditions of political theology grew weaker as their exegetical foundations shrank, dwindling to a few cherished passages (Paul on the authorities, for example) which appeared to have lost any connexion with the messages of the prophets, evangelists and apostles. It had once been very different, as students of the high medieval and Reformation Christian political tradition know well. The success of the more recent enterprise has sprung in part from its willingness to strike out exegetically and deploy (or, better, discover) the political hermeneutic in a wide range of biblical texts. Yet something more than sheer eclecticism is needed, and it is not yet clear that theologians have been able to provide it. If the Scriptures are to be read as a proclamation, not merely as a mine for random sociological analogies dug out from the ancient world, then a unifying conceptual structure is necessary that will connect political themes with the history of salvation as a whole. Political hermeneutic has to yield theology – and I don't say 'a' theology as though any improvisation upon theological themes would do, but 'theology', an account of God's dealings which has the authenticity to command Christian faith and conscience. Otherwise it will never be more than a fashion for the idle.

There has been no lack of interest in the beckoning fruitfulness of Israel's political categories. We have seen World Council of Churches documents brim over with *shālōm*, evangelical Protestants become eloquent about the jubilee, and, more widely noticed than either, Exodus stride across the pages of the Latin Americans. Yet the problem of integrating them theologically has not been solved. Many of those who first thrilled to Guttiérez's famous celebration of the Exodus (*Theology of Liberation*, pp. 155–60) wondered how this 'paradigmatic . . . valid and contemporary event' could be authoritative for a Christian theologian, for whom the uniting paradigm of all experiences that befall God's people must surely be the cross and resurrection of Christ. To which it was not enough to answer that other paradigms, too, besides the Exodus, were taken up by Liberation Theology. What was needed was an architectonic hermeneutic which would locate political reflection on the Exodus within an undertaking that had its centre of gravity in the Gospels.

It would seem that the materials for this were not far to seek. Almost the whole vocabulary of salvation in the New Testament has a political pre-history of some kind: 'salvation' itself (*yᵉshūāh*), 'justification' (*tsᵉdāqāh*), 'peace' (*shālōm*), 'faithfulness' (*hesed*), 'faith' (*ᵉmūnāh*), and above all the Kingdom of God. Israel's knowledge of God's blessings was, from beginning to end, a political knowledge, and it was out of that knowledge that the evangelists and apostles spoke about Jesus. Does this not provide us with the unifying hermeneutic principle that we need? Yet how far can the appearance of conceptual continuity be trusted? Concepts can evolve and change, using the same words as they do so. The proclamation of the reign of Yhwh in the Psalms is different from Jesus' announcement of God's Kingdom in the Gospels. And, of course, even the continuity of vocabulary is broken by one major factor, the translation from Hebrew into Greek. In place of *yᵉshūāh* the New Testament speaks of *sōtēriā*, in place of *tsᵉdāqāh*, *dikaiosunē* and so on. How much of the political content which those Hebrew words originally conveyed is carried forward into the Greek of the New Testament? This is not really a question about the semantic equivalence of Hebrew and Greek vocabulary, or even about the supposed contrast of Jewish and Hellenistic worldviews. It is a theological question about the substance of religious hope in Israel and the early church. In the Palestine of Jesus' time much had changed since Yhwh's anointed used to celebrate his Lord's, and his own, monarchy standing by the pillar to the accompaniment of First Temple psalmody. The very sense in which Israel was still a nation had changed, and looked differently perhaps to the Jews of Roman Palestine, the inhabitants of Herodian Galilee, the Jewish communities of Asia Minor, and the Gentiles who became associated with their worship and belief in each of these regions. And there were differences as to whether, and to what extent, their hope for the removal of Israel implied new institutions of government. We have to reach a judgment, then, on how much the terms in which Jesus' community spoke of God's purposes still resonated with the political energies of the cry *Yhwh mālak*.

As it stands this question is narrowly focussed on the use of *Israel's* political categories; but it has wider implications for the place of political categories as such within the Christian message of salvation. For in the church's understanding Israel's political categories were the paradigm for all others. Jesus belonged to Israel; and Israel was, for him as for his followers, the theatre of God's self-disclosure as the ruler of nations. Always implied in the hope of a new national life for Israel was the hope of a restored world order. The future of the one nation was a prism through which the faithful looked to see the future of all nations. The early and patristic church, then, in taking a position on Israel's political hopes, was deciding between alternative ways of situating politics within the Gospel. On the one hand the 'earthly promises' to Israel could be taken as an elaborate symbolic language for the proclamation of a hope that lay beyond all experience of the public realm. Thus Augustine, in a statement representative of this emphasis, states: 'In the Old Testament we read of earthly and time-bound promises, goods of this corruptible flesh, though they prefigure the eternal and heavenly goods which belong to the New. In this age it is the heart's own good that is promised, the mind's good, the good of the spirit, that is to say, of the intelligible realm' (*On the Letter and the Spirit* 21.36). On the other hand the language of political success could be read in terms of an earthly rule of Christ; from which ensued a struggle to establish that it could not be the old, unbelieving Israel, but the true Israel, the church, that would be the context of these social and political promises.

These two hermeneutic options, negative and positive, are foreshadowed in the New Testament itself. The Epistle to the Hebrews uses systematically negative language in order to proceed from the social institutions of the Old Covenant to the Gospel of the New. The Levitical ordinances were no more than 'a shadow of good things to come' (10:1); the gift of the land of Canaan to Joshua's generation was equally insubstantial (4:8). Abraham never settled in Canaan at all, because he 'looked for a city which has foundations' (11:10); and the whole patriarchal generation, which was to this apostle the most important period of Jewish history, desired 'a better country, that is, a heavenly one' (11:16). Their hope for an 'inheritance' was concerned with final blessing, not with the provisional blessing of Israel's subsequent settlement. The cult and the land in ancient Israel's history are symbols, pointing us and them to a 'kingdom that cannot be shaken' (12:28). By contrast with this the political legacy of Israel is taken up quite concretely by the evangelists in the narrative of the event which we commemorate on Palm Sunday. By the manner of his entry into the royal city Jesus set himself self-consciously in the role of the coming king expected in Zechariah 9:9. According to St Mark and St Matthew this gesture was understood as a reference to the long-suspended Davidic throne. As David's dynasty was the form in which earthly political authority had been given most decisively to Israel, so, when God acted through his anointed to assume authority to himself, David's house was represented in the act. By this narrative we are forbidden to dismiss Israel's political expectations as an irrelevance to Jesus' Gospel.

It would be too easy to see in this contrast of hermeneutic strategies the foundation of a later opposition between 'pietist' disinvolvement and 'theocratic' political legitimation. But that would overlook the theological setting in which the tension of negative and positive arises: the need to envision the glory of the last times in relation to the presence of God in

Israel's past. For the author to the Hebrews, although Israel's institutions were symbolic, the symbolism was not a simple allegory but a prophetic symbolism. The concrete social reality of the past contained a promise of something greater in the last times. The evangelists, for their part, in situating the Palm Sunday narrative at the head of the Passion story, do not allow us to suppose that David's rule could be, as it were, revived and reconstituted, but point us forward to its resumption in a climax of a quite different kind. The consciousness, then, of Israel's history as the pre-history of the Christ and his church mediated the tension between negative and positive hermeneutics and allowed them to complement one another in the elaboration of a theology of promise and fulfilment.

St Paul's extended discussion of the place of Israel in the age of the church (Rom. 2–4, 9–11) allows us to see the negative and positive treatments of Israel's legacy carefully juxtaposed. The public tradition of Israel ('the law') both does and does not confer an advantage on the Jew over the Gentile. It has been, and yet has not been, superseded by the Gospel of faith in Jesus Christ. This age is not one empty of public witness to God's work, a mere space for faith in which all social forms are indifferent; but neither does the church itself and on its own constitute the sole public sign. The church exists *vis-à-vis* the social structures of Israel, once the locus of God's self-giving to mankind and still bearing their public witness to his purposes. For its own part the church does not confront those structures already garbed in structures of its own (still less clothed in garments claimed to have been inherited at Israel's decease!) but appears rather underdressed politically, waiting for a fuller clothing when the public form in which it has placed its hope is made available by Israel's own self-giving to God. The public tradition of Israel carries an unrealised promise for the full socialisation of God's believing people, the appearing, as another prophet puts it, of the New Jerusalem from heaven. This means that any question about social forms and structures must be referred to a normative critical standard: do they fulfil that will of God for human society to which Israel's forms authoritatively point us?

It is in later generations of the church, when the consciousness of belonging to Israel's history faded, that the negative–positive tension could no longer be contained and Christians found themselves forced to decide between a strategy of political disinvolvement and a strategy of political affirmation. Tertullian and Eusebius of Caesarea, perhaps, afford the clearest examples of each. It would, however, be a mistake to suppose that the difficulty of the situation was avoided merely by avoiding the extremes which these two represent. It is more instructive to observe how negative and positive poles exert a magnetic pull on sophisticated political theologies that are far removed from pietism or theocracy, generating an idealist and a realist current within Western political thought.

An example of the first is furnished by John Wyclif, one of the major figures (and a sadly neglected one) of the high period of political theology. Wyclif founded his doctrine of political right on the concept of 'dominion by grace', by which he meant that human justice depends upon God's sanctifying of our relations to material possessions. Political right must spring directly from the charity to God and neighbour which the Gospel imparts; *ius* must flow from the fountain-head of *iustitia*. Only the righteous (elect, forgiven and sanctified) can have a full title to 'dominion' – a word which, in the manner of the period, embraces the two notions of property and jurisdiction. For dominion is given by God, and God grants no rewards to sinners. So 'the whole corpus of human law ought to rest upon the evangelical law as its essentially directive rule' (*De civili dominio* 1.20). To use property in defiance of the law of love, though within the terms of human legality, is to lose legitimate right. The law of love validates and invalidates in detail decisions made under the authority of secular law. Thus, for example, the right of a monarch's son to inherit the throne is determined at the time by a judgment as to whether God has in fact rewarded the deceased king with a *godly* son to succeed him! Wyclif is the first modern Christian idealist, the first to come to terms with what might follow if the traditional guarantee of a public structure for the church, the papacy, is denied its commanding position. Now that the divine right of judgment has been transferred, as it were, from the pope to the law of love, no institution is quite secure against interference, least of all the ecclesiastical institution of bishops and clergy which must be first, in Wyclif's view, to feel the weight of its criticism.

In contrast the great sixteenth-century Thomists, Vitoria and the Salamanca school which followed him, believed they must affirm God's purpose to strengthen institutions of government and law, not always to challenge and overrule them. Wyclif was in their minds when they seemed to hear in the great slogan of their own day, 'justification by faith', an echo of that same destructive atomism which made political right dependent upon the mystery of election and grace. To escape from this they found a basis for political order in creation, especially in the sociality of human nature and its natural capacity for justice. This allowed them to look for universal categories of political experience while still maintaining a relation to the Gospels, for grace, they held, restores and perfects nature. Political theory was to be constructed as the Natural Law of social existence. Here was a Christian secularism – still decisively Christian, though it is easy to see how a later generation would find in it the *point d'appui* for an autonomous political science – unrevolutionary, for it had no place for the intervention of divine judgment, but far from uncritical as its noble protest against colonial slavery and conquest makes clear.

If this admirable venture lacks the excitement that the idealism of a Wyclif can afford, it is because it lacks a comparable sense of divine immediacy. To have

God present in judgment, it seems, makes political institutions unstable; to have stable institutions requires that God's purposes be kept at ground level, as the founding cause of political existence, so allowing conscientious agents almost unlimited endorsement in fulfilling them. The tension between the two traditions needs the mediation of a political order which *itself* discloses and reveals the judging presence of God in society. One may claim that role for the church – as the medieval papalists did, and as it is now fashionable to do once again – but the church's bona fides as a political structure cannot simply be taken for granted. It has to be shown to arise out of the church's relation to Israel, a relation which itself safeguards the church against dangers of theocratic tyranny and inauthenticity that arise, as history shows, from its flexing of political muscle. Failure to attend to Israel is what left Christian political thought oscillating between idealist and realist poles.

The hermeneutic principle that governs a Christian appeal to political categories within the Hebrew Scriptures is, simply, Israel itself. Through this unique political entity God made known his purposes in the world. In relation to the crisis facing this unique entity, the church proclaimed those purposes fulfilled. Or, to express the same point differently: the governing principle is the kingly rule of God, expressed in Israel's corporate existence and brought to final effect in the life, death and resurrection of Jesus. This general statement allows us to add four more precise comments about right and wrong ways of using the Old Testament in political theology:

(i) If political theologians are to treat ancient Israel's political tradition as normative, they must observe the discipline of treating it *as history*. They may not plunder the Old Testament as though it were so much raw material to be consumed, in any order and in any variety of proportions, in the manufacture of their own theological artefact. They are dealing with a disclosure which took form in a succession of political developments, each one of which has to be weighed and interpreted in the light of what preceded and followed it. To dip into Israel's experience at one point – let it be the Exodus, the promise of *shālōm*, the jubilee laws, or, with Thomas Cranmer at the coronation of Edward VI, the reign of Josiah of Judah – and to take out a single disconnected image or theme from it is to treat the history of God's reign like a commonplace book or a dictionary of quotations. We may not appeal to the Exodus for the deliverance of the poor and then avoid mention of the conquest of Canaan; we may not appeal to the conquest to make a distinction between the dynamic pilgrim *melek* and the static *baʿalīm* and then avoid mention of the tribal settlements; we may not appeal to the tribal period for the decentralised republican spirit of the amphictyony and then avoid mention of the monarchy, and so on.

(ii) Nor can theologians do justice to it as a history by constructing a subversive counter-history, a history beneath the surface which defies and challenges the official history of Israel. That will not be the history of the people, but (at best) of a class within the people or (at worst) of a purely suppositious class that they are inclined to think ought to have existed. Actually, the documents we possess are, as they stand, critical of the exercise of government to a remarkable extent, a fact owing to the influence of the prophetic movement in the Deuteronomic literary culture. But we must listen to the affirmations as well as to the criticisms. To do otherwise is to impose a sceptical perspective *ab initio* and procedurally, and to set our face against the thought that in this people's history God has effectively made his rule known. A decision to take *Israel* with special seriousness implies a willingness to have done with perpetual unmasking. After all, why would one trouble to unmask *this* people? If our minds are made up to find nothing but ideology, then let us study the Chinese or the Egyptians whose ideology can, at least, boast monumental cultural achievements. To turn to Israel is already a step of faith on the theologian's part – a step which it is foolish to undo by setting trip-wires across the path.

(iii) Nor may they rewrite Israel's history as a 'Whig' history of progressive undeception, in which the normative principle is simply the emergence of rationality from barbarism. To take as an example of this the secularisation of political institutions: the Jews of the First Temple sang 'The kingdom is Yhwh's', while the author of 1 Peter spoke of all kingdoms as 'human institutions'. Shall we seize upon this change of orientation, and elevate it into an overarching principle of development: sacred institutions are more primitive, secular institutions more differentiated? This hermeneutic policy (which can be repeated with numerous other topics, such as holy war, relations to foreign powers and so on) is 'historicist', not 'historical'. It makes the process of history the sole content of history. The political faith of the First Temple can have no meaning for us, save as a memory which tells us what we have escaped from. The past is recalled solely to justify the present against it, and has no standing as a point of disclosure. Consequently, even the secularist pole within biblical history is distorted, since it is lifted out of its theological and historical context and absolutised to become the law of the future. If, however, we attend to the *history* which made this shift of understanding necessary (exile, return, the oppression of the world-empires, Messianic expectation), and if we make it our business to understand how it lay within the *logic* of Israel's faith to look to sacral institutions at one point and at another point away from them, then we are in a position to treat her historical political experience as normative.

(iv) Yet Israel's history must be read as a *history of redemption*, which is to say, as the story of how certain principles of social and political life were vindicated by the action of God in the judgment and restoration of the people. The difference between this approach and that of the 'Whig history' is that the theological coherence is allowed to arise from within the history and is not imposed upon it from the existing norms of our own historical period. It is not assumed that God's purpose was to make ancient Israel as like modern Europe and America as could possibly be done within the constraints of the time and the material. Yet we must not let go of the theological assertion that God had a purpose with Israel. The history of a nation, even the history of the ideas that were important to that nation, will not constitute a theology on its own, but only as we trace the truth of God's rule unfolded in the sequence of events and cultural periods of that nation's life. But *what* purpose and *what* truth must be told us by Israel's own voices and the voices of the apostolic church (which are also Israel's) in response to them.

The ancient writers themselves used, as a matter of instinct, to express truth about the relations of things in narrative (so that Adam's race ate only vegetables at first, but meat after the Flood); while in the narrative of their own people's history they discerned truths about the relations of things (so that the monarchy, supervening on the tribal period, was a kind of Noachic covenant for political institutions). This interconnexion of history and truth the theologian must be prepared to explore with them, not simply re-narrating Israel's history as the outcome of a purely historical enquiry, nor simply re-reading the documents in an enterprise of literary exegesis, but finding the truth within the unfolding patterns of the history. As the structures of Israel's experience pass by us in their historical sequence (tribe, monarchy, cultural–ethnic enclave, movement of world-renewal), the concepts deployed by Israel's writers in the interpretation of those structures (peace, judgment, possession, worship) allow us to find the sequence of happenings intelligible. And from those concepts we may derive an orientation of political principle through which the legacy of Israel regulates our own political analysis and deliberation. Yhwh's victory lays hold on our intelligence and claims us still.

2.   The revelation of God's kingship

'Yhwh reigns'

In taking up the concept of divine kingship, a concept at once fundamental to Israel's political self-awareness and to Jesus' proclamation of the fulness of time, I propose, as I have said, to 'recover the ground traditionally held by the notion of authority'. What kind of ground is that?

It is important to describe it with a sufficient width to include such ideas as 'moral authority' and 'epistemological authority' as well as political authority. Authority is 'the objective correlate of freedom'. That is to say, it evokes free action, and makes free action intelligible. As such it has to be distinguished both from 'force' and from 'power'. Force overrides the agency of those against whom it is brought to bear, treats them as passive objects, imposes its purposes in such a way as to make their capacity for action irrelevant or even to destroy it. Power is the most general term for an ability to get things done by any means, whether by force, by authority or by persuasion. 'Persuasion', too, must be distinguished from authority, since, although it aims to evoke free action, it is not itself the ground of acting, but the rhetorical exercise of presenting such grounds to the mind. Someone who persuades me does not exercise authority, but appeals to it. In describing authority this way I deliberately draw a circumference much wider than a political discussion taken by itself would seem to warrant or demand. That is in order to stress that a political discussion must not be taken by itself; it needs a background in the ontology of human freedom, action and the good. Without revisiting all that territory now (for which I have sketched an itinerary in *Resurrection and Moral Order*, ch. 6), I must be content with the bare assertion that authority in society is *one* form in which the intelligible ends or grounds of action, the created goods to which our action is oriented, lay claim upon us. Obeying a law has in it something that invites comparison with painting a picture or engaging in scholarship, or with any other action that needs no further justification than its own end self-evidently gives it.

Yet that comparison immediately draws our attention to the differences. The authority which lays claim on us in society does not lay claim on us simply like a moment of beauty or an intuition of truth. It is a distinct phenomenon, irreducible to any other, a 'mystery', as we might say, in its own right, that we *freely defer* to the commands of society even when to do so prevents the pursuit of self-evidently good ends of action that are available to us, so that these commands, by contrast, do not present themselves as goods to us, but as impositions or constraints. Political authority, too, mediates good to us, but it is a distinct form of mediation which can have the immediate character of a limitation. The task of any theory of authority is to explain how the good can and must present itself to us in this alienated and alienating form, and yet without ceasing to be *our good*, that to which our action is oriented.

The humanist family of political theories that have shaped the modern West has sought to find an explanation in the self-alienating character of the human will. It is our own wills, bound together in a voluntary compact, that are reflected back to us in the authoritative institutions of society; and they come back to us in an alien guise because the will is always innovating, forgetful, breaking with the past, and incapable, as such, of recognising its own anterior commitments. Yet the authority of political institutions is precisely the authority of our own wills over ourselves, exacting acknowledgment and recognition from us however inconsistent with the new engagements that we would now like to make. The strength of this approach is its location of the claim of authority in self-recognition. But the recognition is ambiguous at best, because the opposition of person to society has struck back deep into the individual soul. The alienation of each of us from authority is simply the alienation of each from ourself. This essentially pessimistic view cannot tell us what is good about political authority, since its theory of the good, founded on the free choice of the undetermined will, is itself inadequate to survive the division of the will. Neither authority nor rebellion can be 'good' in any substantial sense to the self that wills against itself.

The older theistic family of theories, characteristic of the late medieval and early modern periods in the West and of other theistic societies, tended to find an explanation for the alien character of political authority in the gulf between God and his human creatures. The command strikes us like a meteor from outside our world, cutting across our projects and ambitions, precisely because it is not the human will that has generated it, but the divine will mediated through human agents. The strength of this approach is its emphasis on the objective otherness of what confronts us in political authority. It has aligned this otherness, not incorrectly, with the great otherness that we discover in existence itself, the otherness which religion responds to of the human and the divine. But its failure is the failure of an underdetermined theism on every front: how to present the otherness of God as propitious to mankind. The presence of political authority is like a symbol on earth of the vaguely threatening inscrutability of the divine purpose for the human race.

When the Jews of the First Temple period used to sing the refrain *Yhwh mālak*, 'Yhwh is king', a liturgical act in which political and religious meanings were totally fused, not only did they not take the first of these approaches to authority, but they did not take the second either. The kingship of Yhwh was not an expression of the *potentia absoluta* which philosophical theology ascribes to the divine creator on the brink, as it were, of creating, able to bring about this world of meaning that he has brought about but equally able to bring about alternatives. It is divine authority, not divine power, that is communicated by the idea. This authority evokes free action because it holds out to the worshippers a fulfilment of their agency within the created order in which their agency has a place and a meaning. Yhwh's kingship is not a creation *ex nihilo* but an act of providence, keeping faith with creation once made. It is, therefore, true to say that the goodness of his authority lies in the fact that it demands what is recognisable – but not recognisable as a reflection of the worshippers' *wills*, rather as a calling to their *fulfilment*. They are summoned to fulfilment from beyond themselves, a fulfilment that is recognisable and yet unknown. Hence the alien–familiar character of Yhwh's command: the purpose it expressed was not their purpose, but it was a purpose that corresponded to the *telos* of their own beings. That purpose was that they should live together as a people, that they should be 'Israel'.

The cry *Yhwh mālak* carried with it three kinds of association. In the first place it offered a geophysical reassurance about the stability of the natural order; in the second place, it offered a reassurance about the international political order, that the God of Israel was in control of the restless turbulence of the nations and their tutelary deities and could safeguard his people; in the third place, it was associated with the ordering of Israel's own social existence by justice and law, ensuring the protection of the oppressed and vulnerable. In the third of these lines of association lay the calling and the demand. It was at this point that Israel's king laid an authoritative claim upon his worshippers. Later in Israel's experience the second will be perceived also to comprise a task for Israel, but at this initial moment of political faith it is simply a reassurance. Yet the two political levels on which Yhwh's kingship was seen, the international and the national, were held together by an analogy which consistently characterises the political thought of the Hebrew Scriptures: as Israel is situated among the nations, so are the poor and defenceless situated within Israel. He who cared for the welfare of a servile nation in Egypt cares for the welfare of a servile class in Israel.

In one small group of psalms the words *Yhwh mālak* form the opening chorus which effectively governs all that follows; and this makes them the leading texts for an exposition of the idea. Psalm 93 thinks at once of the stability of the physical world, unshaken despite the turbulence of the ocean. This displays the permanence of Yhwh's throne and its transcendence over the chaotic energies of nature and (by implication) history. How is this experienced within the community of Israel? Through Yhwh's unchanging 'testimonies' (*ēdōth*) and in the holiness of the Temple itself. Psalm 97 makes a different, and more dynamic, reference to the geophysical order, taking the thunderstorm as a demonstration of the forcefulness of Yhwh's rule. His destructive fury at his enemies rides on his righteousness and judgment like lightning on a lowering bank of storm-clouds. Before this cosmic display the different peoples of the world are affected differently: the idolatrous nations covered in shame, but Judah (only!) filled with delight. As the storm divides the quarters of the sky between light and darkness, so Yhwh's judgment causes the darkness of dismay to fall in one place and the light of vindication in another.

Psalm 99, thirdly, passes rather briefly over the geophysical and international dimensions of Yhwh's reign before its thought turns to the 'judgment' (*mishpāt*), 'equity' (*mēshārīm*) and 'right' (*tsᵉdāqāh*) which he has established, not only in Judah this time but in Jacob too. From here the hymn remembers the early lawgivers of Israel, the mediators of Yhwh's rule who preserved his 'testimonies' (*ēdōth*) and his decree (*ḥōq*), concluding with a prayer acknowledging Yhwh's forgiveness of the nation's sins and a renewed call to the people to worship on the 'holy mountain'. To be read together with these three psalms is Psalm 96, which, by contrast, has a strongly international interest. The words *Yhwh mālak* are to be spoken among the foreign nations, together with the warning that they, too, face the equitable verdict of Yhwh's court (*dīn*). They are to come with offerings to worship Yhwh, admitting that their own gods are nothing but idols. Again, the stability of the geophysical order demonstrates Yhwh's rule, and, in a climax of great force, representative features of the natural world join with the 'families of the nations' to offer him praise as he approaches the judgment-seat.

Scholarly convention assigns these psalms (conjecturally, but not without

reason) to the 'enthronement ceremony' of pre-exilic times which, it is supposed, cemented the link between Yhwh's reign and the reign of Yhwh's
anointed. On the debate about the precise meaning of *mālak* (on which see J.
Day, *Psalms*, pp. 75–82), I find it difficult to get worked up. Not even the hypothetical context of a ceremonial enthronement of Yhwh – and we should not
forget that this context is purely a hypothesis – can quite make sense of Yhwh's
'having become' king. The verb may have other senses which equally convey
the idea of an event, and intelligibility should have the decisive voice, not a
demand for exact parallels. I favour: 'Yhwh has exerted his rule', 'has proved his
royal authority', or something of that kind.

Should the hypothesis fail, and the pre-exilic provenance of these psalms be
put in question, we would still have no cause to doubt that the ideas expressed
in them are continuous with conceptions prevalent in the monarchy and
before. The link between Yhwh's kingdom and the cosmic order is associated,
both in the ancient Psalm 29:10 and the later Psalm 74:12ff., with echoes of the
myth of the conquest of the dragon and the binding of the flood. Once Yhwh
appears as a high-king among the gods (Ps. 95:3). His assertion of his rule in
battle (cf. Pss. 44:4; 74:12) appears in the remarkable processional hymn from
the First Temple, Psalm 24, where Yhwh enters the gates of Jerusalem as a conquering 'king of glory'. The commonplace that Yhwh's reign lasts for ever (Pss.
10:16; 102:12; 145:13; 146:10) runs back to one of the most ancient Hebrew
psalms (Exod. 15:18). In this connexion we are also reminded of the conquest of
Canaan (ibid., cf. Pss. 10:16; 47:3), and, in a text from the Northern kingdom,
of the lawgiving at Sinai which preceded it (Deut. 33:5, cf. Ps. 99:6f.). When the
title 'king' is, at a later period, associated with the assertion that Yhwh is Israel's
'maker', it may be that these formative events are in mind (Ps. 149:2; Isa. 43:15).

Yhwh's kingdom is 'over all the earth' (Ps. 22:8) and he will 'judge the
nations' (Ps. 9:7, cf. 96:10). Does this mean simply that he will condemn them
as idolaters? That he will certainly do (Jer. 10:7, 10, cf. Pss. 96:5; 97:7). But there
is a suggestion of something more in the pre-exilic ceremonial Psalm 47, where
the leaders of the nations are summoned to join with the people of Israel in
acknowledging Yhwh's rule. Still, in the exilic and post-exilic texts that take up
the tradition of Yhwh's kingship from the pre-exilic psalms, what is principally
in question is the fate of the nation itself: the gathering of the scattered exiles,
the return to Jerusalem (Isa. 52:7; Ezek. 20:33), the rehabilitation of the city (Isa.
24:23; Zeph. 3:14), the aiding of the oppressed (Ps. 146:7ff.) and perhaps even
the restoration of the monarchy (Mic. 4:7f.). Even so the international aspect
is not lost sight of. Psalm 22:28, with its description of Yhwh's kingship as
'ruling among the nations', may possibly be post-exilic; in Zechariah 14 there
is envisaged a pattern of annual pilgrimage from all the nations that were for-
merly Israel's enemies; while Malachi, forever practical, draws the inference
that, since Yhwh is 'a great king, respected internationally' (1:14), his Temple
ought to have decently furnished cult.

As we survey the texts which speak of Yhwh's kingship, we notice a reluctance to make direct connexions with any concrete form of political order. Where, for example, do we find a mention of Yhwh's anointed, 'the' king as we are tempted to call him, the one who occupied David's throne in Jerusalem, whose victories were Yhwh's victories and whose fortunes were the theme of the royal psalms? There is certainly no great haste to use the language of Yhwh's kingship to 'legitimate' him. Texts which mention the two thrones, heavenly and earthly, in one breath are not very frequent, and they sometimes create the impression of putting the human throne in question. Here, as elsewhere, Israel aspired to be free of images of God.

So it was possible for Martin Buber (*The Kingship of God*) to interpret Yhwh's kingship as an anti-monarchical idea. Literary traditions from the pre-exilic period which associate the heavenly and earthly kingdoms allege Yhwh's kingship as a reason to oppose a central monarchy (Judg. 8:23; 1 Sam. 8:7; 12:2, with a sympathetic post-exilic echo at Ps. 146:3,10). Buber's suggestion, that the cry *Yhwh mālak* originated in the pre-settlement period and expressed Israel's sense of nomadic faithfulness, does not account for everything that came to be associated with the phrase. The psalms of Yhwh's kingship are not short of local references to 'Zion' (74:21; 97:8; 99:2; 102:12f.; 146:10; 149:2, nor should we overlook the testimony of Ps. 24). Still, his argument that *melek* and *baʿal* are two different types of God, the one leading a nomad tribe and giving it identity in battle, the other tied geographically to a settled community, gives us a very important caution. We should not assume that talk of Yhwh as *melek* is secondary to the experience of human kingship. I find nothing in M. Z. Brettler's study *God is King* to justify the hypothesis expressed in its subtitle: *Understanding an Israelite Metaphor*. From the undoubted fact that it is metaphorical to speak of Yhwh's 'throne', can we conclude that it is metaphorical to speak of Yhwh as 'king'? We would be wise to keep ourselves open to the thought that Saul and David were called *mᵉlākīm* by virtue of some relation to Yhwh rather than vice versa.

But this may seem to make it perilous to appeal to Yhwh's kingship as a *political* idea, rather than a *religious* one, at all. Can we learn anything from it to shed light upon the structures by which Israel was governed? We can, if we explore the resonances of a wider range of terms that are used to develop the idea. Consider, for example, the fine prophetic declamation: 'Yhwh is our judge! Yhwh is our lawgiver! Yhwh is our king! He it is that will save us!' (Isa. 33:22). We recognise this grouping of words as a typical one. A poetry that depends especially on parallelism develops regular patterns of association, which offer a way to explore the connexions of ideas. 'Kingship' leads quite naturally to 'judgment', 'lawgiving' and 'salvation'.

We can explore the idea of Yhwh's kingship further, then, by identifying some leading political terms that are habitually grouped with it. We shall take three common Hebrew words as primary points of reference: *yᵉshūᶜāh* (salvation), *mishpāt* (judgment) and *naḥᵃlāh* (possession). Yhwh's authority as king is established by the accomplishment of victorious deliverance, by the presence of judicial discrimination and by the continuity of a community-possession. To these three primary terms I add a fourth, which identifies the human response and acknowledgment of Yhwh's reign: *tᵉhillāh* (praise). Around these points of reference other leading terms which concern the law, the land and the city group themselves in ways that may be explained in due order. The words themselves, of course, serve only as indicators of trains of thought, and in each case could be exchanged for others. If anyone objects, for instance, that *niphlā'ōth* (mighty deeds) is a more comprehensive term than 'salvation', or that *tsedeq* (right) is more appropriate than 'judgment', these are points on which nothing need be staked. But if someone says that the judicial idea as such is not central to Israel's political life, or that the praise of the community is irrelevant to Yhwh's rule, then we have a disagreement. And since this exegetical framework is to play an organising role in our exposition of political theology, the disagreement may turn out to be a serious one that will touch on the very nature of the political act itself.

1. Let us begin with 'salvation', the usual translation of a Hebrew word which often bears a military sense, 'victory'. Yhwh's kingship is established by the fact that he delivers his people from peril in conflict with their enemies. To be sure, this starting-point should not be construed in too narrowly military a sense, as though Yhwh's power was confined to the battlefield (though 'warrior' is a title given him at Exod. 15:3; Jer. 20:11; Zeph. 3:17). Rather, as Buber expressed it (*The Kingship of God*, p. 101): 'His natural potency is contained in his historical potency.' To Yhwh belongs the power to initiate. He initiates and leads his people in the face of opposition and obstacle. They come to be, and they go forward, in the wake of his call to follow, in defiance of all that would destroy and disintegrate them. The miracle of the Exodus, which is a military event only in an unconventional sense, is the paradigm of Yhwh's *yᵉshūᶜāh*. Miraculous and providential deliverance are a part of what that 'right hand' and 'strong arm' have accomplished, as much for the individual worshipper, beset by his 'pursuers', as for the people as a whole.

Yet, equally, it is clear that the primary political implication of *yᵉshūᶜāh* is Israel's power to win military engagements, especially engagements against the odds. 'You are my king and my God, who decree victories for Jacob. Through you we push back our enemies' (Ps. 44:4). In the holy-war traditions which shape both the conquest narratives and the cycle of stories about the ninth-century prophets, there is a special relish for triumphs which defy the reasonable expectations of human military prowess and depend on the scrupulous performance of sometimes bizarre ceremonial. These are Yhwh's victories *par excellence*. But for Judah of the monarchical period it is enough that Yhwh's salvation is seen in the victories of the Davidide monarch. 'Yhwh, the king rejoices in your strength. How great is his joy in the victories you give!' (Ps. 21:1).

Taking 'salvation' as a point of reference, we can follow subsidiary parallels which help us explore the meaning of Yhwh's military victories. They were, in the first place, a sign of his *ḥesed*, or 'favour' (Pss. 13:5; 85:7). As has been constantly stressed, Yhwh's *ḥesed* is more than a momentary or occasional disposition of goodwill. It is his enduring commitment to those who lived within his covenant. (*Ḥesed* in turn often stands in parallel to *ʾemūnāh*, 'faithfulness' (Ps. 98:3 e.g.), and the two words occur together in parallel with *yᵉshūʿāh*.) In the second place it was an exercise of Yhwh's *tsedeq*. The group of words formed on the root *tsdq* are traditionally translated 'righteousness' or 'justice'; but their sense is often better caught by 'vindication' or 'justification', as Luther famously discovered. If with *ḥesed* we are in a relation known only from within, inscrutable to the outside world and private to Yhwh and his people, with *tsedeq* we are in the fully public realm of a world court. When Yhwh's right hand and holy arm have effected a victory for his people, it is a matter of international notice (Ps. 98:2). Future generations, too, must have Yhwh's vindication, victory, mighty acts and power put on record for them (Ps. 71:15–18). When we leave the context of the First Temple and move forward to the exilic period, the connexion of victory and vindication becomes especially prominent. For Deutero- and Trito-Isaiah the victory that Yhwh promises must inevitably have the force of a public rehabilitation of a disgraced and humiliated people (Isa. 45:8; 46:13; 51:5–8; 56:1; 61:10; 62:1). 'My *tsedeq* is near; my *yeshaʿ* springs forth; my own arm shall judge the nations' (Isa. 51:5).

2. This brings us to our second primary point of reference: judgment. The *tsdq* words appear in connexion with the *yshʿ* words from time to time; but they are continually associated with words formed on the root *shpt*, which have to do with judging. 'To judge with *tsedeq*' is the usual phrase for 'judging justly', as it might apply to anybody responsible for making decisions of any kind. But the successful discharge of judicial duties, especially

those of the monarch, is described in the Deuteronomic period by a favourite combination of two nouns and a verb, as 'doing judgment and justice' (2 Sam. 8:15; 1 Kgs. 10:9; Jer. 22:3,15; 23:5; 33:15; Ezek. 45:9). The same phrase describes Yhwh's own exercise of kingship (Ps. 99:4), and is echoed in the psalmists' assertion that 'justice and judgment' are the foundation of his throne (Pss. 89:14; 97:2). That Yhwh, as king, exercises royal judgment in the causes of individual worshippers who call upon him is the very heart of the personal soteriology of the Psalms (Ps. 9:4 e.g.). He is 'a righteous judge . . . who is angry every day' (Ps. 7:11), which is to say that, like his earthly counterpart, he is scrupulous to hold daily assizes (Zeph. 3:5, cf. Ps. 101:8). But his judicial role is also taken to include international and military exertions on behalf of his people as a whole. 'Yhwh judges his people', the Psalms proclaimed (using another verb, *dīn*), and added, as the immediate inference, that 'he has compassion upon his servants' (Deut. 32:36; Ps. 135:14).

A very similar assertion, however, can yield a very different inference. 'He stands up to judge his people; he enters into judgment against the elders and leaders of his people', says Isaiah of Jerusalem (Isa. 3:13). The pre-exilic prophets often return to the theme of Yhwh's 'controversy' with his people (Mic. 6:2; Jer. 2:9), which is taken up memorably in Psalm 50, where Elohim testifies against the consecrated people that makes sacrifices to him. Here the notion of an *objective right* comes to the fore. If it is true that Yhwh's *tsedeq* is his vindication of the righteous against their adversaries, it is also true that it is his vindication of the *righteous*, and that a faithless nation, though chosen of God, cannot escape God's judgment of its ways. Out of this delicately balanced tension springs the whole dynamic of Israel's election-consciousness – one could say, without exaggeration, the dynamic of the Gospel itself, which, through God's act in the death and resurrection of Jesus, addresses not only our need for comfort but our need for objective justice, that paradoxically twofold need which refuses, existentially or ontologically, to be reduced to simplicity one way or the other.

To judge is to make a distinction between the just and the unjust, or, more precisely, to bring the distinction which already exists between them into the daylight of public observation. 'He will make your *tsᵉdāqāh* shine like the dawn and your *mishpāṭ* like the noonday sun', the righteous man is promised (Ps. 37:5). Just as Solomon, in the story of the two whores and the baby, displayed that 'the wisdom of God was in him to do *mishpāṭ*' by devising a way to clarify which of the contenders was lying (1 Kgs. 3:16ff.), so Yhwh exercises his judgment by making the just and the unjust causes manifestly distinct, ending the irresolution of public ambiguity which the cunning of the evil-doer has cast around his deeds. The bad judges of Isaiah's day, on the other hand, so far from clarifying distinctions, show their true genius by being good at mixing drinks (Isa. 5:22f.)!

It is impossible to overestimate the importance of this concept for a study of biblical political ideas. It is often obscured by the influence of a quite different conception of justice, classical and Aristotelian in inspiration, built on the twin notions of appropriateness and proportionate equality – justice as receiving one's own and being in social equilibrium. *Mishpāt* is primarily a judicial *performance*. When 'judgment' is present, it is not a state of affairs that obtains but an activity that is duly carried out. When it is absent, it is not imbalance or maldistribution that is complained of but the lapsing of a juridical function that always needs to be exercised. So, for example, when Amos calls for *mishpāt* to 'roll on like a river', he means precisely that the stream of juridical activity should not be allowed to dry up. Elsewhere (5:16) he has demanded that it should be 'set up' like a fixed monument in the town's public place, always to be found there. Very comparably, Isaiah of Jerusalem demands that the citizens of Jerusalem should 'seek *mishpāt*', explaining this as a commitment to giving judgment in the cause of the fatherless and litigating on behalf of the widow (Isa. 1:17); and he promises that Yhwh will 'bring back judges' to the city 'as in the days of old', because Zion is to be 'redeemed by *mishpāt*' (1:26f.). The secondary sense of the noun has still not lost touch with the context of litigation. *Mishpāt*, having been proper to the judge, now becomes proper to the plaintiff: it is his 'claim', which the judge is bound to attend to (Isa. 40:27 e.g.).

Judgment is an event, a performance, but not for that reason transitory or ephemeral. The judgments of Yhwh have a lasting validity because all Yhwh's acts have a lasting validity. The distinction between law and history was by no means so sharp in Israel as we may be tempted to make it out to be, and the growth of a law-culture in later Judaism was not such a surprising development from the salvation-historical emphases of earlier periods. If history, for Israel, is the telling of Yhwh's acts to future generations, then law is the telling of his judgments, which, once given, are to be handed on. We may be able to detect, behind the jumble of 'casuistic' laws in the Pentateuch, a concept of law founded on occasional precedent, quite different from the all-encompassing 'codes' which marked strong acts of legal foundation elsewhere. Perhaps what differentiated Israel's idea of law from that of other societies was simply that it never abandoned its historical rationale, but remained an avowed testimony to the experience of Yhwh's past judgments.

Among the variety of words for law in Hebrew, the proliferation of which entertained the poet of Psalm 119, two are of special philological interest: ' *ēdūth* (testimony) derives from a root meaning to 'repeat' or 'rehearse'; *ḥōq* or *ḥuqqāh* (decree) is connected with the verb meaning 'to engrave'. The two are found together, with *mishpāt* as a third, in the first two verses of the Northern Psalm 81, in which it is said that the celebration of the New Moon festival is a 'decree' for Israel, a 'judgment' of Jacob's God, founded as a 'testimony' among the Josephite tribes at the time of the victory over Egypt (81:4,5). The still vital sense of ' *ēdūth* is clear from what follows: a recitation of the first command of the Decalogue (9). Recitation and engraving were both features of the ceremony on Mount Ebal which was of importance to the Deuteronomic historian (Josh. 8:22). The inscribed law-stones which were read out there are a kind of paradigm of all the law-texts, at once historical, liturgical and legal. They linked the twelve standing-stones near the Jordan, which had a recitation associated with them but no inscription (Josh. 4:7f.), with the written law-book which provided the text for the reform movement with which the Deuteronomic literary culture aligned itself (2 Kgs. 22:8–13). When, eighteen years after Josiah's initiation of the reform in Jerusalem, a group of high-placed reformers from the families of the late king's court attempted abortively to force a renewal of the programme on his son, Jehoiakim, the text they chose to base their attempt on was not another law-text but something at the time quite new, a systematic collection of prophecies delivered over the past two decades announcing Yhwh's judgment on Jerusalem (Jer. 26:1ff.). To us the literary genres of the two reformers' texts are quite distinct. To them they seemed to do precisely the same thing: attest the judgments that Yhwh had declared in Israel's more remote or more recent history.

The permanence of the law, then, was not a reflection of Yhwh's eternal unchangingness as such, but of his divine decisiveness. There is, as I insisted in *Resurrection and Moral Order* (p. 189), a theme of legal and cosmic stability in Israel's faith; yet it is not self-standing, but rests on the self-consistency of Israel's God, his *'emeth* and *'emūnāh*, truth and faithfulness, in confirming and upholding his own judgments. The sequence of thought in Psalm 96:10 follows quite naturally: the nations are to be told that Yhwh is king, that he has established the world on firm foundations and that he will judge the peoples with equity. The law-culture of later Israel comes to conceive this record of divine judgments as a possession, which can be reflected upon as a whole, called upon as a present resource and handed on from generation to generation, and it is this emphasis, rather than any departure from the salvation-historical foundation of law, that gives it its distinctive flavour. The post-exilic Psalm 147 locates the special identity of Israel in the divine act which made known his 'instructions' (*dᵉbārīm*), his decrees and his judgments; so that Israel is unlike all other nations, which 'do not know his judgments'.

3. This brings us to our third point of reference: without the consciousness of something *possessed* and handed on from generation to generation there could be a theology of divine judgments but not a political theology, since it would never be clear how the judgments of God could give order and structure to a community and sustain it in being. It was not always the case that this traditional possession was identified primarily as the law. Originally and fundamentally the existence of Israel as a people was mediated through the land. But between these two ideas there was more connexion than at first meets the eye. Possessing the land was a matter of observing that order of life which was established by Yhwh's judgments; possessing the law was a matter of enjoying that purchase on the conditions of life which was Yhwh's gift. W. D. Davies has said that the law was 'an effective symbol of the land' and 'served as a perpetual call to the land' (*The Gospel and the Land*, p. 58). Those in whose mouth was wisdom, and in whose heart God's law, would 'dwell in the land' (Ps. 37:29ff.). The material and spiritual aspects of the Israelite's possession are held together, a thought which will deeply affect John Wyclif two millennia later.

We may say that the land was the material cause of Yhwh's kingly rule, as judgment was the formal cause and his victories the efficient cause. There never was a pure nomad-ideal in Israel's history. The stories of Abraham are already organised around the promise of a settlement (see von Rad, *The Problem of the Hexateuch*, ch. 2). The land was Yhwh's sovereign gift to his people (Josh. 24:13 etc.), even though, exceptionally, it could be thought of as given solely on leasehold (Lev. 25:23), emphasising Yhwh's sovereign right of disposal. Two Hebrew words sum up the people's relation to the land: *naḥᵃlāh* ('possession' and often 'inheritance', i.e. possession by tradition) and *ḥēleq* ('share'). They often appear together, sometimes in parallel and sometimes in contrast, indicating an idea that has two complementary poles to it. On the one hand Israel as a whole possesses the land as a whole. On the other hand each tribe and family has its share, its own way of participating in the gift of God to his people. The gift is both collective and distributive.

Corresponding to the notion that the land as a whole is Israel's possession as a whole is an assertion that Israel itself is Yhwh's possession. Possessing the gift, she is possessed by the giver; and this is something that is either to be true of the whole nation or not to be true at all. Hence the stress on the common act of conquest, the military self-commitment of the nation to the claiming of the land which preceded, according to the Deuteronomic historian, the act of division. And hence the emphasis, which became very important for the Deuteronomic reformers, on a united nation based on a single cult-centre.

The conception of the conquest as an act of religious self-bestowal is perfectly recaptured in Robert Frost's poem about the colonisation of North America:

> The land was ours before we were the land's.
> She was our land more than a hundred years
> Before we were her people . . .
> But we were England's, still colonials,
> Possessing what we still were unpossessed by . . .
> Something we were withholding made us weak
> Until we found out that it was ourselves
> We were withholding from our land of living . . .
> Such as we were we gave ourselves outright
> (The deed of gift was many deeds of war) . . .
>
> ('The Gift Outright' in *Collected Poems*)

In this sense we should read the conquest texts, which stress the element of sheer religious faith, quite above all considerations of military strategy and human cunning. Joshua, as military commander, takes his shoes off before the captain of the Lord's host (Josh. 5:15) as a symbol that all that is to follow is a liturgy of worship. The failure to eliminate all the Canaanite inhabitants of the land is traced to a failure of religious observance (Josh. 9:14f.).

There was, however, a persistent uncertainty about whether Gilead, the territories east of the Jordan, were part of Yhwh's gift and Israel's possession. Gad, Reuben and half of Manasseh elected to settle there, according to the traditions known to the Deuteronomic history, rather than persist west with their brethren and wait for Yhwh to give in his own time and manner. Ezekiel, in his ideal reconstruction of the promised land, simply left Gilead out (47:18). What was not freely given by Yhwh was not truly the land of Israel. According to the tradition preserved in Joshua 22 anxieties about Gilead were focussed at an early stage on the role of an altar which threatened the unity of the national cult. Later, the celebration of the Feast of Tabernacles at the shrines of Bethel and Dan became the cardinal point of complaint by Southern spokesmen against the Northern kings (1 Kgs. 12:28ff.). The conviction that the unity of the possession and the people required a central focus of cultic pilgrimage for all Israelites, without prejudice to purely local shrines, was one contributory element in the Deuteronomic reformers' programme. The other was the disgust of the ninth- and eighth-century prophets at the character of the local shrines and their cults. Taken together, these two traditions shaped the Deuteronomic ambition to centralise worship into one cult-centre and abolish all other sites, an aspiration realised, as they hoped at the time, by the massive national Passover celebrated by Josiah in Jerusalem in 622 BC (2 Kgs. 23:21ff.).

The strategy of David and Solomon in moving the Ark to Jerusalem and housing it in a temple adjoining the royal palace had been to create a unified centre of worship and government. In doing so they provided a focus of loyalty in which the nation's sense of territorial integrity coalesced with its sense of military security. The victories of Yhwh and the gift of Yhwh both became concentrated on the fortress city. As God's dwelling, it was the place *par excellence* where the people might dwell in safety (Pss. 46:4ff.; 48:1ff.; 76:1ff.). Zion's towers, ramparts and citadels became the possession to pass on to the next generation (Ps. 48:13). Once razed to the ground, the city became the symbol of the lost land to which the affections of the exiled Jews turned magnetically. It was to the city that the greatest prophet of the return addressed his consolation (Isa. 40:2). It was the city which provided the focus for the self-understanding of the small state which provided a home for returning exiles.

If the poets and prophets of the Southern kingdom borrowed mythical elements from the Canaanite traditions of the place in order to represent 'Mount Zion' as victor in a competition of mountain peaks (Ps. 68:15 e.g.), this imagery was carefully integrated into the conviction that Yhwh was sovereign both in judgment and deliverance of his people. The image of Jerusalem surrounded by invading armies and throwing them back was, therefore, a kind of pre-existing interpretative matrix into which Isaiah of Jerusalem could pour his interpretation of Assyria's invasion and defeat as the direct doing of Yhwh (29:1–8). Isaiah's Zion-theology expressed a subtly balanced view of the city's destiny which commanded repentance, humility and confidence at the same time. In the last years of the seventh century, after the failure (as they saw it) of Josiah's reforms, the prophets of the time felt they had to attack what had become no more than a complacent confidence in the impregnability of the city, either head-on (Jer. 7:3–15) or by damning silence (Ezekiel, who speaks of the 'mountains of Israel' instead of 'Mount Zion', and refuses to call the holy city of his final vision either Zion or Jerusalem).

At the opposite pole from this unitary focus on the possession in the city, there is the tradition of tribal and family landholdings, which still deeply engaged the interest of the Deuteronomic historian. Those chapters of the Book of Joshua which describe the original process of distribution (13–21) are, in their way, an eloquent document. Preserved in this form at a time when the hope for an ordered tribal land-system had been irremediably shattered in the débâcle of the Chaldean invasion and the exile, they incorporate ancient territorial designations which can hardly have been current coin but to which the memory of the faithful clung tenaciously. For tribal and family landholding established, in principle, the membership of Israel. As the prophetic oracle had said: 'Every man shall sit under his own vine and under his own fig tree' (Mic. 4:4). To lose the patrimonial small-holding was to let a name disappear from the clan (Num. 27:4), a consid-eration which dictated the practice of female inheritance. The beautiful Psalm 16 associates the worshipper's oath of loyalty to Yhwh ('You are my lord; apart from you I have no good thing') with his possession of his holding: 'Yhwh, you have assigned me my share and my cup. You have guaranteed my allotment. The boundary-lines have been drawn for me in pleasant places. Surely I have a delightful possession' (Ps. 16:2,5,6).

> In the story of Ruth the duty of the next-of-kin under the law of levirate mar-riage is raised in connexion with the disposal of a parcel of land of which the story has told us nothing at all (Ruth 4:3ff.), a curious reminder of how this pro-vision was conceived in terms of maintaining the distinct identity of family holdings. If the absorption of one holding into another even by inheritance was discouraged, there was very strong hostility to such a development as a result of sale. The practice (or principle, if it was never literally practised) of the 'jubilee year' (Lev. 25:8–34) meant, in effect, that land could be alienated only on lease-hold and not freehold. The eighth-century prophets opposed the development of a market in land, with an expansive proprietorial interest as one of its con-sequences and the creation of a landless class as the other. This controversy touched the powers of the monarchy itself. It was no personal whim that barred Naboth from selling his patrimonial inheritance to the Omride king, but the principle of inalienability. Ahab's offence, in the view of the early prophetic circles who told the story, did not begin with his plot to take the farmer's life, for he had already transgressed in his ambition to consolidate the royal estate – no doubt a necessity, as he saw it, to finance the operations of the monarchy (1 Kgs. 21:1ff.). The same conflict seems to have shaped a composition that has a good deal to say about land, Psalm 37, in which the proverbial traditions of Wisdom are curiously woven together with the themes of conquest and distri-bution of land. Yhwh's act of judgment is seen in his placing the 'meek', i.e. the dispossessed, in secure holdings and in ejection of the usurping proud. Security of tenure will be based on inexhaustible resources, a reminder that alienation was likely to arise from the insufficiency of smallholdings to support their owners (cf. Lev. 25:25).

There was one group of Israelites who, it was universally asserted, had no landholdings: the Levites. According to an ancient tradition there were forty-eight 'Levitical towns' in which they might own houses, attached to which there was pasture-land (presumably common, and absolutely inalienable), more, we may assume, to provide a banking facility than to provide an income (Lev. 25:32ff.; Num. 35:1–8; Josh. 21:1–42). The Deuteronomic law-code does not know of these towns, but envisages the Levites as fully dispersed throughout the villages and towns of Israel, dependent on the tithes of their neighbours. Their relative propertylessness and lack of a tribal territory spoke eloquently of a symbolic status in the community. Yhwh himself was their possession (Deut. 8:1f. etc.), which was, on the one hand, to say simply that their place in the community was assured by their religious service rather than by their landholding; on the other, it meant that they represented the inner truth of Israel's possession of its land, that it was a mediation of their relation with Yhwh. Alternatively it could be said that the tithes were their possession (Num. 18:21). In the light of the disaster of 587, in which every Israelite came to be landless, the Levites' status was a model for the faithful. Poets contemplating the stricken city took upon themselves the profession, 'Yhwh is my possession' (Lam. 3:24, cf. Ps. 73:26). And a later poet, who thought of his possession primarily as the law, found that similar words suited his purpose: 'You are my share, Yhwh; I have promised to obey your instructions' (Ps. 119:57).

We have identified, then, three affirmations which shape Israel's sense of political identity and define what is meant by saying that Yhwh rules as king: he gives Israel victory; he gives judgment; he gives Israel its possession. We have seen how each of these affirmations can be tilted towards either of the others: the notions of victory and judgment come together in the idea of Yhwh's 'vindication'; the notions of judgment and possession meet in the conception of Yhwh's law; and the notions of possession and victory are associated in the role played by Mount Zion as the focus of Israel's security. This analysis of concepts cannot, of course, claim to be directly authorised by the text of the Hebrew Scriptures. Like all exegetical structures it can only claim to comprehend the text and illuminate it by allowing one aspect to shed light upon another. But that claim can, I believe, be sustained for this analysis, which, furthermore, will provide an important clue for the development of the affirmation of God's kingship in the New Testament. Our view here, however, stretches beyond this exegetical claim to a theoretical one. The threefold analysis of divine rule as salvation, judgment and possession will provide a framework for exploring the major questions about authority posed by the Western tradition. The unique covenant of Yhwh and Israel can be seen as a point of disclosure from which the nature of all political authority comes into view. Out of the self-possession of this people in their relation to God springs the possibility of other peoples' possessing themselves in God. In this hermeneutic assumption lay the actual continuity between Israel's experience and the Western tradition. In what follows it will be our business to reclaim it from oblivion.

The direction to be taken can be indicated at this point in two theorems, to which we shall quickly add a third, which appropriate, in terms adapted for general theoretical use, the threefold analysis of kingship on the one hand and the ascription of kingship to Yhwh on the other. They will be given a fuller expansion and development at a later stage. The first theorem can be expressed as follows: *Political authority arises where power, the execution of right and the perpetuation of tradition are assured together in one coordinated agency.* When one of the three is separated from the others, there can be no authority. The 'mystery', as we have presumed to call it, by which we freely defer to the command of social organs (even at the cost of pursuing accessible and worthy ends of action) can be realised only under conditions in which these three concerns of society are held together. But although any actor either may make it a matter of conscious intention to keep power, the execution of right and the perpetuation of tradition together in his own hands and so to exercise political authority, or may intend to keep them together in the hands of someone else and so to be a loyal subject to political authority, in neither endeavour does success come merely by intending it. All regimes, however well constituted and conducted, are dogged by the possibility that their authority may be eroded under the pressure of changing social circumstances. And so our second theorem follows: *That any regime should actually come to hold authority, and should continue to hold it, is a work of divine providence in history, not a mere accomplishment of the human task of political service.* In this second theorem can be recognised an important doctrine of William of Ockham, which defines the distinction between the human and divine roles in the constitution of governments (*Breviloquium* iv.6). Behind every historically successful regime, there is the divine regime of history. The continuity achieved by the one presupposes the operation of the other, because it does not lie within the power of political orders to secure the social conditions for their own indefinite prolongation.

4. From this comes a corollary necessary to complete both the exegetical and the theoretical outline. Political authority, with its associated authorisations of power, right and tradition, its demands for deference and the various social benefits it confers, is simply presented to us as a fact within history. Whatever the role of political agents, whether rulers or subjects, in determining the shape and form that political authority shall take in any

time and place, no one can pretend to have invented political authority or to have devised it as an instrument to serve some pre-political purposes of his or her own. The Thomist tradition of political theology expressed this insight by relating politics immediately to our created sociality through 'Natural Law'. We will express it in a third theorem: *In acknowledging political authority, society proves its political identity.* Acknowledgment is the fundamental relation that obtains between a society and its own political authorities. It recognises them – not in the constitutive sense of conferring existence on them by recognition, but in the much more basic sense of simply acknowledging that they are *there* and that they are *theirs*. 'This government is our government' it acknowledges, with whatever mixture of complacency and ruefulness, simply as a fact about itself from which it may begin its political tasks but which it cannot get behind.

So Yhwh's rule receives its answering recognition in the praises of his people. In a telling phrase a psalmist describes Yhwh as 'enthroned upon the praises of Israel' (Ps. 22:3), an adaptation of the conventional designation, drawn from the sacred furniture of the First Temple, which has him 'enthroned upon the cherubim' (i.e. of the Ark). The link which ties the exercise of Yhwh's kingly rule to the praise of his people is that as the people congregate to perform their act of praise, the political reality of Israel is displayed. 'To you belongs praise, Elohim, in Zion . . . to you shall all flesh come' (Ps. 65:1f.). The gathering of the congregation is the moment at which the people's identity is disclosed (as in the late Psalm 149 the distinct identity of the warrior-saints (*ḥᵃsīdīm*) is seen in the fact that they have their separate assembly of praise). Hence the importance of 'gathering', both on annual pilgrimage and in a final and complete return from exile, to the hopes of the post-exilic community: 'Gather us from the nations, that we may give thanks to your holy name and glory in your praise' (Ps. 106:47). The community is a political community by virtue of being a worshipping community; while the worship of the single believer, restored from some affliction and desiring to thank God, must, as it were, be politicised by being brought into the public arena of 'the great congregation' (Pss. 35:18; 40:9f.) in 'the gates of the daughter of Zion' (Ps. 9:14). Otherwise, the poet says, Yhwh's righteousness, faithfulness, salvation, love and truth would be 'hidden' and 'concealed' (Ps. 40:10).

The congregation, however, forms the centre of a much wider community of praise which runs out as far as Yhwh's kingly rule is manifest. It is as though the assembly can extend itself to include communities of worship everywhere that have seen evidence of the divine rule. So the thought of the poet of Psalm 48 moves from the Temple, where worshippers 'have thought on' Elohim's favour – 'Like your name, Elohim, so your praise reaches to the ends of the earth. Your right hand is occupied with vindication' – and then back to the focal place of worship again: 'Mount Zion shall rejoice' (9–11). Deutero-Isaiah, having introduced a psalm of praise in a conventional manner – 'Sing unto Yhwh a new song!' – at once invites praise *from* the ends of the earth', especially from sailors and island-dwellers and desert cities (Isa. 42:10f., cf. his models at Pss. 96, 98). Some visions of the universal rule of Yhwh envisage a world-assembly of nations in Jerusalem, on the model of Israel's own pilgrim-feasts (Isa. 2:3 = Mic. 4:2, taken up after the exile in Zech. 14:16ff.). 'The name of Yhwh will be declared in Zion, his praise in Jerusalem, when the peoples and the kingdoms assemble to worship Yhwh' (Ps. 102:21f.).

Praise is a kind of proving or demonstration of the fact of God's kingly rule. At no point is the suggestion allowed that the people, by their praises, have *made* Yhwh king, nor should that suggestion be inferred from the speculative hypothesis of an 'enthronement ceremony'. This fourth section of our discussion, then, has to be set apart from the three which preceded it, for it does not relate to them as they relate to each other. Victory, judgment and possession are what God has done 'by his own right hand'. In one sense everything is complete when he has done them. If Israel's praises did not follow, or were radically defective, then, as the prophet of Psalm 50 very well understands, God's position would not be weakened in the slightest. 'The heavens' are sufficient to 'declare his vindication' in an assembly where the supposedly 'consecrated ones' can expect nothing but judgment for their meaningless attempts at worship (Ps. 50:6). Yet the people's praise is more than 'confirmation', if by that word we mean no more than a kind of public notification of something that has happened quite independently. The kingly rule of Yhwh *takes effect in* the praises of his people, so that, to complete the classical analysis we began on p. 41 above, praise is the final cause of God's kingdom. Deutero-Isaiah can say that Yhwh 'formed' the people for himself 'that they might declare my praise' (43:21). This is what God's reign is directed towards, an acclamation that unites the whole community. In giving himself as king, God sought acknowledgment from mankind. We can say that much without derogation from divine sovereignty, since it is the implication of the covenant by which sovereign and subject are bound together. So that even Psalm 50, which knows that Elohim will get his tribute of praise regardless of what Israel does, must renew the summons of the covenant: 'He who brings thanksgiving as his sacrifice, honours me; to him who orders his way aright I will show Elohim's victory' (Ps. 50:23).

Shall we conclude, then, that within every political society there occurs, implicitly, an act of worship of divine rule? I think we may even venture as far as that. 'State-authority', remarks Stephen Clark, 'is what emerges when households, clans and crafts first recognise a sacred centre in their lives together and then forget where the centre gets its authority . . . The voice of the High God reminds us that the land is his' (*Civil Peace and Sacred Order*, p. 90). Certainly it explains, as very few attempts at theorising the foundations of politics ever do explain, the persistent cultural connexion between politics and religion. And it allows us to understand why it is precisely at this point that political loyalties can go so badly wrong; for a worship of divine rule which has failed to recollect or understand the divine purpose can only be an idolatrous worship which sanctions an idolatrous politics. It sheds light, too, on the nature of the impasse into which a politics constructed on an avowedly anti-sacred basis has now come. For without the act of worship political authority is unbelievable, so that binding political loyalties and obligations seem to be deprived of any point. The doctrine that *we* set up political authority, as a device to secure our own essentially private, local and unpolitical purposes, has left the Western democracies in a state of pervasive moral debilitation, which, from time to time, inevitably throws up idolatrous and authoritarian reactions.

The mediators

The authority of Yhwh was, like Yhwh himself, imageless. Nobody could represent it. Yet it was shown forth on earth through cataclysmic events, not only of a natural but also of a political order. Human acts as well as earthquake and fire demonstrated his rule among his people. Immediacy and human mediation complemented each other in a delicate balance. Even the covenant-giving at Sinai, it was remembered, needed a human mediator, who could relate the speech of God to a people unable otherwise to hear it (Exod. 20:19). Yet Sinai was the case *par excellence* of immediate divine presence.

Mediation was necessary, because God was holy. So taught the priestly tradition, which was interested primarily in the mediation afforded by religious ritual; yet the same conception served easily as a paradigm for government. This is strikingly apparent in the narrative of Numbers 16, which brings together two distinct challenges to Moses' authority: one from a Levite source, which aims to get possession of Aaron's priestly privilege, the other from a Reubenite source, in which Moses' political leadership is in question. The earth swallows Dathan and Abiram, the political challengers, while Korah and his followers, like other pretenders to the priesthood (cf. Lev. 10:1–3), are consumed by fire. The theoretical posture of the two challenges is represented in the same way: the whole community is holy; there can be no place for persons who are 'above the assembly'. It is, on the one hand, an egalitarian philosophy, while, on the other, it lays claim to Yahwist faith in the immediacy of divine presence. Moses' reply seizes on the theoretical weakness of the attempt to join these two strands. Is it not precisely an expression of Yhwh's immediacy, he asks, that he 'will cause to come near him that man whom he will choose' (5)? And does not the Levites' position in society already depend upon the distinction Yhwh makes between those who are, and those who are not, admitted into a cultic role? The cultic tribe is itself the proof of Yhwh's sovereign decision to do with each group or individual as seems good to him. The matter is not left there, however, for the outcome shows us why it has in fact seemed good to Yhwh to 'bring near' a group who will mediate between himself and the community. Moses and Aaron are intercessors, who stand in the way of the divine wrath (21f.), a function concentrated in Aaron's priestly incense, with which he 'stood between the living and the dead' (46–8). The mediatorial role is justified not only by Yhwh's destruction of those who would oppose it but by the softening of the judgment against the whole community.

But how could immediacy and mediation be understood in a complementary way when the people were no longer at Sinai, when the thunder and lightning and the sound of the trumpet were no longer to be heard? Must Yhwh's people be kept at a distance from their proper king when they enter the promised land, ruled through intermediaries and without awareness of the divine presence? That question is explored with marvellous subtlety in two complex and haunting chapters of the Sinai literature (Exod. 33, 34). The answer they reach is: Yhwh is immediately present in conquest; his presence is mediated in judgment; and he is present in a kind of concealed immediacy in the law.

> One simple way of saying that the God of Sinai would authorise and empower the conquest of Canaan was: he would send his angel ahead of his people to bring them in (Exod. 23:20, cf. 32:34). This way of conceiving things was meant to be unproblematic: the God of Sinai is not confined to the place of his revelation, and so must have angels through which he acts in any place. The discussion between Moses and Yhwh in Exodus 33, however, begins by finding a problem with it. Yhwh will send his angel to effect the conquest; but does that not imply that he will withdraw *himself*? Apparently it does: 'If I were to go with you even for a moment, I might destroy you' (5). Before the discussion is taken further, the editor (if such a word may be used of so powerful a literary

and theological presence) has placed a description of Moses' encounters with Yhwh in the Tent of Meeting 'face to face' (7–11). The bearing of this upon the discussion is clear: it is through Yhwh's unique relation to the mediator that his own 'presence' or 'face' is secured for the community as a whole. That is the presence that will be withdrawn, then, if Yhwh should act through an angel alone. Moses complains that by offering the leadership of a conquering angel, rather than his own immediate leadership, Yhwh has put in doubt the relationship which marks his people as special: 'If your presence does not go with us, what will distinguish me and your people from all other people on the face of the earth?' Yhwh then yields: 'My presence will go with you.' The primary question is settled: the conquest will be in Yhwh's own hands.

Two further questions follow: first, will the presence of Yhwh destroy his people in judgment? Moses demands: 'Show me your glory!' (18), to which Yhwh replies with a distinction. Moses may see his 'goodness' and hear the proclamation of his 'name', Yhwh. But, in a vivid image, he is to see Yhwh's back and not his face. Are we to understand that the original 'face to face' claim is now in doubt? We are to think of it, at any rate, as qualified. There is a kind of face-to-face encounter with the divine that is simply destructive. But the covenant-name is a form of mediation by which divine judgment communicates itself in forbearance, yet without abnegating the truth of judgment in the long term (34:6f.). This is the second sense in which Yhwh will 'go with' his people and 'possess' them (8,9): he will provide them with a judgment mediated in covenant for their protection.

There then intervenes the so-called Ritual Decalogue (34:10–26), the significance of which at this point in the argument is shown by the final section, which takes up, from yet another point of view, Moses' face-to-face encounter with Yhwh. The question that underlies this stage of the discussion is how the immediacy of the Sinai encounter can be prolonged when Moses no longer leads the people across the desert and goes to Yhwh at the Tent of Meeting. The answer is: the act of lawgiving has brought the radiance of the divine presence out among the people once and for all. The shining face of Moses, returning from the mountain with two tables of stone, is an image of the law itself, through which God is immediately and continually present. As the law is spoken to the people (with *unveiled* face!) the presence of Yhwh, terrifying, inspiring, sustaining, is palpable. This is the 'face' by which Yhwh 'goes with' his people. But the veiling of Moses shows how this decisive act of revelation is experienced, after Sinai, only indirectly. In the promised land the law conceals the divine radiance, though that radiance was never lost since it was founded on the hidden correspondence between the divine legislator and the human lawgiver. St Paul later seized on the negative element in this allegory, stressing the indirect character of the 'ministry of condemnation' and so allowing only half of what this apologia for mediation wanted to say. The indirectness of God's self-disclosure in the law, it would tell us, does not detract from its underlying

immediacy. For Paul that underlying immediacy needed to be given an eschatological twist; immediacy belongs to that moment when the ministry of condemnation is superseded by the ministry of righteousness which 'with unveiled
face behold[s] the glory of the Lord' (2 Cor. 3:18).

The three questions about mediation which concern this passage, then,
correspond to the three elements of Yhwh's kingly rule as we have traced
them: salvation, judgment and possession. Indeed, Moses' role throughout
the Book of Exodus, as we now have it, corresponds to the same pattern:
he leads the people out of Egypt to the victory of the Red Sea; he judges
their cases in the wilderness; he lays before them the pattern of their new
life in possession of their land at Sinai. But whereas Moses is conceived as
the unitary mediator of divine rule in its three aspects, the prospect for the
future is a diffused and differentiated mediation. The force of the allegory
of Exodus 34:29ff. is that Moses is always present, though concealed, in the
law, and that no replacement of him is conceivable. Moses the lawgiver is
the sole bearer of the divine radiance. Two important Pentateuchal narratives (Exod. 18; Num. 11) address the transmission of Moses' functions to
others. Their problematic is partly the relation of local to central authorities; but behind that there lies the more fundamental question of how different elements in government have sprung from the unitary mediation of
Yhwh's rule by Moses.

On this account Moses has no true successor. Yet that conclusion is challenged by some interpretations of the role of Joshua which see him, not
merely as a military leader, but as a complete successor. The tension here
reflects precisely the tension that was felt over the institution of monarchy
in its initial phases. For the claims of monarchy were precisely to hold
together military, judicial and, ultimately, tradition-bearing functions in
one pair of hands. Those who argued against monarchy that where Yhwh
was king there was no place for any other (1 Sam. 8:7; Judg. 8:23) did not,
of course, challenge the idea of human mediation of divine kingship. They
challenged the erection of an image of Yhwh, one whose mediation held all
Yhwh's kingly functions together, so that he, too, was a king. The debate
was comparable to that which emerged in modern political thought in
terms of the 'separation of powers'. Can sovereignty that belongs to a spiritual body (whether God or the people) be exercised whole and entire by
one representative person, or must it be diffused among different offices?

It is a textbook commonplace that we can distinguish two competing strands
of thought about the monarchy within the Hebrew Scriptures. There are texts
of anti-monarchical provenance (e.g. 1 Sam. 8) and texts of pro-monarchical

provenance (e.g. 1 Sam. 9, 10). The strong division of opinion in the late pre-monarchical period emerges explicitly in the stores of Gideon and Abimelech (Judg. 8:27–9:57) as well as in those about Samuel and Saul. The parable of Jotham expresses the anti-monarchist case: only the ignoble become kings, and then either humiliate or destroy the noble (Judg. 9:7–20). The beautiful little psalm entitled 'the last words of David' expresses the monarchist case: 'one who rules in righteousness and in the fear of God is like the light of dawn at sunrise on a cloudless morning' (2 Sam. 23:3f.).

More importantly, whole story-cycles display a leaning, supportive or critical. The masterly narrative of David's decline, the 'succession-narrative', which begins with the story of Uriah and Bathsheba and ends with Solomon's effective possession of the throne (2 Sam. 11–1 Kgs. 2), shows sustained contempt for the monarch's incapacity to control events, even while its author knows how to draw out all the pathos of the king's situation. On the other side, three different cycles of stories, woven together in our history, tell how David came to replace Saul in a manner that clearly legitimates his throne. One shows how David provided protection for the exposed and harassed farmsteads of southern Judah: the story of Abigail (1 Sam. 25:2–42) is an allegory of how these communities made a king out of a brigand by offering him kingly responsibilities and teaching him kingly virtues. A second shows how David's rise was the result of the madness visited on Saul as a judgment by God. A third shows how David, though himself anointed by Samuel, respected the anointing of Saul and resisted the temptation to remove him. The historian, by skilful use of these three cycles, has claimed for David the three constitutive elements of Yhwh's kingly rule: victory, judgment and the tradition of Yhwh's possession.

Yet simply observing these differences of viewpoint does not help us address the most important question about the monarchy: how the imageless faith of Israel became reconciled to the institution. After all, in the end nobody opposed the monarchy. The prophetic movement of the Northern kingdom in the ninth century, notorious for its confrontations with the Omride kings, was credited with having blessed the foundation of a new dynasty (2 Kgs. 9:1–13), while Hosea, in whose mind the new dynasty had proved itself as bad as the old (1:4f.), subscribed to something very like the account of monarchy that had been offered in 1 Samuel 8 (Hos. 13:10f.).

1. Especially offensive to the opponents of the monarchy was the institutionalising of a *military function*. The ironically named 'king's *mishpāt*' in which Samuel warns the people against the monarchical ideal (1 Sam. 8:10–18) is essentially to do with the implications of a standing militia: to maintain it requires an extensive household and an extensive estate, and to maintain them requires staff and taxation, which drain manpower and real estate out of the family-based agrarian economy. But more important, to

assume permanent military leadership is to challenge the supreme sign of Yhwh's sovereignty. For the ideal conception of Yhwh's battles consciously minimised the scope for military initiative. We find this idea consistently presented in the battle stories of the wilderness and conquest periods, in the traditions of the judges, and occasionally in stories connected with Saul and David. The military commander depends upon immediate divine direction (Num. 14:40–5; 2 Sam. 5:22–5 e.g.); the military array assumes a quasi-liturgical character; the sacred battle is paradoxically unexpected in its course and outcome; the forces of nature are involved in securing Yhwh's victory (Josh. 10:13; Judg. 5:20). Gideon's triumph is that of the perfect fool (Judg. 7:5–8); the siege of Jericho is the perfect liturgy (Josh. 5:15). Correspondingly, the Pentateuchal traditions restrict Moses' role in battle to that of a priestly intercessor, who 'stretched out his hands' to invoke Yhwh's victory for his people (Exod. 14:26f.; 17:10–13). Not even the decision to strike camp is his to take, since the presence of the Ark gives it a military significance (Num. 9:15–23); Moses is restricted to invoking Yhwh to battle (10:35f.). It is in this context that the grim institution of 'the ban' is intelligible: as a response to Yhwh's sovereign initiative, the destruction of the enemy becomes a solemn sacrifice from which nothing may be withheld.

> The law-text of Deuteronomy 20 clearly presupposes this understanding of warfare as a sacral performance initiated by Yhwh, while at the same time it qualifies and ritualises the provisions for making war in a way that marks a retreat from the expectations of divine immediacy which the narratives suggest. The purgation of the army (20:5–9) ensures Israel against the ceremonial liabilities of undedicated houses, unharvested vineyards and unconsummated marriages, while excluding the fearful as a compromising element in Yhwh's army. Despite the characteristically humane gloss that these provisions are given, their sacral character is quite in evidence. The interpretation of the ban which follows, however, represents a softening of the ancient law that nothing 'devoted' (*ḥerem*) may be ransomed (Lev. 27:28f. – an initial softening is already visible at Num. 18:14). An offer of peace is required before the ban is imposed, and, when it is, women and children as well as livestock are considered subject to redemption. The exception for the case of the conquest of Canaan (Deut. 20:16–18) is an editorial reconciliation of the law with narrative traditions such as the story of Achan (Josh. 6) and Saul's failure in the war against Amalek (1 Sam. 15). The provision for the protection of fruit-trees in a siege (Deut. 20:19f.), though also humane in its tendency, is probably original to the sacral regulations. Thus the Deuteronomic law developed the sacral conception in the direction of an elementary 'just-war' code.
>
> The ideal of Yhwh's sole initiative in battle was revived and cherished by the

ninth-century prophetic movement in Northern Israel, and is the subject of a lengthy story in the book of the prophets, later incorporated into the Deuteronomic history. A Northern king (identified by the Deuteronomist as Ahab), who spares enemy kings magnanimously according to the rules of an international brotherhood of kings (1 Kgs. 20:32), is pitted against Yhwh's prophets, who demand the right to dictate the course of the battle, give assurance of victory, and exact final and decisive judgment against Yhwh's enemies (20:42). In a sub-plot concerning the fate of a hesitant prophet the moral is underlined: when Yhwh says 'strike', one must strike (20:35f.). Jehu's sanguinary revolution, the original climax of the little book of the prophets, represents a triumph for the ideals of war promoted by his prophetic supporters. Later generations were less impressed than was the prophetic narrator with Jehu's 'zeal for Yhwh' (2 Kgs. 10:16; see Hos. 1:4f. and even, from the Deuteronomist, 2 Kgs. 10:28–33). This was the last attempt at a direct revival. In subsequent generations the theological tradition of the unmediated presence of Yhwh in battle was cut loose from Israel's sacral warmaking and turned by the prophets into an account of his sovereign disposition of the world-empires. The story of Sennacherib's discomfiture before the gates of Jerusalem (2 Kgs. 19:14–36), Jeremiah's designation of Nebuchadrezzar as Yhwh's 'servant' (Jer. 25:9) and Deutero-Isaiah's claim that Cyrus was Yhwh's 'shepherd' (Isa. 44:28) all continue the conviction of Yhwh's sovereign initiative – 'His own arm worked salvation for him' (Isa. 59:16) – but without the ritual context.

The challenge to the sacral concept of war seems to have arisen originally from an alternative ideal which, in the end, made rather little headway in Israel, despite its powerful appeal elsewhere in the Mediterranean: the ideal of the warrior-hero. The characters of Jonathan and of the young David reflect a heroic concept of battle, which demanded a major role for the individual warrior's courage and decisiveness, in defiance of the abnegation of military prowess demanded by the sacral conventions. There is a distinct shift of perspective from the view taken of warriors in the narratives of the Book of Judges, where even Samson's personally motivated outbreaks are driven by the Spirit of Yhwh on an occasional basis. Jonathan, always accompanied by his armour-bearer, belongs to a nascent warrior-culture, which is prepared to take military initiatives of its own, given the opportunity. Curiously sandwiched between two episodes which criticise Saul for disregard of the cultic proprieties in warfare (confirming, from the opposite point of view, that there was a major controversy about the matter at that time) we find a lengthy narrative (1 Sam. 14) which sets Saul up as the representative of an immobile, priest-bound and altogether self-destructive approach to battle, contrasted with the heroic *élan* of his son, who is prepared to venture his life on the insecurity of a 'perhaps' (1 Sam.

14:6). This bitter satire holds that the father was prepared to slay his victorious son for a breach of ritual; but the good sense of the people prevailed, which knew that 'he wrought with Elohim this day' (14:45), a phrase eloquent of the new claim made for the warrior-hero, right down to its use of the more neutral term for God.

Yet, curiously, warrior-heroes are no part of Israel's history until, in the Maccabean period, the *ḥᵃsīdīm* unite some of the characteristics of heroes with some of sacral warriors (cf. Ps. 149). The reason for this must be the absorption of all the hopes vested in military initiative into the person of the king. If there is any figure who is allowed to mediate Yhwh's victories, it is he. Yet there is always a great deal of theological sensitivity as to how this mediating relation is expressed. The royal psalms conceive these victories as won by Yhwh and granted by him as a favour to the king. It is Yhwh who 'lays hold on his enemies', while the king is represented, like Moses, as almost permanently in a posture of supplication (Pss. 20:5f.; 21:2,4,8). From rather later in the monarchical period, perhaps, comes the king's admission that Yhwh 'trains my hands for war and my fingers for battle'; and with this there goes the more world-political understanding, characteristic of the period of the great empires, that God 'gives victories to kings' – as a generalised phenomenon (Ps. 144:1,10).

> About the situation prior to the monarchy we can only be hesitant. If there was, as appears, a confrontation at the time of Saul's reign, between the aspirations of the warrior and the aspirations of the priest in the control of warfare, that may have something to do with the convergence of the roles of priest and judge which we see in the person of Samuel. If Samuel brought the control of military initiatives into priestly hands, the conflict is explicable. No military leader before that period seems to have depended very much on priests. Yet religious authorisation and ritual accompaniment for battle there certainly was, though of a more charismatic kind. Samson drew authority from his Nazirite status, and the young Saul, we are reminded by the proverb, was associated with 'prophets'.

2. The exercise of *judicial functions* played an important role in the monarch's position as Yhwh's representative. In the pre-monarchical period the nearest approximation to a continuous governmental function that can be discerned was provided by 'the judges', and it was a crucial element in the case for a monarchy that they had failed to provide not only the security necessary for Israel's identity but even a consistent standard of justice itself. Effective judgment, then, was to be the ordinary content of the monarch's exertions. The king was required to promise just judgment not

only in his own daily assizes, but through making worthy appointments to his household (Ps. 101:3–8). Criticism of the monarchy centred on the exercise of justice, too. A recurrent story-pattern has the king beguiled into giving a judgment against himself by being asked to rule on a hypothetical case. The unnamed prophet tricked the Northern king into condemning his own peace-treaty with Syria (1 Kgs. 20:39–43). Nathan lured David into pronouncing on his own murder of Uriah (2 Sam. 12:1–16); and in the same way Joab tried to lure David into ordering Absalom's return, but the great story-teller of the succession-narrative shows us that the old king had now lost his innocence and become complicit in his own beguiling (2 Sam. 14:4–19). 'The king is like an angel of God in discerning both good and evil', said the woman of Tekoa (14:7), echoing a suitably amoral commonplace of Near Eastern wisdom which associates monarchs with a wide-ranging knowledge of every kind (cf. Prov. 25:2). But in Yahwism this commonplace was interpreted morally, in terms of just judgment: 'When a king sits on his throne to judge, he winnows out all evil with his eyes' (Prov. 20:8; cf. 16:10,12f.; 20:26; 29:4,14; 31:4–9). Solomon, in the story of the two whores and the baby, is the archetypal king of Yahwist wisdom: he can work out what is going on, and put it right (1 Kgs. 3:16–28).

> That the judges of the pre-monarchical period did, in fact, 'judge Israel' as they were said to, we should not doubt. It is true that the Deuteronomic historian, or his source, in keeping with a generally monarchist interest in depicting the era as one of turmoil and conflict, throughout which Yhwh had repeatedly to rescue his people from the jaws of disaster, combines the succession of judges with a series of battle narratives. But it entirely begs the question that the period poses to him and to us if we paraphrase his verb *shpht* as 'rule' – as though the whole question of whether there could be any 'rule' apart from Yhwh's had already been settled! The figure of Deborah gives an insight into another and more ordinary function than that of charismatic military leadership, which served to hold Israel loosely together in times of peace. And the work of Samuel, the last of the judges, was taken to be judicial even more than it was taken to be priestly. (The criticisms made of his sons leave no doubt about that (1 Sam. 8:3, in contrast to what Eli's sons were charged with, 2:12–17).)

The role of judge is not very prominent in the depiction of Moses; but in two narratives where it does arise, it has to do with the same question, evidently felt to be a difficult one: how are the variety of figures who in fact exercised judicial responsibility in Israel related and responsible to the central judicial authority? The first of these is the unexpected, and self-standing, narrative of Exodus 18, in which Jethro, Moses' Midianite father-in-law, visits the Israelite camp in the wilderness and teaches Moses the art of delegation. It is hard not to think that the placing of this story is the result of a conscious editorial decision that the transition from the Exodus victory-material to the Sinai lawgiving-material needed a reference to the activity of judgment. The concern of the narrative is entirely with hearing cases and giving decisions; even the reference to 'decrees' and 'laws' (*ḥuqqim tōrōth*) envisages precedents and rulings primarily. One of the most striking features of the narrative is its use of the term 'princes' (*sārīm*) to describe the officials to whom Moses is to delegate. The other narrative is in Numbers 11, and the conception, both of the task and of the nature of the devolution of authority, is slightly different. Yhwh shares the 'spirit' of Moses, his own Spirit, that is, which has equipped Moses for his role, with seventy others who are already 'elders' or 'administrators' of the people (*zᵉqēnīm, shōtrīm*), though where we might expect a reference to the tribal structure, none is to be found. They are to assist Moses to 'carry the burden of the people', a description which is more administrative than judicial, though we should not stress this distinction too sharply as the concept of 'judgment' was the matrix in which a whole range of administrative tasks was conceived. The story then recounts how, on their attendance at the Tent of Meeting, the seventy 'prophesy', though they never prophesy thereafter. Their office is not charismatic in its manner of exercise, though it can still claim a charismatic origin. Here is a way of insisting upon the fundamental religious homogeneity of all Israel's institutions: even those that are most 'routinised' are derived from the same Spirit of Yhwh. The sequel to the story tells how two of the seventy, Eldad and Medad, not having been in attendance at the Tent, prophesy in the camp. Moses refuses to censure this breach of the principle of central authorisation: 'Would that all Yhwh's people were prophets!' Even a devolved authority, we are told, can be open to the charismatic immediacy of the divine presence. The judicial–administrative organs of Israel are still open to the incalculable possibilities of divine initiative through prophecy.

But who were these subordinate judicial figures? Tribal leaders? Royally appointed judges? Prophets? Levites? Priests? Perhaps all of these 'gave judgment' at different times and in different contexts. It was a city council that Jezebel rigged to condemn Naboth of Jezreel (1 Kgs. 21:8–14, though this role may have fallen to it uniquely under the blasphemy law, cf. Lev. 24:13–16). What of the 'assembly' that would give judgment in the ancient law of the manslayer? Was that also a city council of the city of refuge (Num. 35:24; Josh. 20:6)? Solomon appointed a group of 'princes' (*sārīm*, 1 Kgs. 4:3–6), with administrative functions. We have a tantalising glimpse of a council of 'princes' in 604 BC, meeting separately from the king's household in the palace and initiating independent policy (Jer. 36:11–19). Isaiah of Jerusalem knew that the rule of the king was accompanied by the rule of 'princes' (Isa. 32:1), who sat in the capital city and disgraced it with their conduct (1:21); it may be the same group that he calls 'judges' and 'counsellors' (1:26). Solomon also initiated twelve regional governors, ignoring tribal boundaries in a pointed attempt to unite the country by destroying its natural divisions (1 Kgs. 4:7–19). The historical record makes them responsible for supplies; but even if their functions went no wider than that, they would have judicial implications.

There must also have been a locally based judicial function, a 'squirearchy' of leading figures in tribe and village, whose judgment 'in the gate' would be the first resort of small litigants. Job is presented as the ideal-type of such a figure (29:7–25). It is a class that we know especially from the witness of its critics and rivals. The prophets at certain points associate the sins of wealth and land-accumulation with the standard corruptions of judicial maladministration, bribery going together with drunken feasting (Amos 2:7; 5:11f.; Isa. 5:22f.; Jer. 5:27f.), which points to the exercise of judicial functions by local men of substance. There are also two highly suggestive Pentateuchal stories, both concerned with the Levites, which shed important light not only on that group but on the local and tribal structures which they challenged.

In the crisis over the Golden Calf, we read, the Levites rallied to Moses' side and went through the camp 'each killing his brother and friend and neighbour', whereupon Moses pronounces, 'you have ordained yourselves this day' (Exod. 32:26–9). Ordained themselves to do what? To be judges, apparently, for it was their ferocious display of impartiality that qualified them for their office. But, of course, the Levites' brothers (and neighbours?) were other Levites, not in line for execution. Killing the brother, friend and neighbour is merely a colourful phrase for impartial vengeance. But it gains a great deal more point if we suppose it is directed against another class of judge for which partiality to brothers, friends and neighbours was a problem, a class rendered ineffective by cronyism and patronage, bound too closely into the economic and familial ties of local community. The narrative is making a case for the independence of Levitical jurisdiction, dispersed through the countryside but removed from local loyalties, as against the court of landed squire or tribal elder.

This is more explicitly the case in the second story, which has to do with the matrimonial, and so religious, alliance of Israelite men with Midianite women. Moses orders the 'judges' to put to death 'each his men' who are guilty of the crime; these judges, it appears, are tribal, or have a jurisdiction determined by some other principle of locality. The order, apparently, goes unheeded. Then Phineas the Aaronite takes the lead in executing an especially blatant offender, putting a stop to the plague which Yhwh has sent as punishment. As a result Yhwh makes a 'covenant of lasting priesthood' with the Aaronites (Num. 25:5–13). Once again the point is to stress the preferability of Levitical judgment over ineffective tribal jurisdiction; but here another argument for associating the roles of priesthood and judgment is developed: the execution of the offender is an act of atonement, and so requires a priest to perform it.

> The priestly jurisdiction was especially associated with 'enquiring' of Yhwh, when there was need for a directive to supplement or replace what law or courts decreed. In post-exilic times this aspect of the priestly role was remembered through the Urim and Thummim, the stones of divination, which were worn by the high priest on his 'breastplate of judgment', and a great deal of store was still set by them (Exod. 28:30; Ezr. 2:63; Neh. 7.65). Yet divination had lost the connexion it originally had with discerning innocence and guilt, a memory of which was preserved in the stories of Achan and Jonathan (Josh. 7; 1 Sam. 14). The extent to which divination had been a more general feature of priestly judgment is uncertain; but it seems to be implied by some prophetic criticism of priests. Instead of giving 'knowledge' and *tōrāh* (meaning, in this context, direction) to those who enquired of Yhwh, they practised degenerate types of divination (Hos. 4:6,12). Direction is proverbially associated with the priest (Jer. 18:18; Ezek. 7:26; Mal. 2:7); and the prophets did not challenge the appropriateness of the priest's 'enquiring' of Yhwh on the applicant's behalf. Jeremiah criticised kings for not enquiring enough (10:21); and it is clear that the prophets themselves assumed some of the traditional priestly role as a resort for those who sought authoritative direction (Jer. 21:2; Ezek. 14:7 e.g.). Their criticism had to do with the way the enquiry was conducted and the direction come by: 'the priests did not ask "Where is the Lord?" Those who handle *tōrāh* did not know me' (Jer. 2:8).

Jehoshaphat of Judah was credited with a reorganisation of the courts that established firm royal control over these competing jurisdictions. Appointed judges were to hold court in the larger towns, thus squeezing out the traditional jurisdiction of the landowners, while the Levites were to be responsible for a central court in the capital, which would function apparently as a court of second instance. The wording of 2 Chronicles 19 bears witness to what this reorganisation had in view: the unification of the system required that a dangerous gulf between Yhwh's judgment, administered by priests, and the king's judgment should be overcome. Great stress is laid on the principle that all judgment is Yhwh's, especially that of the king's judges. Correspondingly all judgment, including the judgment of the Levitical court, is subject to the king and answerable to his legal officer. The distinction between Yhwh's and the king's concerns is retained only to permit the Levitical court to refer certain matters of obviously cultic significance to the high priest's decision (11). In this way the king, by asserting his jurisdiction over all others, establishes his role as the unique mediator of Yhwh's judgments.

3. The most important thing the monarchy had to offer Israel was the *function of continuity*, ensuring an unbroken tradition in the occupation of the territory and the perpetuation of the national identity. The case is made in the simplest form in Psalm 78: the constant infidelity of Israel, calling down on its head the judgments of Yhwh culminating in the fall of Shiloh, threatened its very existence; the situation required a new initiative on Yhwh's part in the founding of the Zion sanctuary and the choice of David as his people's 'shepherd'. The monarchy was not to substitute for law as the principle of continuity in the possession, but to reinforce it. It afforded the prospect that the statutes and law which Yhwh had commanded would no longer be flouted in future generations as they had been in the past (5f.). Yhwh's 'covenant' with David, of which Psalm 89:34 speaks, provided a defence against the instability of the covenant with Israel. The king was Yhwh's 'son' (Ps. 2:7). This was a role of double representation: he represented Yhwh's rule to the people, ensuring their obedience, and he represented the people to Yhwh, ensuring his constant favour.

So far as we can judge, all parties in First Temple Judaism accepted this understanding in outline. There are no anti-monarchist voices among the scriptural witnesses; notably, there is no attempt to disown Solomon, for all the criticism that he comes in for. The famous observation at Hosea 8:3, 'They set up kings without my consent and choose princes without my approval', should be understood as a rejection of the quick-changing dynasties of the Northern kingdom in its declining years, not a rejection of monarchy as such. Even the narrative of 1 Samuel 8 is in fact an apologia for the monarchy addressed to its natural antagonists; it intends to leave no doubt that the monarchy came to existence by Yhwh's decision. The principle, therefore, that the monarch could provide unitary representation of Yhwh's rule was an accepted one. Nor is there any need to confine that summary to the Southern kingdom. Although, inevitably, the historians who shape our knowledge of the period shared a general presumption of the moral, cultic and political superiority of Judah, they respected testimony to the view that Jeroboam's dynasty in Samaria was, in its inception, a legitimate parallel to the Davidic line in Jerusalem, willed by Yhwh and eligible for the same blessings (1 Kgs. 12:34–9).

But in the minds of the Deuteronomic theologians, whose retrospective view of the period formed the classic theological reflection upon it, the monarch could never be more than a safeguard for what Yhwh had given his people. Yhwh's own rule safeguarded the possession; but it also constituted and defined it. Yhwh *is* Israel's possession, and Israel, in turn, is Yhwh's possession. Into this core-relationship between the people and God the mediator could not intrude himself. He could safeguard what was Yhwh's on Yhwh's behalf, but it was not his to define or determine it. The possession had an inner as well as an outer form; it was law as well as land. The monarch could defend the land but could only keep the law. It was an aspect of Yhwh's kingly presence that the king could not take into his own person or eclipse. He was answerable to it; and his answer, the prophetic schools maintained, had continually to be given before the bar of history in palpable successes and failures. Jerusalem's fall showed that in principle the people's liability to Yhwh's judgment was as it had always been.

The Deuteronomic history sees the period not simply as a history of kings, but as a history of the interaction of kings and prophets. The prophets shared the task of tradition-bearing with the monarch; and, indeed, theirs was the more significant part, since it was through their words that Yhwh himself defined and redefined in each new circumstance the moral content of the tradition to which the kings were answerable. That content was the law. One way of expressing the prophets' role was to say that they acted and spoke like Moses (Deut. 18:14), who was himself, according to some prophets' perceptions, a prophet (Hos. 12:13). There appears more to us, perhaps, than to the Deuteronomists to be a certain tension between the claims they upheld for prophecy and their demand that monarchs should study the *written* law (Deut. 17:18f., cf. Josh. 1:7f.). Living in an age when an extensive literary culture was becoming a possibility for the first time, they had no sense of dissonance between written and spoken authority; prophecy they had known as a friend of writing, and writing as a servant of prophecy. At any rate, there was a residuum of Mosaic authority which the monarch's authority could not absorb or occlude. Its form was the law, and its social voice was the prophetic movement.

The prophets' own conception of their role in relation to the law can be viewed through the prism of the criticism they make of the priests. The priests were the natural guardians of the law because of their role in ceremonial recitation (Deut. 27:14) and because the Temple was the depository of law-texts. Hilkiah was appropriately the one to produce the law-text which was to be the centre-piece of Josiah's reforms in 622 BC (2 Kgs. 22:8). After the exile the authority of priests as guardians of the written text was greatly enhanced in a vacuum of all other authority, as can be seen from the standing of Ezra, armed with a text, in imposing stricter marriage laws in Judah (Ezr. 9, 10). But the way in which the priesthood discharged its responsibilities to the law – it is not always clear, nor need it be, which sense of *tōrāh* is in play – was criticised in prophetic circles, and especially on one point. The sacrificial law was secondary, the prophets argued, to the law's moral and social provisions. The cult was not part of the original Sinai revelation (Amos 5:25; Jer. 7:22). The articulate testimony of thanksgiving, the discharging of judicial obligations and loyal dependence on Yhwh's practical guidance, these were what Yhwh sought from his people rather than the ritual performances on which the priests laid too much stress (Ps. 51:16; Mic. 6:6–8; Hos. 6:6). In Judah under Josiah the prophets were suggesting that the law-texts preserved by the priests were contaminated (Jer. 8:8). When Hilkiah found the crucial law-text in Yhwh's house, no doubt it was after a long search for an adequate one! The identification of his text with Deuteronomy can never be more than conjecture; but that code at least gives us some idea what the converging legal and prophetic interests which produced the Deuteronomic literary movement thought to be an appropriate law-text.

Ezekiel, who like some others had a foot in both priestly and prophetic camps, produced a judicious evaluation of this critique for the new circum-stances of the exile community in 591 BC. Yhwh gave two kinds of law to Israel: laws which the obedient might live by, and, as a punishment, 'laws that were not good . . . that they could not live by' (20:11,25). We may be slightly surprised that his example of the latter kind of law is human sacrifice, which Jeremiah thought 'never entered into [Yhwh's] mind' (7:31 etc.). But this constitutes a clear recognition that the legal tradition as it stood contained material that could not possibly represent Yhwh's good purposes for his people. Yet the orig-inal law, Ezekiel maintains, was not moral and social only. In a distinction that was to have a long future he recognises a ritual element; it contained 'a sign between us' which marked the people out as Yhwh's special possession. That was: 'my sabbaths . . . so that they would know that I, Yhwh, had made them holy' (20:12). The prophet of Isaiah 56, extending the promise of Yhwh's favour to Gentiles and eunuchs, makes the same distinction between a moral require-ment, which is 'the covenant' proper, and the keeping of the sabbath (2,4,6).

The rival claims of priest and prophet to represent the continuing authority of Moses in the law were not let pass without a corrective. The story of Miriam and Aaron's revolt (Num. 12) constitutes a warning against tendencies to auton-omy on either side of the religious culture. Neither could lay claim to the orig-inal immediacy of Yhwh's presence to Moses. Moses had no true successor.

The ninth-century prophets distinguished themselves from another tradition of prophecy, relentlessly satirised in the story of Micaiah and the battle of Ramoth-Gilead (1 Kgs. 22), in which the prophet appeared to be a dependant of the court, retained to lend support for the king's military initiatives. In a text of great pregnancy Elijah is commanded (and at Mount Horeb, Moses' Sinai!) to anoint Hazael king of Syria, Jehu king of Israel and Elisha as his own successor. 'Him who escapes from the sword of Hazael shall Jehu slay; and him who escapes from the sword of Jehu shall Elisha slay' (1 Kgs. 19:15–17). This is to say that three forces coincide in Yhwh's dispositions to purify and safeguard the tradition of his people: conquest by external powers, reform by the monarchy, and prophecy itself, which has its own independent sanctions and is responsible for unleashing the other two. This uncompromising insistence on the independence of the prophetic voice did not necessarily imply a posture of permanent confrontation between prophet and king. The Northern prophets claimed credit for Jehu's revolution and admired his 'zeal for Yhwh'. And in the South there was more for the prophets to place their hope in, not least the 'covenant with David' itself. Nathan's relation to David is an ideal portrait of the kind of co-operative relationship that was realised most triumphantly between Isaiah and Hezekiah. The prophet counsels, rebukes, gives promises to the monarch, all from a position of independence, living in his own house (2 Sam. 12:15). In a paradigm story for prophet–king relations, the prophet who confronts Jeroboam at Bethel foretells Josiah's destruction of the altar, is miraculously protected when the king attempts to arrest him, then heals the king's withered right hand, before finally declining a polite invitation to lunch (1 Kgs. 13:1–10)!

Yet the ideal of such a relationship did not long survive the rise of the great empires and the growing conviction in prophetic circles that Yhwh would sweep his people away. What has changed between the expectations focussed on the figure of Elijah in the ninth century and those of Hosea a hundred or so years later is that Jehu has dropped out of the picture. The unstable Northern dynasties are now seen as unauthorised impositions in which Yhwh takes no interest, political idols to match the cultic furniture of Samaria (Hos. 8:4). A centrally led reform has ceased to look like a possibility in the North. The situation in the South, more hopeful for a while, founders somewhere in the darkness of the mid seventh century, leaving the prophets sharing the same bleak outlook. By the time Josiah attempted to reconstruct the old relation between king and prophet on the basis of his reform programme, the radical wing of the prophetic movement had become committed to an unqualified expectation of the kingdom's fall.

Support for his reforms he won; but it was offered *ad hominem* and provisionally, without longer-term prospects for the support of the throne. The response of the prophetess Huldah to the king's overtures (2 Kgs. 22:14–20), though often dismissed as a *vaticinium ex eventu*, must in fact represent very faithfully the mood in which prophets like Jeremiah took up the cause of the reform. Much of his later behaviour is unintelligible on any other basis – not least the immediate rejection with which he, and at least one other before him, greeted the accession of Jehoiakim in 609 (Jer. 26:1–24). As prophetic expectations for the throne declined, criticism of the 'false prophets' became more vehement. The central tradition, Jeremiah coldly assured Hananiah in 594 BC, was one of prophesying doom (28:6–9). Here was a prophet – and he was not the only one of his time – who believed himself called from the start to be 'a fortified city, an iron pillar and a bronze wall to stand . . . against the kings of Judah' (1:8)!

That, in outline, is the alternative way that classical Yahwism found to resist the dangers of making an image of Yhwh out of the monarch. It constitutes a rejection of absolutism: we may contrast the classical image of the ruler as the founder of his society with the image of Moses as the faithful steward in God's household (Num. 12:7). But instead of rejecting the absolutist temptation by distributing powers, it permitted a unitary government subject to the independent authority of Yhwh's law, which had its independent voice in society through the prophetic movement. Essentially the same alternatives have confronted modern political reflection when it has sought strategies to avoid absolutism. The constitutional separation of functions within government has risen in favour when confidence in the effective authority of a common social 'possession' of moral principle has been weak. If we are to express Israel's experience in a theoretical way, we must do so by reaffirming the political significance of such a moral tradition. *The authority of a human regime mediates divine authority in a unitary structure, but is subject to the authority of law within the community, which bears independent witness to the divine command.* This theorem corresponds to what has often been said in the West in terms of 'Natural Law'. It is important to grasp that it is a *political* reality in society to which government is answerable. Absolutist regimes violate the individual consciences of their subjects, no doubt; but it is the common conscience, which is a constitutive factor in the political identity of the community, that they violate most directly. The wrong they do is therefore a political wrong, attempting to override the rule of God within the community.

But this theoretical generalisation of Israel's experience presupposes that Yhwh's law can be extended in principle to other nations than Israel, in apparent despite of the psalmist's claim that 'he has not dealt so with any other nation, nor have they knowledge of his statutes' (Ps. 147:20). This presupposition cannot be avoided simply by speaking of a 'Natural Law'; for the term 'law' itself clearly supposes an analogue to the *tōrāh* in the general experience of the nations, an act of Yhwh which reaches beyond the limits of his elect people. Can this presupposition be made consistent with Israel's own understanding of its relation to foreign peoples?

'King over the whole earth'

'Yhwh Elyon is awesome, a great king over all the earth. He subdues peoples under us and nations under our feet' (Ps. 47:2f.). We may be tempted to suppose that these two assertions amount to precisely the same thing: that Yhwh's rule over the nations consists in nothing more than his assertion of Israel's superiority over them. Undoubtedly it included that, and at times of affliction that aspect of things had a strong purchase on Israel's imagination. In the course of the exile we find a prophet in Babylon promising that Yhwh Sabaoth will 'litigate their case at law' to bring 'rest to their land and unrest to the inhabitants of Babylon' (Jer. 50:34); while another in Jerusalem says that he will 'punish the powers in heaven above and the kings on earth below . . . and will reign on Mount Zion' (Isa. 24:21–3). A prayer with some currency at this period pleaded that Yhwh would 'pour out your wrath upon the nations that do not know you' (Jer. 10:25; Ps. 79:6). At a later time of tribulation the substance of the prophet's promise is the same: 'judgment was given for the saints of Elyon' (Dan. 7:22).

But at no time was this the whole of the matter. Psalm 47 ends with a further account of Elohim's reign, which declares that 'the princes of the nations shall assemble with the people of the God of Abraham' (9). This is meant to suggest a common worship, almost certainly in Jerusalem or Samaria. Though less developed, it can be compared with what was envisaged in the Zion oracle (Isa. 2:2–4; Mic. 4:1–3), in which the nations 'flow' towards Zion for instruction in Yhwh's ways and judgment among the nations. It was a sign of Yhwh's majesty that he could elicit co-operation, on terms of his own deciding, between his people and the nations that surrounded them.

This theme is explored in the patriarchal narratives, notably in the thrice-told tale of the marriageability of the patriarchs' wives (Gen. 12:10–20; 20:2–18; 26:7–11). Abraham (or Isaac) allows Abimelech, a local king in the Beersheba region, to take Sarah (or Rebekah) as a concubine. The intervention of Yhwh, by warning dream or chance discovery, prevents the union; and in each case a treaty results. (The version in which Abraham and Pharaoh of Egypt are the protagonists ends with Abraham's expulsion from Egypt, and so has a different point, which is to anticipate the Exodus.) The background of this story, as of that of the 'rape' of Dinah in Genesis 34, is the difficulty of relations between semi-nomads and settled communities, a difficulty conventionally overcome by a discreet trade in the attractions of women. This way of securing safety is closed to Yhwh's people because of their sacred duty to preserve the succession of holy seed. But by Yhwh's own act it is made unnecessary, since he himself secures them the treaty-relations which they had hoped to negotiate by these inadmissible means. It is illuminating to lay this story alongside the historian's view of the reign of Solomon, in which the spontaneous regard of Hiram of Tyre and the Queen of Sheba signify Yhwh's blessing on the reign, but the foreign marriage-alliances are the betrayal that undermines it (1 Kgs. 5:7–12; 10:1–10; 11:1–8).

Thus Israel's awareness of its own distinctness as Yhwh's chosen is held in a careful equilibrium with a hope for co-operation with surrounding peoples. Notwithstanding the cries for vindication at crisis-moments in its history, Israel's sense of its own dignity does not imply a national monism; but neither is there ever a pluralism which renounces that sense of dignity altogether. Perhaps the memory of such a pluralism is preserved in the fossilised traces of Canaanite 'henotheism' at Deuteronomy 32:8f., in which the high-god Elyon divides the nations 'according to the number of the sons of God', among which Yhwh receives Jacob as his possession. In its present form and context, however, the text identifies Elyon and Yhwh; so that, while other gods receive other nations, Yhwh-Elyon reserves Jacob, whom he 'found' in the desert without the help of any other god, as his own (10–12). Something similar happens on a larger scale in the early chapters of Genesis. Constructed on a Yahwist framework, the primeval history of mankind prepares the way for the history of the nation. It was Yhwh who made Adam and Eve, Yhwh who drove them from the garden into a life under judgment – a life in which there were slave-nations and master-nations, diversity of languages, and every other feature of international conflict and confusion – but all to prepare the way for Yhwh to summon Abraham. Into this structure are fed narratives and records with a cosmopolitan Elohist character (such as the catalogue of nations in which Israel makes only a disguised appearance (10:24–30)), but these gain a new significance from the setting into which they have been introduced.

When Israel calls on God, then, to 'judge the earth, for to thee belong the nations' (Ps. 82:8), something more is implied than a simple defence of the chosen people. It was understood that judgment meant equal responsibility. On the one hand, the political structures of other nations had the same vocation to exercise just judgment as Israel's did. The 'sons of Elyon' who stand before Elohim in his court are castigated for their failure to observe obligations parallel to those which Israel acknowledged under the covenant: 'Judge the weak and the fatherless! Vindicate the poor and the oppressed!' (Ps. 82:3). The late wisdom-writer who warned that the kings and judges of the earth would be condemned as 'servants of [God's] kingdom' who 'did not rule rightly' (Wisd. 6:1–4) was simply drawing the obvious inference from that psalm. On the other hand it meant that Israel was subject to judgment by the same standards as the nations that offended her. Amos drew out the implications of this most brutally, lining Israel up for criticism alongside Syria, Philistia, Tyre and other cruel neighbours (1:3–2:8), suggesting scornfully at one point that Israel's Exodus was no different from any other national migration (9:7), at another that Israel's favoured covenant-status exposed her uniquely to punishment (3:2). The great 'day of Yhwh', on which people hoped to see him judge the earth, would be a doubtful blessing to Israel (5:18–20). But others in Amos' time were looking in the same direction. The poem on the day of Yhwh which we find in a later anthology of foreign oracles (Isa. 13:2–16) is notable for its lack of any comforting suggestion that Israel will be spared its rigours, while Isaiah's great composition on the same theme (2:6–22) takes Jacob's rejection as its starting-point and expands its vision to a total confrontation between Yhwh and the pride of man in every quarter.

Against the background of this general understanding of her place among the nations Israel's prophets confronted the dramatic rise of the Mesopotamian empires. These events evoked a very great interest among them.

One could almost say that the rise of the empires created classical prophecy in Israel, for it demanded a new assessment of the state of the covenant, and with that a longer-range prediction for its future which drove the prophets, and their disciples, to writing. International developments became the occasion for the prophetic vocation. Even Jeremiah, who has less to say to the nations than some, believed himself a 'prophet to the nations' (Jer. 1:5). Events which did not immediately involve Israel still attracted prophetic commentary. Isaiah predicted an Assyrian conquest of Egypt in 711 BC (Isa. 20:1–6). Nahum is known solely as the prophet of Assyria's fall to the Medo-Babylonian alliance in 612 BC. In 605 BC Jeremiah spoke about the defeat of Egypt by Babylon at Carchemish (Jer. 46:2–12), and that event may have precipitated his attempted intervention in domestic politics in the following year. During the very siege of Jerusalem in 587 BC Ezekiel gave his attention no fewer than three times to the likely outcome of Babylon's further ambitions in Egypt (Ezek. 29:1ff.; 30:20–6; 31:1ff.). The interest extended even to the internal affairs of other countries: the dominance of Ethiopia in Egypt interested Isaiah at its inception (Isa. 18:1–7) and Ezekiel who predicted its end (Ezek. 29:13–16). The experience of exile, of course, sharpened this interest even further. It is from Babylon, in all likelihood, that the three substantial collections of foreign oracles which attach to the major prophetic books originated. Ezekiel himself, whose interest in other nations was very keen, may well have set the fashion, editing his book in a pattern which the guardians of the Isaianic and Jeremianic corpora aspired to imitate: domestic oracles, foreign oracles, oracles of restoration.

Of course, the rise of the empires was viewed primarily as a sign of Yhwh's judgment against his people, a development of the role assigned by ninth-century prophets to 'the sword of Hazael'. The purification, or rejection, of Israel was the prophets' leading idea, and the closer disaster came, the more completely it occupied their horizon. Nebuchadrezzar, for Jeremiah, was Yhwh's 'servant' to execute judgment long promised (Jer. 25:9; 27:6). The title that belonged to Israel's king (Pss. 78:70; 89:3 etc.) is applied defiantly to a foreign conqueror who has become the only mediator of Yhwh's judgments to his people! This led Jeremiah to adopt a provocatively pro-Babylonian stance throughout the quarter-century that separated the death of Josiah from the fall of Jerusalem, a fact which was recognised, and rewarded, by the conquerors (Jer. 39:11f.).

Yet it would have been impossible for a prophet in the classical Yahwist tradition of Judah to make the fall of the city and the abrogation of the covenant the ultimate horizon of his vision. Certainly, Jeremiah resisted with extreme thoroughness any premature invocation of the traditions of hope to mitigate the severity of the judgment. But the reverse side of his demand for the city's surrender was the encouragement he offered to the exiles (24:1–10; 29:1–23). His promise that 'after seventy years' Yhwh would visit the exiles (25:12; 29:10, and NB 51:59–64, with its implied message, authentic to the prophet, that the promise was hidden and buried until its time should come) is part and parcel with his conception of Nebuchadrezzar's role, and is directly in line with a tradition which had its roots in the pre-monarchical period (Deut. 32:19–43) but was canonised by Isaiah's interpretation of Assyria (Isa. 10:5–19). Yhwh lays hold on the arrogant conqueror and makes him 'the rod of my anger'; but because the conqueror has no conception of his place and is elated with pride, he must in turn be punished. In Jeremiah's day the same argument was taken up by Habakkuk (1:5–2:5): the one who has forced Yhwh's cup of wrath on others must drink it himself (2:15–17, cf. Jer. 25:15–26).

In this context the so-called Book of Consolation is by no means to be denied to Jeremiah's authorship (Jer. 30–3, and note especially ch. 32). He is not a credible figure if wrenched out of the tradition, as a rather stiff-jointed historical dialectics has liked to wrench him, and turned into an iconic abstraction, a prophet of 'pure' doom without horizon or hope.

As a natural implication of this more comforting side of the prophetic message to Israel, we find a developing critique of empire. This was not a radical novelty; its foundations were already laid in the legacy of myth and primeval legend. The story of the tower of Babel reminds us that the threat of imperial domination from the Mesopotamian basin was ancient. The plurality of languages, defining the separate identity of separate peoples and making co-operative endeavour difficult, was Yhwh's safeguard against the titanism of imperial pretensions (Gen. 11:1–9). The mythological figure of the foe from the north provided a conceptual point of reference for the classical prophets' thought about the encroachment of the Mesopotamian empire. A similar myth, that of the fall of the day-star, was used by one prophet of the Babylonian period to denounce the ambitions of Nebuchadrezzar (Isa. 14:12–15). But there was something more to fear in a world dominated by great powers than a simple infliction of military might; there was the threat to cultural integrity. Isaiah had shuddered at the unintelligible sounds of the Assyrian language in Judah (28:11), and had placed the great Mediterranean trading ships on a par with military fortifications as symbols of pride (2:15–17). Now Ezekiel, with a flash of imaginative insight that must have struck some of his fellow-exiles as wholly perverse, seized not on the military achievements of Babylon but on the great commercial networks of Tyre as the nerve-centre of the age of titans (Ezek. 26:1–28:19). Tyre had attained to an astonishing cultural beauty by means of the promiscuous intermingling of cultural influences through commercial enterprise (its 'harlotry', as a sharper voice called it (Isa. 23:15–18)). In Tyre Ezekiel found nothing mean, but all the created splendour which God had destined for Adam in the Garden of Eden, now hardened and made callous (Ezek. 28:13–18).

When John of Patmos christened his symbolic portrait of Rome 'Babylon' but painted it in the colours of Ezekiel's Tyre, he was influenced by this moment of penetrating insight. But he was also heir to another train of thought about empire which takes its rise at this time: understanding the sequence of world-empires as a continuity, and accounting for God's dealings with Israel in terms of the history of empire as such. It begins simply with the editors of the Isaianic collection of foreign oracles, who found an oracle against Assyria and attached it to contemporary denunciations of

Babylon under the overall title 'the oracle concerning Babylon that Isaiah son of Amoz saw' (13:1; 14:24–7). Ezekiel added a new element, climaxing his vision of Israel's restoration with a frank recapitulation of the mythological assault by the northern foe on Mount Zion, as though the whole history of the empires must be summed up in one last great one. And Daniel, under the Seleucids, elaborated the history of four successive empires as a progressive degeneration or bestialisation of human rule, which must prepare the way for the final confrontation with the Kingdom of Yhwh (Dan. 2:29–45; 7:2–18).

From this follows the conviction that the order of the future, when Israel shall have returned to her home, will be an internationally plural order, free from the unifying constraints of empire. The events of Israel's overthrow by the empire and her subsequent restoration will serve as a lesson and a model by which Yhwh will instruct the nations of the world. A family of humble nations will creep out from under the wreckage of the empires, and Israel's own humiliation and recovery will provide a kind of paradigm for the fate of others, if they will accept the evidence of Yhwh's hand at work. 'The nations shall know that I am Yhwh', is the refrain of Ezekiel's promise of Israel's restoration (36:23 etc.). And Deutero-Isaiah famously has Yhwh's servant assigned, as a second task supplementary to his role in Israel, to be a 'light to the nations' (Isa. 49:6).

Modest speculation begins about the shape of a future international order. Ezekiel anticipates a withdrawal of the Ethiopians to Upper Egypt, where they will cease to dominate the Mediterranean coast (29:13–16). A writer who knows something of the sixth-century Jewish colonies in Egypt predicts a reconciliation between Egypt and Mesopotamia ('Assyria', Isa. 19:16–25). Another anticipates the recovery of Tyre from her humiliation at Babylon's hands and a renewal of her commercial activity for the material benefit of Israel (Isa. 23:15–18). The most expansive vision was that of the collectors of the Jeremianic foreign oracles, an editorial undertaking preoccupied with the question of which peoples will, and which will not, have a place in the reconstructed order. Egypt will (46:26); the Philistine Tetrapolis, because it lay within Israel's original inheritance, will not; Moab will (48:47); Ammon, despite its disappearance from the map by the editors' day, will (49:6); Edom will not, because of its treachery towards Judah in 586 BC; Damascus is left uncertain – historically it is Israel's northern border, and the ancient prophecy spoke only of the firing of its fortifications (49:27); Kedar and Hazor, as nomadic peoples, have no place; Elam (Media, for these Babylonian editors) must certainly have a place as Babylon's ancient foe (49:39); and, equally certainly, Babylon itself must not.

Later than this conception of a reconstructed international order there arises the thought that the internal political arrangements of the foreign powers can be reformed by Yhwh's laws. Faced with the reality of absolutist regimes, the Jews of the diaspora reflected that the nations had no knowledge of Yhwh's laws (Ps. 147:20); yet they thought it part of their own role to encourage a more humble and humane approach to government. The stories of Daniel are full of none-too-gentle satire at the ways of autocrats; their theme is the conflict of this style of rule with the true service of Yhwh. But they tell also of the almost pathetic gratitude of these all-powerful figures to those honest and forthright advisers who could liberate them from the insupportable logic of their own supposed omnipotence, like Nebuchadrezzar restored from animal to human form. The story of Esther sharpens the satire further. Wretched Queen Vashti, condemned to be put on show as the Persian king's chief acquisition, represents the demoralised and undignified state of a kingdom that is viewed as a royal perquisite. Esther proves the alternative possibility, of a free and loyal kingdom that can take initiatives for the good of the realm. The poet of Psalm 138, who lives in a Gentile court and so, like Daniel, has to worship Yhwh 'before the gods', turning his face towards the Temple in Jerusalem, can boast that foreign kings have 'heard the words of [Yhwh's] mouth', that is, from Jewish advisers like himself. Now it is only a matter of time until the ancient promise is fulfilled and they, like Nebuchadrezzar in the Daniel story, adopt a Yahwist liturgy of praise as their official cult.

To summarise, the rule of Yhwh was conceived internationally; it secured the relations of the nations and directed them towards peace. But at the international level there was to be no unitary mediator. Israel never entertained the apologia for empire which we find developing in patristic and medieval sources, that the rule of a single world-power represented and mediated the universal rule of Yhwh as high-god. Yhwh's world order was plurally constituted. World-empire was a bestial deformation. It was in the providential disposition of events that Yhwh's rule was seen; and it was mediated only through the authority of prophets and the prophetic people. Israel did not speak of a 'Natural Law' because it felt no need to go back behind its own prophetic role to explain how Yhwh made his name known; Israel was itself the messenger. But it thought in terms of a law which could and would bind the nations universally. To propose a generalised statement: *the appropriate unifying element in international order is law rather than government.*

This leaves a difference between the ways in which Yhwh's national and international sovereignties were understood, the one mediated by the monarch, the other not susceptible of unitary mediation at all. This difference was to be explained in terms of Yhwh's special providence in protecting his covenant people. The imageless ideal of rule by law and providential action alone could be suspended to protect Israel's existence, but there was no comparable reason for suspending it to justify a world-empire. Two observations follow from this. One is that if Israel's experience of government is to be taken as a model for other societies, then we must allow that divine providence is ready to protect other national traditions besides the sacred one. Reasons for thinking this, and limits which need to be set around a thought which can be dangerous if cut loose from a proper framework, will need to be considered at a later stage. The second is that the particular national traditions are apparently susceptible of a kind of protection which the tradition of human society as a whole is not. In securing the total tradition of humanity, we are in a context in which it is out of place to invoke the commanding role of a government; but it is not out of place to invoke the role of law and to conceive relations between particular national communities in terms of a law-structure. This says something about the limits of our collective identities. To be a human being at all is to participate in one or more collective identities. But there is no collective identity so overarching and all-encompassing that no human beings are left outside it. In that sense it is true that to speak of 'humanity' is to speak of an abstraction. Only in that sense, for in fact 'humanity' has a perfectly conceivable referent, and we should not hesitate to say that 'humanity' is real. But it is not a reality that we can command politically. We do not meet it in any community, however great, of which we could assume the leadership. We meet it only in the face of Christ, who presents himself as our leader and commander. The titanic temptation which besets collectives needs the check of a perpetual plurality at the universal level. There are always 'others', those not of our fold whom we must respect and encounter.

The individual

To speak of 'the individual' among the political concepts of Israel is, perhaps, imprudent. The various ideas associated with 'individualism' in Western thought – the individual contracting into society from a state of nature, the primacy of the self-interested will etc. – are all quite inappropriate to Israel's self-understanding. In the Hebrew Scriptures the holy community is the prior and original fact; the individual member finds his or her significance within it. Yet that significance develops in the course of the First Temple period. The individual becomes, as it were, load-bearing, so that at the exile the future of the nation has come to depend on individual faithfulness. The logic of the development is perfectly expressed in the question of Psalm 11:6, 'When the foundations are destroyed, what shall the righteous one do?' (*hatstsaddīq* in the singular, following the Massoretic text). It is a clear illustration of the principle that, to treat Israel's political tradition as normative, we have to wrestle with its history.

The fact that individuality developed should not lead us to imagine that it was ever absent. Any society must, of course, pay its single member the elementary notice of attending to his grievances; for, if no attempt is made to reconcile him, his anger will be turned destructively on the community and its institutions. Organs of judgment serve this purpose in general; but in Israel appeal to them became clothed in a liturgical form and assumed the character of prayer. It is impossible to pronounce, of course, on precisely how the complaint-psalms were used within the process of judicial appeal. But their importance lies in the fact that the plaintiff could experience himself as calling directly upon Yhwh, having access to the ultimate tribunal over the heads of corrupt ones. The eleventh psalm illustrates the genre. The destruction of the cosmic foundations is brought about by the manipulation of tribunals by a malicious conspiracy of defamation. No longer able to count on the processes of human judgment, the plaintiff appeals to the judgment-seat of Yhwh himself before whose narrowed eyes not only he, the righteous one, but also his detractor, 'the wicked one', are reduced to singularity.

The isolation of the sufferer, neglected by his friends and assailed by his foes who are sometimes also his accusers, is a commonplace of the Psalter. The consciousness of individuality is born in suffering, and especially in the sense of being wronged, which drives a wedge between the unreliable institutions of society and the reliability of Yhwh himself. Comparable to the psalms of protestation are the laments of the sick (Pss. 38, 88 e.g.). These psalm-types are notoriously difficult to disentangle from one another. Guilt, physical misery and isolation by hostility are conflated; accusation and guilt can be an implication of sickness, and sickness can result from hostile enchantment. Together the three create a state of soul in which the sufferer stands alone against mankind and calls on Yhwh for his right.

> Not until much later, in the Book of Job, do we meet a suspicion that this state of soul may be an unhealthy one. Job's resort to a formal liturgy of self-vindication at the climax of his protestations (31) is no haphazard literary effect. The author is intent on probing the curiously hostile state of mind which lies behind the persecuted sufferer of the liturgical tradition. In the folk-legend which we may assume provided the author with his framework it appears that Job's three comforters may have accused him of wrongdoing – that, at any rate, is what hundreds of commentators, pious and learned alike, have claimed to find them doing in the book as we have it. What has happened there, however, is that the roles have been reversed. It is Job who unjustly accuses his friends, alleging that

they are taunting him, dragging out of them the hostility that he is determined to complain of. The problem of suffering, for this author, is not 'why does it happen?' but 'why does it make the sufferer so angry?' The failure of the three friends, from Elihu's point of view which is the poet's own, lay in their inability to overcome Job's self-righteous pathos; and this they could not do because they shared his anthropocentric perspective (32:3).

Yet the author keeps faith with the legend (to which he returns at the end with moving effect) and also with the liturgical tradition of the protesting innocent. For when Job meets Yhwh, not as his vindicator but as his accuser, the sufferer and the world are set in harmony again, a world now discovered to be much richer and fuller of extra-human purposes than could be seen from the enclosed viewpoint of self-pity. Thus Job ends up where the liturgy of self-vindication had intended to bring him: not locked into the isolated hostility to which it gives voice, but discovering in Yhwh's judgment the ground for reconciliation with his accusers and reintegration in society. The psalms of protest are a moment in a dynamic spiritual process. The grievance they express is taken seriously, but not as an end in itself; the aim in expressing it is to bring the complainant and his adversary together before the throne of God.

The anger of the self-perceived victim is respected in the liturgy. His protest is a possible moment of revelation, at which the bearing of Yhwh's judgments may be seen. The mediators of Yhwh's rule do not monopolise the knowledge of Yhwh's *mishpāt*, but must concede the relevance of individual insight in discerning it.

In quite a different context the wisdom-tradition celebrates the possibility of individual insight, this time as a gift of character which befits some people, irrespective of their birth or office, to be a counsellor to those who bear official responsibility. The stories of Joseph and Daniel epitomise the role of the upwardly mobile wise man who ends up as the minister of kings – foreign kings in both cases, reminding us of the broadly international character of this ideal. Joseph, the slave, instructed princes and taught Pharaoh's senators wisdom (Ps. 105:22). The divine gift singled him out for this role; he became the model for all those whom Yhwh 'raises . . . from the dust and seats . . . with princes' (Ps. 113:8). (The comparison with the barren woman should not escape our notice: in that case, too, the personal favour of Yhwh to one individual had political consequences, and Sarah, Rachel, Manoah's wife and Hannah were all history-shaping individuals.) In the Proverbs that reflect on the role of the counsellor, however, something more than practical genius is expected. Skill and wisdom are a prerequisite – a king delights in a wise servant, a skilled man will stand before kings (Prov. 14:35; 22:9) – but there is an emphasis on moral qualities as well – kings take pleasure in honest lips, one who combines attractive speech with a pure heart will have the king as his friend (16:13; 22:11). And that expectation prepares the way for a transformation of the role of counsellor into keeper of the king's conscience, a development we see clearly enough in the Daniel stories. When the poet of Psalm 119 declares that he will speak of Yhwh's statutes before kings and not be ashamed (46), he grafts the claims of the law directly onto the functions of the counsellor; but it is only a hair's-breadth from that to the protestation, 'princes have persecuted me without a cause, but my heart trembles at your word' (161). The wisdom role has become absorbed into the prayer of self-vindication.

There is a third role in which the individual's knowledge of Yhwh's judgments is recognised, and that is the role of the prophet. The prophet drew to himself some of the traits of the king's counsellor and of the isolated sufferer. The ninth-century prophetic movement championed his lonely voice against the flattery of the court (1 Kgs. 22:15ff.), and the story of Elijah's prayer for death invested this position with a memorable pathos (1 Kgs. 19:3–18). But it is in the seventh century with the figure of Jeremiah that the combination of interior isolation and moral certainty comes to its fullest expression, often in close interaction with the psalm tradition.

The prophets had a dramatic convention of announcing an event of cataclysmic dimensions with excited shouts or cries of grief, as though the prophet, wholly caught up in his vision, were present at the tumultuous scene himself. Jeremiah, inheriting this convention, screwed it up to a pitch of personal involvement which strikes us as quite new: 'Oh my anguish! my anguish! I writhe in pain. Oh the agony of my heart, pounding within me! I cannot keep silent. For I have heard the sound of the trumpet; I have heard the battle-cry!' (Jer. 4:19). What has made the difference? Surely, it is Jeremiah's belief that this battle will be Judah's last, that Yhwh has finally rejected his people, and that there is no reprieve to hope for. And so his prophetic involvement in the calamity goes far beyond the moments of prophetic ecstasy in which he acts out Yhwh's message to the people. He has to proclaim his own destruction in the destruction of the people, and to look that prospect in the face through many years of suspenseful waiting.

And so, in Jeremiah's experience, the prophet's role heightens his individual self-awareness in quite a distinctive way. He becomes a kind of mediatorial representative: on the one hand he expresses the anger of Yhwh against the people, on the other the misery and despair of the people under the blow of Yhwh's anger. 'I am full of the anger of Yhwh, and I cannot hold it in' (6:11); and at the same time, 'Since my people are crushed, I am crushed . . . I would weep day and night for the slain of my people' (8:21; 9:1). It is like a negative image of the role of the king, who represented the obedience of the people before Yhwh and the favour of Yhwh towards the people. As Yhwh's messenger the prophet is set apart from the people, marked out and threatened. One aspect of his vocation is to sever the bonds of affinity which tie him to his people, and to cease praying for them (7:16 etc.). But that harsh distance merely increases his sense of painful identification, creating a corresponding isolation from Yhwh himself, with whom he remonstrates urgently (17:14–18; 20:7–10). Contributing to this is the long delay in the fulfilling of his prediction, with consequent loss of public credibility and self-confidence. His experience is summed up in what we could think of as the finest of the complaint-psalms (15:10–21, excluding 13f. which are intrusive). In it he reflects on the isolation he has incurred by taking delight in the words of Yhwh. He can no longer lose himself in the common pleasures of a 'company of merry-makers' but must sit apart, filled with indignation and unceasing pain. His protestation is met with a word from Yhwh renewing his prophetic commission; it offers only further hardening, his sympathies with the people to be denied once more.

Jeremiah's isolation is profound, but not in the least atomistic. He is isolated, paradoxically, because he is too much identified both with the people and with Yhwh in their conflict. Here the mediator's role is put in a startling new light. To speak for mankind to God and for God to mankind is to be thrust into perilous loneliness, emerging from the whole to which one belongs but not free of it, bearing vicariously the pain and responsibility of its fault but without being able to put it right.

Jeremiah's experience, one supposes, must have contributed to the most famous picture of vicarious suffering in the Hebrew Scriptures, the Servant of Yhwh in Deutero-Isaiah. Despised and rejected of men, he was also considered to be stricken by God. Nor was that view of his position a mistake, since 'it was Yhwh's will to crush him' (Isa. 53:3,4,10). The sacrificial system provides the prophet with a clue to the meaning of this role: as a representative of his people he was made a 'guilt offering' for their sin (10). But (and here the sacrificial analogy fails to go far enough) since he has been appointed by Yhwh for this role and has discharged it with unflinching patience, the outcome must be his vindication (52:13; 53:11). Here, then, is one figure who might, without ambiguity, have demanded vindication from Yhwh – but he has borne responsibility for his oppressors' offences! That is why the Servant is the focus around which a shattered and condemned people – and with it the Gentile nations, too – can hope to be reconstituted in a holy world order.

The prophet has, in effect, taken over the mediatorial role, a sign that the monarchy, which was to mediate Yhwh's rule to his people, has been set aside. Yhwh has discarded King Jehoiachin like someone tearing a ring from his hand and throwing it away (Jer. 22:24). The sole obedience now required of the people is to heed prophecy. And the prophet's demand is simply that they acknowledge Yhwh's refusal of themselves, their city and their institutions. By the time Jerusalem was under siege, it had come down to this one stark demand: 'whoever will surrender to the Babylonians will live' (Jer. 21:9; 38:2). In this way the prophet threw his authority into head-on collision with the authority of the institutions, and forced each member of the community to make a choice. Those who listened to the prophet had to share the isolation of the prophet. The gesture Jeremiah required of those who were shut up with him in the besieged city was eloquent: to escape from within its walls and to walk out alone into the Babylonian camp, a symbol of what belief in Yhwh's word had come to mean.

We know a surprising amount about those who did associate with this most lonely of prophets, and they were not at all what one might expect the disciples of a prophet to be. The disciples of Isaiah we imagine as a scribal class, who conserved the prophet's oracles, developed his message, and made sure that its relevance to the changing situation continued to be appreciated; finally, they will have edited collections of oracles in scrolls. Jeremiah had such followers: Baruch's role in propagating his words was immense; he was, one might say, the greatest of the 'Deuteronomists', and the only one we can put a name to. There were also younger prophets dependent on Jeremiah: Ezekiel, Uriah the martyr-prophet (Jer. 26:20) and probably Habbakuk. But there were also many men of action, statesmen from high-born families, sons and grandsons of the leading figures of Josiah's reform movement. In 604 BC the continuity between that movement and Jeremiah's message still seemed sufficiently marked to unite them around a concerted attempt to wrest the direction of foreign policy from King Jehoiachin's hands and tilt it towards Babylon. The publication they relied on was Jeremiah's first book (Jer. 36). By the middle of Zedekiah's reign, however, the coherence of the group had broken up. Some were on Zedekiah's staff, and may have believed that his reign marked a new start for Judah. Others were in Babylonia, siding with the exile community's hopes for an early return. Both groups may have thought they could find some support from the prophet. At one stage Jeremiah encouraged the view that the line between Yhwh's favour and disfavour lay precisely between the exiles and the city, the good and the bad figs. But when the exiles began to agitate for return, he qualified that distinction: Yhwh would make the city-dwellers like bad figs because they had not listened to his words; 'but you exiles have not listened either!' (24; 29:19f.). The division ran through all the communities, the prophet's own supporters not excepted. Not even the reforming movement remained intact.

Those who heeded the prophet to the last experienced an isolation akin to his own, as we sense from the poignant final chapter in Baruch's last edition of

Jeremiah's book, where the editor identifies himself by reporting an oracle addressed to himself. It dates from 604, the year of the abortive palace coup against Jehoiachin and the publication of the first edition, after which Jeremiah and Baruch had had to go into hiding (36:26). Baruch was in despair, and Yhwh's word to him suggests why: 'I will overthrow what I have built and uproot what I have planted throughout the land. Should you, then, seek great things for yourself? Seek them not.' The ambition which Baruch harboured was that modest one which decent men harbour: that the structures of society will provide them with a place in which to shine. But those structures were collapsing, and all that he could hope for was his 'life as a prize of war' – that is to say, his bare existence, snatched out of the context in which living might have been constructive and satisfying (Jer. 45:4f.). Escaping the fate of others, he is to be thrust out to live alone and unsupported as a refugee.

Jeremiah was not the only Jew of his era to understand what an unaccustomed isolation the coming catastrophe would thrust upon the faithful believer. Habbakuk's lapidary oracle, 'the righteous one shall live by his faithfulness' (2:4), though difficult to interpret with precision, suggests something close to what was promised Baruch: the faithful individual will come through with his life and with nothing else. And this implied a new concept of moral responsibility. In a brief oracle preserved in the Book of Consolation, Jeremiah quoted a proverb, 'the fathers have eaten sour grapes and the children's teeth are set on edge'. In the present time of crisis, he declared, that would no longer be true. The very continuity of the moral life of the nation, in which generation inherited the legacy of generation, was now to be broken, and each individual would find himself thrust alone into the world, answerable only for himself (31:29f.). Ezekiel, possibly before his departure for Mesopotamia, composed a commentary on this brief oracle, in which he denied the principle of inherited responsibility altogether (Ezek. 18:1–20).

Yet the solitary wandering of the refugee was not to be the end of the story. There would be a community to be the subject of Yhwh's favour again, and words of comfort would finally be addressed to Jerusalem. There is no reason to doubt that Jeremiah himself anticipated as much. But the character of this remnant-community was radically affected: it had faced the challenge to heed the voice of the prophet against the totality of its national institutions, and had seen the prophet vindicated by events. From that point on an element of confessional voluntarism enters into Israel's sense of itself. The reconstruction of the community had to be grounded on a new covenant, Jeremiah taught, which would reach to hidden personal depths of understanding and motivation, bypassing the perilous mediation of community tradition: 'I will put my law in their minds and write it on their hearts . . . No longer will a man teach his neighbour or a man his brother, saying "Know Yhwh", because they will all know me' (31:33ff.; Ezekiel again softens the eschatological contrast in his imitation, Ezek. 36:25–7). The question of who is a true Jew (as St Paul later put it, 'inwardly' and 'in the heart' (Rom. 2:24f.)) had been raised and could not be put down. Quite naturally the great prophet of the return, in calling the ransomed to believe, addresses them in terms which invite a new, committed people to emerge from the midst of the old: 'Who among you fears Yhwh and obeys the word of his servant? . . . Listen to me, you who pursue righteousness . . . you who have my law in your hearts!' (Isa. 50:10; 51:1,7, cf. 56:1–8).

It is important to understand the emergence of the individual in Israel historically, but equally important not to succumb, as we have said, to 'Whig history', supposing that the trend from community to individual could simply be extrapolated to authorise any kind of radical individualism as its final term. For what Israel affords is a strong concept of the individual on a quite different basis from the individualism of the West. The community is the aboriginal fact from beginning to end, shaping the conscience of each of its members to greater or lesser effect. But when the mediating institutions of government collapse, then the memory and hope which single members faithfully conserve provide a span of continuity which can reach out towards the prospect of restructuring. The fractured community which fashioned the individual's conscience is sustained within it and renewed out of it. And from having been preserved through single members' memory and hope, Jeremiah anticipates, it will be the stronger, for it will incorporate that direct knowledge of Yhwh's ways which each has won by his, or her, faithfulness. (We add the words 'or her' at this point without gratuitousness; for Esther is one of the models by which this faithfulness was commended.) The distinctive strengths of a voluntary community have been grafted on to the racial stock.

To generalise, as we have done before, we may say that *the conscience of the individual members of a community is a repository of the moral understanding which shaped it, and may serve to perpetuate it in a crisis of collapsing morale or institution.* It is not as bearer of his own primitive pre-social or pre-political rights that the individual demands the respect of the community, but as the bearer of a social understanding which recalls the formative self-understanding of the community itself. The conscientious individual speaks with society's own forgotten voice.

The six general theorems which we have drawn from Israel's political experience provide an outline of what theology may need to put in the place traditionally held by a notion of political authority. We have spoken of divine rule finding complementary expression in the rule of government and in the consciousness of law: on the one hand, claims of power, right and tradition are held together in a given community by a single agency, which, functioning as an effective organ of public judgment, elicits popular acknowledgment as a mediator of divine government; on the other, the community at large, and those of its members who are morally attuned to it, have knowledge of what God requires and authorises, not only in that political community but in all communities. A 'theological concept of authority' if we will have it so, but with the warning that nothing can be presumed about affinities with any other concept of authority. It is remote from both poles of the authority-dialectic in the modern tradition: state sovereignty on the one hand, popular sovereignty on the other. Those poles, indeed, are best understood as residual fragments of an original theological whole, which owe their opposition and their arbitrariness to the loss of their common centre of attraction.

But political theology must go beyond such general conceptions, and take on the character of a proclamatory history, attesting the claim that Yhwh reigns. Its subject is God's rule demonstrated and vindicated, the salvation that he has wrought in Israel and the nations. Unless it speak in that way it can only advance a theological type of political theory, not an evangelical political theology, a 'Law', in the theological sense, rather than a 'Gospel'. What we have done in this chapter is simply to abstract from Israel's experience a general understanding of what the divine rule is which is to be the subject of the proclamation. We have, as it were, examined the design of the vehicle; now we must see it move.

3.   Dual authority and the fulfilling of the time

Dual authority

Jesus proclaimed the 'fulfilling of the time' which had brought the 'Kingdom of God near' (Mark 3:15). The problem with the question – which continues to be discussed and answered today in terms very little different from those used by the church Fathers – whether the kingdom which fulfilled Israel's time was a 'political' or a 'spiritual' one is that it treats the terms 'political' and 'spiritual' as known quantities. As though the competing answers, 'political', 'spiritual', or 'both political and spiritual', could make us wiser, when in fact we need to know what the alternatives posed by the question could mean! Political theology must explore the meaning of the alternatives and show why the question, though of fundamental importance, could never be given a straightforward answer. For the terms 'political' and 'spiritual' take us to the very substance of the proclamation of the Kingdom of God, which spans the two. We have to let ourselves be instructed, even surprised, by what each of them contains: to rediscover politics not as a self-enclosed field of human endeavour but as the theatre of the divine self-disclosure; to rediscover God as the one who exercises rule.

Yet, as in speaking of the Incarnation itself we cannot affirm the hypostatic union without the two natures, so with the Kingdom of God we cannot conceive the henosis of political and spiritual without the duality of the two terms held together in it. That is why those who have asserted that a conception of Two Kingdoms is fundamental to Christian political thought have spoken truly, though at great risk of distorting the truth if they simply leave it at that. The unity of the kingdoms, we may say, is the heart of the Gospel, their duality is the pericardium. Proclaiming the unity of God's rule in Christ is the task of Christian witness; understanding the duality is the chief assistance rendered by Christian reflection.

St Augustine canonised the experience of Israel in Babylon as the archetype for the duality of this-worldly and divine rule, and gave special emphasis to one text arising from that experience, the letter of Jeremiah written to the exile community in 594 BC (Jer. 29:1–23). The context of that letter was a moment of special unsettlement in a generally unsettled political situation just after the first capitulation and captivity of Jerusalem. Among the exiles there were prophets who promised a speedy return, while prophetic elements at home echoed the hope. The government's policy tilted dangerously away from its Chaldean patrons to an alliance of local states hoping to throw off the yoke (27:1–29:32). Jeremiah, as usual, deprecated the suggestion that Yhwh's judgment could be quickly or painlessly got over. Nebuchadrezzar is Yhwh's servant; the nations must all bend their neck under his yoke. 'After seventy years' Yhwh would visit the exiles (29:10), and in the mean time they must settle down to a social life in their new political context. They must also 'seek the welfare (*shālōm*) of the city where I have sent you into exile, and pray to Yhwh on its behalf, for in its welfare you will find your welfare' (29:7).

Augustine did not misread the text in taking it as the model for his conception of two political entities coexistent in one time and space (*C. Faustum* XII.36; *City of God* 19.26). We need only enter the caveat that there are two ways of identifying the duality in this situation: on the one hand, there are two 'cities', the social entities of Israel and Babylon which live side by side; on the other, there are the two 'rules' under which Israel finds itself, that of Babylon and that of Yhwh. These two interpretations of the situation make it flexible as a model, capable of illuminating not only the situation in which Israel shared social space with others, but also the situation at home where it sensed its own provisional political institutions as alien to its true calling.

It would be difficult to exaggerate the significance of the Babylonian experience for Israel. One could even say that it became the paradigm of Jewish existence thereafter, even with the resettlement of Judah and the rebuilding of Jerusalem. 'The exile', N. T. Wright observes, 'has continued long after the "return"' (*The New Testament and the People of God*, p. 270). The presence of Esther in the canon and the use of the Daniel stories to confront the Seleucid tyranny both attest how even Palestinian Jews looked to the experience of exile to instruct them in their conduct. The Jeremiah text, too, played a central part; the seer of Daniel was prepared to read the 'seventy years' of the prophecy as extending right through the era of the great empires (Dan. 9:24). The diaspora Jew, of course, quite naturally saw his experience in this light. The Songs of Ascents, a collection of pilgrim-psalms (120–32), conjure up poignantly the sense of an alienated geographical identity and its corresponding rootlessness. Two of these psalms (122, 132) are processionals from the First Temple put to new use as prayers for the city of Jerusalem and the restoration of David's throne. The others speak directly of the pilgrim's perception of his situation: living in far-flung places, offering his neighbours the *shālōm* which Jeremiah commanded but met with continual hostility (120:5f.); protected on his journey to the Judaean hills by the maker of heaven and earth who guards his comings and goings (121:8); experiencing the protection of Yhwh in every place as though he were in Zion itself (125:1f.). For these diaspora Jews the liberation of 538 BC has been inconclusive (126); they express their hope for an end to foreign domination of the Holy Land, which must, however, be patiently borne in the mean time (125:3). Israel is now, as a nation scattered through the world, the oppressed one of the pre-exilic psalms, the righteous sufferer who lifts up his eyes to the king in heaven (123:1). Not only occasionally, but as a pattern throughout history, Israel's experience has been oppression, alleviated by Yhwh's protection (124:7; 129:1–4). Israel's faithfulness is a continuing hope for redemption from the result of its sins (130:7f.; 131:3).

The situation may seem to be quite different when we listen to the voices that celebrated the great deliverance, that of Deutero-Isaiah in particular. From time to time the prophet seems to go as far towards the reaffirmation of the traditional sacral kingship as he can: in the oracle where Cyrus is called Yhwh's 'shepherd' and 'anointed', in which Yhwh takes him by the right hand to subdue nations and in which Cyrus orders the rebuilding of Jerusalem, one could imagine oneself back in the days of Hezekiah and Isaiah, with nothing changed except for the oddity that the king is a Persian (44:24–45:8). Yet this would be to mistake the force of the prophet's message. He is the last of that sequence of nameless exilic prophets, to whom he often appeals for support, who anticipated Babylon's fall (Isa. 13:1–14:23; 21:1–10; Jer. 50, 51). The importance of Cyrus is not that he will rule Israel but that he will bring the dominance of Babylon to an end. He conquers on Israel's behalf, but the other activities of Israel's monarch, especially that of judgment, are attributed to the Servant of Yhwh (42:1–9). As for the future of the now liberated Israel, it is left open. Deutero-Isaiah keeps faith with the refusal of Jeremiah and Ezekiel to encourage resistance; Yhwh's sovereign decision to restore Jerusalem has been given through events quite independent of the people's restless machinations. What the foreign sword has given is an *opportunity for separation*, a moment in which Israel can withdraw from the idolatrous society in which it has dwelt. To go home will be to affirm that it is still Yhwh's holy people, and so to excite universal wonder at what Yhwh has done through its history. Beyond making use of the moment, Israel has nothing further to do with Cyrus. Its future life is for itself to determine, in obedience to Yhwh's prophet and following Yhwh's servant.

A parallel to this can be found in the thought of Zechariah, preaching to the earliest community of returned exiles. The prophet has visions of four horses and four chariots, going at Yhwh's behest to the four corners of the earth (1:8–17; 6:1–8). These speak of how divine providence has secured favourable conditions of world peace in which the restoration of Zion can proceed. The emphasis then falls upon the people's own act of self-purification. The vision of the woman in the ephah (5:5–11) reverses Jeremiah's vision of the two baskets of figs. Now the corruption within the people must be left behind in Babylon. But it is this continuing stress on separation that makes the admission that what Yhwh has done through Cyrus is only a first instalment. It postpones to a later day the time when 'ten men from all languages and nations will take hold of a Jew by the hem of his robe and say "Let us go with you"' (8:23). The ideas of separation, on the one hand, and of international inclusiveness on the other, ideas which were blended together in the exilic prophets and even in Deutero-Isaiah, are now separated out into a 'now' and a 'hereafter'. The way must be prepared for the latter by a more stringent insistence on the former.

The prophets of the sixth century, before, during and after the exile, had had some clear conceptions about the shape of the future restoration. It would involve the gathering of scattered Israelites from Egypt and Mesopotamia to their home (Isa. 27:12; Zech. 2:11), and the healing of the centuries-long rift between Northern and Southern communities (Jer. 50:4f.; Ezek. 37:15–23). It would involve the long-anticipated worship of the nations at Jerusalem, an event anticipated, as it seemed, by the accession of proselytes to the community (Isa. 44:5; 14:1; 56:3). And there was a third element which should not be overlooked: the restoration of the Davidide monarchy. Ezekiel was very definite that this must be the case (34:23f.; 37:24–8; 45:7f.). Few others spoke with his insistence on the matter; nevertheless, the point keeps coming up.

There are exilic prophecies of a renewed monarchy at Micah 4:6–13 and Isaiah 33:17–19, and the Deuteronomic historian seems to have found significance in the favour shown to Jehoiachin by Amel-Marduk in 560 BC (2 Kgs. 25:27–30). The collection of oracles referred to as Deutero-Zechariah keeps the hope alive after the return (Zech. 9:9; 12:7–9), while the Chronicler, devoted to the Davidides in his history, preserves a genealogy that traces their line well into post-exilic times, presumably because he expected something to come of it (1 Chron. 3:17–24). The anointing of Josiah and Zerubbabel (Zech. 4:11–14) may be intended discreetly to suggest the hope, never realised, of a partnership between the two as priest and king; and it may even be speculated that behind the broken text of Zechariah 6:9–14 there lay a suppressed coronation of Zerubbabel.

The post-exilic community found that though a gathering of scattered exiles had occurred, there was still a substantial diaspora; though the Persian kings extended tolerance, even a measure of patronage, there was nothing like a world-wide conversion from idolatry; and there was no son of David on the throne. They therefore understood themselves to be living in a state of preparation, charged to maintain the purity of their own life in readiness for the dawning of that later day. This led to the policy of separation from the existing inhabitants who had occupied the land for the duration of the exile and who claimed, as Yahwists, the right to worship in Jerusalem (Ezr. 4:1–3; Neh. 2:20). This policy reached the point of stirring up internal conflict in the fifth-century crisis over mixed marriage (Ezr. 9, 10; Neh. 13:23–31). To understand this policy, which grates as much as anything in the Old Testament upon our expectations, we have to understand the place in salvation-history which the community believed itself to occupy: still living in hope, it was preoccupied by its own unreadiness for Yhwh's reconciling act.

There was another inference which was drawn from Yhwh's use of the foreign sword, paradoxically related to the first. It provided an *opportunity for influence* with the imperial power, offering constructive assistance on the one hand and securing protection for the holy people on the other. The roles of Mordecai and Esther are a fictional paradigm of how Jews saw themselves earning the gratitude of the imperial power and using their position for their nation's benefit – but not only their nation's, for Esther, as queen, is a symbol of a frank and free-spirited subject people, which renders better service to rulers than the pathetic doll-like subservience to which Eastern potentates were accustomed, symbolised by Vashti. A historical example of such a figure is Nehemiah: a reforming governor who used his place to strengthen the colony's position among its neighbours, but who owed his authority to Artaxerxes I. A quite remarkable instance in literary practice is afforded by the opening chapters of the Book of Ezra, which laboriously establish the legitimacy of the colony in Persian terms by quoting imperial documentation: the Cyrus decree itself (1:2ff.); a letter from a local governor to Darius, quoting in turn a document of Cyrus' reign (5:7ff.); a letter to Artaxerxes I and his reply (4:7–23); the mandate for

Ezra's mission from Artaxerxes I (or II) (7:12–26). But what does it all prove? In Ezra's astonishingly sombre words, 'For a brief moment Yhwh our God has been gracious to us, leaving us some survivors and giving us a foothold in this holy place . . . some chance to renew our lives in our slavery' (Ezr. 9:8). Yhwh had not, in fact, renewed his rule over his people. 'We are slaves, slaves here in the land which thou gavest to our forefathers . . . All its produce now goes to the kings [sc. of Persia] whom thou hast set over us because of our sins' (Neh. 9:36f.).

The poet of Psalm 138, who lives in a Gentile court and so, like Daniel, worships Yhwh 'before the gods', turning his face towards the Temple in Jerusalem, can boast that foreign kings have 'heard the words of [Yhwh's] mouth', that is, from Jewish advisers like himself. Upbeat as this is, the poet still knows that he walks on a knife-edge (7). When we come to the stories of the Book of Daniel, the sense of peril is all-present. The twin conceptions of separation and influence still provide the frame of reference; but in the crisis precipitated by the Seleucids they have ceased to seem unproblematic. Daniel and his friends maintain their purity, but at great risk; they enjoy high influence, but it is acquired in the teeth of opposition and lost more easily than it is won. Daniel in Babylon prays with his window open to Jerusalem; but now it is a dangerous and defiant thing to acknowledge the claim of the one city within the other's walls. We can read here a warning against optimism about the compatibility of the two kingdoms, bred, perhaps, by too facile a reading of the stories of Joseph or of Esther. The co-operative relation between Israel and the empire is not a right, and to make a priority of preserving it can lead to fatal compromises.

Why this instability? Because empire itself is unstable. The Book of Daniel is remarkable for its interest in empire as a distinct phenomenon. Emperors one after another fail to recognise that 'the Most High is sovereign over the kingdoms of men, and sets over them any one he wishes' (5:21). They divinise themselves, and then the mind of the emperor is 'changed from that of a man [and become] the mind of a beast' (4:16). In the visions of chapters 7–12 the empires appear as beasts, but the vindication of Israel is the vindication of humanity against bestiality; the one favoured of the Ancient of Days appears as a 'son of man', and the kingdom of God is, at the same time, a kingdom of man (7:13–27). And in subtle ways the stories point us to a purely human knowledge of the instability of empire. It is not as a prophet that Daniel serves Nebuchadrezzar, but as a counsellor who interprets dreams, like Joseph before Pharaoh. The knowledge given in those dreams is Nebuchadrezzar's own knowledge. But, in a deft adaptation of the dream-interpretation motif, the king needs to be told not only what his dream meant but what it was (2:5). Empire cannot articulate to itself its suppressed knowledge of its own fragility; the king as dreamer knows something that the king as ruler cannot repeat. Yet at the same time empire cannot abide anyone having secrets, but must drag everything into the light by threat and cruelty so that it may be controlled. Thus it works its own undoing, eliciting the suppressed knowledge that will subvert its own fraudulent pretensions.

In projecting his reflections on empire back onto the stage of the sixth century, the author allows himself to make two complementary points. In the first place, empire has always been like this, and it is wrong to look back to a golden age of co-operation. The normal situation was not the Persians' hands-off policy but the perilous insecurity of life under the Chaldeans. In the second place, empire has its own internal history of degeneration, each successive empire being baser than the last. There is a historical necessity in the worsening situation which must lead to 'a time of distress such as has not happened from the beginning of the nations' (12:1). The vision section of the book intends to establish the uniqueness of the crisis now impending, and to warn the faithful that there is no *modus vivendi* that can somehow be sustained. In this section, then, Daniel ceases to be an interpreter of other people's dreams and becomes a dreamer himself, a prophet who can awaken Israel to the crisis which is overwhelming the Two Cities settlement. To treat the coexistence of Israel and Babylon as a permanent ordinance was, in effect, to accept the emperor's own assessment of himself, to bow down before his image of gold. To arm itself against that temptation Israel must, once again, heed prophecy, alert for the culmination of Yhwh's purposes in which the Ancient of Days will entrust his Kingdom to a son of man, who should also represent the people of the saints of the Most High.

The fulfilling of the time

When Jesus announced the coming of God's Kingdom, according to St Mark, his words were greeted with astonishment 'because he taught them authoritatively, not like the scribes' (1:22). This report is reinforced a moment later, somewhat paradoxically, when the crowds respond to an exorcism with the exclamation 'What is this? A new, authoritative teaching' (1:27). The paradox consists in the *non sequitur* between the display of miraculous power and the authority of the teaching. St Luke was the first of many to feel that something in this connexion needed to be clarified. He rephrased the exclamation: 'What is this word, that with power and authority he commands the unclean spirits?' (4:36). This paraphrase, while easing the *non sequitur*, still preserves the connexion between Jesus' miracle and his speech, the 'power' and the 'word'. What Jesus had to say about the reign of God was authoritative because it was confirmed by an exercise of power that demonstrated it.

Our own difficulty in grasping the connexion between word and power, the connexion which St Mark sums up in the term 'authority' (*exousia*), is sharpened by the fact that we are used, following an important legacy of medieval legal analysis, to distinguishing two quite different kinds of authority: epistemic and political, the authority of word and the authority of act. Canon lawyers made the distinction explicit, partly to clarify the proper scope of theological and episcopal authority respectively: when the pope tells us that we are obliged to observe certain fast days, we obey the pope; but when he claims to demonstrate the obligation from Holy Scripture, we follow the best theologians. This distinction is an important Christian gain. It did not, of course, need canon lawyers to make the point that those in political authority are not a reliable source of intellectual instruction, for Socrates knew as much; but it was a Christian insight that the capacity to give instruction was actually a kind of *authority*, parallel to, though different from, the capacity to give effective commands. This is because both kinds of authority mediate the command of God. Our concept of a differentiated authority, epistemic and political, is derived from an originally united authority in which truth and power are one, that is to say, the authority of God. It is the divine word, powerful because true and true because powerful, that surprises us when we meet it so baldly in St Mark's account of Jesus' authority. His miracle is not distinct from his teaching, and his teaching assumes miracle as its natural expression. It is God's rule that is the content of his teaching, in which word and act are one.

Jesus' teaching-ministry, then, is taken by the evangelists to be something more than instruction. It is a disclosure of the reign of God, through which the authority of God asserts itself. Jesus' authority consists in his capacity to bring us directly into contact with God's authority. That most subtle of narratives from the 'Q' category of Gospel material, the story of the Capernaum centurion, whose servant (or son) Jesus healed at a distance, tells us how the quasi-political character of Jesus' authority was recognised by a representative of the authority of the empire. The centurion, in St

Matthew's comparatively unelaborated version (8:5–13), declines to let Jesus come into his house because that would be an unnecessary and unfitting condescension on the part of one who commands a superior authority to his own. The same word, *exousia*, is employed, and it is elaborated in a way that does not allow us to miss its political significance.

> Authority is the capacity to give effective commands, we are told; those who can call upon it are used to having their commands obeyed without attending in person to watch over their execution. Not to be overlooked is the phrase used for 'being in authority': *hupo exousian tassesthai*, literally, being set 'under' authority. An important insight is captured there: to be *in* authority you have to be *under* it, and if you are under it you are in it. To be subject to authority is to be *authorised*. In that Jesus exercises the powers of God's Kingdom, he shows himself subject to that kingdom. So God's Kingdom is made known by a true subject of that kingdom, wholly under God's authority, wholly authorised to act in God's name.
>
> As I have referred to the 'Q' material, I should make it clear that I have no pretension to intervene in scholarly arguments which by their very nature seem incapable of decisive resolution. But those of us who would prefer to be told by specialists what we are to think of synoptic sources must, when the specialists are unable to give clear guidance, assume something not too implausible for the sake of argument. When I use the term 'Q' I intend to assume rather little: merely that there is Gospel material which Luke and Matthew both found somewhere, but not in Mark. Sometimes I assume just a little more, namely that this material existed independently in some form (goodness knows what), and that an intelligent conjecture may be made as to whether Luke or Matthew has, in one or another case, kept closer to that form. Readers of these pages who may stumble across references to such things as 'the "Q" community' are invited to consider them as jokes in poor taste!

Near the heart of Jesus' message lies a recurrent and important reference to the Son of Man of Daniel's vision. No one could hear this without understanding that imperial oppression was to be replaced by the rule of the saints, the restored Israel which would exercise a humane authority granted it by God. Expectations of such an event were a part of the context into which, and out of which, Jesus was speaking. We may not interpret Jesus in a way that denies him that context, but neither may we simply assimilate him to it, especially as it is itself diverse, comprising more than one movement of renewal and more than one strategy of preparation for it. Yet the fundamental orientation, common to Jesus and others of his contemporaries, was to look for the intervention of Yhwh's rule to rectify Israel's political and social situation. That implied challenging the Two Kingdoms settlement with the promised unity of God's all-sovereign rule.

And in Jesus' preaching the challenge was immediate. The time was at hand.

An important saying from the 'Q' source declares that John the Baptist was the threshold between two ages, 'the law and the prophets' and the age of the proclamation of the Kingdom (Matt. 11:12f.; Luke 16:16). The sense of the historical significance of that moment was present in John's own preaching, as Christian recollections of him insisted. The evangelists all report that John described his own role in terms drawn from Deutero-Isaiah: 'the voice of one crying in the desert, "Prepare the way of the Lord"' (Mark 1:3; Matt. 3:3; Luke 3:4; John 1:23), and that he anticipated one to follow, who would 'baptise in spirit and in fire'. It is possible that he saw this figure as the 'Elijah' whom Malachi had promised 'before the great and terrible day of the Lord comes' (Mal. 4:5, cf. John 1:21). Jesus, in turn, was reported to have cast John himself in the role of the Elijah (Mark 9:13||Matt. 17:12; Matt. 11:14), which implied that the day of the Lord had now come.

Jesus' attitude to existing structures of authority can be traced more closely through the two synoptic stories about payment of taxes. The more famous of the two, that about the census-tax (Mark 12:17ff.||), tells of a question put to Jesus as a trap by Pharisees and 'Herodians': whether it was right to pay the census-tax to Caesar. Jesus' reply is sufficiently elusive to have allowed of many interpretations; but it is also sufficiently decisive to exclude some, and among those, in my view, is one that was canonised by medieval theories of empire and papacy – the view that civil government can claim certain secular rights and that those rights should be respected, though not demands which exceed them. Within the context of a Christendom understanding of authority divided between secular and spiritual powers, this may be asserted with perfect truth; but it is not what Jesus, speaking in a different context, said or meant.

The key to the story is to decide what the trap was that his answer avoided so successfully that, the narrative tells us, his audience was 'astonished'. There seem to be two possibilities. Either his tempters intended to seduce him into expressing opinions which were dangerous in the eyes of authority; or they intended to make him come down on one side of a disputed question with a clarity that would alienate half his supporters. The choice between these turns on the historical question whether the issue of census-tax, which had given rise to sanguinary insurrection a generation earlier, was widely and freely debated in Jesus' own day. If it was, then Jesus is supposed to be hedging on a matter which divided his contemporaries; if it was not, then he is supposed to be harbouring dangerous views in secret. But if Jesus actually meant to say that the Romans had a right to exact a secular tax without prejudice to the claims of God to rule Israel, then, on the one hand, his opinion was not dangerous in the eyes of authority, while, on the other, he publicly avowed an opinion likely to be repugnant to many of his supporters. Whichever of the two traps was set for him, he deserved no admiration for evading it. In the one case, there was no cause for suspicion of his views; in the other, there was no ground for admiring his neat-footedness. But the answer really was neat-footed if, while not appearing to deny the imperial power its claim, it could be widely understood as brushing that claim aside.

The census-tax story, then, allows us to rule out the view that Jesus assigned Roman government a certain uncontested sphere of secular right. It does not allow us to clarify his opinions more precisely. Various accounts remain possible, of which two in particular are worth considering. One supposes that Jesus disapproved of paying taxes to Rome, and expressed his disapproval in circumspect terms which could be understood by those with a mind to understand them: 'Give back' to Caesar this taxation he has introduced, with which Jews have no truck! The other would suppose that he treated the question as an irrelevant distraction from the real business of receiving God's Kingdom. If Caesar put his head upon the coin, then presumably it is his: let him have what is his, if he asks for it (for such transactions are not the stuff of which true government consists), but give your whole allegiance to God's rule!

The reasons for attributing the second of these views to Jesus lie elsewhere, in the story of the didrachm tax. In this story, told by St Matthew alone, Jesus enunciates some clearer principles of political action. The 'sons' of any kingdom, he argues, are free of all claims made by that kingdom on its subject peoples. To recognise the coming of God's Kingdom is to be a son of the Kingdom, and so emancipated from the order in which God's rule was mediated through such alienating institutions as taxation. But purely as a concession Jesus and his disciples will pay taxes 'to create no scandal', i.e. lest they be misunderstood as mere rebels, who refuse God's mediated rule as such. As it were to emphasise the purely peripheral character of this compliance, their payment is provided for them by the almost comic intervention of a miracle (Matt. 17:24–7).

A modern parable, perhaps, may clarify the thought expressed here. Imagine an official of the Russian Government in October 1991, confronted with some demand from the foundering Soviet authorities. 'This is ridiculous!', he thinks to himself. 'We will be running that ourselves by next week!' Yet to display open contempt would give the impression that the new authorities did not believe in constitutional government at all. So confident is he of the shape of the coming order, that he has no need of an insolent posture to assert it against the order that is vanishing. Jesus, similarly, believed that a shift in the locus of power was taking place, which made the social institutions that had prevailed to that point anachronistic. His attitude to them was neither secularist nor zealot: since he did not concede that they had any future, he gave them neither dutiful obedience within their supposed sphere of competence nor the inverted respect of angry defiance. He did not recognise a permanently twofold locus of authority. He recognised only a transitory duality which belonged to the climax of Israel's history, a duality between the coming and the passing order. So the duality inherited from Israel's past underwent a transformation. The Two Cities, with their concomitant Two Rules expressing Israel's alienation from its calling, gave way to the Two Eras. The coming era of God's rule held the passing era in suspension.

> Discussion of the didrachm story is complicated by the initially disconcerting fact that Jesus' generalised political reply answers a question apparently about a temple-tax. It is possible to think the form of the question secondary. But it resolves the difficulty sufficiently to reflect that temple authorities were also political authorities, and that Israel's whole structure of social and political order, not only colonial domination, had been felt as alienating and provisional.

Yhwh's rule over Israel, as we analysed it earlier (pp. 30–49), was founded on his acts of salvation and judgment and on his gift of an inheritance. That is to say, Israel enjoyed its existence as a nation because Yhwh overcame its enemies, ordered its common dealings by judgment, and secured its common possession of land and law. That same analysis will serve to clarify how God's Kingdom was demonstrated in Jesus' ministry.

1. Jesus' *works of power* (*dunameis*) were identified in the Gospel tradition as acts of exorcism and healing. They were taken to be victories over the demonic powers, and as such significant of what Jesus believed about that 'strong man' from which Israel stood in need of liberation (Mark 3:27||). By comparison, as we have observed, he treated the fact of Roman occupation casually, with little respect and less urgency. Israel was enslaved to spiritual enemies, and of this its colonial status was, at most, a secondary symptom. Here is a double hermeneutic difficulty. On the one hand, Jesus' preference for addressing the demonic rather than the colonial oppressors looks, from the point of view of our own narrowed conception of politics, like a decidedly apolitical inclination. On the other hand, our

materialist interpretation of disease and dementia makes it hard to take seriously the thought that there are enemies to confront within this realm at all.

We may, however, overcome the limitations of our modern perspective by a sympathetic engagement with the problems of deeply depoliticised societies, especially those in which hunger and disease have contributed in a major way to depoliticisation. It is a Western conceit to imagine that all political problems arise from the abuse or over-concentration of power; and that is why we are so bad at understanding political difficulties which have arisen from a lack of power, or from its excessive diffusion. There is no abuse of power that can be blamed for the ills of Somalia. True, such power as there has been has, as a matter of course, been abused. That is a part of the pathology of depoliticisation. But political power was never strong enough to cope with the daunting natural obstacles. To say that the chief enemies of Somalia are disease and famine would be a metaphor – but only just! Disease and famine are not enemies in the way that tyrants and invaders are enemies; but they are, quite literally, depoliticising forces. They prevent people from living in communities, from coordinating their efforts to the common good; from protecting one another against injury and maintaining just order; and from handing on their cultural legacy to their children. Political organisation and authority is founded, only partly but necessarily, on political power; and political power is founded on power over nature. If the ink in the dictator's pen won't flow when he wants to sign the decree, if his gunpowder won't explode, if his military jeep won't start or the radio fails when he wants to broadcast, then his dictatorship will come to a humiliating end. But the power the tyrant depends on is that which all political organisation depends on.

In the argument about Beelzebul Jesus appealed to a simple political principle, well known to the ancient world, as it was, indeed, to earlier phases of the modern tradition: the establishment of multiple centres of competing power is a recipe for political weakness. The kingdom divided against itself is bereft of resource; the conflict between one household and another leads to social collapse. The point of his argument was that his own intervention by miracle could not have been effective unless it represented the intervention of a superior and coordinated power which was capable of sweeping the predatory rule of demons before it. 'If I cast out demons by the finger of God, the kingdom of God is upon you' (Luke 11:20||Matt. 12:28). His audience had to observe the effect of what he did and draw its own conclusions: were they seeing signs of collapse, or of a new injection of power into the nation's life?

Yet that new power was directed against the forces which most immediately hindered Israel from living effectively as a community in God's service, the spiritual and natural weaknesses which drained its energies away. This was not an apolitical gesture, but a statement of true political priorities. Jesus' departure from the zealot programme showed his more theological understanding of power, not his disinterest in it. The empowerment of Israel was more important than the disempowerment of Rome; for Rome disempowered would in itself by no means guarantee Israel empowered. The paradigm of the Exodus was, we might say, being read with an emphasis not on the conquest of the Egyptians but on the conquest of the sea. The power which God gave to Israel did not have to be taken from Egypt, or from Rome, first. The gift of power was not a zero-sum operation. God could generate new power by doing new things in Israel's midst.

The fashion for aligning Jesus with zealot revolutionaries – giving academic respectability, one might say, to the views of Pontius Pilate! – has now deservedly passed. Not only is it incompatible with certain famous texts: the Gethsemane story (in all its four different versions) and 'Q' sayings from the Sermon on the Mount/Plain which must surely have a bearing on attitudes to Roman impositions (Matt. 5:38–45‖Luke 6:27–30). There is also a pervasive emphasis in Jesus' teachings encouraging his disciples to expect the Kingdom to shine and manifest itself without being forced. The parable of the lamp set on the lampstand refers, in its Markan context (4:21), not to the witness of good works, as at Matthew 5:15, nor to the manifestation of faith in perseverence, as in Luke 8:16, but to the 'coming' of the light of God's Kingdom which will not be left hidden or concealed. The seed growing secretly grows in a way of which the farmer is unaware, so that the land bears fruit 'of itself' (4:26–9). The Kingdom is like the mustard seed which, though insignificant in its inception, comes to dominate the natural landscape by its own integral development (4:30–2).

Nevertheless, the 'zealot development' – if we may call it so without prejudging open scholarly debate about the forms it may have taken – could appear to Jesus (so the 'Q' saying of Matt. 11:12f.‖Luke 16:16 suggests) as a sign of the times. It was a temptation precisely because the age of the law and the prophets had closed and the age of the Kingdom had come. This 'Q' saying actually makes a historical claim: it was since the coming of John the Baptist that 'violent men' had begun to lay hold on the Kingdom (following St Matthew; St Luke's version identifies the period as that of the Kingdom's proclamation).

There is some reserve expressed in the Gospels (and especially in St Mark) about Jesus' exercises of power. It is by no means as strong a reserve as some idealist-inspired interpretations have liked to make it appear, and it is, at most, a qualifying parenthesis to the assertion of the presence of divine power in Jesus' ministry. The point at issue is publicity and the way in which it may distort what is publicised. Jesus' powers were deployed as a demonstration of God's rule, and their function was to draw attention not to themselves but to the preaching of the Kingdom. But power often attracts a public interest of a politically destructive kind, restless and dissatisfied, heedless of justice and authentic community. A popular movement drawn to power but not to the Kingdom of God would be implicitly hostile to the Kingdom. By focussing attention on this danger Mark prepared his readers for the ambivalence of Jesus' triumphal entry into Jerusalem.

> In the synoptic Gospels the reserve is found primarily in the Markan 'secrecy-motif': a half of the eight examples of commanded secrecy in that Gospel have to do with miracles, the other half with Christological confessions, and the two types should be distinguished, though they are not unconnected. Apart from this, it is merely that in the Markan apocalypse false prophets are said to perform miracles (Mark 13:22‖), while Herod is said by Luke to be idly curious to see one (23:8). The saying that an evil and adulterous generation seeks a sign does not have to do with miracle but with a 'sign from heaven', i.e. an unmistakable public verification of Jesus' authority by God (Matt. 12:38f.‖ 16:1–4‖Mark 8:11ff.‖Luke 11:16,29)). St John provides more explicit criticism of a faith dependent upon miracles (4:48, cf. 20:29). Theological commentary on the question often takes its lead from John, and locates the Gospels' reserve within the epistemological problematic of the nature of faith and its difference from sense-based knowledge. But there is an alternative context for it, more immediately germane to the Markan secrecy-motif, and that is precisely the significance of miracle as power. The commands of secrecy in relation to Jesus' miracles, unlike those that relate to Christological confessions, are said to be disobeyed, so that Jesus' reputation spreads widely on the basis of reports of his miracles (Mark 1:44; 7:36). In the case of one miracle Jesus commands the opposite of secrecy: the Gerasene demoniac is told to report what has been done for him at home (5:19), the point of the difference, in all probability, being that he did not live within the geographical borders of Israel, where Jesus' ministry was exercised.

2. Jesus proclaimed the coming *judgment of Israel,* as John had before him, in terms which have their sources in the Hebrew Scriptures and in Israel's history. The long apocalyptic discourse in the synoptic Gospels, announcing the fall of Jerusalem, moves within this field of expectation: Gentile enemies would besiege the city and sack its Temple as they had in the past, and the faithful would find themselves in flight to the hills. The Gentiles

play another part in this projection: the establishment of God's Kingdom would be marked by a 'gathering' of the Gentiles to acknowledge the place of Israel in the divine plan. 'Many will come from the East and from the West and will sup with Abraham, Isaac and Jacob in the Kingdom of Heaven' – while judgment within Israel itself means the exclusion from power of some who thought they had a claim to it: 'the sons of the Kingdom will be expelled into the darkness outside' (Matt. 8:11f.). Blocks of polemic against the governing establishment, 'lawyers' and 'Pharisees', identify those who bear responsibility for Israel's misdirection. In a parable from the Markan tradition we read how the master of the vineyard (the vineyard is Israel, as always) will come and remove those who had failed in their responsibility and replace them (Mark 12:9).

> St Matthew's interpretative note on this (21:43f.) suggests that they will be replaced by another 'race', something that the parable does not say; but that is no more than a combination of two contentions, each of which had its place in the preaching of judgment: that Israel's inadequate leadership would be removed, and that some Gentiles would honour, and be honoured in, the Kingdom while some Jews would not. By his physical assault on the precincts of the Temple Jesus undertook to demonstrate the presence of God's judgment. In the synoptic tradition this action was explained by a quotation from Jeremiah's denunciation of the Temple as a 'robbers' den'; the parallel between the fate of the First Temple in Jeremiah's day and the fate that was subsequently to fall on Herod's Temple was not lost on the synoptic evangelists. The position in which they placed the narrative of this event interpreted it as the opening of the Passion, the supreme act of judgment. St John makes the same link but differently, by recalling its connexion with the saying about Jesus' destroying the Temple and building a new one in three days, a prediction, as he saw it, of the resurrection. Still, the incident also looks back and forms a climax to the controversial side of Jesus' ministry as a whole – especially in St Matthew's Gospel, where it marks the crisis of a period of growing confrontation. St John recognises this aspect by locating the incident in a programmatic position at the beginning of the Gospel, where it shares with the story of the miracle at Cana the task of anticipating the character of all Jesus' subsequent ministry. The significance of the episode has been highlighted by the work of E. P. Sanders, *Jesus and Judaism*.

If judgment fell against the governing classes, in whose favour was it given? In the first place it was given for the 'crowds', who are seen throughout the synoptic Gospels flocking around Jesus, often making themselves a nuisance and sometimes forcing him to withdraw, but never simply repulsed. Jesus 'has compassion' on them (Matt. 9:36; 14:14||Mark 6:34), and constantly teaches them. At the centre of the Gospel tradition, both synoptic and Johannine, there stands the miracle of the feeding of the crowds, which acquires a special weight and importance in St Mark's narrative from its repetition.

More specifically, Jesus' support was said to be directed to 'the poor', echoing words from Trito-Isaiah, 'to preach good news to the poor', which lie behind Jesus' message to John the Baptist (Matt. 11:5||Luke 7:22) and are quoted directly by St Luke as a programme for Jesus' ministry (4:18). The Beatitudes begin with a blessing pronounced on the poor (Matt. 5:3||Luke 6:20), followed in St Luke's Gospel by a corresponding woe upon the rich (6:24). When Jesus sends his disciples on their mission of preaching and healing, he requires them to travel in a condition of poverty (Matt. 10:9f.). And at the climax of his ministry in St Mark's Gospel there is placed a story of how he appreciated the temple-offering of a poor widow (Mark 12:42). We must be careful not to read the term 'poor' in a narrowly economic sense. In the Isaiah text, as in the synoptic passages that depend upon it, 'the poor' are accompanied by other needy classes: crippled, blind, captives etc. Yet neither can the economic sense be set aside. When St Matthew qualified the first beatitude with the words 'in spirit', he did not mean, as has sometimes been suggested, to dissociate the idea of poverty altogether from material want, but rather to situate the experience of want within a context of moral disposition appropriate to it. 'Spiritual poverty' is not a mere analogy to material poverty; it is material poverty that has generated a spiritual orientation: dependence upon God and openness to his Kingdom.

There was one class in which Jesus took a notorious interest, who were, as a rule, the opposite of poor, those described as 'irreligious tax-collectors'. These were predatory profiteers from whom the poor especially must have suffered. Their claim on Jesus' interest was that they were 'lost sheep', effectively excluded from participation in their national culture by the disapproval and contempt in which they were held. They illustrate clearly enough that Jesus' demonstration of divine judgment was not only to be a matter of forcing divisions (Matt. 10:34–6), but of recovering and reconciling the alienated. He was the physician who came to attend to the sick, not to the well (Mark 2:17), the shepherd who went in search of the sheep that strayed (Matt. 18:12ff.||Luke 15:4ff.). Thus to pronounce God's judgment on the rich is not to close the door upon them finally; for though it is 'easier for a camel to pass through the eye of a needle than for a rich man to enter the Kingdom of God', yet 'with God everything is possible'. His judgment creates new situations and new conditions, in which it may come to be seen, as in the case of Zacchaeus, a representative figure from this class, that 'this man too is a son of Abraham' (Luke 19:9).

What of that largest of alienated classes, the Gentiles? The Gospels are remarkably direct in their assertion of the difference between Jesus' practice in relation to the Gentiles and that current in the church of their own day. The authorisation for the Gentile mission was given, according to Matthew and Luke, only after the resurrection; and even so, as St Luke reports the matter, the decision to embark upon it was not easily taken. (The mission of the seventy in St Luke's Gospel probably does not have anything to do with the Gentile mission; but if it does, it anticipates it only symbolically.) Matthew insists that Jesus did not permit any approach to the Gentiles in his lifetime (10:5f.). Mark shows him on a journey outside the boundaries of Israel to the north, hesitant about engaging with a Gentile woman who approached him (7:24ff.). Luke supposes that the centurion from Capernaum was received by Jesus only because a strong case was made for him by his Jewish friends (7:4f.). With respect to the rather different question of the status of Samaritans Jesus was known to have taken a liberal attitude (Luke 9:52; 10:25f.; John 4:1ff.), but this had to do with the reunification of Israel, and is not an indicator of how he related to those who were outside Israel by any reckoning.

But this ought to increase our confidence in the two stories in which Jesus performs healing miracles for Gentiles, the Markan story of the Syrophoenician woman and the 'Q'-source story of the Capernaum centurion. The scholarly tendency to regard them as apologetic compositions from the period of early Gentile mission is an example of that tidiness of mind which is such a dangerous liability in historical discussions. All great questions have their gestation periods as well as their moments of crisis. Imagine scholars of a future generation to our own discovering an English episcopal letter which permits, in liberal-minded manner, women to preach in church 'occasionally, and from the lectern'. Will they be well advised to date it to the early 1990s, when, as independent evidence assures them, the controversy over women's ministry was at its height in England? Those of us with a native's nose for the period know instinctively that the concessions offered are too small to be intelligible in that context. Similarly, what is allowed the Gentiles in the two synoptic narratives is too little to be an invention of the late forties. They must derive from an earlier period, when the question was looming on the horizon, but had not broken. But that points us back to Jesus' own day. What precipitated the question of the Gentiles was precisely the preaching of judgment on Israel, drawing with it such themes as the gathering of the nations to Jerusalem. There were Gentiles all around – Capernaum itself, after all, was the neighbouring city to Jesus' home – and those with an eye to the signs of the times would be alert to any indications that they might gather. The Gospels present Jesus as ready to welcome faith on the part of Gentiles, but not ready to take an initiative, which is more or less what we would expect.

St John describes an apparently inconsequential moment shortly before the Passion, when some 'Greeks' who have come to Jerusalem to worship seek an audience with Jesus through his disciples. Jesus greets the request with an exclamation that 'the time has come!' (12:23). The world is to be judged; he himself will be exalted; he will draw all to himself. The status of these visitors is left vague; presumably they must have been proselytes at least, but to the evangelist they represent the Gentile world as a whole. In the event they are never actually brought into Jesus' presence; the reader is left thinking they are just about to be. But it is most important that they asked spontaneously; their arrival was the sign of the moment of crisis. St John, as always, has clothed the moment in theological reflection; but it is the precise moment, the moment of theological history in which Jesus operated, that he has successfully captured in that incident.

3. That Israel should be put more effectively *in possession of the law*, the mark of its national identity, was a concern characteristic of Jesus' age. Perhaps it was a reaction to the loss of territorial independence before the encroaching waves of Roman colonial control. Unlike the Seleucids two centuries earlier, the Romans were not ambitious for cultural transformation of the communities they ruled. It suited them, as it suited Israel's own self-understanding, that the national self-consciousness should be poured into the construction of a law-culture, an alternative manner of self-determination to armed struggle. St John represents 'the Jews' as taking offence at Jesus' suggestion that they were in need of liberation: 'We are Abraham's descendants . . . we have never been enslaved to anyone' (8:33). That such an assertion was thinkable is a testimony to the effectiveness of the law-culture in conferring a sense of autonomy.

Jesus' own work was undertaken naturally in this context. He, too, confronted the task of making God's law accessible to God's people. It was never right to see this project in general merely as a matter of regulating details of behaviour by precise application of the text. The enterprise was a more broadly hermeneutic one. Jesus' famous 'summary' of the law in the two commands of love to God and neighbour recalls similar attempts by rabbis to find a central point from which the whole law could be grasped imaginatively. Other hermeneutic distinctions current among the rabbis, such as that between 'heavy' and 'light' commands, were equally intended to achieve a discerning, intelligent use of the text rather than clinging *au pied de la lettre*. Of course there was a fair measure of casuistic enquiry, and Jesus criticised some of its proposals (e.g. Mark 7:9–13) as well as a preoccupation with it at the expense of the moral priorities that the law expressed. To this extent Jesus approached the law with a prophet's rather than a lawyer's mind. Nevertheless, he, too, was an interpreter of God's law, who believed that national restoration had to come through the reappropriation of the law. Yet there was something which set his interpretation apart. Associated with the proclamation of the dawning Kingdom, it acquired a claim of ultimacy. There was no room left for the discussion of alternatives. As an exposition of God's law for the moment when the crisis of the Kingdom was imminent, it was, in effect, the final exposition. Anyone who 'built his house' on the foundations of this teaching would see it stand in the storm of judgment, while anyone who did not would see his house fall (Matt. 7:24–7; Luke 6:47–9). This sharpened his quarrel with some Pharisaic contemporaries, who, he claimed, in trying to make the law clear, concealed it: 'you do away with God's command and cling to human tradition' (Mark 7:8).

E. P. Sanders (*Jesus and Judaism*, especially pp. 270–81) has recently called into question the historicity of the ascription to Jesus of the anti-Pharisaic polemic in the synoptic Gospels. Much of his reserve is based on dissent from the unfavourable portrait of the Pharisees which has been current in some modern theological writing. No one who knew the Pharisees, he argues, could have criticised them in such terms; therefore the polemic is a later invention by those who did not know them. We need not deny a tendency, especially in St Matthew, to concentrate criticism on the Pharisees which could have been more widely directed against the Jewish establishment as a whole. St Luke often prefers the less specific term 'lawyers'. This merely attests early Christian recognition that in the Pharisees were opponents who, from a religious point of view, had to be taken seriously. Nevertheless, it seems to me unthinkable that this polemic does not reflect actual conflict between Jesus and the representatives of a programme of legal renewal with which he undoubtedly had much in common. We are often most severe on those who stand close to us but fail to grasp the one point on which we believe everything hangs. We might expect such polemic to arise even if we did not have evidence of it. And we do have evidence. Even discounting all the 'Q' material which underlies Matthew's ferocious anti-Pharisaic speech, there is still the saying, 'Beware of the leaven of the Pharisees and the leaven of Herod' (Mark 8:15).

Not only the Pharisees themselves but the critique of the Pharisees, too, have been carelessly represented in modern scholarship under the influence of the Kantian doctrine of motive. The word 'hypocrite' does not have the modern implication that the Pharisees are only *pretending* to an interest in holiness. It means that their interest functions, like the performance of an actor, solely at the level of representation, and so cannot achieve real holiness because it attempts to construct from outside what can only become manifest from within. If there is a modern analogy to what Jesus is reported to have said about the Pharisees, it is not the Kantian morality of motive but the Freudian critique of repression. (On this see further pp. 109f. below.)

Could Jesus have attributed such a programme to the Pharisees? We may, of course, reply: Could the 'Q' community, could Matthew, have done so? There is no obvious reason why Sanders' excellent principle that an account of Jesus must yield an account of the early church should be suspended at this point. But there is a stronger reason why Jesus could; and that lies in the prophetic prediction that God would write the law on the hearts of each Israelite, so that there would be no need for laborious legal pedagogy. To one who believed that the time had now come, the pedagogy of the Pharisees was bound to appear in the light in which the Gospels see it.

The central accusation against the Pharisees was that they attempted to construct holiness from outside in. But the holiness acceptable to God was God's own new work, in which, as the prophets had predicted, he would write the law upon the people's hearts. A constructed holiness could only be a futility. Appearances would, in the end, correspond to the life that generated them: 'the good tree bears good fruit; the bad tree bears bad fruit' (Matt. 7:17‖Luke 6:43; cf. Matt. 12:33). Parodic analogies for the lawkeeping exercise (decorating prophets' tombs, cleaning the outside of cups) were meant to show it up as comically pointless rather than sinister.

From this there followed a series of secondary criticisms of current fashions in casuistry, which are charged with emptying the law of moral seriousness (Mark 7:1–23‖; Matt. 23:16–22). This is the context in which the Pharisees, for all their moral intensity, are accused of evading the law which they profess (Matt. 23:3). It is consistently claimed that their emphasis on externals has led them to fall in love with their own social standing, but it is only St Luke, not Jesus, who goes so far as to say that they were financially greedy (Luke 16:14). There is no reason to deny that precisely when he criticises their moral views in detail, Jesus shows himself nearest to their ideals. St Matthew, who heightens the polemic the most, also underlines most clearly the similarity of moral reasoning. Jesus answered his opponents from within, rather than from outside, their tradition. Jesus cares about the law of God, and he cares about understanding it precisely. But it cannot be understood without the hermeneutic key which will order its demand comprehensibly: the 'weightier matters' of disposition taking priority over detailed casuistic resolutions (Matt. 23:23‖Luke 11:42). In saying which, Jesus hardly departs from the terms of a discussion going on around him. Nor need he; for it did not require the coming of the Kingdom to teach the Pharisees what they might have learned from Hosea (Matt. 12:7). Jesus does not pay these opponents the compliment that he paid John the Baptist: he does not think their service could, at any rate, have been appropriate for a historical moment that was now past.

Jesus' relation to the legal tradition and its guardians is shown most clearly in his attitude to the sabbath. About this the Gospels have a great deal to tell us;

the sheer bulk of the information there, compared with the comparative lack of interest in the subject in early Christianity as a whole, is a confirmation, if one be needed, of the historical fact that Jesus acted and taught about it in a way that was controversial. There are two stories in Mark (2:23–8; 3:1–6, both with parallels in Matthew and Luke); there are two stories unique to Luke (13:10–17; 14:1–6) and there are two Johannine stories (5:1–18, with further comment at 7:22f.; 9:1–39). Five of the six stories concern healing miracles. The sixth deals with the controversy caused by the disciples' picking and eating corn. Despite the extent of this material we may reduce the approaches to two.

In the first place Jesus argues that deeds of mercy may be performed on the sabbath, and appeals to accepted practice to provide analogies. It is possible within approved interpretations of the law to rescue a sheep from a pit, to water an ox or an ass, or to circumcise a child. Why, then, should he not heal the sick? It is common to these healing stories that it is Jesus' action that provokes the argument; he does not launch into criticism of Pharisaic sabbath-rules unprovoked. One saying that appears three times sums up the argument: 'Is it permitted to do good on the sabbath, or ill, to save life or to kill?' (Mark 3:4∥Luke 6:9; cf. Luke 14:3). The force of this pronouncement is not that the only alternatives that confront us are doing good and doing harm, that abstention from action is not a possibility. Such a claim really would have struck at the root of the sabbath as an institution! It claims simply that there are *some* demands, those of mercy, to neglect which would amount to doing positive harm – not a very radical principle in the context of Jewish convictions. Here Jesus is one interpreter of the law among others, bringing the best possibilities of the tradition to expression.

The story about picking corn, however, is more radical. In Mark's telling it concludes with the words, 'The sabbath was made for man, not man for the sabbath; therefore the Son of Man is lord also of the sabbath.' There are secondary differences among the synoptic evangelists in their presentation, which illustrate different nuances of interpretation. Mark is the only one of the three to include the first half of the concluding statement. By it he indicates that Jesus' conduct rests on the humanitarian, Deuteronomic understanding of sabbath-observance as a duty of charity, rather than on the concept common to Ezekiel and early post-exilic writers that it is a ritual expression of covenant loyalty. Matthew adds to the reference to David two other Old Testament precedents which are meant to show that the law itself qualified the sabbath-restrictions, and so that the disciples were 'guiltless' on the law's own terms. But for neither evangelist are these considerations sufficient justification in themselves; they need (what for Luke is the only explanation required) the assertion of the coming of the Son of Man. Jesus could do what he did because the age of the Son of Man had arrived. The time was past for ritual symbols of loyal waiting on God's intervention; the time had come for the royal prerogatives of David to be reasserted. 'A greater thing than the temple has arrived!' (Matt.

12:6). It goes without saying that St Mark and St Matthew had no doubt that the Son of Man was personally identical with Jesus, nor, in my view, is there good reason to think that Jesus understood it differently; the text itself, however, can be understood, though awkwardly, apart from this assumption. Yet, with or without the self-reference, Jesus' use of the title 'Son of Man' must be taken seriously. In fulfilment of the prophecy of Daniel ('obviously pregnant with the meaning of Genesis 2' (N. T. Wright, *The New Testament and the People of God*, p. 292)), God has conferred his authority upon *mankind*, represented in the triumphant Israel. In the exercise of this authority mankind is now free to interpret God's law in a way that realises God's purposes for mankind's welfare. The legal tradition which had prepared God's people for this moment could transform itself to accommodate its own fulfilment.

The argument of the story about plucking grain is curiously related to the discussion of the healing of the paralytic in John 5, where Jesus justifies his action with the enigmatic utterance, 'My father is working still, and I am working' (5:17). This is presumably an allusion to the eschatological sabbath, the climax of history when God's providential work of sustaining the world will be complete, and the immediate implication is that that moment has not yet arrived. But that is quite irrelevant as a reason for ignoring the sabbath, except, as 'the Jews' immediately recognise, for God himself, who alone continues his work uninterrupted till the end of history. However, Jesus continues, 'the Son' does what he sees the Father do. The sabbath healing signals the appearance of one whose work precisely parallels the work of God. The climax of history has therefore arrived, though the peace of the eschatological sabbath has not.

If the law was Israel's national possession, those who possessed it were Israel. Jesus' decisive account of God's law had as its corollary the formation of a decisive Israel, a community which would be the spiritual centre of the restored people. Disciples were a common enough phenomenon among the rabbis – 'Be deliberate in judgment, raise up many disciples' (*Aboth* 1:1) – but Jesus' disciples had a representative function in his programme. Around them the renewed Israel was to take shape. 'You are the salt of the earth', he told them, '. . . you are the light of the world' (Matt. 5:13f.). St Mark explained that the creation of such a body of disciples lay behind Jesus' choice of parable in instructing crowds. It was a method of teaching designed to sort the hearers out into those who were able to learn and those who were not, to draw some in and to send others away. To his associates, those who had shown themselves 'fruitful' hearers, he offered direct explanations of the coming Kingdom of God (Mark 4:10–13,33f.).

Such were the 'disciples' as we meet them in St Mark's Gospel. They accompanied Jesus on his journeys, shared his hazards, assisted him practically, mediated between himself and those who wished to see him, asked him questions privately and received straight answers, and were entrusted with his most demanding teaching, especially that which concerned the quarrel between himself and the Jewish establishment and his anticipations of the final conflict. Affectionately, he called them 'children' (10:24). If St Matthew and St Luke both seem to cast the net wider in their use of the word 'disciple', it is only, perhaps, to put less weight on the social intimacy of disciple and teacher and to make more of the response to the teaching itself. For Luke, the whole crowd of supporters that cheered Jesus into the city of Jerusalem consisted of 'disciples' (19:37). Yet they were still distinguished from 'crowds', though they mingled promiscuously with them (6:17–20; 7:11). For Matthew, the audience for the Sermon on the Mount could be viewed as disciples (for they followed him when he withdrew to the highlands in order to hear him teach) and also viewed as crowds (5:1; 7:28). The disciple occupies something of an ambiguous status in this evangelist's view, interested in Jesus' teaching and yet not wholly shaped by it. The interest may turn out to be superficial; and in that case adherence to the company of Jesus' associates will be seen to have meant little (7:21). The salt may lose its savour, the light may be hidden (5:13ff.). In St Matthew's Gospel it is a *disciple* who would like to postpone joining Jesus' company until his father is dead and buried (8:21). Taking up some indications from St Mark that Jesus' disciples sometimes disappointed their master, St Matthew underscores them with a favourite word: *oligopistoi*, 'small in faith' (8:23; 16:5).

The gathering Israel is focussed in twelve, their names remembered in the Gospel tradition, though with variations: called 'apostles' by St Luke because of their missionary activity, 'the twelve disciples' by St Matthew, but usually just 'the twelve' because the number itself, evoking the twelve eponymous tribal patriarchs, explains sufficiently their role in the new community. Of the three things that St Mark attributes to them – proximity to Jesus, mission and authority over demons (3:14f.) – none is their exclusive prerogative. Rather, they focus representatively the life of the restored Israel living under the authorisation of the coming Kingdom. St Luke knows of a wider circle of seventy called into existence for one missionary enterprise at least; these probably correspond to the seventy elders of Numbers 11, and so complete the authority structure of the revived Israel.

If 'authority structure' seems to venture rather far on the basis of a symbolic identification of the twelve with the patriarchs, we need to remember their authority to cast out demons, reflecting the divine power by which the Kingdom of God made itself known. The authority to preach carried judgment with it, too; the preachers were taught to make a sign of divine judgment against those who rejected them (Mark 6:11). In the combination of power, judgment and the continuity of Israel's identity the authority of the coming Kingdom resided, and the Kingdom's representatives bore that authority in a representative form. In an important 'Q' saying Jesus assigned them twelve thrones to judge the twelve tribes (Matt. 19:28||Luke 22:29ff.).

Yet the nature of this authority is subject to further interrogation in the Gospel tradition. St Mark recalls an exchange, which seems to presuppose the 'Q' saying, between Jesus and two of the twelve who wished to occupy the two thrones nearest their master (10:35ff.). Jesus' response makes a general contrast between authority as commonly understood and the authority exercised among his disciples. In the pagan world rulers 'bear down' with their authority (*katakurieuousin, katexousiazousin*); but those who wish to be 'great' and 'first' in this community must be servants and slaves, following the example of their master. (To St Luke's version of this saying we shall return on pp. 138f.) The point is to change the disciples' expectations of what the exercise of authority consists in. Within the people of God's rule authority is directed to providing for the weak. But this is more than an extrinsic end; it is an intrinsic end which characterises the way authority-holders proceed about their business. So when Jesus held up a child and called it 'the greatest in the Kingdom of Heaven', the paradox worked in two ways. On the one hand, it meant that the child *commanded the interest* of authority to protect it from harm; on the other, it meant that the child, being simply at the command of others, was the *model of humility* which authority had to emulate (Matt. 18:1–6). So the fixed opposition between greatness and lowliness is disturbed. In its place there is a dynamic disposal of authority into the place of need, a dialectic in which authority spends itself in action for those who need it. The notion of authority has not been abolished, but it has been refashioned on the model of how God exercises his own. It has taken on pastoral lineaments: the shepherd seeking his lost sheep, a picture of God's search for the scattered Israel, has become the emblem for a community leadership urgent to recover its lost sheep before the night of judgment falls (Luke 15:4–6; Matt. 18:12–14).

What, then, are the controlling features of Jesus' teaching of the law, which defines and shapes the new spiritual centre of Israel? We take as our leading text the collection of 'Q' sayings which St Matthew used for his Sermon on the Mount and St Luke for his equivalent sermon in the lowlands. Luke's version, which I assume to be less developed, gives us a clear basic structure: (a) a striking series of blessings and woes (6:20–6); (b) a block of sayings about generosity: loving enemies, turning the other cheek, advancing money and so on (27–36); (c) criticisms of pretentiousness: judging other people, the blind leading the blind, the parable of the tree and the fruit (37–45); (d) finally, following naturally from these, a warning of insincere discipleship (46–9). Matthew's much longer reworking, drawing on other material in the 'Q' source as well as independent material, is designed to turn this collection into a comprehensive law for the new community. Presented near the beginning of Jesus' ministry, it is a kind of repetition of the Deuteronomic lawgiving, with Jesus in the place of Moses. Yet the integrity of the speech is retained. It is still generated by the interaction of two themes prominent in the Lukan version, which we may refer to as 'generosity' and 'hypocrisy'.

Placed at the centre of St Matthew's composition (6:9–13), between the second and third sections of Luke's structure, is the teaching of the prayer which is to enshrine the moral attitudes of the community. In the 'Q' material which provided the prayer there were sayings to encourage persistent petition (7:7–11||Luke 11:9–13); and to these Matthew has added some further sayings which discourage anxiety and an exaggerated sense of practical responsibility (6:25–34). The community is to show a carefree attitude towards difficulties, based on its total trust in the protection of God and enhanced by its expectation of the dawning of God's Kingdom. This attitude is found in the central petition of the prayer itself, 'Give us today our bread for today' – 'today' being the unit of time with which the community can properly concern itself. Before this central petition stand three petitions for the speedy coming of the Kingdom. After it stand two petitions anticipating judgment and asking for forgiveness and correction. An important parenthesis, which is singled out for special comment (6:14f.), links prayer for forgiveness with a forgiving spirit in the petitioner. Israel approaches God's judgment with the assumption that it levels us all. Its own sense of need for mercy is evidenced by its readiness to show mercy.

St Matthew has exercised great sensitivity in integrating this prayer into the context of the Sermon as a whole. The theme of forgiving those who offend us is, of course, already echoed in the teaching on generosity. New material against hypocrisy in worship introduces the teaching of the prayer, and this serves to forge the link with the existing teaching on hypocrisy that follows. But the linchpin which holds the prayer in place at the centre of the Sermon is the little group of sayings which contrast two possible orientations of the heart: seeking treasure on earth and seeking treasure in heaven, the single eye and the corrupt eye, the serving of two masters (6:19–24). For St Matthew the Sermon coheres around the decision between two competing frames of reference for our action. Generosity and hypocrisy represent the outcomes of the one and the other choice. To choose the Kingdom (and God's righteousness, Matthew explains (6:33)) is not only to secure our own freedom from material anxiety but to orient ourselves to the 'perfection' of our heavenly Father's law.

At the beginning of the Sermon stand the Beatitudes, intended, by both evangelists as by their source, to set the context for the whole. (St Matthew's omission of the corresponding 'woes' is due to his sense of the function the Sermon fulfils in determining the law of the community. Condemnations addressed *ad extra* would not be to the point here.) They are marked by a series of future tenses: 'they shall be comforted', 'shall inherit the earth', 'shall be satisfied'. These contrast the present state of things with that which will obtain when the Kingdom is fully come, a contrast emphasised in St Luke by the addition of the word 'now' to the blessing. The Kingdom will turn everything upside-down: those that weep shall laugh, those that are rich shall have exhausted their resources, and so on. The Beatitudes, then, do not speak of 'life in the Kingdom', as has often been said, but of the essential contradictions of that life which is seriously preparing for the Kingdom. But the first and (in Matthew) the eighth beatitudes are followed by a present tense: 'theirs is the Kingdom of Heaven'. This is not a mere stylistic variation on the future tense, but balances the predominant emphasis on reversal with a corresponding emphasis on continuity. Attitudes *now* displayed in adversity shall *then* be shown to have been the appropriate attitudes; so that already those who display them, not merely 'the poor' but 'the poor in spirit', are those who belong to the Kingdom of God.

The most striking of St Matthew's adaptations is his use of the teachings on generosity. These are made to answer a question which is very much his own: how does Jesus' interpretation of the law improve upon traditional understandings? The evangelist is commonly taken as a spokesman for the point of view of Palestinian Christians who held that the *tōrāh* was still binding on Christian believers. 'Do not suppose that I have come to destroy the law and the prophets. I have not come to destroy them but to fulfil them' (5:17). Clearly he thinks the law is binding; but to say 'still' binding suggests, misleadingly, that nothing has changed. It is 'fulfilled'.

Two accounts of how 'fulfil' should be understood go back to St Augustine: performing all that the law requires; and adding to the law that in which it falls short (*De sermone Domini* 1.8). The interpretative question comes to be framed this way because Augustine, like many commentators since, assumed that the verb 'fulfil' must make sense with 'law', standing on its own, as object. But in fact the text speaks of fulfilling 'the law and the prophets', a phrase which sums up the legacy of Israel's tradition as a whole. This encourages us to understand fulfilment in a third way: *expectation* is what Israel has inherited, *fulfilment* is the satisfaction of that expectation. In the strange saying that not a yod or a serif will pass from the law 'until all be fulfilled', the law itself is treated as a kind of promise. It anticipated a righteousness for which the faithful hungered and thirsted, a righteousness in which all would be subject to God's command. That promise is now to be made good, and the life of the new community is to demonstrate it.

That life is an advance both upon the bare text of the law and upon current interpretations of it (5:20). Here St Matthew guides us to what he understands as the heart of Jesus' polemic against current legal interpretation. It is this: that interpretation is content to require a form of obedience within a public frame of reference. Being content with that frame of reference is what Jesus meant by 'hypocrisy'. Properly understood, the law demands obedience within the hidden sphere of attitudes and actions that are open to God's eyes alone. The distinction between the publicly observed and the secret means nothing to God, and so neither should it to us. For there is a judgment coming, in which God, who sees what is done in secret, will reward 'openly' (6:4,6 – the last word is supplied by a glossator, but it expresses the force of the saying exactly). The distinction between the hidden and the public is of very short duration, and soon everything will be made public (10:26f.). The private dissensions which might have been ignored while the public business of worship went forward can be ignored no longer (5:23f.). They must be treated at once with the seriousness due to problems that are about to be subjected to the full glare of publicity.

This is the 'perfection' required of Jesus' disciples (5:48). It corresponds to the 'generosity' which is required of them in Luke's version of the same saying (6:36). Generosity means: not staying within the limits which public rationality sets on its approval of benevolence. An extravagant, unmeasured goodness, corresponding to God's own providential care, defies the logic of public expectation. St Matthew has understood that this implies adherence to the spirit of the law beyond the law's susceptibility to public implementation. Thus he has found a point of unity between the twin themes of the Sermon: generosity and the rejection of hypocrisy. For 'hypocrisy' is conforming simply to public expectation. An almost perfect synonym would be 'performance'.

Jesus' teaching about the hidden sphere of attitudes and actions risks being misunderstood by moderns, since it, and especially the criticism of hypocrisy, is too easily sucked into the magnetic field of the modern ideas of 'motive'. A motive, as we use the term, is a reason for doing a particular act located within the purposes of the agent. To understand the inner purpose from which an act arose, it appears, is both to grasp the truest meaning of that act (what it 'really' intended) and to simplify the task of passing judgment upon it. For though an act may have its own inherent goodness or badness, the goodness or badness of the motive, which does not necessarily correspond, always trumps it in the final evaluation. An evil deed done from a good motive is, at worst, well meant; while a good deed done from a bad motive displays the worst of all evils, hypocrisy. As Eliot put it, in a couplet worthy of Alexander Pope in sentiment as well as form: 'The last temptation is the greatest treason: To do the right deed for the wrong reason' (*Murder in the Cathedral*, pt. 1).

We must be clear that Jesus did not share this modern idea of a motive lying behind each act. When he speaks of what is hidden that will be made plain, or what is 'inside' that will come out, he is referring to one of two things, different from each other and different from our 'motive'. He is referring, in the first place, to '*the heart*', which is the ultimate disposition of the self, the attitude which finds expression in our acts. It is an attribute of the agent, not of particular acts; but it is known, over time, through the agent's acts. The idea that contrary values may attach to the acts and to the heart is consistently rejected in a parable which occurs in the source of the Sermon and which St Matthew reuses elsewhere: 'A good tree cannot bear bad fruit, nor a bad tree good fruit' (7:18||Luke 6:43, cf. Matt. 12:33–5). The hypocrite may attempt to construct morality from the outside in, without conversion of the heart, but the attempt will be a failure; it is precisely his acts that will betray him. In the second place, Jesus refers to *private acts* that are not open to public enquiry and judgment: secrets which are whispered, angry words that are muttered, lies told when the speaker is not on oath and so on.

Jesus' interpretation of the law, then, as St Matthew presents it, challenges any reading which, expressly or by implication, excludes unjusticiable attitudes and acts from consideration. This is the key to the series of six contrasts between the legal tradition and Jesus' own teaching, which include, but with much expansion, the material of Luke's section on generosity. The law's prohibitions of murder and adultery (5:21–30) condemn certain publicly objectified deeds; but they must be supposed to condemn, by implication, the attitudes which underlie those deeds as well as secret words or thoughts which express the same attitudes. The case is slightly different with the prohibition of divorce (5:31f.). Here the law licenses a practice which we understand to be contrary to God's will. According to the explanation preserved in the Markan tradition, presupposed here, it licenses it because it cannot eradicate it (Mark 10:3–9). But the law's intention is to secure the permanence of the marriage-bond, and it is this intention that Israel must respect. The prohibition of oaths (Matt. 5:33–7) follows the pattern of the first two examples. The law condemns the use of an oath to win confidence that is then betrayed. But this is merely an outrageous instance of the general project of using oaths to secure the confidence of others when one's own unaided word will not suffice, a project we should eschew altogether.

> This seems the more satisfactory interpretation, taking a lead from the observation of vv. 34–6: the things we swear by are entirely under God's control, not our own. This suggests that the oath-taker pretends to have control over these things, presumably to secure belief or credit to which he is not otherwise entitled. This account assumes that the oath was intended to win credit for a *promise.* The alternative, which goes back to Justin Martyr, assumes it is a *statement* that is in question (cf. Justin, *1 Apology* 16.5). The law defines a solemn sphere in which false statement is open to public sanction. But this, by implication, tolerates false statement outside that sphere, something Jesus' disciples ought not to tolerate. They will, therefore, abjure the institution of oath-taking for the same reason as they will abjure divorce: it is an institution that accommodates to human sin, not an expression of the law's true intention.

Passing over the fifth contrast we come to the last, in which Jesus denies that the duty of love of neighbour implies a permission to hate one's enemy (Matt. 5:43–7). Here alone among the six examples Jesus quotes not only the text of the Hebrew Scriptures but an interpretative gloss on it. Yet this makes very little difference. In each case the quarrel has been about the hermeneutic approach that is appropriate in the age of the dawning Kingdom. Did the law not, in fact, license the pious hatred of the Jew for those who made themselves God's enemies (Ps. 139:21f.)? If the interpretative gloss was inappropriate, that was only because it failed to hear and believe the word of promise. When God himself had dealt with his opponents, there could be no scope left for anyone to cherish pious hatred on his behalf. To extend the scope of love to embrace the enemy was to demonstrate hope: the end of enmity was now at hand.

We have left a discussion of the command 'not to resist the wicked', plausibly interpreted as forbidding prosecution in court, to the end, because it sums up so well the new approach to law which Matthew understood Jesus to have taken. The early Christian distrust of litigation exemplifies the way in which what we have called 'generosity' combines with the suspicion of 'hypocrisy' to create a reserve about the institutions of public justice. The law permits 'an eye for an eye, a tooth for a tooth', that is, precisely limited damages, and no more. But, Jesus claims, the fulfilling of the law will mean the end of all our thirst for public vindication. God's coming judgment will give us more than our entitlement if we are the meek who inherit the earth; so we may be generous to those who exploit us. The human court can only see what breaks the surface of public order, whereas God's judgment will penetrate beneath it. To win our case now is to risk losing it later. 'Judge not, that you may not be judged!' (Matt. 7:1). The community is therefore told, in a parable which borders on the literal, to think of itself as a nervous litigant eager for an out-of-court settlement: 'make peace with your adversary while you are on the road . . . lest your adversary hand you over to the judge' (5:25–7). As a parable this points to the final judgment which we hope to avert; as literal instruction it advises us on how to avert it: by not rushing into court! The desire to secure a judgment in one's own favour, on the other hand, is prompted by 'greed', as Jesus tells the man who asks him to arbitrate a property dispute. It cannot wait for the final word of God's true judgment, but must get its hands on the award here and now. Judgment of this order Jesus refuses to provide: 'Who made me a judge or divider over you?' (Luke 12:13–15).

> That saying, of course, echoes the rebuke delivered to Moses when he interfered between the quarrelling Israelites in Egypt (Exod. 2:14). Neither in Jesus' nor in Moses' case is there any doubt that God has in fact sent him as a judge; but everything depends upon how and when the judgment is to be given. To desire a judge who is a 'divider' is to desire to secure one's own portion; it does not amount to that hunger and thirst for final and universal judgment which characterises the people of God. Jesus' reticence contrasts strikingly with the assumption that is made in much rabbinic teaching that the student of the law will act as a judge (*Aboth* 1:7; 4:5,7,8) and that responsibility for interpreting God's law resides with courts (*Harayoth* 1 e.g.).

Yet the reserve about courts is not a reserve about the law as such, nor about the principle of judging in accordance with the law. St Luke, with great insight, prefaces the parable of the litigants on the road with a short saying: 'Why do you not judge for yourselves?' (12:57). Those who settle on the road are, in one sense, 'judging not'; in another sense they are 'judging for themselves'. Precisely their knowledge of the law of God enables them to reach a judgment that is wiser, because more full of honest self-knowledge, than the judgment they might get from a court. The community has not lost its confidence in judgment; but each member has to exercise judgment for himself in the light of God's judgment upon him. It is a community of God's law, but does not need litigation in order to give law expression in the community. The judgment each member makes on his own relations with his neighbour expresses it. This, then, is the community promised by the prophets in which the law would be written on their hearts.

4. From our explorations of the idea of Yhwh's rule in Israel we reached a working analysis of kingly rule, or political authority: power, judgment and the conferral of community identity. We have now applied this analysis to Jesus' proclamation and demonstration of the Kingdom of God. But in those first explorations we also identified a fourth factor in the analysis: the praise of the people, which was not a constitutive element in Yhwh's kingly rule but a demonstrative proof of it. Corresponding to this is *the faith with which Jesus was received*, faith which, according to one saying, the Son of Man came looking for (Luke 18:8, cf. Matt. 8:10‖Luke 7:9). As in the case of Yhwh's rule over Israel, we must be careful not to suppose that reception conferred authority. The authority of the Kingdom and its messenger lay in itself, not in the reception that it found. But it proved itself by eliciting faith: from the crowds that thronged round, from the sick and their relatives who came for help, and from the disciples who came to learn. In certain striking cases Jesus drew attention to it: the friends of the paralysed man who let him down through the roof (Mark 2:5‖), the woman with the haemorrhage (Mark 5:34‖), Bartimaeus the blind man (Mark 10:52‖), the Syrophoenician woman (Mark 7:29‖), to which instances in St Mark's Gospel the other synoptic evangelists added that of the centurion at Capernaum from the 'Q' material (Matt. 8:10‖Luke 7:9). In two further cases St Luke thought it appropriate to recall the words of Jesus spoken to the woman with the haemorrhage, 'your faith has saved you' (7:50; 17:19).

A contrast has sometimes been made between the emphasis on repentance in the message of the Baptist and this emphasis on faith in Jesus' ministry (see e.g. Sanders, *Jesus and Judaism*, p. 206); and, provided it is understood as a contrast in *emphasis* on categories not mutually exclusive, we may accept it. John was known for his practice of baptism, which was understood as a sign of repentance (Mark 1:4; Luke 3:3); but Jesus, according to John's emphatic note (4:2), did not practise baptism himself. This corresponds to a notable absence of instruction on the need for formal repentance, restitution and sacrifice. St Luke emphasises this especially. Zacchaeus offers restitution spontaneously, after Jesus has entered his house and not as a condition (19:18). When the Prodigal Son tries to deliver a speech of penitence, it is brushed aside (15:20–4). If there is, in Jesus' teaching, anything like a condition for being forgiven other than faith itself, it is, as we find St Matthew emphasising, forgiving others. And this is a condition only because it shows we have taken God's act of forgiveness seriously as a world-changing event which leaves no relations in the state that they were. On this understanding, however, it is clear that faith implies a change of life. Repentance is included in, rather than excluded by, the priority of faith.

The recognition which Jesus sought and welcomed often consisted simply of confidence in his power to meet the petitioner's need, and entailed no statement about Jesus' identity. In the case of Bartimaeus, however, something more was involved: he persistently called Jesus 'son of David' (Mark 10:47ff.ll). In the narrative structure of the synoptic Gospels, following the pattern set by St Mark, the attribution of a special role to Jesus occurs only at rare and highly charged moments – apart, that is, from the acknowledgments of demons which hail him as the bearer of a divine power sent to destroy them (Mark 1:24; 3:11; 5:7; cf. 1:34). These demonic acknowledgments Jesus consistently silences; they come from the wrong source and are wrongly focussed, directing attention away from the coming of God's Kingdom. They do not assist the recognition of Jesus by human beings. Neither, strangely enough, do the words from heaven which acknowledge Jesus at his baptism as God's Son (1:11) – about which St Mark presumably wished us to understand that such a disclosure could be grasped only retrospectively by those who had recognised Jesus for themselves. Human recognition begins within the small circle of Jesus' disciples that witness the miracle of the stilling of the storm (4:41). It is made explicit in the confession of Peter, 'You are the Christ', elicited by a direct question from Jesus (8:29). It is then extended more widely: Bartimaeus' unexpected declaration while Jesus is on his way through Jericho prepares the way for the crowds which accompany him in his entry to Jerusalem with their celebration of 'the one who comes in the Lord's name and the coming kingdom of David' (11:9f.).

It is commonly observed that one major difference between the synoptic Gospels and St John is that the former contain no self-announcements of the kind exemplified in the 'I am' statements of the fourth Gospel. Indeed, in one story Jesus snubs an apparently well-meant acknowledgment of his standing as a religious teacher, because it implied no acknowledgment of the coming Kingdom of God: 'Why do you call me good? No one is good but God alone' (Mark 10:18). If the enquirer wanted only to understand the moral demands for 'eternal life', then he had no business looking for any revelatory teacher or 'good master'; God's law should have been sufficient for him. But if he was hungry for the realisation of God's work in history, then he should throw in his lot decisively with those who waited for the Kingdom. Yet within the company of those who waited for the Kingdom a growing recognition of Jesus' own role was a sign of their emerging faith. Jesus, far from discouraging it, is presented as encouraging it. His role has become a public issue in his trial, where he is taxed directly by the high priest with claiming to be 'the Christ, the Son of the Blessed'. Directly in St Mark, indirectly in the other two synoptic evangelists, Jesus accepts this designation, but accompanies his acceptance immediately by a renewed proclamation of the coming of the Kingdom of God (14:62||).

The content of these titles is fairly clear: they amount, as Pilate, with a somewhat limited political imagination, expresses it, to a claim to be 'the King of the Jews'. The hope of a successor to the throne of Judah continued to be a factor, though often a suppressed one, in post-exilic expectation. If in later periods it fell from view, it is, nevertheless, a natural one to have cropped up in Jewish culture at a time of enhanced political agitation and speculation, not only because of those explicit hopes to which the prophetic literature pointed but also because of the devotional and liturgical use of the pre-exilic royal psalms, which must have encouraged the faithful to look for some development in their own experience to correspond to the recurrent figure of 'David'. The Gospel narratives simply assume such speculation as a part of the cultural background. There will be many who claim to find, or even to be, 'the Christ' (Mark 13:21; Matt. 24:5), of whom the disciples must learn to be suspicious.

> There is also a curious saying of Jesus himself, which can only be understood as a contribution to a debate of pressing current interest, the details of which are not clear to us now. Jesus appears to say that the Christ is not David's son (Mark 12:37||). Many commentators have been reluctant, and understandably so, to take this at its face value; it would place the saying in contradiction to all Jewish understanding of 'the Christ', making it difficult to see why Jesus should have taken any interest in discussing the figure at all. But if it is difficult to be sure of what Jesus was intending to deny, it is clear enough what he intended to affirm: that 'the Christ' was David's lord. That fits well enough into a controversy about the character of the new order: was it to arise from the leadership of a *David redivivus*, a military leader who would draw the nation together again in the way that David had? Or was it to arise from a new work of God that superseded the kind of leadership that such a figure could provide? Jesus spoke for the second: the Christ, when he appeared, must be a representative of the total rule of God in the hearts of his people, a decisive step forward from anything that the political history of Israel had known. (The sceptical explanation that the Davidic origins of the Christ were denied in order to accommodate Jesus' own non-Davidic claims creates great difficulties. Are we to suppose that this argument was promoted by Jesus himself in order to advance his own

claims on the throne? Or by the early church, which from an early date became confident that it could demonstrate his Davidic lineage? And again, why should anyone be interested in this title if they were not interested in the Davidic associations of it? It could have been left aside. If Jesus himself took it up, it must have been to respond to some point that was being founded on it in other quarters.)

St John records *en passant* a moment in Jesus' ministry at which he was forced to withdraw from the crowds because he became aware of an intention 'to seize him to make him king' (6:15). The verb 'seize' sums up what it was that Jesus had to reject in the movement of Messianic enthusiasm. The kingship could not be restored to Israel at the initiative of a popular movement, laying claim to the powers of a divinely gifted leader and turning them to its own political account (very much as Judah had laid claim to David's powers according to the allegorical story of Abigail and Nabal, cf. p. 53 above). It had to come by the arrival of God's rule. 'The Christ' would derive his authority from that rule and not from the people's search for a successor to David, from above and not from below.

There is some truth, then, in the old theological commonplace that 'the Jews' expected a military Messiah, while Jesus presented himself as a suffering Messiah, even though, as it stands, it is defective in both members. It is too general, on the one hand, about what the Jews as a whole expected: some of Jesus' contemporaries looked for a military solution around a military leader; Jesus was among those Jews who did not. On the other hand, the idea of a suffering Messiah was not part of his public proclamation, whatever he may have said privately to his disciples. But the truth of the commonplace is that the notion of a successor to David was an ambiguous one, and that Jesus would neither endorse nor reject everything that could be inferred from it.

The title which Jesus preferred to use in respect of his own role in the coming Kingdom was 'the Son of Man', taken from the vision of Daniel 7. This could, of course, converge with the idea of a Davidic heir; the Son of Man was given 'sovereignty and glory and kingly power' (7:14), which envisaged, therefore, a structured form of political leadership for authority to be exercised by 'the people and saints of the Most High' (7:27). This picture lay behind Jesus' promise to the twelve of thrones in proximity to his own. Yet the Daniel motif had the advantage of giving priority to the Kingdom itself and to the restoration of Israel, placing the Son of Man in a clearly representative role. It has, of course, been doubted whether Jesus' references to the Son of Man were intended to refer to himself. This doubt seems to me unnecessary; but the element of truth behind it is that the Son of Man sayings function like compressed arguments, in which the premise is the given fact of the coming Kingdom of God and the conclusion about Jesus' own authority, or fate, is inferred from the representative role. 'The Son of Man' is, therefore, more than a 'title', which might in principle be interchanged with other titles that could be given to the same person. It is a role that had to be fulfilled; and, in understanding himself to be cast in that role, Jesus was prepared to conform his expectations to its demands.

On the other hand, Jesus laid claim to the legacy of Davidic expectation in his great entry into Jerusalem, a demonstration of popular support staged to evoke the memory of the king's coming in triumph to Zion in Deutero-Zechariah (9:9). If the Davidides were the vessel by which political authority was given to Israel in the first instance, then they must be the vessel by which it would be restored. The coming of the Kingdom must at least *satisfy* the lack in Israel's life created by the long disappearance of Judah's monarchy. In directing his path to the Temple on that occasion Jesus placed himself at the centre of socio-political and religious authority in Israel. It is not to be understood as a preference for religious rather than political reform. Jesus' concern, on that occasion as hitherto, was with the reauthorising of Israel rather than with the deauthorising of Rome. The Temple, not the praetorium, was the seat of Yhwh's authority among his people. The appearance of true authority in Israel meant the unity of political and religious spheres under the rule of God. Obedience and worship were to be one and the same. But that is to say: the Kingdom was the Lord's! The Two Kingdoms period, in which Temple without power and praetorium without worship coexisted in some kind of parallel, was declared closed.

Faith in the coming of the Kingdom, then, implied an act of political recognition directed to Jesus himself. The dawning rule of God was experienced in his ministry. To recognise God's rule was to see him as the figure who satisfied the hopes and expectations which had been vested in the reappearance of traditional monarchical leadership. In that sense the coming of the Kingdom was proved by the acknowledgment of Jesus as king. Yet that acknowledgment presupposed the recognition of the Kingdom itself; otherwise it would have been a rebellious bid for autonomy against God's rule.

Exemplifying the subtleties of this acknowledgment we may pause, in conclusion, over the birth narratives, stories full of political overtones, through which the church told of Jesus' origins in a way that allowed the inference of his royal standing to emerge as an implication paradoxically related to the actual circumstances. In St Matthew's Gospel Jesus is introduced, by way of the genealogy, as the climax of Israel's history, the fulfilment of the unfinished business of Israel's past, and especially of the covenant with the patriarchs, the Davidic throne and the return from Babylon. In the story of Joseph's betrothal the Immanuel prophecy of Isaiah 7 is taken as the leading text, because it binds together three elements: a royal figure, with a name that evokes the covenant, who gives his people hope in the face of foreign oppression. The story of Herod opposes the two rival authorities: Herod's own and the authority which God has vested in the child. Herod resists the announcement of the new-born king because it implies divine judgment on his own authority; but his resistance is incapable of overcoming the authority of the challenger, while it has the effect of aligning him with those foreign invaders who (in the text from Jeremiah) had caused Rachel, matriarch of the Northern tribes, to mourn the loss of her children. The exile, the patriarchs and the kingdom, then, form the context of Jesus' appearance as the new intervention of God into Israel's affairs.

In St Luke's story the theme of kingship is only discreetly present in the background, though the title 'Saviour' carries political overtones (1:74), and it is said to be through 'the house of David' that God has intervened (1:69). Bethlehem, indeed, as the city of David's birth, is as important for St Luke's story as it is for St Matthew's. Augustus, rather than Herod, represents the alien rule; his tyrannous desire to 'enrol' the people of God ironically provides the occasion for the city of David to witness the Saviour's birth. Events conspire to make a public spectacle of what would otherwise be a private event: the holy parents are thrust into the street where the birth of their child will be noticed. The angelic announcement to the shepherds serves the same function as the appearing of the star to the magi in St Matthew: it provokes a journey of enquiry which will bring God's act to public attention. It also provides a suitable political interpretation: God's glory and peace on earth together constitute the meaning of the Saviour's birth (2:14). Israel's integrity implies a unity of the liturgical and political aspects of its life (as also at 1:74).

The birth narratives pose many questions which I cannot address or even raise properly in this context: where did they come from?, why are they different? and so on. The Christology which they express has to be laid, in the first instance, at the door of the two evangelists, without prejudice to whatever sources may lie behind them. But it is worth saying that what strikes us most forcibly is their lack of any post-Easter Christological perspective. With the exception of the words spoken by Simeon to Mary, 'the sword will go through your own heart also', the perspective is purely that of Jesus' fulfilment of the hope of Israel. If one asks to whose faith these stories are most likely to bear witness, the answer appears to be: to the faith of the crowds that waved palm branches as he entered the city in triumph.

We return, in summary, to the question from which this chapter began. When we speak of Jesus' ministry by deploying the categories of power, judgment, community identity and political recognition, are we exploiting essentially hard-edged political concepts to illuminate spiritual realities with such a use of analogy that the effect is to construct an elaborate metaphor? Our response has been that we must diffract this spectrum of analogy as much for the sake of political understanding as for spiritual. It is precisely the impact of Jesus' proclamation to make us (and Israel) think again about where the *political* deployments of such terms really lie. The problem is with the assumption that we move from 'core' political concepts to the Kingdom of God as from the known to the unknown. Precisely the opposite movement is called for. Can we not be introduced to a kind of rule that is unlike, as well as like, the kind of rule with which we are familiar? And can we not be taught to conceive of living within law in a manner unlike, as well as like, the litigious culture we associate with lawcourts? The first assumption of political theology must be that these analogies are valid, and that through them the Gospel of the Kingdom offers liberation to an imprisoned political culture. Political aspirations find their true satisfaction in these unlikely likenesses.

4. The triumph of the Kingdom

The representative

Jesus proclaimed the coming of the Kingdom of God, but the apostolic church did not. It told the story of what happened when the Kingdom came: its conflict with the established principalities and powers and its vindication at God's hand through Jesus' resurrection. What the church proclaimed was not what Jesus had proclaimed, because it stood on the other side of that great crisis which his proclamation evoked. Yet it claimed continuity with his proclamation, because he, and his message of the Kingdom, had been vindicated.

It has been one of the chief concerns of New Testament theology this century to express the balance of continuity and discontinuity correctly. A spectrum of emphases is defined at one end by Schweitzer's suggestion that Jesus and his hopes were simply disappointed, and that the church's message of a risen Lord and an indwelling Spirit was a consoling substitute. At the other end lie attempts to smooth out the articulation of the pre- and post-Easter faith into simple continuity, and this in one of two ways, either by championing the message of the coming Kingdom in what has been called 'Jesuology', or by championing the message of the cross and resurrection in a Christology which overwhelms Jesus of Nazareth.

The distinction between Jesus' message and the message of the apostolic church does not, of course, correspond to the *literary* distinction between the Gospels and the rest of the New Testament literature. The Gospels themselves, as we have often been reminded, are the story that the apostolic church told, a story which began from John the Baptist and reported how Jesus' effective demonstration of the authority of God's Kingdom was confronted and challenged by entrenched worldly authorities, political, religious and demonic; and how, in fulfilment of God's hidden purpose, it was overthrown, only to be vindicated and shortly, to the shame and disgrace of the principalities and powers, to be manifest universally. St John's Gospel is unique as a literary composition in the way that it tells this story with a self-conscious knowledge of the end overarching the whole, whereas the synoptics provide more articulation of the phases. Yet the synoptics, too, believe that the story forms a meaningful unity, while St John, too, stresses the difference between the time of Jesus' bodily presence and the time of the Spirit. All have a Passion narrative linked to anticipations of the Passion in the course of Jesus' ministry. All have a resurrection narrative, and all point to earlier moments at which God acknowledges Jesus at key points in his work.

Neither, we may add, does the distinction correspond to a distinction of *doctrinal* emphasis between Christology 'from below' and 'from above'.

Political theology has its own *Tendenz* at this point. Just as it finds a greater wealth of politico-conceptual resources in the Old Testament than in the New, so, within the New, it tends to find more of immediately political interest in the message of Jesus. During the past century it has been a natural ally of Jesuology in various forms, from the idealist pacifism of Tolstoy to the Liberation Theology of our own time. This, however, was not always the case. In the eighteenth century 'political' Christianity was associated with high trinitarian doctrine and with the civil establishment of religion; and those who fought against these did so in the name of individual conscience, not of society. The late-modern disposition of forces reflects continued impatience with the older models of political theology now compounded by disillusion with the social agnosticism of liberal pietist individualism. It was the impatience of a reaction; and, like many reactions, arose largely in ignorance of the conceptual strength and flexibility of the high tradition, responding only to a shrunken and hardened old age. And it could provide no answer to the theological question. It could produce analogical parallels between Jesus' announcement of the change of the times and the various moments of social opportunity that have come upon the world since. It could encourage hope for new acts of divine creativity. But it could not speak meaningfully of the defeat of Jesus' programme, nor of its vindication. In the end every political Jesuology offers a helpful illusion: let us model ourselves on Jesus, ignoring Caiaphas and Pilate; then we will at least achieve something, even if it is not what we hope to achieve. The transition of mood from that point back to a bleak and hopeless 'realism' requires no more than a slight shift in the barometer (as is illustrated clearly enough in the thought of Reinhold Niebuhr, whose great merit was to understand perfectly the logic of the idealist formulations for which he could find no substitutes). A secure political theology must base itself on 'the hidden counsel of God' which worked also through Caiaphas and Pilate.

It may seem at first sight that to extend the Gospel of the Kingdom to encompass the death and resurrection of Christ is to lose its political dimensions. The resurrection of Jesus gives the individual believer an indefeasible confidence in the face of death. The gift of the Spirit gives the believer inward certainty of God's presence and will. Israel's rejection of the Christ and God's approval of him opens up entry to the Kingdom to believers of every race on equal terms. Each of these three consequences seems to weaken the role of the community. How can an immortal individual depend upon the community to sustain the conditions of life? How can those who have God's Spirit in their hearts need the knowledge of God that is gained in the public realm? How can a community without local or national limits avoid evaporating into an indeterminate ideal with no concrete social presence? These are the objections which classical republicans, ancient and modern, have made to Christianity, accusing it of replacing political society with a communion of immortal souls with divine thoughts, defying political structures.

In their way the classical republicans are right. But, of course, their challenge can be turned round. By what right is the term 'political' claimed exclusively for the defence of social structures which refuse the deeper spiritual and cosmic aspirations of mankind? The price to be paid by classical republicanism is that of pitting political order against human fulfilment, of making the polis constitutionally hostile to philosophy, theology and artistic vision. It confines the social good to something that would satisfy an assembly of slave-holding landowners. A 'pure' political theory which can make it a matter of intellectual conscience to disinterest itself in the transcendent is not one that any humane thinker need feel guilt about rejecting. If political order must be conceived in that way, it would be well, perhaps, that theology should be anti-political.

But political order need not be conceived in that way. Our notions of the public and political may be made wider and more generous. That is what a political theology shaped by the Christ-event must undertake. In the first place it must criticise existing notions of political good and necessity, not only classical republican notions but imperial and theocratic notions too, in the light of what God has done for the human race and the human soul. Public norms must be adjusted to the new realities when ordinary members of society may hear the voice of God and speak it in public, even, according to the prophet, men and women slaves. Ideas of what government is must be corrected in the light of that imperious government which the Spirit wields through the conscience of each worshipper. This is political theology in its liberal mode, attacking and overcoming the pretentiousness of the autonomous political order. But there is also a constructive side to its task, which is to show how the extension of the Gospel of the Kingdom into the Paschal Gospel elevates, rather than destroys, our experience of community. Political theology has an ecclesiological mode, which takes the church seriously as a society and shows how the rule of God is realised there. The independence, then, of the individual believer is not antisocial. It arises from the authority of another community, centred in the authority of the risen Christ. From that community the hope of immortality and the consciousness of God's presence spring. Personal security is rooted in social identification. Only apparent, too, is the lack of definition and centre in this world-wide community, where Jew and Gentile mingle indiscriminately. The life, death and triumph of Israel's representative have defined that community precisely; it exists by participation in that one focal event.

The key to these assertions, as to much else, is Christology. If political theology cannot perform its task by striking out on its own into Jesuology, it must learn how to perform it Christologically, making its way along that stream which flows from the apostles' proclamation of Christ as 'Lord' to the later, ontologically developed definitions of the ecumenical creeds. But in order to perform its own special task, it cannot simply draw from that stream at its most convenient points of access, the Chalcedonian doctrine of the Two Natures, for example. It has to show how the Christological tradition belongs to the proclamation of the Kingdom of God. If Christian theology as a whole has sometimes allowed the careless or sceptical to conclude that the church changed its proclamation from Kingdom to Christ somewhere around AD 50, it is the special task of political theology to efface that impression.

There meet in Christ two roles with which we are already familiar. There is the *mediator of God's rule*, the role focussed centrally upon the Davidide monarch, though also borne in lesser and partial ways by other authorities in Israel, priestly and administrative. And there is the *representative individual*, who in lonely faithfulness carries the tradition of the people, its fate and its promise, in his own destiny; this was the role of Jeremiah and of his exilic imitators, summing up the tradition of the isolated sufferers in Israel's liturgy. That these two roles could, and must, meet was the momentous discovery of Deutero-Isaiah whose Servant of Yhwh, clothed in royal characteristics, bears the suffering incurred by the people's sin. In this meeting the mediator–representative bore at once the divine rule and faithful response to it; the outline of the Two Natures conception can already be discerned in the two functions. But when to this formal duality is added the eschatological presence of God's Kingdom, then the two functions are transformed into more than place-holding roles. We must then speak of Christ as the *decisive* presence of God and the *decisive* presence of God's people.

Does this amount to the ontological assertion that he was 'very God and very man'? To answer that question fully would take us beyond the scope of political theology. But we can say, I believe, that whatever surplus of meaning may be contained in the ontological form of the assertion is not a political surplus. From the point of view of political theology there is nothing that the ontological assertion could, or should, mean that is not stated in the eschatological claim that the very presence of the ruling God is present to the true people of God once and for all time in the person of Jesus. But if someone is tempted to infer from this that political theology must therefore align itself with a purely functional Christology, I would suggest that he or she has not grasped the import of the *eschatological* affirmation and needs to go back and wrestle some more with the Gospel of the Kingdom. To think of Christ's mediatorial representation as a function, simply, is to treat the announcement that the Kingdom of God is at hand with something less than full seriousness. A function is a paradigm for action to which more than one actor can be accommodated. But when we speak of God's decisive presence in Christ we leave all other actors behind: they turn out to be anticipations and types for what happens *only* (for that word cannot be dispensed with) here.

Here the mediatorial role is elevated to transparency. God's rule was discerned through the judicial tasks of angels and kings in all the nations; it was discerned in special covenant through the vocation of the Davidide line. But now the last layer of the veil is drawn back. The divine authority is irreplaceably immediate in the dying, rising and future disclosing of Jesus. The Davidides are not forgotten at this moment, but consciously recalled. Yet what we see there is nothing like a revival. It carries the role forward to a moment of revelation that is of a different order entirely.

Appropriately, then, Ezekiel's prophecy of the coming David is situated in an oracle devoted to *denouncing* the monarchs of Judah and their officers (34:1–31). (Quite probably it is a conscious expansion of the oracle of Jeremiah, 23:1–6, and composed in Jerusalem before Ezekiel's migration to Mesopotamia. If so, it is of considerable incidental interest as a witness to the authenticity of Jer. 23:5f. Another instance of an expansion by Ezekiel of a short prophecy by Jeremiah is found in 18:1–31, cf. Jer. 31:29f.) The people have scattered because there was no shepherd; the supposed shepherds, instead of tending the flock, have tended themselves and made themselves more like predatory beasts. So Yhwh will remove them from their positions and rescue his people from their control (34:10). There follows a series of strong assertions that Yhwh will intervene *personally*: 'Behold, I, I myself will search for my sheep . . .' (11; Hebrew: *hinnī 'anī*: 'Here I am! I myself . . .!'); 'I myself will be the shepherd of my sheep . . .' (15); and a powerful sequence of twelve further verbs in the first person singular, all in ten lines of Hebrew text: 'I will seek . . . I will rescue . . . I will bring . . . I will gather . . . I will feed . . . I will make them lie down . . . I will bind up . . . I will strengthen . . .' etc. The reproof is then directed briefly from the shepherds to the flock itself, before the divine intervention, this time as judge, is emphasised afresh: 'Behold, I, I myself will judge' (20). And then, quite unexpectedly, the promise turns to the future David: 'I will set over them one shepherd, my servant David', and the traditional covenant pledge is adapted to include a mention of him: 'I, Yhwh, will be their God, and my servant David shall be prince among them' (23f.; Ezekiel consistently refuses to use the term 'king', *melek*). The impact of this unexpected turn, carefully crafted as always with Ezekiel, is to reproduce and comment on the equally unexpected throne prophecy of Jeremiah 23:5f. What Ezekiel understands by it is that the Davidide line could become something that it had consistently failed to be, a vehicle for the immediate disclosure of Yhwh's rule. Yhwh's servant David will become completely transparent to Yhwh's own direct intervention as saviour and judge.

The other side of the role, that of representation, needs some further exploration. It can be expressed in two complementary and mutually necessary statements: (a) The representative *alone* constitutes the presence of the represented; (b) The represented are *really present* in what the representative does and experiences on their behalf. The two sides of the idea must be kept in balance if it is not to collapse into meaninglessness. If the first is taken on its own, representation is a kind of fiction; the represented are not really present, but we pretend they are. If the second is taken on its own, representation is diminished into paradigm; the representative does and experiences nothing more than the represented do and experience, but he serves as a point of reference, a heuristic instance of the pattern. As the early church conceived Jesus' role, it was new, creative and irreplaceable, an innovation which defied repetition and defined new reality and possibility.

As such it was atypical; the representative had to contribute something that was not already there. He could not represent by being the supremely *average* figure that some modern Christologies have thought to be implied by the formula, 'very man'. Atypicality was traditionally expressed in the doctrine of Christ's sinlessness. It required an innocent person to represent a guilty race, because only the innocent can confer upon the guilty the public standing that they lack. To represent is to transcend the represented; it cannot be done from a position of complicity. In the identification of the representative with the represented there is something fitting, but there is also something innovative and unforeseen. For the author to the Hebrews it was necessary for the heavenly high priest to be 'made like' his brothers, not simply to *be* like them; and for St Paul Christ was 'in the likeness of' men or of sinful flesh, suggesting not that the likeness was superficial or unreal but that it had to be achieved by an act of identification that went beyond simple conformity to type (Heb. 2:17; Phil. 2:7; Rom. 8:3).

Yet this does not mean that the representative merely stands in for those he represents in such a way as to dissimulate their effective absence. Christ's role provides a *hupogrammos* (1 Pet. 2:21), not, that is, an 'example' simply, but a mould or template; it gives determinative presence to the life of God's people which thus becomes available for all. He is the *prōtotokos*, the 'first of many brothers', according to St Paul (Rom. 8:9 and elsewhere in the apostolic writings with various nuances). But if the represented is not simply absent while the representative stands in, neither does the representative absent himself in order that the represented may return. Dorothee Soelle invited us to consider the decision between representation and substitution in these terms: 'To represent someone means to take responsibility for him temporarily, while he is on leave or ill. It is regarded as a temporary expedient . . . Substitution demands permanence . . . The replacement represents the other person completely and unconditionally' (*Christ the Representative*, p. 20). But to frame the decision as one between two forms of *replacement*, one temporary the other permanent, is to misunderstand political representation, which is not replacement but co-presence.

The idea that our relation to Christ might be temporary is not, of course, original to Soelle. It is to be found in Origen and, on the other side of the trinitarian controversy, it was thought to be implied in the Sabellian doctrines of Marcellus of Ancyra which provoked the clause 'whose kingdom shall have no end' in the Nicene creed. It is theologically deficient because it brings a defective political imagination to bear on the idea of Christ's representation. The static monarchianism underlying the Sabellian version is matched by the static individualism underlying Soelle's, each failing to conceive representation as a creative innovation. Public existence is seen as a zero-sum operation: if my representative disposes of my fixed ration of freedom, I cannot dispose of it myself. There is, of course, a kind of representation that this describes, but it is sub-political. Political representation is not a zero-sum operation. As Hannah Arendt understood so well, to found a structure of political representation is to multiply freedom and authority, leaving everyone with more. But this perception itself seems to depend on the eschatological transformation of politics by the Christ-event. It is not clear how we can see political authority as conferring freedom, rather than taking it away, unless we have first learned to think in terms of a rule that is salvific. Here, I would judge, is one of those points at which this pre-eminent republican critic of Christianity trades in theological contraband. But however that may be, freedom is perfected in the act of representation. Christ is not first alone and then together with his brothers, first representing them and then handing back the representative function; he is at one and the same time alone and accompanied, always representing, always together with those he represents.

> About the term 'substitute' it is enough to say that it singles out a moment within the concept of representation. It has to be understood in relation to the more inclusive term, and is misleading if used in isolation. Yet it identifies one of the two necessary poles of the representative role, the point of initiative and innovation where the representative moves in to fill the breach left empty by default: 'I have trodden the winepress alone; no man, no nation was with me' (Isa. 63:3).

In the history of theology Christ's mediatorial representation has been explored most consistently in connexion with his death. The need to speak of a unique and all-sufficient sacrifice, on the one hand, and of the church's reliving of it on the other, especially in the celebration of the Lord's Supper, has caused a familiar chapter of theological controversy to be written. Some of the controversy could have been avoided if it had been recalled that representation is a feature not only of Christ's death but of the whole drama of the coming, the conflict and the triumph of the Kingdom of Christ. (It is, indeed, in the context of the resurrection that Paul achieves his most lapidary statement of Christ's representative role: 'Since by man came death, by man came also the resurrection of the dead' (1 Cor. 15:21).) If Christ alone upon the cross bore the judgment upon sin, that is because he alone was acknowledged as God's Son by the Jordan, he alone rose from the dead, he alone took his seat on the right hand of majesty on high when 'a cloud hid him'. Correspondingly, if it is true that we were 'crucified with Christ' (Gal. 2:20), it is also true that we have risen with him, that we are seated with him in heavenly places (Col. 3:1; Eph. 2:6); and, indeed, that at his Advent we were found to be God's children as he was found to be God's Son. All these moments of the Christ-event are included by the author to the Hebrews in his description of Christ as *archēgos*, 'pioneer'. That writer's famous *hapax*, 'once only', by which he underlines the definitiveness of Christ's self-offering, extends from the moment of the cross to the moment of ascension (9:12), and defines the unrepeatable aspect of Christ's work, illuminating, purifying and judging the world, at every point (6:6; 10:2; 12:26).

Yet it is legitimate to focus the drama, and with it the representative role of Christ, more closely upon the Paschal mystery. The condition is that the events of Good Friday and Easter should be articulated as a *double* event, death and resurrection, without succumbing to the persistent Western temptation (evident in atonement theories from Anselm to Moberly, and not excusing the excellent Grotius) to abstract the death of Christ and interpret it on its own, thereby radically depoliticising the central saving event of the Gospel. This is the focus adopted by St Paul throughout the towering central section of the Epistle to the Romans, and from his argument there two points emerge with special clarity. The first is the connexion between representation and authority. The new life lived under the sway of Christ's resurrection is a life commanded of us as a 'service' to righteousness. By participating in the triumph of Christ we find ourselves under the 'reign' of grace. The second is that the two moments, death and resurrection, are complementary but not isomorphic. It is the resurrection that establishes the authority of the new life. The death, on the other hand, is understood as a severance from the old, destroyed authority, that of law with its twin oppressions of 'the flesh' and 'condemnation'. Christ's death, therefore, takes place within the sphere of the old authority; it represents the point at which the old is confronted and challenged; in the resurrection the challenge issues in the assertion of the new.

The key passages for this conception are Romans 6:1–7:6 and 8:1–17. The discussion arises initially out of the extended contrast between the two representative figures, Adam and Christ, in chapter 5. There Christ's act is described as an eschatological act of grace (*charisma*) which effects righteousness (*dikaiōma*), overwhelming the protological act of transgression (*paraptōma*) which has produced condemnation (*katakrima*). The typical juridical contrast between justification and condemnation reminds us that we are within the sphere of the divine act of rule. The eschatological age is one in which 'grace reigns'. The question is then posed whether the historical dialectic of grace overwhelming transgression can be projected as a permanent law of the operation of grace in our moral experience. Does the triumphant presence of grace presuppose an ongoing encounter with transgression?

In arguing for the negative answer Paul appeals: (a) to the articulated structure of Christ's saving act as death and resurrection; (b) to its representative character as a decisive historical act determining our existence as a death and resurrection too. Our moral experience is articulated biographically by the diremption of sin and grace, as decisive in our case as in Christ's. His death and resurrection were a representative act in which we participate – beginning at our baptism and culminating in the last resurrection of the dead (6:2–8). Since in the representative's case the transaction from death to life was a final and decisive act of history (*ephapax*), we have to conceive our lives as radically transformed, free of the compelling authority, the 'reign', of sin (6:9–14).

The conception of the two eras in terms of two rival authorities is then explored in a pair of self-consciously developed metaphors. The first is of household service. We have passed from one service to another, through 'heart-obedience to the outline of instruction [we] received'. The old indenture is annulled now that the new has taken effect. Each employment carried its rewards: death and life respectively (6:16–23). The second is of the legal marriage-bond. Death releases from it – and not only the deceased, but the widow, too, who is, as it were, dead so far as that particular legal bond is concerned. So Christ's death has put an end to a nexus of relations; we have entered a new context which makes a new set of demands (7:1–6).

After a digression on the moral inadequacy of the law and its place in God's purposes for history (7:7–25) Paul returns to the original contrast between condemnation and justification (8:1–4). They represent two realms within the terms of which we cannot live simultaneously. Each has its bent of mind (*phronēma*), death and life respectively. The contrast is now redefined in terms of that between 'the flesh' and 'the Spirit'; but this is not an anthropological contrast, but an eschatological one. The Spirit is the Spirit of Christ, manifest in the divine action of the resurrection. He dwells within those who are Christ's, directing their behaviour in ways that accomplish the 'death' of 'the flesh', and their prayers by which they discover that they are, indeed, true children of God (8:5–16). The indwelling Spirit turns out to be the ground of our participation in Christ's representative act; and so Paul reverts, in concluding his discussion, to the twofold sharing in suffering and glory, though expanded, now, towards a further horizon, a shared inheritance (17).

Is the logic of the argument, then, that we reverse the Western concentration on the cross at the expense of the resurrection, and constitute the resurrection as the central fact, in relation to which even the death of Christ assumes an ancillary role? No: the resurrection refuses to be isolated from Christ's death as surely as the death from the resurrection. Admittedly, the primary layer of meaning in the death–resurrection sequence (as we see it expounded, for example, in Peter's speech at Acts 4:10f.) is simply antithetical, throwing all the weight upon the resurrection. Jesus' death was the overthrow of God's cause at the hands of rebellious Israel; his resurrection was the reassertion of God's triumph over Israel. Here the conflict between Jesus and the Jewish authorities was simply the last act of that long tussle between Yhwh and his people, in which they finally overreached themselves and were finally overcome. But this layer of meaning then entails another.

The logic of the situation generates a complementary set of statements: Yhwh's self-vindication was always, in the end, *for* Israel rather than against it; it was judgment against Israel, certainly, but for Israel's ultimate good. The vindication of God carried with it the vindication of Israel's true calling against Israel's corruption. But if Jesus' resurrection restored not only God's cause but Israel's, his death, correspondingly, meant not only God's defeat but Israel's, self-willed and self-inflicted, the terrible judgment on its constant refusal of its call. So the death of Jesus summed up the condemnation of Israel at God's hands. In representing God, he represented Israel, too, 'in the likeness of sinful flesh, and for sin' (Rom. 8:3); for their two causes, by God's act, had been made one.

> To spell it out like that is to look at it from the point of view of the post-Easter community. But the conflict could have been – perhaps we may even say 'must have been' – anticipated. Opposition was a reality in Jesus' ministry well before the final crisis broke. According to the evangelists Jesus taught his disciples that it was necessary. It did not deflect him from his conviction about the triumph of the Kingdom, but seemed to serve it. The triumph of the Son of Man would be the triumph given by God to Israel; but the bestial and demonic forces over which he would triumph were currently in possession of the soul of Israel. Israel's triumph, then, would be over itself and over its own enslavement. The conflict was God's struggle against Israel for Israel, and the struggle of Israel against God and against itself. The Kingdom's representative must suffer the resistance of Israel on God's behalf; but representing Israel's cause, too, he must suffer God's resistance on Israel's behalf. The lines of this double representation are already sketched in outline in certain experiences of Israel's past, the confessions of Jeremiah, for example. But now, Jesus taught, the time was fulfilled. The representative act, too, must be fulfilled finally and decisively.

We have spoken of the representation *of Israel.* But that opens out to the representation *of the human race.* By receiving the Kingdom on Israel's behalf the Son of Man in Daniel's vision was to vindicate humanity against bestiality. Yet if the bestial and demonic forces are in possession of Israel too, and the struggle is *against* Israel, can it continue to be *for* Israel at the same time, or is it simply for humanity as a whole? Has the 'catholic church', gathering believers from every race, replaced Israel as the people of God, embodying the new humanity of Christ on its own as a proof of Israel's failure to embody it? It was easy for the predominantly Gentile church of the second century to draw this conclusion.

> The little document called 5 Ezra (=2 Esd. 1, 2) illustrates very well how the Gentile church had come to think of the Jews. They are 'beyond correction'

(1:8) and the Lord's forbearance with them has come to an end. 'Condemn them to be scattered among the nations, and their name to vanish from the earth because they spurned my covenant' (2:7). The Gentile church had dispossessed Israel as the heir of God's election promises: 'I will hand you over to a people soon to come, a people who will trust me, though they have not known me; who will do my bidding, though I gave them no signs; who never saw the prophets, and yet will keep in mind what the prophets taught of old' (1:35f.). The same message is heard in other writings of the period. The Epistle of Barnabas points to the destruction of the Temple in AD 70 as proof of it, and is eager to deny that Jews have any claim whatever on covenant-promises of the Old Testament: 'Take heed and do not be like some who say that the covenant is both theirs and ours. It is ours . . . They turned to idols and lost it' (16:3f.; 4:6f.). Ignatius of Antioch, reflecting the indignation which some Christians felt at the continuing survival of Judaism after the fall of the Temple, regards contemporary Jews as impostors: 'Christianity did not base its faith on Judaism, but Judaism on Christianity' (*Ad Magnesios* 10). From which it is a shock to turn back to St Paul's question, 'Have they stumbled so as to fall?', and his answer, 'By no means!' (Rom. 11:11).

The argument of the Epistle to the Romans, much of which is directed to the question of Israel's identity in the light of the claim that 'there is no difference' between Jew and Greek (3:22; 10:12), reaches its climax in the affirmation that Israel can never be replaced. The continuing Israel, which does not yet believe – a contradiction, it might seem, to the fulfilment of the nation's hope in Christ – is not to be dismissed as an irrelevant survival from the past: 'God has not rejected the people whom he foreknew!' (11:2). The present phase of Israel's history is marked by a 'partial hardening' (11:25), but there exist Jewish Christians who anticipate the final reconciliation (11:1), and the dialectic of the two communities in the mean time is not to no point but serves the end of world-redemption. It is to 'make them jealous', and so bring the Jewish people 'as a whole' to salvation (11:13,26). What Israel has yet to accomplish, however, is a shift of understanding about the centre of its own identity. If at an earlier stage it came to see the possession of the land as transcended and fulfilled in the possession of the law, so now it must come to see the possession of the law fulfilled in Christ, the 'end of the law' (10:5). His coming brings to its goal the covenant of God with the patriarchs. He it is who *is* Israel, 'the root' (adapting an old metaphor). Israel must learn to see itself in terms of him; and when it does so, the struggle for Israel will have borne fruit. In the mean time the 'grafting' of the Gentiles onto Israel's root cannot change the fact that it is Israel's root that they are grafted onto.

What this striking argument implies is that Israel's *public* tradition – 'the adoption, the glory, the covenants, the giving of the law, the worship and the promises . . . the patriarchs and . . . the Messiah' (9:4f.) – is continuous. If we have been misled by Paul's insistence on the inward obedience of the 'true Jew' (2:28f.) or by his assertion of a righteousness possessed 'independently of law' (3:21) to think of a purely subjective, interior experience of salvation, the apostle will show us we misunderstood him. Gentiles who had faith challenged the Jews to pass from outward to inward membership of their own people. But faith did not nullify the public tradition; it filled it with its necessary content, the 'faith of Abraham'. History, then, was a struggle for the soul of Israel. The tradition and its guardians were claimed by the church for their foredestined fulfilment. Even Gentile Christians, Paul argued – he who more than anyone defended their right to *be* 'Gentile Christians'! – cannot ignore the community into which they have themselves by faith been grafted. So until the last reconciliation the two communities must coexist, the one with the witness of its public institutions, the other with a witness founded on and attesting faith, the community of circumcision and the community of baptism.

The comparative unfamiliarity of this picture, to which only Christian Zionists have paid consistent attention, may hide from us its fruitfulness for the politico-theological task. For it does not allow us to conceive the age of the church as one to which social order is irrelevant. The public tradition of Israel still confronts the church, and it is not wrong to look for the fulfilment of that public tradition under the rule of Christ. The age of the church is one of striving to reclaim the public tradition of Israel for the faith which completes Israel, an age in which faith and social structure wrestle with one another in the hope of being fused into each other.

> Nor is this picture seriously modified by a consideration of the Epistle to the Ephesians, with its classically 'catholic' emphasis upon the unity of the church (2:11–22). The unity of the 'one new humanity' is constituted out of two founding identities, Jewish and Gentile. But they are not equal co-founders, but are described (with a reference to Isa. 57:19) as 'the near' and 'the far'. The Gentiles entered the union from a position of complete disadvantage in relation to Israel's public tradition: 'without the Messiah, excluded from the community of Israel, strangers to the covenant of promise, having no hope and no knowledge of God in the world'. In bringing the two together God breaks down the 'dividing wall' – but that does not stand for the distinctness of the two identities, but for their hostility. Abolished is only 'the law of commandments and ordinances', and with it (it is implied) such ceremonial distinctions as circumcision. In all this the problem that presents itself is the exclusion of the Gentiles

from *the public tradition of Israel.* The idea of Israel's replacement by the Gentiles has not even appeared on the horizon.

In the Christ-event we found the elements of God's rule: an act of power, an act of judgment and the gift of possession. But these elements are presented in the narrative account of a decisive act, an act in which God's rule was mediated and his people reconstituted in Christ. We are told of the Advent of the one in whom the possession was vested, the conflict that his coming evoked and the vindication that he received at God's hand. To speak of God's rule from this point on must mean more than to assert divine sovereignty, or even divine intervention, in general terms. It means recounting this narrative and drawing the conclusions implied in it. And so we face the task of tracing its chief moments. We cannot discuss the question of 'secular' government, the question from which Western political theology has too often been content to start, unless we approach it historically, from a Christology that has been displayed in narrative form as Gospel. Christ's road to victory, then, and the subjection of the nations are the subject of what follows.

The moments of the representative act

In following the narrative which the early church told of Christ and the Kingdom, we shall mark four 'moments', which I shall refer to as Advent, Passion, Restoration and Exaltation. This division is purely an exegetical schema; it has no theoretical function and adds nothing that is not in the story itself – unlike the analysis of the Kingdom in terms of power, judgment and possession, which, though intended provisionally, does propose an interpretation of political authority not simply given in the concept. The story of the Kingdom's coming is the story the evangelists tell, not some formalised scheme derived from it. Nevertheless, as an exegetical summary the four moments can claim to represent the essential structure of the story, for the purpose of theological discussion, in a way that achieves an optimum balance of economy and fidelity.

1. The *Advent* of the Christ who mediates the rule of God occupies most space in the evangelists' narration. We have already devoted some attention to it in the second part of chapter three. We might think ourselves free at this point simply to refer back to that discussion and proceed on our way. However, so as not to miss the shift in perspective when we see the Advent from the viewpoint of the apostolic proclamation as a whole, we will pause

briefly over one important incident. All four evangelists mark the coming of the Christ by telling of Jesus' baptism by John the Baptist.

As we read the story in St Mark, the event is focussed upon the divine act of authorisation. The voice of God hails Jesus in words that echo the royal servant-song of Isaiah 42: 'You are my beloved Son, in whom I am well pleased', and the Spirit rests on him as the sign of his empowerment. In St Matthew and St Luke this thought is present still, but each gives additional weight to the point that Jesus represents not only God before mankind, but mankind before God. St Matthew (3:14f.) recounts an argument between Jesus and the Baptist in which John, recognising 'the one that is greater than I', demurs at the task of baptising him. But Jesus insists, because he must 'fulfil all righteousness'. He must represent before God the longing expectation of his penitent people. To be the answer to their prayers, he must first articulate them. So Jesus takes upon himself the role of Israel before he appears as Israel's Saviour. St Luke introduces the detail that Jesus was praying at the moment of revelation (3:21). That prayer expressed faithful Israel's prayer for the coming of the Kingdom. St John, in pursuit of his wider concern with the Baptist's role as 'witness', puts the whole incident upon his lips. He has been told the meaning of the descent of the Spirit, and identifies Jesus as the 'Son of God'. The political meaning of this title emerges soon enough. The movement of disciples away from the Baptist's leadership to Jesus signals the gathering of Israel to the coming Kingdom. 'We have found the Messiah', Andrew announces to Peter (1:41). When Jesus meets the sceptical Nathanael who has doubted that 'the one of whom Moses and the prophets wrote' could come from Nazareth (because, of course, a Davidide must originate in Judah), he acknowledges these hesitations as appropriate to 'an authentic Israelite' (1:47). The combination of titles, 'Son of God' and 'King of Israel', with which Nathanael makes his submission sums up what the coming one was to mean to this group of authentic Israelites which the Baptist had prepared.

An apparently quite different approach to describing the Advent is taken by a few self-consciously reflective passages in the New Testament, where it is asserted that Christ existed from eternity in the presence of God as his Word or 'image'. These incarnational passages (sometimes thought, but inconclusively, to be hymns of the early Hellenistic-Jewish church) were responsible for the normative shape of classical Christology, so that the Gospels' emphasis on the dawning of the Kingdom of God tended to be lost sight of. Yet, without prejudice to questions about development in Christology which these passages raise, we can discern a continuity which links this approach to the other.

As an example we take the 'Christ-hymn' of Philippians 2:5–11. Here the understanding of the Advent is dominated by the idea of condescension (*kenōsis*): Christ was in the form of God and accepted the form of a slave. The double use of the word 'form' expresses the double representation performed by Christ: of God to mankind and of mankind to God. Why is the 'likeness of men' a servant-form? Because servitude would be our experience of God's sovereignty on that (entirely conceivable) alternative hypothesis that the mediator of God's rule had *not* taken it on himself to represent mankind. God could be perfectly good, his sovereignty over the universe unimpugnable, and he could dispose of the human race as a master would dispose of a slave, not taking it into his head to think that the household might be governed for the slave's welfare. But Christ has assumed the representation of mankind; he is 'obedient' to the commanding God, but he is not a slave. This act of condescension is articulated into two moments: he has condescended in becoming man before the logic of that step has led him to the further condescension of the cross. Advent and Passion are distinct, though inseparable, moments. The representation effected through them both carries through to the moment of vindication: it is as *Kurios*, 'Lord', that he is exalted, acknowledged by every tongue. The story has told of how God's rule progressed from glory to greater glory. A self-sufficient divine sovereignty, self-justified and complete, has come to be a rule in which all human nature finds itself represented.

It would be possible to regard the narrative form of this passage merely as a device to show up the significance of double representation. Exegesis has sometimes taken this course in the past, not least the exegesis in the fourth century of Apollinaris, for whom the condescending divine nature could be spoken about only by way of abstraction, to facilitate the analysis of the union of natures in Christ. In that case we would wish to say that the Incarnation was, in the fullest sense, a 'myth', that is, a narrative which had the purpose not of reporting happenings but of disclosing permanent realities. In saying that this is not what those who fashioned this narrative intended, we need not deny them any trace of mythopoeic imagination. Indeed, any story which travels from heaven to earth and back again must have a symbolic element in it to the extent that it coordinates in one time–space field the being of God on the one hand and the earthly events which reflect his being on the other. The earthly time–space field is imaginatively extended to accommodate the ultimate source and end of what happens within it. But this is very far from saying that the narrative is not about what happened at all. What happened is the starting-point for all Christian reflection about God – as it was also for Jewish reflection. The

extension of the narrative structure is the appropriate, indeed, the only possible way to trace events back to their divine source and forward to their
divine end. In true myth the narration is form but not substance. The
Incarnation is not true myth, because the point to be communicated was
the coming of the Kingdom, an event which could, indeed, be dated.

The reason for taking the event back to its source outside this world's
events is that Jesus wholly mediates the Kingdom in his personal being, and
that the Kingdom has its origin in God's eternal purpose. It fulfils all that
God intended in Creation. It is necessary, then, to say not simply that the
Kingdom has appeared, but that it has been waiting to appear. And as with
the Kingdom, so with its mediator: Christ, too, has been in waiting. Yet in
the debates that this assertion gave rise to, the church became clear that it
did not mean to say that he had pre-existed *as a man*. His pre-existence had
been as the 'Son of God', the Kingdom itself, who came *to be* man, 'taking'
the form of a servant.

2. The *Passion* of Christ upon the cross introduces 'the judgment of this
world' (John 12:31); but the act of divine judgment cannot be restricted to
the Passion-moment alone. Judgment has two aspects to it: the separation
made between innocence and guilt, which overcomes ambiguities and clar-
ifies the nature of their opposition, and the affirmation of the innocent
against the guilty in an act of vindication and condemnation. These two
aspects are expressed in the sequence of cross and resurrection: Christ set
in opposition to the guilty Israel; Christ vindicated against the guilty Israel.
The resurrection can, therefore, be presented as the *sole* moment of divine
judgment, the point at which God intervened to overthrow a judgment
falsely passed by Israel on Christ (Acts 2:24; 3:15; 4:10 e.g.). But a more profound analysis traces the judgment of God already at work in the conflict
which pitted Jesus against the established authorities. It is a favourite theme
of St John that the judgment between light and darkness has happened
'already' when darkness refuses the light (John 3:18–21), so that the conflict
between Jesus and his contemporaries has brought judgment upon the
world. (Just so, according to St Paul, God's judgment was already in play
when Pharaoh hardened his heart against Israel, shaping the opposition
that was to result in Israel's vindication (Rom. 9:17).) And since the very
fact of conflict between innocence and guilt is already the work of divine
judgment, the innocent, who suffers most from the conflict, is suffering the
judgment invoked by others' guilt. His unmerited rejection makes him a
representative; so that subsequently he represents others in his vindication,
too. This is what underlies the profoundest twist given to the doctrine of

representation in the New Testament, the claim that Christ suffered as a 'propitiation' for the sins of mankind (Rom. 3:25).

'Already', of course, takes us back behind the cross to the first opposition to Jesus' ministry. Three out of the four evangelists signal this opposition formally at the beginning of their accounts of Jesus' work: St Mark by the struggle with Satan in the wilderness (1:13), St Luke by the story of the rejection at Nazareth (4:16–30), and St John by the story of the cleansing of the Temple, moved forward to a programmatic position (2:13–22). St Matthew makes a fourth, if we count the infancy narrative dominated by Herod's plot to kill the child. Otherwise Matthew reserves his account of conflict for a section in the middle of his Gospel (chs. 11–17), where, however, the theme of looming crisis is strongly marked. St Luke achieves something of the same effect by putting most of his non-Markan material within the framework of Jesus' final journey to Jerusalem (9:51–19:48), so emphasising the apocalyptic and conflictual elements within it. There were, of course, smaller collections of conflict-stories in Mark, notably the one which he located in Jerusalem directly after the cleansing of the Temple (11:20–12:44). The force of all this is to show how the division excited by Jesus' ministry was an essential implication of his work. In gathering the scattered Israel the Son of Man had come to force a division: 'Whoever is not with me is against me; and whoever does not gather with me scatters' (Luke 11:23||Matt. 12:30). Yet the division must come to a head. The three formal Passion predictions of the Markan tradition do not stand alone in suggesting that Jesus anticipated a climactic outcome: 'I have come to cast fire upon the earth; how I wish it were alight! I have a baptism to undergo; what strain I am under until it is complete!' (Luke 12:49f.).

Jesus, we have said, unsettled the Two Kingdoms conception, which had, in one way or another, shaped Israel's understanding of its political position since the exile. He announced the coming of God's Kingdom to sweep away existing orders of government. Those orders were of a passing age; they could, from one point of view, be dismissed as 'those who are said to rule the Gentiles' (*hoi dokountes archein*, Mark 10:42). But since their displacement could not happen without conflict, their provisional existence still counted while the moment of confrontation lasted in which the two claimants stood poised over against each other.

For St Mark this moment of confrontation comes clearly into view on the threshold of the Passion when Jesus is challenged to show authority for his high-handed gesture in the Temple precincts. The form of Jesus' answer is subtle. On the face of it he refuses to answer at all because he has failed to get an answer to his counter-question about John the Baptist. In fact his counter-question contains his answer. In it he develops the question, 'on what authority?', by positing a simple alternative: 'from God or from men?'

The question about authority must be answered in one of these two ways in the end. Either one is authorised by the direct intervention of God's rule, or by some provisional structure of human government. But if God's rule is immediately present, the provisional authorities have been swept aside. So everything turns on whether the divine intervention has or has not happened, and Jesus invites them to decide that question with reference to the Baptist, for the answer they reach in his case will be the answer they are demanding in his own. The issue John the Baptist raised about the coming of God's Kingdom had been let disappear in a pacifying, honorific martyr-cult. Jesus will raise that issue again, and will force it to the point of outright decision.

In the next few days the decision of the Jewish rulers is given. This new eschatological pretension was 'from men', only a reflection of the restless crowd-enthusiasm which was always looking for a new divine initiative. The implications of the decision were, as St Mark notices, serious. They forfeited such legitimacy 'from below' as they might otherwise have drawn from those same crowds; they retreated to their claim to mediate God's rule, and could not, as Jesus could, claim to represent God's people. The Roman authorities were the first to seize the opportunity provided by a split between Jewish leaders and people. 'King of the Jews' was written on Jesus' cross, humiliatingly for Caiaphas and his supporters. If, after all, the decision of the leaders was right, and God had not intervened, Caesar's officers would be the ones to benefit, not they.

We follow the theme of the conflicting authorities through parts of two other Passion narratives which bring it sharply into focus, St Luke's and St John's.

Luke collects material about authority, gathered from elsewhere in the Gospel tradition, into his narrative of the Last Supper, where it is introduced by the warning that the Son of Man is about to be betrayed (22:21f.). There follows the Markan saying about Gentile rulers (22:24–7) which Luke has adapted to be a programmatic statement for the Passion as a whole. There is a conflict between the ways in which earthly and heavenly kingdoms operate: the one claims precedence, the other accepts subservience patiently. In rewording Mark's saying Luke takes out the verbs compounded with *kata-*, which had suggested oppression and tyranny. He does not want our attention to rest upon the tyrannous abuse of earthly rule, but on its normal and customary ways of proceeding. For *archontes* (rulers) he puts *basileis* (kings) in order to make the contrast clearer with the Kingdom (*basileia*) of God. Then he singles out, not without irony, the custom of conferring the honorific title 'benefactor' upon rulers. The benefit for which the Gentiles are so grateful is the exercise of 'authority'. Those who expect the assertion of God's authority, on the other hand, should exercise *diakonia*, 'service'. It is the appropriate posture for political expectancy. 'I am in your midst as a servant.' But in case this may seem to remove the prospect of sharing God's rule altogether, Luke continues with a version of the 'Q' saying about twelve thrones to judge twelve tribes (22:28–30), and reinforces it with a saying unique to his source: 'I assign to you a kingdom'. Those who have rejected the pursuit of authority in favour of service, as Jesus has, will, nevertheless, inherit authority, as Jesus will. What Luke has done, then, by combining the two sayings – the one about Gentile authority and the other about the twelve thrones – is subtly different from what Mark did with the first saying on its own. There the contrast was between styles of authority: the overweening and the humble, the oppressive and the serving. Now the question is how the authority of the Kingdom of God will come into being, and the answer is that its servants will renounce the will to seize it. They will turn from the prospect of authority (of any kind) and attend to the prerequisite for wielding God's authority, a willingness to accept subjection for the sake of others. There is a sequence of events which has to be observed. It is the Gentiles who rule now, and the disciples serve. They will rule later, after they have 'persevered' with Jesus through the trial of the cross.

Luke then returns to the Markan outline with the warning to Peter of his coming denial. But this he introduces with a saying that is unique to him (22:31f.): 'Simon, Simon, Satan has desired to have you to sift you like wheat . . . But after you return, strengthen your brothers.' Once again authority rests presently with the apostles' oppressors. Peter has to live through a period in which Satan has authority over him; but beyond that period the outline of a church community with its own pastoral authority comes into view.

Finally we have the section 22:35–8, mysterious and therefore, according to some critical canons, certainly authentic – perhaps we should simply say, lacking any plausible origin in the early church. Jesus announces the moment of crisis in which the apostles will no longer be able to rely on the support of the wider community of disciples. The leader is to be 'reckoned with the offenders', and the basis for community support has gone. Each one has to be equipped individually for survival; the experience of Baruch, wandering alone through the world when Jerusalem fell, is now to be repeated. The dismantling of the faithful community must precede the emergence of true authority. How, then, did St Luke understand the closing exchange about the two swords? The infamous medieval interpretation in terms of the spiritual and secular powers of the pope is only an extension of the misunderstanding which the evangelist attributes to the apostles themselves. They were not being told to defend themselves, but to be self-reliant in their flight. The misunderstanding, however, produces clarification, which comes in the Gethsemane scene, where the disciples' armed struggle incurs Jesus' rebuke (22:51). 'This is the moment when the dark authority prevails' (22:53). Where did this 'dark authority' come from? If the authority of the Kingdom had been manifested, what was this countervailing authority which the Gentile powers wielded against it? In his depiction of Pilate Luke undertakes to answer the question: he shows a man unpersuaded by the charge, three times assuring the crowd that there is no case, offering, nevertheless, to administer a gratuitous minor punishment to satisfy them; and he shows the crowd simply overruling him ('their demands prevailed', 22:23). Again, in an episode unique to himself, Luke shows Herod Antipas, frivolously curious, happy to inflict humiliation although agreeing with the verdict of acquittal. In his darkest remark, worthy of St John for irony, the evangelist tells us that collaboration over the case of Jesus sealed a political friendship between these two rulers (23:12). What bound them together was their mutual consciousness of impotence. They were professional flatterers, who sang to the tune that their masters, the mob, piped for them. This, then, was the meaning of the authority of the kings of the Gentiles; this was the secret of the title 'benefactor'. Their authority was from below, and they held on to it by dutiful obedience to what was required of them.

St John focusses his trial-narrative upon two short dialogues between Jesus and Pilate, to which the question of rule and authority is central. The first of these (18:33–40) begins with Pilate's question, 'Are you the king of the Jews?', which evokes a question in reply, 'Do you make the suggestion on your own account, or have others suggested it to you?' The kingship of Jesus is such as can be recognised only by those who recognise it on their own account; it lacks accessibility to public recognition. When Pilate responds to this by indignantly denying personal interest, the point is made more clearly: Jesus' authority as king is not 'from this world', which would imply that it had to be asserted against other such authorities by force of arms. But then the question poses itself: does this other-worldly authority really constitute anything political at all? Is it *kingship*? Jesus' task, he replies, is to witness to the truth; but truth creates a socially centripetal force; it gathers its following of those who 'belong to' the truth. Thus Jesus commands a social authority – the root of all social authority, in fact – and the answer to Pilate's question is 'Yes'. But Pilate does not see what truth has to do with authority, and assumes the answer is 'No'. Jesus does not appear dangerous to him. He is happy for the Jews to have their 'king', because to his short view nothing of political moment is at stake.

It ought not to need saying that there is nothing here of that sympathetic portrait of Pilate which some modern readers have claimed to find in St John's trial-narrative. Pilate's incomprehension represents the unawareness of the bestial empire against which the Son of Man is to be vindicated. Perhaps only modern readers could find such a portrait sympathetic! The 'greater sin' of Jewry is, of course, the centre of the evangelist's attention, but that is because Jewry is God's elect on whose decision everything of importance hangs; whereas Pilate, for St John as for St Luke, is incapable of meaningful decision. His profession is the wielding of authority, but he has no idea where authority comes from or in what it consists.

His confidence that he can dismiss the whole matter is shaken when he is told (by 'the Jews', of course!) that God's law requires him to act against Jesus (19:7). The troubled question 'Where are you from?', with which the second dialogue (19:9–12) opens, might as well have been put to the law itself as to the prisoner. Together the law and the prisoner confront him with an authority the source of which he must investigate. The answer to his question is that his own authority, which he tries to assert by threatening, is also dependent on a source. Is that source Caesar, or is it God? The question is left open for the moment, but the answer will come: because it depends on Caesar, it depends on God, since Caesar is destined to fulfil the role that God has assigned him. 'From this point Pilate sought to release him', the evangelist remarks memorably. That is his last opportunity to assert the authority he *thinks* he has, to escape the authority of God's law, to avoid taking the authoritative claim of truth seriously. But he cannot pull it off. Caesar himself, the unacknowledged source of his own authority, turns against him: in Caesar's name he is instructed that he cannot ignore the challenge of kingdom to kingdom. The irony of the Jewish leaders' alliance with Caesar is often noticed; no less striking is the irony whereby Caesar's representative is denied, by the logic of Caesar's rule, the final privilege of impotence, the right to decline battle. His position forces him to confront God's Kingdom and to concede its claim. The title 'King of the Jews' on Pilate's lips begins as a joke against the Jewish leadership (18:39) and ends as a capitulation.

3. The *Restoration* of Christ from death is, in the first place, the judgment of God against Israel and for Israel: the overcoming of Israel's sin and the affirmation of Israel's new identity in its representative. When St Paul in the Epistle to the Romans describes Christ as 'given up for our sins and raised for our vindication' (4:25), he has, of course, Israel's sin and vindication in mind. Fulfilling the promises that Abraham believed in, Christ represents Israel equally in both moments of the Paschal crisis, and becomes a new focus of identity for those who inherit Abraham's faith. But the form which this rejection and affirmation take is the conquest of death; and this makes Israel's restoration representative of the wider human hope, a restoration to be claimed by the human race as a whole. And so as he proceeds Paul explores the representative role by analogy not with the national patriarch but with the founder of the race, Adam: 'If because of one man's trespass death reigned through that one man, much more will those who receive in abundance grace and the gift of righteousness reign in life through the one man, Jesus Christ' (5:17).

The same analogy dominates the resurrection chapter of 1 Corinthians: 'Since by man came death, by man came also the resurrection of the dead. As in Adam all die, even so in Christ shall all be made alive' (15:21). The resurrection restores the life of all mankind, reversing the effects of sin; it reorders the disorder of which death is the emblem, and vindicates God's original act of creation. But here there is something further to be said. When Paul returns a second time in that chapter to the comparison of Adam and Christ, he introduces a new thought: 'the first man Adam was made a living soul, the last Adam a life-giving spirit . . . The first man was from the earth, made of dust, the second man was from heaven . . . As we have borne the image of the man of dust, so shall we bear the image of the heavenly man' (15:45ff.). The thought stated in the first contrast is still maintained here. Christ is the life-giver; he restores Adam's children to the life for which they were created. But a new thought is superimposed upon the old one. What is achieved is more than a simple restoration of Adam's life. There is a difference between what was first given, described as 'soul' and 'dust', and what will be given, which is 'spiritual' and 'from heaven'. It would be a mistake to imagine that Paul's use of these terms is intended to lay the basis of an anthropology. The 'spiritual' does not stand for the natural inwardness of human existence, the 'spirit' which could be contrasted with bodily attributes. The categories of 'spirit' and 'heaven' point instead to the authority which belongs to God's reign. Christ, in giving us back our life, has endowed it with authority and power.

In making this second point Paul has not ceased to speak of the resurrection. The two aspects, restoration and empowerment, are both contained in that one event. In St Luke and St John, however, we find the two aspects presented separately. The resurrection is primarily restoration to bodily life: Jesus eats meals, is accessible to sight and touch, is not 'a spirit' which 'does not have flesh and bones as you see that I have' (Luke 24:40); only the strange and unpredictable manner of his coming and going differentiates this risen life from what went before. But this restored existence can only be a stepping-stone to something further. 'Do not cling to me, for I have not yet ascended to the Father' (John 20:17). There is a moment of transition to come, from this restored life to that empowered life at the Father's right hand. Generally the New Testament veils that transition in reticence and refers to it only obliquely, as when Mark and Matthew show knowledge of a special encounter of the risen Lord with his disciples in Galilee, or when St Paul describes himself as 'untimely born'. For the most part it is enough for the New Testament witnesses to point to the fact of the resurrection, without unfolding it into its two elements, the mysteries of Easter and Ascension.

In following Luke and John in spelling out the meanings of Easter and Ascension distinctly, we are, in one sense, attempting to separate the inseparable. St Paul can say everything that needs to be said by means of the simple affirmation that Christ has risen from the dead. However, since the two evangelists do offer us the help of unfolding this affirmation into its two moments, we would be unwise to refuse it, and especially because the distinction is a defence against two mistakes from which contemporary theology is hardly exempt.

The first mistake is to ignore the meaning of Christ's triumph as the restoration of creation, and to convert it exclusively into a doctrine of history. A redemption that has merely the transformation of the world in view will not deal seriously with the fact that what God has done in Christ he has done for his creation and for his own sake as creator. It is not enough to understand the triumph of the Kingdom as improving or perfecting a world that was, as it stood, simply inadequate. The distinct ideas of a good creation on the one hand and a redeemed creation on the other are then collapsed into an undifferentiated ongoing activity of God, in which the lower is raised to the level of the higher, a depressing conception of Manichean character, sometimes dignified with the name of 'continuous creation', though in fact it constitutes a denial of the decisiveness implied in the term 'creation' and is really only concerned to assert continuousness. History as a perpetual movement 'out of' the imperfect and 'into' the more perfect does not provide a substitute for the doctrines of creation and redemption. Only in the light of a restored creation can we take the measure of the ups and downs, its accomplishments on the one hand and its corruptions and degradations on the other.

The second mistake is to lose the balance between what has been accomplished and what remains to be accomplished. It can, of course, be said that only from within the perspective of our time-frame does anything remain to be accomplished at all. Christ's triumph is complete, and in that event mankind has been brought into the presence of God's glory. Nothing remains to be added to what has been done; we wait only for a fuller sight of it. Yet while this is true so far as it goes, it ignores one aspect of the Ascension that should not be missed: it is a bridge between the time of Christ's life and the time of the world's future. This is the significance of the invisibility which surrounds the Ascension. The disciples could embrace the flesh and bones of their risen Lord, but they could not observe his entry into the glory of the Father. St Luke, who alone braves the task of description, goes so far as to take us to the top of the Mount of Olives and report Jesus' parting words. But we see nothing, less even than Peter, James and John saw on the mount of the transfiguration. 'A cloud hid him from their sight' (Acts 1:9); and two messengers from God told them that they were to expect . . . the Parousia! As an event with only one foot in human time and space the Ascension is strictly indescribable, and this accounts for the general reticence of the New Testament to describe it. To grasp the Ascension whole would mean that we should behold the glory of the Son in the Father's presence; but this in turn supposes the resumption of our time-frame into the last time of God's manifest judgment. The unfolding of the resurrection into its two moments warns us against a complacent settlement with the present. The Christ-event, though accomplished, is still an event for the future, and our faith in it must still be marked by a hope, and not a hope for our own private futures only but for the future of the world subject to God's reign.

4. The *Exaltation*, undescribable in itself, is clothed in the imagery of royal coronation. The ascended Christ takes his throne, as the Davidide monarch was summoned to do in the ancient psalm (2:1), on the right hand of the divine majesty. The Son of Man is presented before the Ancient of Days and receives the Kingdom. Precisely because it attracts this political imagery to itself, the Ascension is of great importance to political theology, but also, it may seem, somewhat alarming. What are we to make of the assertion that the promise of the Kingdom of God, the heart of Jesus' political Gospel, was fulfilled here and at this place – at the top of the Mount of Olives? Is this a simple sublimation of all the political themes of Jesus' preaching, a volatilisation of political substance into the ether of religious sensibility?

We need not rehearse the well-known arguments surrounding the claim that in the early church's talk of the Ascension, as with the Incarnation, we have to do with a mythical framework in which the earthly reality of Jesus was clothed by religious interpretation. Such a line of thought, whatever its claims to be taken seriously on other grounds, can offer nothing but disappointment to political theology. The political expectations of Jesus, denied validation within the immediate course of Israel's history, have to be laid aside as altogether ill-founded unless some validation for them is to be found within the history of Jesus himself. But if the story of this validation is said to be not a history of event but a myth of interpretation, then those political expectations were, after all, insubstantial. There has been no political achievement; the hope of it has merely become the conceptual material out of which is spun a religious validation for a life of frustrated efforts and fruitless self-sacrifice. Not every version of this account denies the event-status of the *resurrection*. Some allow to Jesus a historical, not merely an interpretative, vindication. But without the Exaltation such vindication can only be a personal affair, not in the realm of public achievement. This demythologising of the Gospel is, inevitably, a depoliticising of it, since political affirmations are classified among the religio-mythical concepts that must be shed.

Very different from a theological point of view is the proposal to understand the language of coronation as a *symbolic* expression for happenings which cannot be spoken of. An account of the climax of Christ's history must be given in symbols, since its manifestation to sight is a matter for the future; yet it can be marked as an event in Jesus' history, located at the end of the forty days of resurrection appearances. The coronation imagery drawn from Psalm 2 is stylised, and serves an overtly symbolic function; nevertheless, it directs us to what happened; and the use of political imagery to describe what happened is not arbitrary. This unspeakable event had political significance. It was not a private vindication but a public one; it was the fulfilment of the political promise which Jesus had come to bring, and his own authorisation as the representative of the Kingdom of God. We may develop this in two short complementary statements:

First, the Ascension is the *conclusion* of the story of Christ, the story that we have summarised under the heads of Advent, Passion and Restoration. As its conclusion, it expresses the meaning of the story in a climactic way. There is one story, not four, and the division into four moments is an exegetical device only. It is not, therefore, surprising that the language of kingdom, which gives the story its unity, is focussed especially upon its concluding moment. It has told of an act of divine rule: power put forth, judgment effected and the gift of communal identity secured. The coronation of Christ expresses the accomplishment of that act as a whole. Naturally, there are anticipations: already in the appearance of Christ by the Jordan and again on the mount of transfiguration, the divine affirmation of the royal Son has been heard. It is wrong to ask at what point in the story Jesus *became* endowed with the authority of the Son, before the resurrection or after it, because the whole story is the story of how he came to be so, and the final moment confirms what the whole story has been about.

Secondly, the Ascension is the *foundation* which determines all future time. Its logic leads from Christ's absence on the Mount of Olives to his unqualified presence at the Parousia. The contrast between these two moments is mediated by his 'presence in absence' at Pentecost, so that not only ultimate future, but intermediate future is governed from the moment of the Ascension: the time that lies between ourselves and his past time, the time which we ourselves now inhabit and the time which is still future up to the point at which the Kingdom is published universally. In one sense it is a secret foundation, since that ultimate publicity has not occurred; yet in no sense is it a private foundation, but one which determines all public existence. It determines the ultimate and most truly public existence of all, when the contradiction between private and common is to be resolved and disorder overcome. Prior to this it determines the public existence of the church, which participates in the coming of the Kingdom and witnesses to it; and through the church it determines the provisional public life of the world, in which the authorities are subdued, reformed and given a limited authorisation.

The subjection of the nations

The kingly rule of Christ is God's own rule exercised over the whole world. It is visible in the life of the church, to which we shall return in the next chapter, but not only there. St Paul declared that God has 'disarmed the principalities and powers and made a public show of them in Christ's triumphal procession' (Col. 2:15). That must be the primary eschatological assertion about the authorities, political and demonic, which govern the world: they have been made subject to God's sovereignty in the Exaltation of Christ. The second, qualifying assertion is that this awaits a final universal presence of Christ to become fully apparent. Within the framework of these two assertions there opens up an account of secular authority which presumes neither that the Christ-event never occurred nor that the sovereignty of Christ is now transparent and uncontested.

The description of secular authority in the New Testament follows from the understanding that the authority of the risen Christ is present in the church's mission. The question, then, presents itself like this: to what extent is secular authority compatible with this mission and, so to speak, re-authorised by it? If the mission of the church needs a certain social space, for men and women of every nation to be drawn into the governed community of God's Kingdom, then secular authority is authorised to provide and ensure that space. Consider the logic of 1 Timothy 2:1ff. The apostle exhorts that, before all else, there should be prayers, i.e. public intercessions on behalf of all mankind, within the church which represents mankind under God's rule. Ultimately the church will pray for the consummation of the Kingdom, that goes without saying. Immediately, however, it prays for kings and all in authority. How, then, are these supposed to serve the ultimate horizon? By facilitating a 'quiet and peaceful life' – for their subjects, that is – 'in all religion and sobriety'. 'This', the apostle goes on, 'is good and acceptable to God our Saviour, whose will is for everyone to be saved and to come to recognise the truth.' Whether it is the role of kings or the church's prayer for kings that is 'acceptable to God' is not quite clear; but it hardly matters, since the principle is the same either way. When we have overcome the customary affectation of dismay at the supposed 'quietism' of this picture, we may allow ourselves to be impressed at how the goals and conduct of secular government are to be reconceived to serve the needs of international mobility and contact which the advancement of the Gospel requires.

The same idea underlies the most famous, and most disputed, discussion of political authority in the New Testament, Romans 13:1–7, a passage which it is necessary to read with fresh eyes, forgetting what has thoughtlessly been said about its 'conservatism' in order to see how it contributes to a reconception of political authority in the Gospel era. It is necessary to read it in the context in which Paul himself has set it, which is his claim for the continued significance of Israel as a social entity in God's plans for final redemption. St Paul's famous paragraph about the authorities arises naturally from his claim for Israel. Christ's victory, after all, is the same victory that was promised to Israel over the nations, the victory of a God-filled and humanised social order over bestial and God-denying empires, a victory won for Israel on behalf of all mankind. As Israel is claimed for faith, then, so the authorities are claimed for obedience to Israel, chastened and reduced to the familiar functions that were once assigned to Israel's judges.

Paul's first words describe secular government in a way that ought to catch the ear. The natural way to refer to political leadership in the ancient world was concretely, speaking of 'kings', 'princes', 'magistrates' or, as Paul himself does, 'rulers'. It has often been suggested that Paul's choice of the term 'prevailing authorities' alludes directly to the angelic character assigned to national governments in ancient Hebrew culture. By posing the question of political authority in these terms, Paul is placing it in the context of the victory of Christ. Given that Christ has overcome the principalities and powers by his death and resurrection, what rights can they still claim? The question is parallel to the question he has just asked and answered about Israel, a question that arises from the dawning of the eschatological age. And, in this case as in that, Paul undertakes to show that it is by God's purpose that the structures of the old age 'continue to exercise their sway' (*eis auto touto proskarterountes*, 13:6), serving the church's mission.

That purpose is judgment. Government is 'an avenger to visit wrath on the wrongdoer'. Correspondingly, as judgment in the ancient world always has in mind a decision between two parties (as in our civil rather than our criminal jurisdiction), it is also to 'praise' the party who has acted rightly. This exactly reflects the concept of *mishpāt* in the Old Testament. What has now changed is the privileging of this aspect of governmental authority, so that the whole rationale of government is seen to rest on its capacity to effect the judicial task. Here, it seems to me, is a novelty not anticipated either in classical or in Old Testament sources. If one of the three elements of political authority could be seen as privileged over the others in ancient Israel, it must surely be that of possession. Government was given to safeguard Israel's existence in relation to the land and the law. Similarly in the classical world the end of government was the protection of the polis. Plato called his ideal rulers 'guardians', and perpetuated the famous metaphor of the political 'helmsman' (*kubernētēs*) from which our word 'government' derives. St Paul's new assertion is that the performance of judgment alone justifies government; and this reflects his new Christian understanding of the political situation.

For the *possession* – of Israel and therefore of the world – was Christ himself, the true Israelite and the true representative of the human race. Membership in Christ replaced all other political identities by which communities knew themselves. No respect can be paid to the role of government, then, as a focus of collective identity, either in Israel or in any other community. Judgment, on the other hand, must be respected, for it is the form in which God expresses his wrath; and that wrath cannot cease yet, for, as we will learn from Paul elsewhere, it is a restraining element in society which preserves the social order that furthers the spread of the Gospel. The apostle does not go on to say of secular government what he has said about the Jewish law in Israel, that wrath, by 'making sin appear more sinful', prepares the conscience for the law of the Spirit of Christ. Luther made that connexion, not unreasonably.

Christians, too, are subject to the regime of divine wrath ministered through secular government. That is an assertion, as Paul is aware, which will surprise Christians taught to see themselves as free members of a perfectly governed society, 'sons of the Kingdom'. 'Rulers inspire no fear', they would say, 'in those whose work is good.' (A parallel to this sentiment occurs at 1 Tim. 1:9.) Very well, Paul replies, the Christian community, with its sense of freedom from the 'fear' which rulers command, had better make sure that its work *is* good! The subjection expected of it is not the subjection of fear (*dia tēn orgēn*) but the cordial recognition of the judicial function based on respect for its place in God's purposes, a respect born of 'conviction' (*dia tēn suneidēsin*). If Christians refused this recognition, they would not be acting under the government of Christ, and so would deserve to be subject to the regime of wrath. The payment of taxes Paul sees as a symbol of their recognition of the judicial function. We are reminded that Jesus was said to pay taxes ironically (Matt. 17:24–7, cf. pp. 91ff.). Here, however, there is a more positive affirmation of the government's role than there could be at the moment of the Kingdom's challenge to all settled authorities.

The life of the Christian community itself, on the other hand, functions on an almost totally opposite principle to the judicial principle that serves the general needs of the world. The paragraph on secular government comes as a parenthesis in between two paragraphs on the life of the church which make the sharpest contrast with it. There is to be no retaliation for evil received, no seeking of vengeance or vindication (*ekdikountes* in 12:19 anticipates the governmental *ekdikos* in 13:4), but only love for the enemy, which entrusts the whole of judgment to the decisive act of God. The precise payment of dues within the secular order contrasts with the unmeasured and uncalculating bestowal of love within the community. ('Owe no one anything' (13:8) is a demand not for strict accounting of debts, but for a determination not to be outdone in rendering benefits to others.) Here we can recognise the community that Jesus founded: unwilling to engage in litigation, motivated by the operations of the law written on their hearts and suspicious of external measures of conformity.

The recovery of certain elements of the Two Kingdoms idea of post-exilic Judaism goes a little further in 1 Peter 2:13–17. There is a new conceptualisation of the way in which the church and the world interact: members of the church are seen as 'aliens and exiles', like diaspora Jews, having their own political identity but being resident on alien territory; the structures of secular government, meanwhile, are allowed to be an *anthrōpinē ktisis*, an institution that belongs to humankind as such, so that the common grace of God, rather than his saving purposes, forms the foundations of secular authority. Nevertheless, in evident dependence on Romans 13, the same pair of terms, *ekdikēsis* and *epainos*, 'vengeance' and 'praise', characterise judgment as the sole purpose for which emperors and governors are 'sent out' by God, while the Christian community continues to live in its own social space, free in relation to the authorities of the world and subservient directly to God. The 'respect' paid to the emperor (as it is paid to 'everyone'!) stands in sharp contrast to the 'fear' that is paid to God and the 'love' that is paid to the brotherhood.

The emphasis on judicial functions contrasts, as we have observed, with the community's own dislike of litigation. This was sharply underlined by St Paul, dismayed to hear of a court case opposing two Christians in Corinth (1 Cor. 6:1ff.). That, in Paul's view, was a retreat from the exercise of church authority; it gave to the secular authorities a judicial role within the church which ought to be governed solely by the authority it had received from Christ. But did that mean that church authorities should have their own tribunals to hear cases between Christians? St Paul suggested that that was the answer; and yet he was troubled by the knowledge that this was not how Christ's authority was supposed to function. It was altogether a 'defeat' that the occasion should arise. 'Why not rather suffer wrong?' The Lord who commanded us to make peace with our adversary before we reached the court did not exactly envisage setting up a church court on the road! Yet making peace was also 'judging for yourselves' (Luke 12:57, cf. p. 112). There was a place for judgment among those who had the law written on their hearts, and, when the contestants could not do so, there was a place for a 'wise' Christian to discern between them, contributing his judgment to make good the insufficiency of theirs.

Yet this church judgment would be of an altogether different kind from what went on in the secular courts. The community was not in business to divide the guilty from the innocent, taking vengeance on the one and vindicating the other. For the judgment that counted had already been given by God in the death and resurrection of Christ: 'Who shall lay any charge against those whom God has chosen? When God himself acquits, who is to pronounce condemnation?' (Rom. 8:33f.) The sole purpose of the church court was to make the implications of God's judgment clear, by reconciling the contending Christians in a common understanding of God's right.

An important passage in St Matthew's Gospel (18:15–20) provides an institutional commentary on Jesus' parable of the lost sheep: a Christian who believes himself ill-treated by a fellow-Christian must try to reach an understanding privately first; only if that fails may other members of the church be involved, and then only in such a measure as is strictly necessary to secure agreement, the aim of the whole process being to keep the issue confined and to bring to bear the least weight of public pressure capable of doing the job. Only when public pressure fails to reconcile can the question of sanctions arise, and then only of one sanction, expulsion from the church, because the essence of the offence has been to reject God's judgment in the community, and so, in effect, to reject Christ himself. The only judgment with which the church has to reckon is the final judgment, dividing between belief and unbelief. The secular authorities, on the other hand, deal only in provisional and penultimate judgments. By embracing the final judgment of God Christians have accepted that they have no need for penultimate judgments to defend their rights. The continued presence of such judgments in the world, however, is an important witness to those to whom the word of final judgment has yet to come.

But secular authorities are no longer in the fullest sense mediators of the rule of God. They mediate his judgments only. The power that they exercise in defeating their enemies, the national possessions they safeguard, these are now rendered irrelevant by Christ's triumph. This is what might properly be meant by that misleading expression, the 'desacralisation' of politics by the Gospel. No government has a right to exist, no nation has a right to defend itself. Such claims are overwhelmed by the immediate claim of the Kingdom. There remains simply the rump of political authority which cannot be dispensed with yet, the exercise of judgment.

I summarise briefly what divides my reading of this passage from that popularised on the evangelical left wing by John Howard Yoder, drawing on the traditions of his own Mennonite confession. I take as the principal source for his reading the chapter devoted to this text in *The Politics of Jesus* (1972), pp. 193–214. But if I were to look elsewhere in Yoder I would find statements with which I could be more comfortable: for example, the following brief mention in *The Original Revolution* (1971) pp. 59f., where he thinks the text gives 'criteria for judging to what extent a state's activities (since the state incarnates this semisubdued evil) are subject to Christ's reign. If the use of force is such as to protect the innocent and punish the evildoer, then the state may be considered as fitting within God's plan as subject to the reign of Christ.' Yet in 1964 (*The Christian Witness to the State*) and again in 1972 Yoder made a major break with that line of interpretation. Absent was the reference to Christ's triumph and the state's subjection, or semisubjection. The language of principalities and powers was invoked solely to point up the demonic character of the state, requiring 'at best acquiescence', and the whole text was a call to 'a nonresistant attitude towards a *tyrannical* government' (my italics). With which I find it impossible to reconcile Paul's statements that the authorities praise those who do good, and that obedience is due 'as a matter of principled conviction'.

Much of the force of Yoder's argument rests on its opposition to an exegetical 'tradition' which he takes to be the mainstream tradition of Christendom. The text does not say that God ordains 'a particular government', but only 'whatever structure of sovereignty happens to prevail'. The text does not say that whatever a government asks of its citizens is good. The text does not say that government is instituted 'as a part of God's good creation'. No more it does, and I do not recall that the mainstream tradition ever thought differently, on the first two of these points at least, and only one strand of it thought differently on the third. (One can, of course, find deviant traditions. Yoder's own view of the mainstream seems to have been formed in the post-Nazi era of the German-speaking world, which naturally tended to paint 'the tradition' in Nazi colours.)

More controversially, Yoder thinks the text refers not to the death penalty or to war, but to the 'police function'. This is to impose an anachronism upon a text which knew of no civil order that was not maintained by soldiers. This distinction, like the question whether Christians are permitted to engage in military service, is simply not envisaged by the text. When later Christians argued various positions in relation to those matters, they intended to be consistent with Paul's words but not to claim direct authority from the exegesis of them. Yoder, it must be said, is not beyond dismissing as bad exegesis views that were never meant as exegesis, and in turn claiming Paul's silence as exegetical support for his own alternative views.

The theme of Romans 13 is the authority which remains to secular government in the aftermath of Christ's triumph. It offers no empirical observation about the way in which the limited authority was used or exceeded, for its concern is ecclesiological and, more indirectly, Christological. Elsewhere in the apostolic literature, however, such observations do appear. The abortive attempt of the Emperor Caligula to set his own statue in the Holy of Holies in AD 40 may have prompted the thought of 2 Thessalonians 2:3–9. Before the final public demonstration of Christ's rule rebellion must focus itself (when an unspecified 'restraint' is withdrawn) into a 'man of lawlessness' who will engage in combat with the appearing Christ. Nothing is said to connect this figure with any political ruler; but the overtones of the imperial cult are too strong to ignore.

It is a mistake to set this apocalyptic presentation of the Roman emperor at odds with the view taken in Romans 13 and 1 Peter 2. Those passages were not attempting a description of contemporary politics; they had as their aim the definition of the ruler's right. Precisely those modest judicial accounts of governmental function, indeed, forced the church to see in the accrual of divine titles and religious symbols by the empire a defiance of resurrection order. But neither is it enough to reconcile the two perspectives by remarking on the difference between a law-state and a totalitarian state, nor, with John Howard Yoder, by seeing in them 'the two dimensions of the life of any state' (*The Christian Witness to the State*, p. 77). Just as the conception of a moderate judicial order was shaped by the achievement of Christ's triumph, so the defiant and expansive empire was an eschatological phenomenon, too. The concentrating opposition was a sign of the last times. What Christ's enthronement had effected was to force upon the principalities and powers the alternatives of subjection and outright confrontation and defeat. It had brought in a moment of apocalyptic division.

The conception of a final conflict had its roots in the post-exilic prophets from Ezekiel to Daniel. The theological difficulty was whether the church was free to reappropriate that tradition, given its claims for the finality of Jesus' resurrection. Was a reversion to such themes not a retreat from the central tenet of the Christian faith, that in the confrontation of Christ and Pilate the eschatological climax had come, so that now there remained nothing but the task of letting it be known? That is the question underlying the book written by John of Patmos, at once a towering achievement of disciplined theology and of poetic imagination – terms of praise which do not preclude John's own account of his authorship as the product of a visionary ecstasy. The task he set himself was to integrate the apocalyptic account of current political developments into a Christian view of history, in which Christ's crucifixion was the decisive achievement of God's purposes. His theme is that the evolution of the idolatrous imperial pretensions is a necessary outcome of the Messianic victory itself, a working out of Satan's downfall on Calvary. (What follows is more fully explained and justified in my article 'The Political Thought of the Book of Revelation', *Tyndale Bulletin* 37 (1986), 61–94.)

His opening vision, after an extended preface, displays his concern with the shape of history (chs. 4, 5). The 'sealed scroll' of history, which makes the transparent glory of creation unintelligible, is now opened by the appearance of the slain Lamb. Jesus' death and resurrection are the key to history. Three successive views are then given of the shape of history, each a cycle of seven visions and each adding something to the interpretation of the last. First we see history as a series of worsening man-made calamities (6:1–8:1), originating in the ambition of conquest. Here is the disintegration that human sin has brought upon itself, which will reach its climax in the redemption of a people delivered from the wreckage, a preserved Israel on the one hand and a preserved international community on the other (7:1ff.). But this climax is deflected by an empty pause ('a silence in heaven for the space of about half an hour') which represents the present moment, a breathless intermission, as yet without content, between the sounding of the last trumpet and the appearance of what it portends. The second cycle (8:2–11:19) shows history as a series of judgments invoked by prayer. Here is the retribution that outraged justice demands, which will reach its climax in the critical confrontation between God's witnesses and the apostate city, resulting in the city's fall. This climax, too, is deflected, but this time the intervening space contains something: an announcement, that God has taken his Kingdom. The final appearance of the Kingdom, then, has twice been postponed, postponed at the very point where its arrival has been published. The third cycle (15:1–16:21) runs to its end without interruption. It depicts history as a series of divine judgments, modelled on the plagues of Egypt, and it reaches its climax in the fall of 'Babylon'. But before John will permit us to observe the third cycle and its conclusion, we must be shown the meaning of that crisis at the penultimate point of history, the Christ-event itself, which is the ground for the announcement that God had taken his Kingdom. This is the subject of the long vision which forms the centre of his book (12:1–14:20).

Here John first recounts the birth, conflict and triumph of Christ in a brief allegorical narrative. His ascension to God's throne is followed immediately by the expulsion from heaven of Satan, who, because he 'knows his time is short', persecutes the church and summons from the abyss two beasts, the one from the sea and the other from the land, which herald the arrival of the idolatrous totalitarian political order described in chapter 13. The historical setting of this order, which obviously reflects the early Roman empire, is of supreme importance to the prophet: it belongs to the Messianic age, between the Ascension and the Parousia; it is evoked by the enemy's great defeat, precisely as a reaction to it. To underline this he makes various suggestions that the idolatrous empire is a parodic mirror-image of the Kingdom of God which has just dawned: the beast from the sea is an anti-Christ, on whom the dragon, Satan, confers his throne and his authority, as God the Father had conferred his upon Christ; he boasts a 'healed wound' like the risen Christ; the beast from the land, meanwhile, is an anti-Spirit, a 'false prophet' who propagates a false gospel and maintains the empire's appearancy of legitimacy, sealing its adherents with an imitation of the baptismal seal. The unqualified allegiance which the empire demands and enforces by exclusion challenges the demand of the Kingdom of Heaven itself. Here is the first description of what we have come to call 'ideology', the religious absolutising of political doctrine.

In his portrait of Rome (17:1–19:10) John has taken up the critique of world-empire which he found in the exilic prophets. The characteristics of ancient Babylon, as seen through the eyes of the anonymous prophets of Isaiah 21 and Jeremiah 51, are blended with the characteristics of ancient Tyre, as seen by Ezekiel and the anonymous prophet of Isaiah 23. It is a significant combination: John needs no modern Marxist to tell him that economic domination is a more effective key to world-empire than military might. He has also drawn on the idea of a degenerating history of empire explored by Daniel. But although he thinks the Roman empire continuous with the cruel empires of the past, he also thinks that it presents something new and distinctive to the Messianic age. The old whore of empire is familiar to us from history; but now she comes riding on the beast that has just risen from the sea. Her present manifestation is an anti-Messianic sign. Human empire is put to an unprecedented use by the diabolical forces marshalling to fight the Kingdom of God. So for John of Patmos the penultimate disclosure of evil in the political realm, and its comeuppance at the hands of God and the Lamb, are necessitated and controlled by the decisive triumph of Christ which has just taken place. We see the death-throes of demonic power, the sign that final judgment has indeed come upon the world.

There is a puzzling feature about the interaction of politics and church in John of Patmos' vision. Nowhere in the New Testament is such a broad array of political categories deployed to depict the eschatological triumph of the church. There is the true throne, of God and the Lamb; there is the true warfare which establishes it, and the true judgment. There is, in a luminous enhancement of the prophets' Zion-theology, a true city, conveying the solidity of community self-possession and still allowing for the *vis-à-vis* of international communications (21:24). Yet there is correspondingly less allowed to the solidity of the Christian community in its present form. The 'churches' (John's use of the word only for particular congregations is revealing) turn out to be ambiguously faithful. From them must emerge, like the faithful leaving Babylon, 'the conqueror', the individual who by endurance will prove to be a bearer of the ultimate authority, a truly public person: a pillar in the temple, with the name of New Jerusalem written upon him, an occupant of the Lamb's throne. The great congregations of the Apocalypse are all eschatological, while the church of the present is represented by two witnesses. In the heat of persecution the gap between appearance and reality within the church has opened up. The faithful are as scattered, isolated witnesses before the massive solidity of the idolatrous empire. This is the most disconcerting aspect of John's vision, setting him more or less on his own (though possibly accompanied by the author to the Hebrews). For the majority of voices in the apostolic generation the church is the primary political reality in the Messianic age; but here its social existence seems to have become attenuated.

Still the church gathers, suffers, rejoices in the world's redemption; still its prayers shape the course of public events, though in an exclusively conflictual way. But for its completion in the public realm, the church needs 'the great city'. The curious thing about the two cities in the Apocalypse, Babylon and Jerusalem, is the continuity between them. This emerges most strikingly in the vision of the two witnesses in chapter 11. There the prophet is told to measure the temple of God and the altar and to number the worshippers; but the outer court is to be excluded from his measurements because it is to be handed over to the Gentiles, who will trample 'the Holy City' for forty-two months. The title, of course, belongs to Jerusalem. We then read of the prophecy and martyrdom of the witnesses, who are slain by the beast from the abyss and left to rot in the square of 'the Great City'. Not another city, but the same. Yet the title 'the Great City', here 'symbolically' called Sodom, Egypt and 'the city where their Lord was crucified' (i.e. Jerusalem, though the holy name cannot be spoken in this context), is later given to Babylon (18:21). A subtle but unmistakable point is being made with this play upon names. Three political communities, ancient Israel, the pagan empire and the eschatological church, are being drawn together in a startling identification. In fact there is only one city, which is at once the Holy City trampled on by the Gentiles and the Great City where Christ was crucified. The community in which God and the Lamb have set their throne is one and the same with the community where Satan and the beast have set their throne. The reason why John of Patmos will not allow the church a distinct social presence is that its witnesses claim back the Great City to become the Holy City.

Just as there is only one true throne, so there is but one structured human community, and there can never be a second. Its name and aspect changes as the God who claims it wrests its government away from the pretender. The church is not apart from it; it is the sanctuary within its midst, and by its acts of witness it enables its transformation to begin. The cry from heaven which John heard at the seventh trumpet, 'Sovereignty over the world has passed to our Lord and his Christ', was not only an announcement for the future; it was a commentary on the scene of the two martyrs, at the conclusion of which 'one tenth of the city collapsed . . . and the survivors, filled with fear, gave glory to the God of heaven' (11:13,15). The outcome of the church's martyr-witness is to call forth the first hesitating and abashed confession of the rule of God, the beginning out of which the Holy City will come to be.

In conclusion, it was possible for the apostolic church to look at the relation of church and secular government from one of two angles. On the one hand, government could be seen as thrust back by Christ's victory to the margins, there to be reauthorised to perform a single function of which the church outside the world stood in need for the time being. On the other hand, it could be seen as goaded by Christ's victory to a last desperate assertion of itself, momentarily overwhelming the church's solidarity in an alternative, massively smothering solidarity of refusal. Either way the victory of Christ was the key to the relation. The Messianic age was to be the age of ultimate choices and conflicts, in which the pluriform structures of political mediation would be propelled to a simple decision between two governments: the creative government of the Word of God and the predatory self-destructive government of human self-rule. In this age that decision must underlie all other decisions.

5.   The church

The authorisation of the church

In Jesus' proclamation the duality of Babylon and Israel has become a frontier in time. He stands at the moment of transition between the ages where the passing and coming authorities confront one another: the rulers of Israel representing the one, the Son of Man the other. The same frontier in time occupies the apostolic proclamation, with this expansion: the future age now has a social and political presence. A community lives under the authority of him to whom the Ancient of Days has entrusted the Kingdom.

So dual authority assumes a distinct form. In Israel's experience we observed two forms: an exilic form, in which two communities lived side by side, the one subject to the other until the day of visitation; and the post-exilic form in which the faithful knew that their structures of government were alien. In both these forms dual authority corresponded to the fractured and enslaved condition of God's people. Now it corresponds to the progress of the victory that God has given them. In the post-exilic community the imperial power protected the holy people until Yhwh should exercise his judgment to secure possession for them. Now their possession is secure, judgment given, the power of God at their disposal. The duality assumes a conflictual, aggressive note, as the rule of Christ within the church presses back upon the old and withering authority of empire. It was not protection that was needed, but that the secular authority should give way. It is a meeting, as Augustine described it, of two 'cities', of two powerful and authorised (though differently powerful and unequally authorised) political communities. 'Two there are by which this world is ruled', wrote Pope Gelasius I, giving notice to the emperor that his authority had to come to terms with a rival. The dual-authority tradition which this expressed, though subject to troubling ambiguities and mistakes, was essentially sound.

A theological account of how this world is ruled, then, must proceed from and through an account of the church. It should not lose itself in the complex suburbs of ecclesiology, a branch of theology threatened more than any other by uncontrolled suburban sprawl; but neither can it afford to take a bypass. Decisions made about the nature of church authority have shaped and still shape what is said about secular government. In this chapter we shall take the essential decisions, and in the next consider the character of the church–state relation as it follows from them. This leaves for our final chapter, still in response to the delineation of the church, the shape and ethos of society.

We begin from two complementary assertions about Christ's rule in the church which set us on guard against two recurrent mistakes. These are, first, the political character of the church's social existence, and, second, the hidden and undisclosed status of the rule which constitutes it. Then, thirdly, we shall indicate some positive criteria for ecclesiology, before, in the second section, filling in this outline with just sufficient content to pro-vision our subsequent explorations.

1. We assert first the true character of the church as a political society. This term is used (of course) analogously. The church is not another member of that category which might be displayed, say, by reading a list of the member-states of the United Nations Organisation. But it is not used metaphorically, as, for example, one may use it of societies which have political features to them but are essentially constituted to discharge a special function *within* society at large. A university, for instance, may think of itself as a 'republic' and elect a 'senate' to 'govern' its affairs; but its affairs are limited to education and research, and, when other concerns come into play among its members, it yields place to the due authorities. Describing the church as a political society means to say that it is brought into being and held in being, not by a special function it has to fulfil, but by a government that it obeys in everything. It is ruled and authorised by the ascended Christ alone and supremely; it therefore has its own author-ity; and it is not answerable to any other authority that may attempt to subsume it.

The powerful sense of political independence continually emerges in the reflections of the early church upon its own position. 'Our citizenship is in heaven', Paul famously remarked (Phil. 3:20). The First Epistle of Peter coun-sels Christians, addressed as 'resident aliens and visitors' (2:11), to defer to institutions and to honour the emperor, but 'as free men' (13,16). The sense of this is given in the (certainly metaphorical) expression which balances it: 'as God's servants'. That is to say: their place within the surrounding community is like that of household staff who cannot be held answerable to one domestic regime because they actually belong to another. In 1 Timothy 1:9 we overhear what sounds like a common opinion in the church: 'Law is not laid down for the righteous, but for the lawless and disorderly', a claim to be free from legislative authority, acknowledging its right but from an independent distance, rather as one might acknowledge the right of a foreign government. Current discussions about the sense of the 'quiet conduct' (*hēsuchia*) recommended to the early Christians is much obscured by a failure to take note of its close connexion with independence (1 Thess. 4:11 e.g.). To be led by the sociological question is too often to ignore or misunderstand the insistence of this community that it forms a *distinct* society.

In the patristic era the same sense of distance persists. Like resident aliens, as a second-century writer saw it, taking up the image of 1 Peter, 'living in Greek or barbarian cities as it may be, following local customs in dress, diet and other daily matters, they display the astonishing, even perplexing character of their own citizenship' (*Ep. ad Diognetum* 5). The emphasis in this famous passage falls on alienation concealed under the appearance of full membership; persecution is the sign that they do not belong. Sometimes independence hardens into resistance. The monks who flooded the city of Antioch in 387 grandly informed the emperor Theodosius' inquisitors that *they would not allow* any executions to take place (Chrysostom, *On the Statues* 17). In the previous year Ambrose had remarked disdainfully to Valentinian II that Christians, instructed by God's law, had no need of the emperor's, which at best could cow the fearful and could never turn the heart to faith (*Ep.* 75(22)). As late as the end of the sixth century, when the energy of this idea had abated, Gregory the Great will still echo the saying from 1 Timothy, remarking that earthly authority is not exercised over *brethren* but over *sins* (*Moralia* 26.46).

To later generations this political self-consciousness could be an embarrassing element in the Christian tradition. The romantic Christianity of the nineteenth century did what it could to convert it into an elaborate metaphor for religious sensibility. 'Where'er the gentle heart finds courage from above . . . City of God, thou art!' The seductive attraction of F. T. Palgrave's famous hymn lies in its success in recruiting all the emotional resonances of the 'city of God' theme in order to subvert and destroy it. 'Not throned above the skies, nor golden-walled afar . . .' Those pounding negatives were clearly meant to deny a great deal more than the author to the Hebrews, from whom they are borrowed, ever envisaged. It is not the material images that are set aside there, but the whole concept of political community, too unsusceptible, as the Victorians thought, of that inwardness which, for them, was the criterion of the operations of divine grace.

To understand the church's independent authority we must speak of its authorisation, which is to speak of Pentecost. Pentecost has no place of its own among the narratives of the Christ-event. It does not make a fifth in the series, Advent, Passion, Restoration, Exaltation. One cannot say of the descent of the Spirit, as one can say of the death and resurrection of Christ, that it was done 'once for all' in the first filling of the apostles. Pentecost authorises the church by uniting it with the authorisation of Christ. It belongs, therefore, immediately to the moment of authorisation, Christ's Exaltation. The church can live under the rule of Christ because Christ has ascended on high and led captivity captive. In whatever sense it is correct to speak of the church as 'beginning' at Pentecost, it is so by virtue of the link between Pentecost and the Ascension, through which the Exaltation of Christ was opened to the participation of his community. But since that moment is not isolated, but sums up the whole Christ-event, so Pentecost unites the church not only with the works of power and public display that attest his triumph but with the service, sacrifice and suffering of Christ, too. Through the Spirit the church recapitulates the whole saving event, Advent, Passion, Restoration and Exaltation. In Christ it is represented in that event; in the Spirit it participates in it. These two aspects of the one relation to the representative act confer the church's political identity upon it. Represented, it is authorised to represent Israel, the people of the Kingdom, possessed of the identity promised to the patriarchs. Participating, it is authorised to be the gathering nations, finding the new world order in the rule of Israel's God. If we forget this, our talk of the Holy Spirit floats free of its Christological reference, and the dangers of Montanism are not far away. Too often the church's life has been discussed in isolation from the historical existence of Christ, a distortion which can lead not only to the charismatic waywardness traditionally associated with Montanism but to the institutional stiffness of self-posited church order.

The simplest way of linking Ascension and Pentecost is to understand the special gifts and manifestations of the Spirit as the consequence of Christ's coronation. In the Epistle to the Ephesians, where the stress falls on the diversity of gifts in the church, they are described metaphorically as a distribution of booty after a triumph: 'He ascended on high with captives in his train, and gave gifts to men' (4:8, adapting Ps. 68:18). A similar conception is maintained in the early chapters of the Acts of the Apostles: the promise of 'power' is the theme of Jesus' last words before the Ascension (1:8), and in Peter's Pentecost speech the connexion is made between Ascension and the miraculous tongues. But as Luke's narrative proceeds, the width of the Spirit's operations emerges: not only miracles of healing and judgment, but effective preaching and witness, the direction of the course of the Gospel's outreach, the forging of a common mind, the confidence to confront rulers, the structuring of the community's leadership, and, indeed, the faithful witness of martyrdom. Something more than gifts is in question: the whole authorisation of the church is conveyed by the Spirit, so that Pentecost can be seen as the moment at which the church comes to participate in the authority of the ascended Christ.

In St John this wider understanding is evident. The coming of the Spirit depends on Jesus' 'going away' (16:7). While still maintaining Luke's association of the Spirit with miracle (14:12) and with effective confrontation of the world (16:8–11), John underlines the pedagogical role of the 'Paraclete' as the one who will guide the church into all truth (14:17,26). St Paul carries the widening of the Spirit's role still further, affirming the complete coextensiveness of Christian faith and experience with the Holy Spirit. 'No one can say "Jesus is Lord" except by the Holy Spirit . . . By one Spirit we were all baptised into one body' (1 Cor. 12:3,12). 'Whoever does not have Christ's Spirit is not Christ's' (Rom. 8:9).

To lose sight of the church's rooting in the Christ-event leads in another direction, too, We cease to understand the church as a society ruled by 'another king' (Acts 17:7). Instead it becomes accommodated to existing political societies as a system of religious practice that can flourish within them, a kind of service-agency (inevitably clerical) which puts itself at the disposal of a multitude of rulers. It assures existing authorities that they will not be disturbed by it, since it does not lay claim to the same ground that they occupy. Its authority is distinguished from theirs as 'spiritual' rather than 'earthly'. Any collision between its claims and theirs is due to a confusion of categories: one or the other, priest or ruler, has misunderstood the scope of his responsibility and trampled upon his neighbour's corn.

One of the sources of this mistake is a doctrine to which an embarrassingly distinguished company has subscribed, Augustine himself among them, that the church was already present in Israel before Christ. In this, of course, there is an element of truth: the church represents Israel in the fulfilment of the promises made to the patriarchs. But if we reverse this statement and infer that Israel represented (or contained, or simply was) the church, two major errors follow. One is to think that Israel is sufficiently accounted for in the church, and so to look on its continued presence as a meaningless survival, so that the church, instead of wrestling with Israel for its own fulfilment, turns its back on Israel as a displaced irrelevance. The other is that Pentecostal authorisation ceases to be determinative for the church's self-understanding. It sees itself as prolonging the ancient faithfulness of Israel (or of a remnant within Israel) subject to many changes of regime. It fails to see in itself the regime that answers Israel's hope for freedom, which was what Jesus proclaimed. The tradition that maintained this false identification had to admit, with more or less shame-facedness, that Israel actually hoped for the wrong thing and that Jesus' proclamation was liable to be misunderstood.

In the late patristic and early medieval periods we begin to meet an important innovation in the Old Testament paradigms for dual authority. The church–state relation comes to be seen in the light of a more ancient, and more functional, duality than that of the exile: the relation of priest and king.

This paradigm then encouraged a universalising religious explanation, in which Israel's practice served merely as the most conspicuous example of a general practice, to be filled out by such anthropological and historical parallels as were available. Imperialists and papalists alike furnished their polemic armouries with demonstrations of what the natural relation of priests to kings had always been. So, for example, Honorius Augustudunensis (s. xii), having traced the superiority of priest to king through Old Testament narrative from Abel and Cain, concludes: 'All gentile histories, too, report that kings payed honour to their own priestly orders' (*Summa gloria* 3).

If papalists resisted this turn to natural religion more successfully, it was because, at the moments of high conflict, the conventional appeal to a traditional distribution of roles did not serve their purposes. At such points the radical displacement of the kings of the earth came into view again, and Christ's triumph re-emerged as the basis of the church's claims. So Gregory VII, in a fury of impatience, appealed to Matthew 4:9 to argue that kings of every kind had arisen at the instigation of Satan, while the priesthood rested upon the commission of Christ (*Letter to Hermann of Metz* anno 1081). Later papalists would take up the Augustinian dictum that without justice kingdoms were large-scale criminal syndicates, and urge, in the interest of papal pre-eminence, Augustine's argument that justice required true and revealed religion. The shortcomings of the medieval doctrine of the papacy must be mentioned in their place; what concerns us here is that the Christological foundation of the papal claims preserved for medieval theology a Christocentric understanding of authority in state and church which was otherwise imperilled. With the abolition of papalist pretensions by the Reformation, nothing stood between the Erastian churches and a purely naturalist account of dual authority.

I take as an example one of the most admirable exercises in political theology of the late Reformation period, a work which offers much to appreciate and which has the additional interest of having missed only by the chance of a monarch's hesitation the fate of becoming an official doctrinal formulary of the Church of England: John Overall's *Convocation Book* of 1606, 'Concerning the Government of God's Catholick Church and the Kingdom of the Whole Worlde'.

Overall's leading theme is the sovereign authority of God in Christ (who, as the Second Person of the Trinity, reigns from the moment of creation), and the mediation of this authority in human communities as something co-natural with created human nature itself. A trenchant dismissal of contractarian theory (half a century before Hobbes!) locates political authority in the Garden of Eden; and an uncompromising assertion of the Fall locates revealed religion immediately outside the garden gate. 'If any man shall affirm, that the Son of God having from the beginning a church on earth, did leave them till the Flood without priests, and priestly authority to govern and instruct them in those ways of their salvation . . .', he concludes, with his mild but somewhat over-used formula of anathema, 'he doth greatly erre' (1.canon 4). The dual line of civil and ecclesiastical authority is traced in unified succession through the Deluge, to be differentiated with the founding of the Jewish nation through the twelve tribes, until (after an uncomfortable intermission of civil authority during the period of the judges) God established the normal pattern with the Davidide succession, with princes who practised their 'authority in causes ecclesiastical' (1.canon 21) and priests who were 'rightly and properly subjects' (1.canon 18), but 'both having their bounds and limits appointed unto them by God' (1.22). The government of Jewish exiles by Babylon, though a degenerate form of government, was, nevertheless, a continuation of the line of civil government, and the restored community owed the Persian administration precisely the same obedience that it had owed the Davidides, even in ecclesiastical causes. The same is said of Alexander and his successors, the Maccabees (skating with some embarrassment over the legitimacy of their revolt) and the Romans. Through the whole period the priestly line of authority ran in parallel, and the Son of God reigned through both lines, as 'head and sole (though invisible) Monarch'. There was always 'One Universal or Catholick Church', and 'as many Persons, Families, Societies and Companies as truly believed in the blessed Seed, without . . . distinction of People, were the true Members of the Catholic Church' (1.36).

Which means that, when Overall comes to the Incarnation, there is very little of political import left to happen. The Incarnation was an act of gracious humility, and we should not, as papalist apologists do, 'attribute sundry virtues, powers and branches of authority unto his humane nature, which do not, in truth, belong properly unto it' (11.1). Grace does not destroy nature. 'In the whole course of his life here upon earth we find not any alteration that he made in the civil state', but rather he submitted to Pilate's lawful authority (11.2). His was a spiritual, not a temporal kingdom (11.3). He treated high priests with great respect, and encouraged his disciples to use the 'ecclesiastical courts' of the Jews (Matt. 18:15! (11.4)). The resurrection made no difference to the authority of civil government. But what of the ecclesiastical? There were, of course, sacramental and doctrinal changes; but Overall wants to stress the *continuity of form* in ecclesiastical government between the Jewish priesthood and the Christian church. Christ modelled his threefold ministry of priests, bishops and archbishops (!)

upon that already established in the 'national church' of Jewry (II.6). The *replacement* of the latter by the apostolic ministry is very lightly touched on.

In a self-betraying moment Overall affirms that Christ was 'content' to be 'only' a spiritual king to rule men's hearts (II.canon 8). The customary genteel anathema is pronounced against the idea that 'he did make them (sc. the apostles) any more partakers of his regal authority, whereof his human nature was then actually possessed' (i.e. by the Ascension) 'than he made their natural and corruptible bodies uncorrupt and spiritual . . . or endowed them in this life with any of the glory, power and heavenly estate which they were to enjoy after their deaths and blessed resurrection' (II.canon 8). The influence of the Franciscan ideal of clerical poverty and powerlessness, so strongly evidenced in Wyclif, is still to be seen in this Jacobite Anglican, who dismisses the idea that the apostles might have had political authority as tantamount to thinking that they might have made themselves rich!

The effect is that the church acquires no distinct identity as a society governed by the ascended Christ. It has become the ecclesiastical system within a community that is primarily structured otherwise, as a civil kingdom. The patterns of Christendom have, it is true, been preserved and (notionally) universalised; but the key element which made sense of the Christendom idea is missing: the eschatology which founded dual institutions in the confrontation of the victorious Christ with the defeated world-rulers and protected them against a loss of tension. Even the church appears to be more rooted in nature than in the Gospel (though formally, in deference to Protestant convictions about the Fall, it is not nature but special revelation that instructs Adam on the duties of priesthood as he turns his back upon Paradise). And as for civil authority, all his insistence on the sovereignty of Christ as Second Person of the Trinity cannot conceal the fact that Overall conceives it as given entirely, and without need of improvement, in creation. He is no more ready to connect it with the *Christ-event* than Luther was – Luther, so often blamed for weaknesses in political theology which other Erastians, and pre-eminently Anglicans, shared!

The extent of the similarity between Western Erastianism and the Byzantine tradition has been much controverted, and, no doubt, will continue to be. We can simply say that once the Greek-speaking church withdrew from exaggerated Eusebian concepts of the emperor as a salvation-historical figure, it settled on the priest–king duality as the key to its political self-understanding. Justinian's sixth *Novella* makes the distinction between priestly and imperial spheres in terms of 'things divine' and 'things human'. Three centuries later the Macedonian emperors describe themselves as 'legal authority' and the patriarch as 'a living and animate image of Christ, expressing the truth by deeds and words'. Co-operation between the two is necessary to secure the felicity of subjects both in body and soul. The ontological contrasts of human and divine, body and soul, distinguish the Eastern idea, and allow for different emphases –

the anti-iconoclasts calling for a tighter limitation on the emperor's ecclesiastical role, the imperialists arguing for the emperor's higher dignity as a point of unity between material and spiritual realms.

2. In the second place, however, we assert that the political character of the church, its essential nature as a governed society, is hidden, to be discerned by faith as the ascended Christ who governs it is to be discerned by faith. Experienced from within, the church is a community of obedience and freedom, a society under the law of Christ, heedful of his commands and direction and enjoying the freedom from all other lordships that he has won for it. Looked at from outside, it presents the appearance of a functional religious organism rather than a political one, having no visible source of government and right save that which is from time to time borrowed from or imposed by other rulers. The 'perplexing character of its own citizenship', described by the *Epistle to Diognetus*, turns on the paradoxical combination of independence and conformity to local law and custom.

'We are citizens of heaven, and from heaven we expect a deliverer to come' (Phil. 3:20). How could the paradox be resolved apart from the appearing of Christ, apart from the resurrection when 'he will transfigure the body belonging to our humble state'? And (we must add, in the light of what was said in the last chapter, pp. 131f.) apart from the glorification of Israel? Yet the temptation besets the church to make its hidden government visible by a representative icon of the ruling Christ. Charged to realise the premonarchical confidence of Israel that it had no king but Yhwh, the church compromises itself when it asserts from its midst a ruling entity to act on Christ's behalf, matching the claims of secular rulers with counterclaims. If Erastianism is an instance of the first mistake, papalism is a striking example of this one. Up to this century the kingship of Jesus has been a favourite theme of ultramontane advocates of papal authority. But it has not always been a supreme pontiff that the church has put up, to rival an emperor; it has sometimes been bishops, to rival regional governors; it has been consistories, to rival town councils; it has been synods, to rival national parliaments; it has even been courts of justice.

When Gregory the Great at the end of the sixth century wrote a handbook for clergy (*Regula pastoralis*), he referred quite ordinarily to them as 'rulers' (*rectores*), and to their congregations as their 'subjects' (*subditi*). The episcopal office was 'the apex of rule' (*culmen regiminis*), and his reflections on its duties include penetrating insights into the inherent tensions in any form of rule, a fact which made the book popular with monarchs who promoted its translation in later ages, securing its position as one of the decisively influential texts of the Middle

Ages. He assumes that the task of a Christian priest is to give direction to various classes of people about their duties in society, as well as to control, by confrontation or accommodation, the 'vices' of his subordinates (II.10). The conception is the more remarkable as Gregory, in dissuading the overambitious candidate for the episcopate, draws attention to Christ's refusal of the role of earthly ruler (1.3), thereby driving a wedge of ominous dimensions between the bishop and the Lord.

Yet it was the papacy which illustrated the danger most dramatically. When Gelasius I, a century earlier, declared: 'two there are by whom this world is ruled as princes', he quickly transformed the priest–king duality, 'the consecrated authority of pontiffs and the royal power', into a direct contrast between the emperor and 'the bishop of that see which the Most High wished to be preeminent over all priests' (*Ep. ad Anastasium*). The verbal contrast of 'authority' and 'power' is not of great moment; the pontiff has his 'judgment' as the emperor has his 'sentence', and the pope is happy to describe the priestly office as a 'power' elsewhere. The distinction lies between the respective spheres of responsibility: 'the reception and appropriate administration of the sacraments' on the one hand, 'what pertains to order and public discipline' on the other. Balance between the two authorities, rather than differentiation, was Gelasius' primary concern; and in this he drew the implications of a century and more of Roman practice in which the popes had carefully modelled their office upon that of the emperors. Contrast this with what was said in the East under similar circumstances, confronting a heretic emperor. John of Damascus (s. viii), in denying kings the right to legislate for the church, appeals to clerical authority, it is true; but it is a different *kind* of authority, founded on the Gospel word and apostolic tradition, scriptural and oral. 'Kings have to deal with political welfare; the order of the church is the business of pastors and teachers . . . We have our pastors who have preached the word and given form to the church's constitutions. We do not move ancient boundaries . . . but hold fast to the traditions as we have received them' (*Or. de imaginibus* 2.12).

The remarkable political and administrative exertions of the papacy in the later eleventh century, culminating in the reforms of Gregory VII, introduced a juridical element into the way in which church authority was understood in the West. At the heart of the reform was the creation of a new corpus of law to govern the church as a juridical society, bringing together acts of councils and popes and making a system of them, ruling the church in itself and in relation to the secular jurisdictions of Christendom. The greatest institutional legacy of the Roman empire, the 'civil law' codified and Christianised by Christian emperors, became the model for the new legal enterprise, the 'canon law', originating in the ecclesiastical structure itself and governing Christendom from its newly defined jurisdictional apex. This law claimed as its particular subjects the clergy, who became defined legally as a people apart, fiscally and juridically distinct from other Christians. More generally, it claimed supremacy for the pope over secular authorities, with the right to depose rulers and to absolve subjects from their oaths of allegiance. The bishops of Christ were the true 'princes' of Christendom, senior in authority to secular princes (Honorius Augustudunensis s. xii) and the pope was to be described quite literally as a 'king' (James of Viterbo – his thesis, ascribing to prelates both *sacerdotium* and *regalis potestas*, was based directly on a juridical interpretation of the sacrament of penance).

Yet from the midst of this reform movement voices were raised in critical questioning: the jurisdictional supremacy of the pope was not translucent with the authority of Christ; it enmeshed him in an impenetrable tangle of secular appeals that detracted from his authority rather than enhancing it. Bernard of Clairvaux's treatise *On Consideration* presses on Eugenius III the responsibility of bringing a quite different style to his judicial tasks, one grounded in the stillness of worship. In principle, Bernard affirms, the pope should have no secular responsibilities at all, since Christ and the apostles had none. But since the times demanded it, he must discharge them appropriately to his office and not imitate kings. Church leaders should 'preside' rather than 'rule'. 'Ruling' – again we notice the association of authority and wealth – is a matter of 'possession'; but 'presiding' is a matter of 'caring' for the household and 'providing'. Though Bernard echoes all the Gregorian claims for papal supremacy, this distinction gives them a significant reorientation: 'It is no ordinary sovereignty.'

We must be clear what this mistake is not. It is not a mistake about the order of ministry as such; it does not consist in thinking that there should be a pope or bishops or synods or courts. The questions whether the church needs a local primate among the presbyters, whether it needs a Petrine office or *pastor pastorum*, whether it needs those who can judge among its members: these can be freely addressed on their own terms in their own place. Nor is it a mistake to think that the structures of the church may be thrown into opposition or rivalry with structures of secular authority. That, on the contrary, is a risk to which the Gospel always exposes the church, which cannot be made to disappear simply by precise definition of their respective spheres of responsibility. The mistake is quite simply to posit an order of ministry, of whatever sort, and to deduce the identity of the church from it, as though *that* were the rule of Christ, and what it encompassed were the true form of Christ's bride!

'Those who are God's are with the bishop!' Those fighting words of Ignatius of Antioch, based on a concept of monarchical episcopacy which saw it unqualifiedly as an icon of Christ's rule, sounded the positivist theme in Christian ecclesiology (*Ad Philadelphios* 3.2). The same theme can be heard again, scored for full orchestra, in Cyprian (*De ecclesiae catholicae unitate* 6): 'Whoever is separated and joined to an adultress, is separated from the promises of the church, and no one will attain the rewards of Christ who has deserted the church of Christ . . . If anyone could be saved outside Noah's ark, one could be saved outside the church!' But the bride of Christ descends from heaven. The church's form is disclosed to us; it is the gift of the Holy Spirit, giving social form to the triumph of Christ. Only as we discern this form can we ask ourselves about the order of ministry that such a church with such a form must have. That is not to advocate indifferentism about ministerial order: there are true and false answers to the questions of ministry. The point is, they are derived, not posited. They are the last, not the first links in the ecclesiological chain.

This makes a contrast between political identity as conferred by Christ upon the church and the identity of political societies as we customarily experience them. The identity of the church is given wholly and completely in the relation of its members to the ascended Christ independently of church ministry and organisation. Of no political community can it be said that it retains its identity irrespective of how, or by whom, it is governed. Political communities come into being and disappear, are absorbed into larger units or fragmented into smaller ones, depending on the governmental structures that prevail at any given time. Whether the citizens of Aberdeen are Scottish, British or European depends upon whether the decisive acts of government that concern them are made (at that point in time) in Edinburgh, Westminster or Brussels. Stratified forms of government, of a federal or devolved type, can, of course, produce composite political identities; but the principle remains that if governmental authority is redistributed political identity undergoes change. But the church's ministry can split, fight and excommunicate itself without the church's changing its identity. From which there derives the ecumenical thesis, so important in the twentieth century: the church's unity subsists in Christ despite whatever wounding divisions.

3. How, then, may we describe the church's political character as a community ruled by Christ? One formal principle must be respected: we are to speak distinctly of the church's catholicity, on the one hand, and of its order, on the other. Two different things are meant by those two terms. The ordering of the church's life *follows* its authorisation as a 'catholic' social reality by the Holy Spirit. The catholic identity of the church derives from the progress of the Spirit's own mission. It is therefore always larger than its ordered structures, taking its shape from the new ground that the Spirit is possessing. It remains for the church's structures to catch up with this mission, to discern what the Spirit has done, and to construct such

ordered links of community as will safeguard brotherly love. Informal Christian phenomena are found all around the margins of the structured church, and to deplore the untidiness of these is simply to betray an ignorance of what that rock is upon which the church is founded. But these phenomena are not 'invisible', as the old dogmatic term expressed it; they are merely disorganised and spontaneous manifestations of the church's catholicity.

An important contribution of the later Reformation to the theory of the church allowed the church-society as such, the historical reality of the Christian community throughout the world and throughout the centuries, to come more clearly into focus. Theologians began to propound a threefold analysis of the church: (i) the church invisible; (ii) the church catholic and visible; (iii) the church particular and organised. This disengaged the 'catholic and visible' church from the heavenly invisibility of the church elect, on the one hand, and from the particular structures of its various institutions (including the papacy), on the other. It marked a definite improvement on the early Reformation distinction between the church catholic-and-invisible and the church visible-and-particular. The earliest appearance of this tripartite analysis that I have found is in an unexpected source: the Thirteen Articles agreed between Anglican and Lutheran theologians in 1538. 'Ecclesia praeter alias acceptiones in scripturis duas habet praecipuas: unam, qua Ecclesia accipitur pro congregatione omnium sanctorum et vere fidelium, qui Christo capiti vere credunt et sanctificantur Spiritu eius. Haec autem vivum est et vere sanctum Christi corpus mysticum, sed soli Deo cognitum, qui hominum corda solus intuetur. Altera acceptio est qua Ecclesia accipitur pro congregatione omnium hominum qui baptizati sunt in Christo et non palam abnegarunt Christum, nec iuste et per eius verbum sunt excommunicati . . . Cognoscitur autem per professionem evangelii et communionem sacramentorum. Haec est Ecclesia catholica et apostolica, quae non episcopatus Romani aut cuiusvis alterius ecclesiae finibus circumscribitur, sed universas totius Christianismi complectitur ecclesias, quae simul unam efficiunt catholicam' (art. 5). This same threefold analysis underlies the relevant discussion in Calvin's 1559 *Institutes* (IV.1.7–9). Surprisingly, it did not influence official formularies. The Anglican Articles (in both Cranmer's and Parker's redactions) were content with the old twofold distinction, as were the Irish Articles of 1615. The Reformed Confessions displayed a tendency to characterise the catholic church in a 'visible' rather than an 'invisible' way, but did not make the distinction clearly. Then, in a lapidary statement of the Westminster Confession of 1647, we find it perfectly expressed: 'The Catholick or Universall Church which is invisible, consists of the whole number of the Elect, that have bin, are, or shall be gathered into one . . . The visible Church, which is also Catholick or Universall, under the Gospell (not confined to one Nation as before, under the law) consists of all those throughout the World, that professe the true Religion; and of their children; and is, the Kingdome of the Lord Jesus Christ . . . This Catholick Church hath bin sometimes more, sometimes less visible. And particular churches which are Members thereof, are more or lesse pure, according as the Doctrine of the Gospel is taught and imbraced . . .' (art. 25).

A description must begin, then, from the catholic church as such, prior to any form of order, and with what identifies it as the community which the Holy Spirit authorises. But is there anything here for a description to get a purchase on? Can we do more than gesture to a formless 'relationship' with Christ about which there is no more to be said? This is the doubt which tempts the church, from time to time, to posit ministerial order in place of its own catholic identity. We can overcome it by recalling that the relation of the church to Christ, to which the Pentecostal Spirit admits it, is itself a formed relation: it is a *recapitulation* of the Christ-event, by which the community participates in the acts and experiences which the Representative first undertook on its behalf alone. The shape of the pre-structured church, then, is the shape of the Christ-event become the dynamics of a social identity. In describing that shape, we may follow the heuristic guide we have deployed in speaking of the Christ-event itself: the four moments of Advent, Passion, Restoration and Exaltation shape a society which continually gathers, suffers, rejoices and speaks.

So when the apostle wished to guide Timothy on how to 'conduct the business of God's household' he referred him first to the catholic shape of the church, the '*mustērion* of true religion', which was the proclamation of the Christ-event itself: revealed as flesh, vindicated as spirit, witnessed, proclaimed, believed and exalted in glory (1 Tim. 3:14–16). The 'pillar and bulwark of the truth' is the concrete social form which, like the Temple buildings that declared the presence of Yhwh within them, gives a structured and institutional announcement of the *mustērion*.

This starting-point, however, does not authorise us to conclude that order is a matter of indifference. Here the tradition of Geneva upheld an important element of catholic tradition in resistance to the spiritualising of the church in earlier Anglican and Lutheran Reform. However distasteful the radical reforms of order which emerged from Geneva were to more conservative Protestants, they shared with Rome a witness to a point of principle which Protestant indifferentism had let go. A certain structuring of the church's life is given with that life. Many local and temporal adaptations of church order are conceivable, and many have been practised. Yet we expect some abiding signs, some marks of identification which will stamp a formal identity on the community and confirm, in instituted practices, that we may look for a 'catholic shape' within it. Catholicity and order are related as substance and form. The latter announces the former, like a headline in a newspaper story; it draws our attention to it, and ensures that its significance is not overlooked. Sacramental theology used to speak of 'badges of a Christian man's profession'. It could be said of all church order that it serves as a badge, telling us what we can expect from this community and entitling us to expect it.

But such a badge will bear upon its face the Christ-event, which has become the catholic shape of the church. This helps us take a further step: it is not the order of the church's *ministry* which announces with formal clarity the fact that this is Christ's community; it is the church's *sacramental* order which does so. A saying of Augustine, influential in the Reformation, points the way to a description of church order founded on the practices of worship: 'Our Lord Jesus Christ has knit together the company of new people with sacraments, few in number, easy of observance, explicit in meaning, such as baptism in the name of the Trinity, the sharing of his body and blood, and whatever other practice is commanded in the canonical scriptures' (*Epistle* 54.1.1 – notice the prominent place given by Cranmer to this quotation in the twenty-sixth of his forty-two Articles: see my *On the Thirty-Nine Articles*, p. 146). The sacraments provide the primary way in which the church is 'knit together', that is, given institutional form and order. Without them the church could be a 'visible' society, without doubt, but only a rather intangible one, melting indeterminately like a delicate mist as we stretched out our arms to embrace it. In these forms we know where the church is and can attach ourselves to it. They are at once 'signs' of the mystery of redemption wrought in Christ, and 'effective signs' which give it a palpable presence in the participating church. This conviction underlay Augustine's case for the recognition of schismatic baptism: where the sacraments of the Gospel were practised, there the form of the church had taken shape – even if the schismatic congregation were not the 'true' church but, like the handmaids of the patriarch's wives, bore children *for* the true church (*De baptismo* 1). Here is another ignition-point which set light to the ecumenical movement: a valid line of ministry does not authenticate a church's sacraments; rather the church's sacraments authenticate its ministry.

We may draw a parallel between the way in which the Christ-event authorises the church's life and the way in which the church's life authorises the sacraments. From the last moment of the four, the Exaltation, there arose the community that recapitulated not only that one victorious moment but all four. In Christ's triumph every aspect of his work was given to the church to share in: his coming, his passion, his restoration and his triumph too. Now another sequence of recapitulating moments begins, from the fourth moment of the preceding series. As the church, in its fourth moment, the moment of speech, prays for the powers of the Kingdom and exercises those powers in prophecy, it is granted cohesion and definition, an 'order'. There arises a series of formed acts and observances, through which in acted speech (performance shaped by the interpreting word, word embodied in performance) it recapitulates the saving acts of Christ once more. These are the church's sacraments.

There have, of course, been both few and many sacraments identified in the history of Christian thought. Neither the scholastic seven nor the Reformation two should limit our perspectives. Writers of our own time have rightly argued that sacramental action diversifies, on the one hand, into many acts, and concentrates, on the other, into the one act of encountering Christ. Around the central few are grouped, quite properly, acts of the church, some of them acts of natural religion like marrying and burying, which in the context of the Gospel fellowship take on a sacramental character as proclamations of Christ's presence in the church. In identifying here four practices of worship, more or less universally maintained, which go back to apostolic use and formally place the Christ-event at the core of the community's identity, we do not mean the figure to be hard and fast. This four is no more final than the four moments of the Christ-event or the four marks of the church's identity. It is a heuristic four, which helps us trace the correspondence of the church's formal acts and observances to the shape of the Christ-event. Baptism and eucharist proclaim, uncontroversially, the Advent of the Christ and his Passion. To mention the keeping of the Lord's Day as a celebration of the resurrection in this context will appear a novelty, but only because the term 'sacrament' has usually been restricted to solemn acts, and excluded solemn observances, for no very good reason. The laying-on of hands (which has appeared in sacramental tradition in at least three guises) belongs inseparably with the prophetic identification of vocation, with prayer, and with the gift of Pentecost.

This is the point from which the question of an ordered ministry, which tradition has too often brought forward prematurely, can properly be broached. I shall say more or less nothing about it; but that is not because I think it may be swept downstream into the sea of theological *indifferentia*. Jesus entrusted Peter with a task of oversight. Unfolding the implications of that act will always be a task for theologians, and when they bear in mind the discussions of the apostolate which dominate two Pauline letters and the extensive references to pastoral authority which fill the Pastoral Epistles, they can hardly complain of a shortage of biblical material to work on. For our present purposes, however, it can be set aside. The essential point has been made when we have contrasted the nature of church order with that of secular government. Church ministries do not replicate or parallel in any way the authority of secular rulers. The kingship within the church is Christ's alone.

> I leave the subject on one side, too, because I have some sense of the difficulties that it poses. A theology of ministerial order has at least two tasks to fulfil, neither of them straightforward. It must render intelligible the partnership within the church of ordained ministry and charism, neither eliding their distinctness nor allowing one to push the other out. And it must interpret the forms in which the ordained ministry has historically been recognised: the threefold ministry of bishop, priest and deacon, on the one hand; the universal primacy on the other. It is not enough to say that these came to be, and that God's will can be seen in them. The whole ecumenical question, after all, is whether God, consistently with the nature of the church, could will, or could have willed, otherwise. If they arise integrally from the nature of the church, rather than as historically occasional aids, we would expect to see branches of the church which have lived without them rediscovering their importance – without necessarily being aware they were doing so. I would be open to exploring (though so tentatively that small type is needed even to suggest it) a correlation of this kind: corresponding to the church's gathering, a ministry of recognising Christians; corresponding to the church's suffering, a ministry of fellow-suffering in service; corresponding to the church's glad recovery of creation order, a ministry of instruction and teaching; corresponding to the church's free prophetic speech, a diverse ministry of administration to build up the community. Could we associate these with primatial-bishop, deacon, presbyter-bishop and lay charism respectively? I leave the question open, to be taken up another time.

Moments of recapitulation

By opening the Christ-event to its participation, the Spirit authorises the church: which is to say, places it *under* and *in* authority, giving legitimacy to its existence, effect to its mission, right to the various relations it comprises. The church represents God's Kingdom by living under its rule, and by welcoming the world under its rule. It recapitulates the Christ-event in itself, and so proclaims the Christ-event to the world. The Christ-event, then, is the structuring principle for all ecclesiology, holding the key both to the church's spontaneous 'catholic' existence and to its formal structure.

1. In response to the Advent of Christ, the church is a *gathering community*. It continually adds to its membership from all existing political and natural communities, as the recognition of Jesus as the Christ is communicated throughout the world. Here we speak of the church's 'mission' – to use a term which draws attention to the responsibility which is laid upon the church. But the responsibility is simply the implication of this aspect of the church's being. It can exist only as a community that is always gathering, anticipating the final state in which mankind as totality will gladly be subject to the rule of God. This is what should be meant when, in the context of formal dogmatic definition, the church is described as 'catholic': the church leaps over all existing communal boundaries and forbids any part of the human race – even the church itself, as *presently* gathered and structured – to think of the Kingdom of God as confined within its own limits and to lose interest in what lies beyond them. Within this process there can still be differentiation, as is shown by the example of Israel and the Gentiles; but that differentiation can only be valid as a genuine mutual concern arises, Israel caring for the Gentiles and the Gentiles for Israel. The barriers have to be broken down before they can become those necessary, even delightful, fences which, according to the proverb, make good neighbours.

> Gathering is the dominant motif of the first two major sections of St Matthew's Gospel, from the point at which Jesus begins his preaching in Galilee and attracts to himself the first four of the twelve. 'He went round the whole of Galilee teaching in their synagogues, proclaiming the Gospel of the Kingdom, healing every disease and sickness in the people . . . And they brought to him those who were ill . . . And large crowds followed him, from Galilee and Decapolis and Jerusalem and Judaea and Transjordan. And seeing the crowds he went up into the hills. And as he took his seat there those who wished to learn came to him' (4:23–5:1). The significance of the Galilean setting is twofold: it is the home of the Northern tribes who were first to go into exile, and it is the point of junction between Israel and the Gentiles. Matthew quotes Isaiah's prophecy about 'the land of Zebulun, the land of Naphtali, the road along the coast and Transjordania, Galilee of the Gentiles. The people that sat in darkness have seen a great light' (4:15f.; Isa. 9:1f.). The twofold gathering, of exiled Israel and of the Gentile nations, has begun. After the Sermon on the Mount the evangelist shows us representative figures coming to the Messiah: a leper who represents defiled and humiliated Israel, a centurion who represents the Gentile world (8:1–13). The second section culminates in the mission-charge,

introduced by Jesus' saying about the harvest (9:37f.). The 'harvest' is a symbol of eschatological gathering and judgment. What Jesus recognises in the crowds pressing to hear him is that the time of final gathering has come. Because this is the case, the disciples are to pray that God will make haste with it; and because God is making haste, the community which has so far gathered is to help in gathering others.

A church that really thought itself 'gathered' would conceive that the Kingdom's coming was complete. Charity and good sense demand that when we meet the term in ecumenical discussion, we attribute some less literal sense to it! To speak of a 'gathering' church, on the other hand, is to speak of a community which, for all the permeability of its skin, has a sharply defined core. To gather is to make a centripetal movement; it is altogether different from merely milling around or associating. The church that gathers must have defined the central point to which it gathers. The apostolic confession of Jesus, 'You are the Christ, the son of the living God', St Matthew would have us understand, is the confession that defines the church as such (16:16–19). (There are equivalents which had currency in the earliest church: 'Jesus is Lord' (1 Cor. 12:3), 'Jesus is the Christ come in the flesh' (1 John 4:2).) In making this confession the church takes upon itself the acknowledgment of Jesus made by the Father at his baptism: 'You are my beloved Son.' Each believer in turn, by making this confession at his or her own baptism, gathers to the church which has received and believed God's word about Jesus. This is the criterion of the church's membership. To recognise those who gather and to claim them for the community; to defy, where necessary, other communities which make rival claims on their allegiance; to rule out those who do not make the apostolic confession: this is the authority which the Spirit confers upon the gathering church.

There follow implications for how the church's *unity* is to be conceived. On the one hand it is a unity that only *becomes apparent* as the limits of the church are shaped historically by the gathering of believers. On the other hand it is based on a fixed central point, the uniqueness of the Christ-event itself, in which the unity to which the church aspires has already been given it. 'By one Spirit we were all baptised into one body . . . and were made to drink of one Spirit' (1 Cor. 12:13). The two poles of what is given and what is aspired to are both expressed in this terse statement. The unity of the body, implicit in the unity of the Spirit, is filled out historically as new Christians are baptised 'into' it. Sometimes, of course, the process of historical definition runs the other way, as those who separate from the body make it clear that they were never prepared to take the apostolic confession seriously (cf. 1 John 2:19).

We should never allow ourselves to speak of a 'contrast' or 'tension' between unity and diversity. Diversity is the historical content of unity, the material in which the unity becomes concrete. Even to put the question in terms of a tension needing some reconciliation betrays a misunderstanding, born of the Neoplatonic conception of metaphysical tension between the One and the Many. Plurality, so far from being a diminution of the divine autarky, is its fullest demonstration. The First Epistle of Peter refers memorably to 'the dappled grace of God' (4:10). Unity is proper to the creator, complexity to the created world. But because the world is created, it has its own way of reflecting the creator's unity, a 'universality' that runs through all its parts like the rhythm one can detect in the sound of a waterfall. When the church, therefore, displays 'differences of gifts', 'differences of ministries', 'differences of operations', it is demonstrating how the world itself is being redeemed. Were it not diverse it could never represent the world; did it not represent the world, it could not embody catholic unity but only sectarian division.

In what, then, does the unity of the church inhere? In the word of God acknowledging Jesus as his Son. As that word defines the membership of the church, so it determines its unity. But does it determine it sufficiently? The apostolic church excluded members for grave sexual sin and for unspecified offences against other members. It regarded love of the fellow-Christian as an essential mark of faithfulness, and treated schism as apostasy. On one memorable occasion Paul declared that for a Gentile Christian to accept circumcision was apostasy by implication (Gal. 5:3f.). How are these concrete demands to be reconciled with the avowed principle that 'no one can say "Jesus is Lord" except by the Holy Spirit' (1 Cor. 12:3)?

The answer lies in the relation between the Christ-event and the last judgment. To confess Christ was to acknowledge and accept that final judgment had arrived. There remained, however, the unfolding of its implications: the demonstration of transforming righteousness, the discrimination of works done in Christ from those done in defiance of him. The life of the church was an exploration of all that was contained in that decisive event and simple confession. The unity of the church in confession implied a moral unity for which it had to struggle by discernment. Some who pronounced the confession would turn out to have repudiated it; yet the discipline of the community was not concerned to raise any *other* standard of membership, but solely to explore and expound what *that* standard contained.

Baptism is the sign that marks the gathering community. It was the sign that marked the community when Jesus himself accepted it; for he came to be baptised by John as the representative of God's expectant people. In accepting baptism, each new believer accepts Jesus as his or her representative, and accepts Jesus' people as his or her people. Identified with him in his baptism, the believer is identified with Israel present in him, and so with the church which is Israel baptised with the Holy Spirit. We say 'each' new believer because existing collective identities have to be set aside and replaced with this new collective identity. Even members of existing Israel had to come out to the wilderness to find God's Israel there. In baptism each person makes vows singly, is addressed singly and (by tradition) given a new name. The prophets of the exile expected that the gathering to Jerusalem must take place one by one (Isa. 27:12, cf. Jer. 3:14).

> The characteristic weakness of defences of infant baptism is that they elide this point. The defence which has most influenced Protestant thinking, that of John Calvin (*Institutes* IV.16), is a clear example. Taking as its starting-point the apostle's comparison of baptism and circumcision in Colossians 2:11f., it draws from this an analogy between membership of Israel and membership of the church. This overlooks precisely the most important difference between Israel and the church as political societies. As the eschatological society, the church is entered only *by leaving* other, existing societies. It is not a society anyone can be born into. There is a better way to understand the traditional practice. Because the community is eschatological, the decision of a person to enter it is not one among many decisions; it is the one, total and final decision of life. For this reason no person may be baptised twice. If the virtue of adult baptism is that it throws weight upon the personal decision of the candidate, its danger is that it invites confusion between the *particular* decision to be baptised and the *ultimate* decision which baptism represents. *That* decision is not taken on a Wednesday! Infant baptism, on the other hand, by locating the sign at a moment when there is no possible particular decision to confuse it with, throws into high relief the eschatological character of the decision to follow Christ. Yet it is still *the candidate's* decision, and no one else's, that is treated of.

2. In response to the Passion of Christ the church is a *suffering community*, engaged in conflict with the principalities and powers that Christ has overcome. Here we speak especially of martyrdom. For John of Patmos the church is in its essence a martyr-community. When the 'first resurrection' is given to those 'beheaded for their witness to Jesus and for the word of God' (20:4), the reader naturally wonders what the author thought became of the ordinary faithful who did not encounter martyrdom. But within the terms of the author's symbolism, there are no such; the martyrs stand for the whole church. Yet, when we pursue the apostolic thinking about Christian suffering, we find that it includes a great deal besides. Actual

martyrdom is simply the focal point of a conflict engaged through every variety of endurance. The word *thlipsis* ('pressure') is often used to mean the pressure that an unbelieving society puts on the church by harassment, threat and violence; but it also stands for a wider range of difficulties, such as the apostle's worries over the welfare of the church and the frustrations of physical weakness and mortality (2 Cor. 2:4; 4:17 e.g.). Another term in common use, *peirasmos*, is notoriously difficult to translate: 'trial' suggests conflict with those outside the church, 'temptation' suggests conflict in the soul, and the word clearly embraces both. One of St Paul's most eloquent passages about the meaning of suffering arises from a chronic physical ailment of his own (2 Cor. 12:1–10). The authority conferred upon the suffering church, then, is the authority to confront and overcome resistance to God's saving will by enduring suffering in whatever form.

The suffering of Christians in the church is, like Jesus' own suffering, vicarious; it is undertaken with and for the community for the benefit of others. This gives a special symbolic weight to those sufferings which arise directly out of the apostolic and missionary endeavour. The apostle suffers in order to hold out to the world the sufferings of Christ which were undertaken for the world. It is not merely a contingent circumstance of the apostolic work; it is a part of the apostolic mission, demonstrating the validity of the apostolic message. In taking his place with Christ upon the cross, the apostle proclaims the cross as the answer to the need of redemption. The apostle 'bears around the death of Jesus in the body, that the life of Jesus, too, may be clearly manifest in the body' (2 Cor. 4:10). It is a distinctive missionary boast, that 'Death works in us, life in you' (4:12).

> The magnificent opening chapter of 2 Corinthians develops this idea at length: 'Just as the sufferings of Christ overflow to us, so through Christ our comfort overflows. If we are afflicted, it is for your comfort and welfare; if we are comforted, it is for your encouragement as you endure the same sufferings that we experience' (4–6). The verb 'overflow' controls the train of thought. Neither suffering nor comfort belong to Paul in isolation. They have spilled over onto him from the Passion of Christ. Christ's sufferings have poured out comfort for Paul, but they have also engulfed him in suffering, and that in turn spills over in comfort for the church. In their turn the Corinthians are to receive suffering too: 'Our confidence about you is strong, as we know that participating in the sufferings, you will participate in the comfort as well' (7). A chain of suffering is established: each suffers for the welfare of others; each benefits from others' suffering. But the chain originates in the sufferings of Christ.

More specifically, the suffering of the church imitates the suffering of Christ in its *double representation* of the righteous God and sinful mankind.

The word 'martyr' carries the primary connotation of 'witness': the apostolic church understood its suffering as a witness both to the righteousness of God and to the sin of the world. The church, like Christ, suffered innocently but in identification with sinners. The Two Witnesses of the Apocalypse (11:1–13), who prophesy for one thousand two hundred and sixty days clothed in sackcloth, represent the church's proclamation. Their prophecy concerns God's righteousness, their sackcloth the guilt of mankind. Their death on the streets of the city 'where their Lord was crucified' re-enacts Christ's act of double representation. In the early church the connexion between suffering and sin was expressed in the role assigned to the 'confessors', those who had suffered for their faith without losing their lives, in the rehabilitation of grave sinners. What made this role appropriate was the perception that in suffering an acknowledgment is made of the justice of God. One who had made that acknowledgment for others was the best help for one who needed to make it.

The eucharist is the sign that marks the suffering community. Of all the sacraments none has been so badly misrepresented by the inclination of the Western theological tradition to individualise. The effectiveness of this sign should not be looked for in a 'sacramental grace' which affects the believer in a different way from other kinds of grace; but in the *formation of the church*. The 'one loaf' binds 'many' into 'one body' (1 Cor. 10:17). It determines the identity of this society by reference to the Passion: it is the community of those who have not only gathered to God's Christ, but have died with him.

After individualism the most serious besetting problem of eucharistic theology has been a confusion over the point of Christological reference. In some patristic traditions preserved in Eastern Christendom but influential also in the Reformation the sacrament has been thematised as a feeding on the living, ascended Christ, a train of thought productive of rich religious imagery but, in conjunction with the corporeal language of body and blood, no theological clarity. The New Testament witnesses no other foundation of the eucharist than that reshaping of the Passover on the night the Lord Jesus was betrayed. The words of institution, 'This is my body . . . this is my covenant blood . . .', define the meal as a participation in the events of Good Friday, just as the Passover formula on which they were based, 'This is the bread of affliction . . .', interpets that feast as a participation in the Exodus. Speculation which posits a second source of the Christian eucharist, a fellowship-meal which celebrated the living presence of Christ, has made two things out of one. What does, however, colour the reference to the Passion is its opening to the eschatological Kingdom. If, as we are told (cf. J. Jeremias *The Eucharistic Words of Jesus*, pp. 255ff.), the Passover Hallel was already interpreted in terms of the Messiah's coming, the eucharist fulfils this note of expectancy, seeing through the meal of Christ's betrayal and suffering the great banquet which was the symbol of God's promised reign. This is what made the note of celebration central to the eucharist, and justified its regular use on the Lord's Day. No re-enacting of Christ's death by the suffering church could be without its affirmation of divine victory.

3. In response to Christ's Exaltation the church is a *glad community*. This is an essential qualification to the martyr-consciousness of the church. For communities that find their identity in the fact that they have been unjustly treated come to depend upon the injustice of others; they need to perpetuate the wrong and to ensure that the oppressor shall not cease to oppress, like Jonah trying to ward off the disaster of Nineveh's conversion. What stands between the church and this pathology is the conscious joy it takes in the resurrection life. 'The Spirit of him who raised Jesus from the dead' dwells within it. From this position of strength it has no need of the oppressor's impotent oppression, and so can offer reconciliation. Forgiveness is the sign that all rebellion against God has been defeated, so that the enemy, too, is liberated from its power. That is not to belittle the evil that may have been intended; it is open to resurrection faith to take evil and forgiveness equally seriously.

When we say that the church is glad in the resurrection of Christ, we point to the meaning of that event as the *recovery of creation order*. Gladness belongs essentially to the creature, as glory belongs to the creator. There is something to say about the glory of the church, too, and of mankind's exaltation to participate in God's rule; but we need know nothing of that as yet. It is enough that Adam has recovered the original joy with which he greeted the creator's glory. If the church's gladness is the gladness of creation, that means it is the gladness of Jesus himself; for this renewed order of creation is present in him. He was the 'first-born of all creation . . . in whom all things hold together', and consequently, in his resurrection, 'the first-born from the dead that in everything he might be pre-eminent' (Col. 1:15,18).

Gladness is a moral attitude, a disposition of the affections appropriate to the recognition of God's creative goodness. Recalling Aristotle's observation that virtue is 'feeling pleasure and pain at the right things', we may say that pleasure at the work of God is pleasure at the right thing. But because we are ourselves God's work, not mere observers of it, our pleasure is part of that good order of things that God has made; so that by delighting in created order, we participate in it. Our very joy places us within that order, and by our gladness the ordered creation of God is made complete.

> The connexion between Easter gladness and the moral life shapes the opening section of 1 Peter: 'Blessed be the God and Father of our Lord Jesus Christ, who in keeping with his great mercy has given us a new birth to a life of hope through the resurrection of Jesus Christ from the dead!' (1:3). The resurrection of Jesus confers new life upon mankind. This life we have received, for God 'has given' it to us; yet it looks forward to a completion still to come, an 'inheritance incorruptible, undefiled, unfading, reserved in heaven for you' (1:4f.). Within this eschatological frame, with the resurrection behind us and the full appearance of salvation ahead of us, we live this life: 'in which you rejoice' (1:6). For joy, even in the face of suffering, of which this letter will have something to say, is the decisive characteristic of the resurrection life. 'You rejoice with unutterable and exalted joy, possessing as you do the goal of faith, the salvation of your souls' (1:8f.). Does this imply that our joy is not strictly joy at the resurrection of Christ at all, but a selfish satisfaction at our own security? No, for Peter has just linked joy to the love and faith with which the church views Jesus: 'whom without seeing you love, in whom without seeing you believe'. Rather, the church's joy at the resurrection of Christ is the expression of its inner well-being, the 'salvation of souls', which consists precisely in being free from sin to participate in the delight with which creation entertains its Lord.
>
> The writer then proceeds with a challenge to resolution and sobriety: 'set your hope to the full upon the grace which is coming to you' (1:13). To live in resurrection gladness and hope is not a matter of momentary ebullience of spirit, but of a settled and resolute attitude. Joy must master our purposes; we must hope 'to the full'. Which means: 'as obedient children, do not be shaped by the desires of your former life of ignorance, but as he who has called you is holy, be holy yourselves in every sphere of life' (1:15). It remains an open question for these members of the church whether their lives will be shaped by that exalted delight which is participation in the new creation of God, or whether they will be shaped by the old and habitual dispositions of the affections.

In this connexion, then, we speak of the *moral life of the church*. Church morality is an evangelical morality. In springs directly from the vindication of God's rule (which is also 'our' vindication, cf. Rom. 4:25) in Christ's resurrection. It is not added to it as a preface (as when dogmatic tradition spoke of 'Law *and* Gospel') or as a postscript (as when it spoke of 'justification *and* sanctification'). Protestant, especially Lutheran, objections that to speak of evangelical morality means no more than a promise of inward strength to keep the law, not a 'new relation to God' (see, for example, M. Honecker, *Einführung in die theologische Ethik*, p. 70), cannot be sustained.

This is a morality of new creation in Christ, the life of a new community constituted by God's acceptance of Christ, promising a world made new in Christ and fit for human beings to live and act in. On the other hand, the Gospel is not simply 'apart from' God's law. The Mosaic Law, the possession of Israel, contained the promise of an active life, awaiting fulfilment in an Israel with the law written on its heart. That fulfilment is now offered. In Christ we may live and act acceptably to God.

The church's active life is based on delight at what God has done. Delight is not a matter of contemplation and reflection only, but of active celebration; yet the activity is founded on something *there*, the handiwork of God, and is not simply self-generated. When we care for our neighbour's welfare, it is because we are delighted by our neighbour: by the sheer facticity of this other human that God has made; by the fact that God has given, and vindicated, a determination of our neighbour to health, rationality and relationship. When we make artefacts and machines to exploit the forces of nature, it is because we delight in nature, both in its raw givenness and in its possibilities for co-operation, and we are glad that God has restored it to fulfil his purposes for it. At the heart of making and doing there lies discernment of what the world is and is meant for. Activity is responsive; otherwise it becomes tyrannous and destructive.

As the church participates in Christ's resurrection it is authorised to live joyfully in the order God has made, and to recover it from oppressive and exploitative corruptions. The church of the New Testament self-consciously claimed the created structures of life and work in community, as we may see especially (but not only) in the so-called 'household codes', a common model of ethical catechesis underlying passages in Colossians, Ephesians and 1 Peter. These have sometimes been thought a disappointingly conservative sequel to the proclamation of the Kingdom of God. The reasons for discomfort are various: it arises from direct quarrels between contemporary liberal assumptions and the convictions expressed in the text – as in the matter of the male presidency of the household; but it arises also from a failure to appreciate what these texts undertake to do. They do not treat household structures merely as part of an unnegotiable social context with which the church has to get along somehow. They repudiate aspects of them, and claim back other aspects.

The catechetical form common to these three New Testament books is not confined to the list of household roles but includes a lengthy characterisation of how the moral life of Christians differs from life lived around it. This is rooted, in each case, in an assertion of the church's sharing in the resurrection or ascension of Christ. The object, in other words, is not accommodation to current norms; it is to show how social structures are retrieved within the new context. The roles of household life are to be reconceived. The parallel passages in Colossians and Ephesians approach the household code by way of an invitation to joyful worship (Eph. 5:18–21; Col. 3:16f.). The codes in these two Epistles then address the attitudes of wives to husbands and husbands to wives, of children to parents and parents to children, and, most disconcertingly to modern readers, of slaves to masters and masters to slaves. All have in common an element of hegemony and subordination. The purpose of the catechesis is to defend that order, while stressing three qualifying factors: the mutuality of the duties; the fundamental equality of the persons; and the practical difference that these two factors make to the way the relation is interpreted.

The code in 1 Peter runs in the opposite direction, from government to slavery and finally, with nothing about children and parents, to husbands and wives. The reason for this is the author's special concern for subordinates who have bad, or at any rate non-Christian, superiors to deal with. (Thus he has little to say about husbands, who do not usually suffer worse from their ill-disposed wives than the small trials of patience imposed by 'weakness', whereas wives suffer much from ill-disposed husbands.) Here, then, the church's community of loving fellowship is not the immediate context. The author is interested in the structures as 'human institutions' (2:13), and it is on that basis that he throws his net beyond the household to include government. Christians are 'aliens and pilgrims' in the midst of social structures that are not their own. Yet still in view is the possibility that these may be reclaimed for the lordship of Christ by the patient self-possession of Christian subordinates. What these relations may come to be appears at the conclusion (3:8ff.). In this case, however, the retrieval of created order rests on the witnessing individual, whose suffering with Christ is the source of his or her authority to reconstruct the expectations of others (3:13ff.).

It is worth exploring this interpretation further in the case of slavery, since it is commonly said that the church simply settled for compromise with this institution. That underestimates what the church believed it was doing with it and the concreteness with which it made the claim that the slave called in Christ was Christ's freedman, and the freedman called in Christ Christ's slave (1 Cor. 7:22). The misunderstanding arises in part from the word 'slave' itself, which to us denotes a social institution altogether apart from the normal structures of economic organisation and exceptionally oppressive in the terms on which it governs the exchange of labour for livelihood. 'Slavery' has existed, for most of the last millennium, only on the fringes of civilisation, as a colonial indulgence or as a sub-political pathology. To the ancient world, on the other hand, it was central to any imaginable economic organisation, providing the only skilled labour-market for the chief unit of production, which was the household business. So the word *douleia* appears in contexts where we might speak not of 'slavery' but of 'domestic service', or quite simply of 'employment'.

What the apostolic church wished to affirm was the possibility of reconceiving the traditional household economic organisation in such a way that its participants stood on a new footing of equality. They were both employees of Christ; they owed him the conscientious performance of their respective duties. The master had to ensure that the servant received 'justice and equity' (Col. 4:1), and was not entitled to use threats (Eph. 6:9). The servant had to conceive his service as a benefit he was free to confer upon one to whom he was bound in a covenant of mutual love and trust (1 Tim. 6:2).

It is wrong to think of the church as simply tolerating slavery because it could not abolish it. It believed that Christ had abolished it. The modern conception of what the early church failed to do is dominated by the thought of legal reform; Wilberforce's battles in the House of Commons become the norm by which the early church is implicitly criticised (and, perhaps, indulgently forgiven). Undoubtedly, the early church had no direct power over the law. But it might have claimed to have taken a more direct route. It knew something about law and liberation from it. With this law, as with all law, the key to freedom was the way in which one understood oneself in Christ. It was the slave-mind which produced unfree behaviour, and Christ had abolished the slave-mind. Slaves who were 'called' were now his servants and therefore no one else's. 'You must not be slaves of men!' Paul exclaimed (1 Cor. 7:21). Did Paul hint to Philemon, it is sometimes asked, that he should free Onesimus? No: because Christ had freed Onesimus without consulting Philemon. Paul makes it clear that he feels under no obligation to send Onesimus back, and does so only that Philemon may be party to the mutual charity which affirms the former slave's status as a brother. There is no place for punitive measures (18). (Paul's letter is not as clear as its commentators sometimes are that Onesimus was converted *after* leaving Philemon's house. Possibly it should be read as a rebuke to Philemon for having failed to treat his Christian slaves as brothers hitherto.) Did legal status count for nothing with the early church, then? Not for absolutely nothing, since Paul is prepared to recommend to Christian slaves that they take any opportunity that comes their way to change their position (1 Cor. 7:21). Yet the essential element of freedom is already there. They have been liberated by the call of Christ, and they occupy their economic and social position with an altogether different standing, and as members of a community which affirms their standing. Slaves and free are differentiated in the church only as Jew and

Gentile are, or as married and unmarried are; it is a difference of social role without concomitant difference of dignity or freedom.

The *keeping of the Lord's Day* is the sign of the church's resurrection gladness. As the sacraments of baptism and eucharist adapted existing symbols of Israel's waiting for the Kingdom (Johannine baptism, the Passover), so it is here: the Lord's Day is modelled on the sabbath. From it it draws two strands of meaning which belong to different historical phases of the interpretation of the sabbath. From the pre-exilic understanding, the holy day celebrates creation in its comprehensive completeness: the putting of work aside marks the acceptance of God's finished work, which is the presupposition for all our own. But now it is Christ's resurrection that completes creation and vindicates creation order. From the post-exilic understanding, the holy day is a mark of the community's identity (cf. Isa. 56:1–8); but now the community is given identity not by its loyal waiting for redemption, but by its participation in fulfilment.

The idea that the keeping of the Lord's Day could be listed among the sacramental signs of the church would seem less novel to patristic theologians than it does to us, who are weighed down by memories of the scholastic definition of the sacramental act. Augustine explicitly identifies the *keeping of Easter* as a sacramental observance (as distinct from keeping Christmas, which is a mere commemoration), because in observing Easter we re-enact the death and resurrection of Christ and represent our own delivery from death to life. And that is why Easter must always be kept on a Sunday (*Ep.* 55.2,16–23), and why fasting on a Sunday gives such justified offence (*Ep.* 36.27–9). The Lord's Day was entirely of and for the church. With almost one accord (Origen stands out in dissent (*Hom. in Num.* 23.4) – and note two other examples given by Lampe in the *Patristic Greek Lexicon* s.v. σάββατον C), the Fathers agreed the Lord's Day was not the sabbath. The third (fourth) command of the Decalogue was ceremonial, not moral, now fulfilled and superseded by Christ. The transference of the observance from the seventh to the 'eighth' day (as they liked to think of it) marked the supersession of time by eternity. The Reformers, on the other hand, treated the sabbath-command like the other nine, as a moral command, and identified the Lord's Day with the sabbath. If the Fathers' line of interpretation weakened the moral significance of the institution, the Reformers' tended to over-moralise it. Karl Barth knew what he was doing when he placed a section on the Lord's Day *at the outset* of his volume on the ethics of creation, not as one moral principle among others but as the ground and reason for all moral principles within the church. Our own interpretation follows his lead.

4. In response to Christ's Exaltation the church is a community *that speaks the words of God.* In 'words of God' two directions of speech are included:

the speech that God addresses to mankind and the speech that he invites mankind to address to him. The church speaks God's words in prophecy and in prayer. Here, then, we come to the glory of the church, its enthronement with Christ at the right hand of the Father, its authorisation to deploy the powers of the Kingdom of God. But those powers are displayed through speech, so that the church's authority mirrors Christ's own, establishing God's Kingdom by God's word.

> When I first tried to formulate a statement of this strand of ecclesiology, I proposed to describe the church as a *powerful* community. But in exploring the picture of the Pentecostal church presented in the Acts of the Apostles and elsewhere in the New Testament I found myself driven to attend to one exercise of power in particular: behind the miraculous healings, the missionary expansion, the multiplicity of charismata and ministries, lay the power of prayer. I revised my proposal, then, and described the church of the ascension as the *praying* church (in unconscious imitation of what Barth so memorably did in making invocation the key to his volume on the ethics of reconciliation). But this seemed one-sided. It failed to register the shockingly unexpected appearance of glossolalia and prophecy in the infant church and the dramatic empowerment of its preaching. Are we to say, in pietist fashion, that it is all an answer to prayer, and that the Father gives the Holy Spirit to those who ask him? Of course, we must say that, too; but it needs the complementary assertion that no one says 'Jesus is Lord' except by the Holy Spirit, and that all our invocation is anticipated by God's speech to us. So finally we characterise the Pentecostal church simply by its participation in the divine speech, which is at the same time God's speech to us and ours to him, reflecting the two natures of Christ in hypostatic union.

This speech is *prophecy*, in fulfilment of the oracle of Joel which Peter recalled on the Day of Pentecost. The church that arose from Pentecost is a church of prophets; but prophecy, as the unbidden, unscripted voice of God, cannot be, as it were, built into the church as a form of official function. The presence of prophecy directs us to the concept of the 'charism', the individual gift of service conferred by God upon the individual member 'as he will', that is to say, quite independent of decisions made by bishop, priest or deacon. It was a perilous temptation for the Calvinists of the seventeenth century, whose chief contribution to the Protestant world had been to reassert the normativity of a structure of ministry, to suppose that in so doing they had prophecy accounted for. The strongest card in their Erastian opponents' hands was to accuse them of turning the charism of prophecy (which could be granted to lawyers, parliamentarians, kings and such like) into a mere designation of the priestly office; in place of the wind blowing freely where it list were heard the clerical huffings and puffings of the synod.

To prophesy is to speak a word from God to the church as it is placed here and now; to declare that the present situation is this, and not that. It is not scriptural exposition: it brings forward something new and of the moment, something not wholly predictable. Yet it is not free and exploratory innovation, but is always predicated upon careful attention to the testimony of Israel's prophets and apostles to the Christ-event. In the light of that testimony, it discovers the present. Its deliveries may be rejected, as inconsistent with the apostolic word, and so false prophecy; they may be added to and complemented; but in a certain way they can never be discussed, because the act of recognition ('*We* are those who have incurred this rebuke! *We* are those to whom that promise applies!) is neither a deductive nor an inductive line of reasoning. It is a discernment that comes either from God or from the devil, and has to be taken or left as such.

Out of all its vocations the church prophesies: its administration, its charity, its music, its art, its theology, its politics, its religious ecstasy, its preaching. Prophecy is the archetypal charism, the paradigm of all the others. The church prophesies to the world, discovering the situation of the world and passing judgment on it. But the individual prophet, like all who exercise a charism, does not address the world immediately, but the church, and, by contributing to the church's prophetic identity, addresses the world through the church. There is no *private* Christian counsel to be delivered to the principalities and powers, bypassing their need to confront the social reality of the church. A theologian, for example, who is invited to participate in an exercise of secular deliberation about matters of social concern, has no independent standing to give advice. Such a one either speaks for and out of the church (not for its hierarchy or synods, of course, but for its faith and tradition) or is a false prophet. Yet this does not imply that the *church*'s concern is wholly with its own integrity and not with the redemption of the world. It is true that the church addresses the world with its being and not only with its talking. But the very essence of the church's claim on the powers of the Kingdom is speech, and God's speech, as the psalmist knew, runs into all lands and his words unto the ends of the world.

The church's speech is also *prayer*, speech addressed to God, from whom it originated, from the whole body on behalf of each charism in it. If the speech of prophecy is given through each charism for the whole, the speech of prayer is given through the whole for each charism. The powers of the church mediated through charisms are given and taken away and given again; they are present intermittently. But the power of this speech is not intermittent; it is given to the church to deploy at all times. It is thus the foundation for every other powerful speech which may be given from time to time, the power which calls upon God for power. It is, of course, true that the prayer of the church is exercised in weakness, and that when the church calls on God for power it acknowledges that it has no power. Yet, more fundamentally, the speech which calls upon God *is* power. The apostolic church believed that, when it prayed, the powers of God's Kingdom were at work in the very prayer itself. The Spirit of God 'himelf intercedes' for a church which does not otherwise know how to pray (Rom. 8:26). In John of Patmos' vision the prayers of the church are represented by a censer: it was an angel who hurled the censer to the earth to produce 'thunder, voices, flashes of lightning and an earthquake' (Rev. 8:5).

The term 'power' (the ability to do things) may be predicated of the church quite generally and non-politically, especially in the context of miracle. To cause a mountain to uproot itself and be planted in the sea is an exercise of power in the simplest sense. We are interested, however, in the authority which accrues to acts of power, and which is, itself a species of power, the power to elicit political co-operation and community. By 'the power of the church', then, is meant 'the authority of the church', its effective enablement to be the political community that it is, the community of God's rule, manifesting his Kingdom to the world. But such a power cannot be exercised statically: like the Kingdom itself it is wholly oriented to its own more complete manifestation. It is the power to call upon God *for power*. The prayers of the church seek one thing only, the final manifestation of God's rule on earth. Nevertheless, because it is called into existence in order to witness to that coming manifestation through its own life and word, it prays also for God's power at work within itself. Prayer is invocation of the Spirit, calling upon God's power *now* to witness to God's power *then*. But since the Spirit is known through a differentiated multiplicity of gifts, prayer for the Spirit is also prayer for the various charisms, the graces given to the church's members individually for service. In praying for one of its members, the church prays for the Spirit to give life to the whole church through a particular calling and endowment.

The Aramaic prayer for the coming of the Kingdom, 'Marana-tha' (1 Cor. 16:22), is matched by the closing prayer of John of Patmos, 'Come, Lord Jesus!' (Rev. 22:20), and, of course, by the Lord's Prayer, in which the three petitions, 'Hallowed be thy name', 'Thy kingdom come', 'Thy will be done on earth as in heaven', are to be interpreted in the light of the central one. But the prayer for the Holy Spirit becomes the paradigm prayer in St Luke, who concludes the parable of the son's requests, where Matthew has a promise of 'good gifts', in the form: 'How much more will your Father in Heaven give the Holy Spirit to those who ask him' (Luke 11:13).

The *laying-on of hands* is the sign of the church's empowerment. By this formal means it prays for the gifts of the ascended Christ to be manifest in the service and discipleship of its particular members. In later centuries three different 'sacraments' of the scholastic seven were derived from this sign: confirmation, ordination and the anointing of the sick. (The practice of anointing and laying-on of hands became inextricably interwoven. Some Carolingian thinkers would have wished to count the anointing of kings, too, as a sacramental act.) In the New Testament there is but one sign, used in different contexts but with a single thread of meaning. It signifies the church's privilege of invoking 'the powers of the age to come', and especially the bestowal of the Holy Spirit. The Spirit is invoked in circumstances of weakness, in the face of illness or before tasks impossible to perform without divine aid, and the laying-on of hands calls for the invasion of God's power to break the fetters of impotence. But especially this sign invokes the Spirit to the aid of the individual believer. It singles out someone for whom, because he or she is a new member of the body, faces a supreme threat from the powers of death, or has a particular task of great difficulty to perform, it especially implores the effective working of God. Although it is true that in this sign, as in the others, we have to do with a mark of the community, not with a private transaction of grace, it guards in a distinctive way against collectivism. It forbids the church to lose sight of the needs of its individual members in the mass; it enables the church to single a particular person out and to direct its prayers towards that person's needs. For this reason it is especially suited to accompany baptism (or, in the case of infant baptism, to accompany the later renewal of baptismal vows), for there, too, the responsibility of the individual becomes the matter for the church's corporate act. The wider use of the laying-on of hands (not only in the formal contexts which have become traditional) could do much to maintain the right relation of the individual believer to the community, and protect the church against the dangers of institutionalism and clericalism.

The use of the laying-on of hands has the most impressive of New Testament credentials. On four different occasions we read of Jesus' laying hands upon the sick (Mark 6:5; 8:23; Luke 4:40; 13:13); and on one occasion upon children to bless them (Mark 10:16||Matt. 19:15). In the Acts of the Apostles it is used for healing (9:12,17; 28:8); for commissioning or ordination (6:6; 13:3); and in invocation of the Holy Spirit upon newly baptised disciples (8:17ff.; 19:6). In connexion with ordination it is mentioned three times in the Pastorals (1 Tim. 4:14; 5:22; 2 Tim. 1:6). The Epistle to the Hebrews includes it in a list of basic teachings that are given in elementary catechesis (6:2). Finally, the longer ending of St Mark includes the promise that those who believe 'will lay hands on the sick and make them well' (16:18). References to anointing of the sick should also be noticed in Mark 6:13 and James 5:14. The two incidents in Acts where hands are laid on new believers after baptism make an explicit connexion with the prayer for the bestowal of the Holy Spirit; but it would be wrong to think this association confined to those two cases. At Acts 13:3 Paul and Barnabas were commissioned in response to prophetic direction from the Holy Spirit. The two references to Timothy's ordination (1 Tim. 4:14; 2 Tim. 1:6) both connect the laying-on of hands with charism.

What narrative coherence, finally, can this sequence of church moments lay claim to? It is a serious question; since the Christ-event itself is one drama of redemption, not a series of dramas, an authentic imitation of Christ could hardly take the form of four dissociated tableaux. Unless they recapitulate its narrative coherence, the moments of the church can have no internal relation to each other; and that will mean we end up arbitrarily plumping for one sole mark of the church in preference to the others. The evangelical church of mission, the romantic church of suffering, the bourgeois-liberal church of social responsibility, the catholic-charismatic church of triumph: whichever we choose, it will be *the* church, permanently valid for us against all challengers. Yet not every way of construing the church moments or the sacraments as narrative carries conviction. In the late patristic age it was sometimes thought that the sequence of suffering and glory could be read out of church history, so that since the conversion of the empire the age of martyrdom had passed for ever. This, as Augustine saw, had failed to understand the struggle of the times and had ceased to long ardently for the church's perfection. In medieval scholastic tradition, on the other hand, the sacraments become assimilated to a biographical narrative of human development and growth: baptism for birth; confirmation for growth; eucharist for regular nourishment; ordination for socialisation; marriage for propagation of society; penance for healing; extreme unction for death; dissolving the signs of church identity into rites of passage.

These approaches fail because they look for an *external* narrative, following the apologetic law which demands the explication of the mystery in terms of what is plain already. The narrative we need to discern, however, is the *inner* logic of the sequence, the logic of the dawning Kingdom of God which the sequence itself makes plain. If we approach in reverse, and ask what each church moment presupposes, this logic can emerge more easily. Prophecy must be tested to discern the true from the false, and the true is known by the context out of which it arises. Church speech is authenticated by the moral quality of the society that generates it: happy relations shaped by resurrection, enemies forgiven, community rebuilt, creative possibilities of work and family reclaimed for humane enjoyment. The ethical test proves and reproves what the prophets say. But the moral life, however integrated, cannot speak of resurrection unless it has been won through resistance and suffering. The church's happiness is not the fragile happiness of Eden which we may think we discern in innocent societies spared the degradations of technological and ideological imperialism; nor is it the too-determined happiness of alternative communities that have resolutely turned their back upon the world. It presupposes struggle, it is proved through the pain of treachery and tragedy. But then, again, the struggle is not self-authenticating either. Suffering can be merely stubborn and perverse, or merely pathetic and ineffectual. Church suffering is founded in the welcome shown to the achievement of God's purposes for the world. To suffer well one must suffer for the thing worth suffering for. That requires a recognition of reality (which we call 'faith'), the ground from which the sequence of suffering, joy and testimony flows, each stage adding a completion to the one before. Church existence unfolds in its due and proper order, with its beginning, its middle and its end. In history, as in any individual life, the beginning, the middle and the end are sounded together; yet, like a tune played in counterpoint, the whole consonance is understood because the beginning, the middle and the end can still be heard for what they are.

6.   The obedience of rulers

Christendom: the doctrine of the Two

Christ had gone up on high; he had led captivity captive, and given gifts to men. So the nations and rulers of the world were confronted with the rule of God, triumphantly present in a community that owned no other rule. No account of the pre-Nicene church can do it justice if it overlooks the extraordinary missionary triumphalism to which this faith gave rise. These Christians saw themselves riding on the wave of the future, conquering society with the word of truth and the blood of the martyrs, God's own strategy for success. It was only a matter of time before the pagan empire, too, with its repellent idolatry, would yield before Christ's army. And so it happened (as it seemed) at the Milvian Bridge.

We distinguish two frontiers within the Gentile mission: the church addressed *society*, and it addressed *rulers*. Its success with the first was the basis of its great confidence in confronting the second. The logic of this distinction is given in the very idea of God's rule in Christ. Society and rulers have different destinies: the former is to be transformed, shaped in conformity to God's purpose; the latter are to disappear, renouncing their sovereignty in the face of his. The distinction must, then, be reflected in our systematic thinking about the political content of the Gospel. Political theology must have something to say about society and something to say about rule, and the two must be coordinated. And the best order might, perhaps, be the missionary order: society first, government after. The truth in that order is that Christ has conquered the rulers from below, by drawing their subjects out from under their authority. There is, however, a strong reason for making the opposite approach. Our present situation, conveniently called 'post-Christendom', requires us to address especially the challenge of society; it has as its backdrop that centuries-long engagement with government which we call 'Christendom'. There is everything to be said for our learning to address *this* frontier out of the experience the church has gained from addressing *that* one.

With the vast change of context catalysed by the Edict of Milan the question of how to understand the obedience of rulers came high on the church's agenda. There is no point in regretting this. The church of that age had to do contextual theology just as we do; nor did the evolution of the missionary questions into political ones strike anybody at the time as constituting a volte-face. This was the logical conclusion of their confidence in mission, the confirmation of what they had always predicted. The kings of the earth had come to bow before the throne of Christ, and the empire they had served had lost its most powerful agents. When Nineveh the imperial city repented and believed, Augustine taught, Jonah's prophecy was in sober truth fulfilled: Nineveh was overthrown (*Serm.* 361.21; *In Ps.* 50.12).

What claim has this 'Christendom', this millennium and a half of respectfulness on the part of Gentile lords, upon our interest now? Not the claim of revelation, certainly, which is the claim of Israel and the Christ. Nor even the claim of tradition, since tradition is continuity, and its claim is the claim of what has proved its worth by survival. We now have little continuity with Christendom; it is not our tradition any more; its assumptions are alien to us. Its claim on us is simply that of witness. It attests, as a matter of history, the actual impact of the Christian faith on European politics, and it expounds this impact in its developed political reflections. Those who ruled in Christendom and those who thought and argued about government believed that the Gospel was true. They intended their institutions to reflect Christ's coming reign. We can criticise their understanding of the Gospel; we can criticise their applications of it; but we can no more be uninterested in their witness than an astronomer can be uninterested in what people see through telescopes. And while no testimony to Christ can safely be ignored, this one lays claim with a special seriousness; for although it is no longer our tradition, we are its *dénouement*, or perhaps its *débâcle*. It was the womb in which our late-modernity came to birth. Even our refusal of Christendom has been learned from Christendom. Its insights and errors have fashioned, sometimes by repetition and sometimes by reaction, the insights and errors which comprise the platitudes of our own era.

Christendom, then, offers two things: a reading of those political concepts with which Scripture furnishes us, and a reading of ourselves and of our situation from a point of observation outside ourselves but not too far outside. Either of these readings we are free to question or to doubt; but for neither of them can we find a ready substitute. The more the political character of Israel's hope engages us, the more we need to know how it has actually shaped the government of nations. The more the problem of our own modernity engages us, the more we need to see modernity against its background.

I use the term 'Christendom' (in keeping with a good deal of current discussion) to refer to a historical idea: that is to say, the idea of a professedly Christian secular political order, and the history of that idea in practice. Christendom is an *era*, an era in which the truth of Christianity was taken to be a truth of secular politics. (I note that the *Shorter Oxford English Dictionary* (1993) does not recognise this sense, but only ('Christendom' 3b) the older geographical sense in which the Christian 'domain' formed a parallel to the *dar al-islam*. But it seems to be undeniably in current use.) Let us say that the era lies between AD 313, the date of the Edict of Milan, and 1791, the date of the First Amendment to the US Constitution, though these moments are symbolic only, and others could no doubt be found that would do as well. In the course of this period the idea of Christendom developed and underwent corrections and elaborations; sometimes it was taken to imply more, sometimes less. Yet the idea is always there, giving a unity to the whole era which entitles it to the name 'Christendom': it is the idea of a confessionally Christian government, at once 'secular' (in the proper sense of that word, confined to the present age) and obedient to Christ, a promise of the age of his unhindered rule.

The rulers of the world have bowed before Christ's throne. The core-idea of Christendom is therefore intimately bound up with the church's mission. But the relationship between mission and Christian political order should not be misconstrued. It is not, as is often suggested, that Christian political order is a *project* of the church's mission, either as an end in itself or as a means to the further missionary end. The church's one project is to witness to the Kingdom of God. Christendom is *response* to mission, and as such a sign that God has blessed it. It is constituted not by the church's seizing alien power, but by alien power's becoming attentive to the church.

The sympathetic account of Christendom (*chrétienté*) with which Jacques Ellul opens his book *Les Nouveaux Possédés* is weakened by a failure to grasp this point. In his insistence on the voluntary character of the Christian social order, Ellul conceives of Christendom as a project of the church. 'Christendom is not a religious society emerging from primitive religious impulses which translate themselves into social forms, but the outcome of a conscious and voluntary operation. How is society to be rendered Christian? Or: how can the Christian faith be made to impregnate every level of life, private and collective? What these Christians wanted, in fact, in their gradual creation of Christendom was a "social ethic"; but they took that more seriously than we do, courageously addressing the task of applying the ethic and transforming the structures effectively to correspond to what they understood as goodness and truth. And they succeeded' (pp. 12f.). But I doubt whether anybody asked such overt social-engineering questions. The questions they did ask were of the kind: 'how shall I, as someone responsible for making *these* decisions, make them in obedience to Christ's command?' The traditional structures simply yielded ground as their officers sought to act under the authority of Christ.

In its primary form, then, the Christendom idea supposes the *vis-à-vis* of church and secular government, as distinct structures belonging to distinct societies and, indeed, distinct eras of salvation-history. Until the end of the patristic period this *vis-à-vis* is constantly in evidence, and the meaning of the Christian empire as a *capitulation* to the throne of Christ is not forgotten. With the replacement of the empire in the West by the Germanic kingdoms, however, a new perspective emerges, that of a single, homogeneous society with twin foci of authority. The missionary context falls away, and we are left with a Christian society led by kings and bishops. We can distinguish the two conceptions, perhaps, by borrowing terms from Luther and speaking of a Two-Kingdoms-Christendom and a Two-Governments-Christendom doctrine. The one supposes that the conversion of rulers leaves the underlying social *vis-à-vis* exactly where it was. The other introduces a unified doctrine of society holding the twin peaks of authority together in a common social context. The ambiguities which surround the Christendom idea arise chiefly from this latter development of it.

Yet even within medieval Two-Governments-Christendom a variety of interpretations of the doctrine proved possible, and it is not misleading to see the successive phases through which it passed as a series of attempts to reassert the missionary *vis-à-vis* by establishing further differentiations within Christian society. The papalist revolution of the eleventh century attempted to disengage the clergy from the structures of society in order to establish a distinct juridical order with superior authority. The mendicant movement of the thirteenth and fourteenth centuries attempted to identify an apostolic missionary class set apart from property and rule. And the Calvinist and Tridentine reforms of the late sixteenth century attempted to redefine autonomous structures of ecclesiastical government. Far from seeing Christendom, then, as an age in which the missionary challenge of the church became derailed, we have to understand that it was perpetually preoccupied with that challenge. The question which created the turbulence of church–state relations in the West was how the sign of Christ's victory could be protected against subversion, which would leave the church in a Babylonian captivity to its own Christian rulers. It was always understood that the church had not attained its final glory 'merely because the kings serve it, wherein lies greater and more perilous temptation' (Augustine, *De perfectione iustitiae* 15.35). The temptation was precisely to see the conversion of the rulers as achieved and complete, and to abandon mission. And so the structures set up to recover the church's mission in the eleventh century were attacked as an obstacle in the fourteenth; while the other-worldly de-structuring encouraged in the fourteenth was itself seen as a dangerously restrictive thing by the late sixteenth.

This overall view must be given some more detailed substance.

1. The rout of the demons. The perspective of the church at the height of the Constantinian moment, more especially a Greek perspective, perhaps, but more broadly representative, too, of the enthusiasm generated by the great change, can be judged from two speeches which Eusebius of Caesarea delivered in the fourth decade of the fourth century, subsequently transmitted together under the title *Laus Constantini*. These have come to be seen as the archetype of ignoble theological legitimation, the epitome of 'Constantinianism'. Their faults are certainly glaring: not only the encomiastic halo in their portrait of the emperor, but also the Logos-Christology, 'semi-Arian' as it will come to be called, contribute to the view of Constantine as a kind of Christ-surrogate. The later speech, especially, celebrating the thirtieth anniversary of the emperor's accession, gives the impression that the Christian Gospel amounts to not much more than monotheism. Still, from beneath the surface of this self-conscious culture-Christianity there emerge unexpected traits of Christian authenticity.

The key lies in the passionate challenge addressed to those who doubt the Christian affirmations of the resurrection, to 'decide by manifest effects whether to acknowledge the mighty acts which Christ even now carries on to be the work of a living agent' (16). Eusebius is the apologist for revolutionary events which have reshaped the world around him. 'It is as it were an event of yesterday that an impious and godless race confounded the peace of human society and possessed mighty power.' He challenges us with that disturbing authority which belongs to those who have lived through transformations and have a testimony to give: 'Mine eyes have seen the glory of the coming of the Lord!' Those of us who have not lived through them assess them from a different point of view, knowing more about their context and their outcome; we find fault with the way in which contemporary agents acted and contemporary chroniclers expressed their significance. Yet at a certain point we are simply dared to disbelieve. Later Byzantine apologists drew from Eusebius a cosmic understanding of the emperor's role: divine sovereignty is mediated by the Word of God to the King, who, conforming his rule to God's, becomes a kind of paradigm man, the philosopher-king of the Platonic tradition. They could not replicate Eusebius' sense of shocking novelty. Only now has the royal man appeared. Though man was royal from his creation, it required that the Logos should cherish the seeds of reason he had sown, call out a company of men and women who would follow him, and fill the whole world with his doctrine; only then could the 'transcript' or 'similitude' of the heavenly kingdom appear on earth, conquering the twin evils of barbarian war and polytheism.

Eusebius maintains the view, well known to the pre-Nicene church, that the beginning of the Roman empire coincided with the Christ-event as a sign of the rout of the demons. The plurality of national governments was an aspect of polytheism, the creation of a single empire a fulfilment of the prophecies which pointed to a universal reign of God. The abolition of human sacrifice was another sign of the same kind. Yet these were merely formal indications. The substance of God's sovereignty in the public realm was not seen until Constantine arose 'to follow up the victory' (7). For an undoubted legitimator, Eusebius is reckless with one element in Constantine's legitimacy, the succession of the imperial office itself. But the empire had shed the blood of Christian martyrs. Constantine's predecessors and rival Augusti are dismissed as 'persecutors of Christians' and he is celebrated for defeating them. Eusebius remembered the earlier theory that good emperors were rewarded by God and tyrants punished; but, with the honourable exception of his father, Constantine seemed to have been the *only* good emperor, 'alone of all that wielded the Roman power . . . the friend of God' (*Vita Const.* 1.3). He had grown up (a revealing simile) like Moses in Pharaoh's court (*Vita* I.12). He was God's champion, not the heir of the Caesars. It was not the conversion of the empire that occupied Eusebius' thoughts but the overthrow of its tutelary deities.

The essential factor in the Constantinian moment, then, was the victory of God. Was this victory the Parousia? Structurally, at least, it seems to fill that place. There is no distinct future horizon, and Eusebius is even willing, though with philosophical stipulations, to describe the regime as 'eternal' (*Laus Const.* 6). The divine rule, with all its attributes, had become luminously present in the royal man. It is as though the eschatological horizon of all political theology has, in the moment of astonishment, come to be spoken of as present. Subsequent generations were left with two corresponding tasks: to recover the future horizon and to redefine the present boundary between God and Caesar, yet in such a way as to acknowledge what had changed.

2. Redefining the boundary. In withdrawing from the Eusebian impasse, the church interpreted the contrasting roles of emperor and bishop in terms of the transition from the old age to the new. The anonymous fourth-century Roman theologian known to us as 'Ambrosiaster' put into currency a pregnant phrase: 'a king bears the image of God, a bishop the image of Christ' (*Quaest. vet. nov. test.* 35). (It was precisely as *Christ's* image that Eusebius had celebrated Constantine!) Christ's image is, of course, also the image of God; but God's image in Christ is specific and climactic; it belongs to the end of history and the dawning of the Kingdom of God. It is an older and more universal divine presence to which the authority of government attests. Reminding the emperor that his was the *old* order only was but one strand in the fourth-century redefinition. The other was reminding him that he was none the less expected to behave as a Christian. Skilfully deploying both these strands in argument with a succession of emperors we encounter the commanding figure of Ambrose of Milan.

On the one hand the church existed on its own (that is, the Gospel's) terms and could not compromise autonomy. The icy remonstrance that Ambrose addressed in AD 386 to Valentinian II focusses the point clearly. The emperor proposed to sequester a major church to accommodate an Arian congregation; the bishop declared him incompetent to do so, quoting a formula of the emperor's father, Valentinian I, that 'the judge in a cause of faith or of church order must be sufficiently senior and of the right jurisdiction'. What Ambrose deduced from these words was striking: 'only bishops should judge bishops, only priests priests, and that in cases of other kinds as well, where moral allegations are made against a bishop' (*Ep.* 75(22)). This amounted to a claim for considerable clerical exemption from imperial jurisdiction. The elder Valentinian had intended to allow some immunity against lesser governors; Ambrose determined to establish a complete independence of the church's affairs from secular jurisdiction. He refused to attend the emperor's consistory to defend the catholic cause because it was not the right place to debate the church's business. 'Matters of faith should be handled in the church', he declared, and added: 'before the people'. It was a *public* sphere, this sphere of ecclesiastical jurisdiction! And to rub salt into the wound: he neither knew nor cared to know 'the secrets of the palace'!

Is the church now redefined as a society of clergy? Throughout the fourth century there was a tendency to find a core-church within the church which conserved the church's distinct identity; for others the monks and ascetics played this role. Ambrose struggled, like other bishops, to achieve exemption for his priests from municipal responsibilities, for the sake of which he was happy to accept the severe terms of a law preventing them from inheriting legacies. But it was not the priests as such but the church building (which included the priests' residences) that defined the church. The laity, by gathering with their bishop there, proved their identity as the Christian society. Ambrose discouraged pastoral visiting in the homes of laity. The proper place for Christians to meet their clergy was the basilica, which had something curiously like the status of a modern embassy.

On the other hand, the emperor, refused the privilege of interfering in the church's affairs, was himself by no means immune from interference. 'In a case of faith', Ambrose reminded Valentinian, he was subject to the bishop's jurisdiction. The church expected the emperor to act like a Christian, and when he failed to do so it claimed the right to censure him. On several occasions Ambrose withdrew communion from emperors, sometimes for moral, sometimes for doctrinal causes.

The emperor should act like a Christian, but like a Christian exercising an alien function. Ambrose inherited an established convention which allowed a bishop the right of intercession on behalf of those condemned to death or long imprisonment. The logic of the convention was, in effect, subversive. It expressed three perceptions: that the task of rulers was to judge; that a Christian ruler should show clemency; and that there was an inherent tension between the two obligations. The bishop represented the coming Kingdom of Heaven and the present community of forgiven sinners, both of which pressed in upon the exercise of secular judicial responsibility. 'It is necessary for judgment to yield to religion', he declared in a succinct statement of salvation-history. Christ had neither acquitted nor condemned the woman taken in adultery; he had simply made the prosecution withdraw, so that the trial collapsed. The bishop would not question the emperor's decisions; he would demand nothing of right; he would give the emperor no help in the task of prosecution (Ambrose was appalled to learn that two bishops acted for the prosecution of Priscillian of Avila). He would merely urge the emperor, with all the solemnity he could command, to remember that he, too, stood in need of mercy. The two represented different aeons living by different principles. If in the end these two conflicted, it would be for each to act out the logic of his role, the emperor doing to the bishop 'as royal power is wont to do' and the bishop suffering from the emperor 'the fate a priest has to bear' (*Ep.* 68(26)).

Yet the Christian emperor was, as it were, a spy in his own camp, an uncomfortable situation which the bishop could do little to make more comfortable. It was not for the church, Ambrose insisted, to condemn any secular official who, in that situation, did his best within the terms his role dictated. Christian governors should not have to fear ecclesiastical sanction if they made lawful use of the death penalty, though they deserved credit if they could avoid doing so (*Ep.* 50(25)). However, in his famous confrontation with Theodosius I in 390, which ended in the emperor's doing public penance for the massacre he had ordered of the citizens of Thessalonica, Ambrose drew a line. By the standards of the age Theodosius had been harsh, though not unprecedentedly so. In censuring him the church took up the task of judging judges, and began the slow work of reforming the criteria of earthly justice, marking certain acts of retribution out of bounds. In his lectures to the clergy the following year Ambrose advanced the claim – a legacy from the pre-Nicene church but now charged with new significance – that what pagan philosophers had thought of as justice, retaliation for wrong received, 'has been set aside by the authority of the Gospel' (*De officiis* 1.28.131). Justice is to have a new, evangelical content.

> That Christian emperors should not act against the church seemed obvious; and in that century of heresies and anti-heresies, it seemed equally obvious that this meant not helping heretics, nor, indeed, pagans, now vigorously reacting to their dispossession of the public realm. Ambrose was ready to use the weapon of suspension from communion against rulers who behaved to these groups in ways that strike a modern susceptibility as merely equitable. Perhaps modern susceptibility does not do him justice, for it is quick to assume the possibility of a neutral and impartial relation of government to religious rivals, an idea with its own difficulties and which no party to those struggles conceived of. But this excuse hardly extends to the most notorious case, in which Ambrose used his right of intercession to dissuade Theodosius from punishing a bishop who had roused a mob to burn a Jewish synagogue. The Christian emperor was expected to stand back from his judicial obligations and encourage the forward march of history, of which the outcome, as he knew, must be the overwhelming of the Old Covenant by the New: 'it is necessary for judgment to yield to religion' (*Ep.* 40(74)). Here, as so often, what we must chiefly regret is the lack of an adequately Pauline theology of Israel.

If Ambrose derived his aggressive posture from the confrontation of the two communities defined by 'judgment' and 'religion', Augustine allowed for some slackening of the tension between them. It was, he thought, an inevitable feature of the age in which the good and the bad had to mingle like fish in a net, that the church should suffer a partial lack of visible definition over against the world. It was enough that the two were distinguished by polar opposite moral principles ('Two loves made two cities . . .', *City of God* 14.28) and by final separation on the day of judgment. In the mean time an ambiguous sacramental definition sufficed the church as it passed through the earthly city's realm and made use of its transitory peace in the course of its pilgrimage. It was the duty of Christians in this age to 'tolerate the evil' and to 'bear with sinners' (*Serm.* 4.20; 47.6). This was no time for apocalyptic confrontation with Christ's adversaries, who might yet, before the end of the age, become his friends. As he urged the military commander Boniface: 'We should not before the appointed time desire to live only with those who are holy and righteous' (*Ep.* 189).

But toleration was compatible with a certain pastoral correction, which was the discipline extended by the church in love to its wayward members. And with the emperor a member of the church, it was possible to see his role, too, as part of the 'moderated severity or rather clemency' which the church practised. The sharp distinction between political and pastoral tasks began to be smudged over as emperor's and bishop's roles converged upon a single end, 'the common good and the security of the republic', an end which was, in fact, nothing other than God himself (*Ep.* 137:17; 138.10). The soldier's office, too, has become an office of mercy to those who require protection (*Ep.* 189). Again, the story of the adulterous woman was a paradigm. Jesus did not suspend the course of judgment, as Ambrose had suggested; he himself exercised judgment, ruling like a higher court upon the inadequate proceedings of the lower one (*Serm.* 13.4; 16A.4; *In Ps.* 50.8; *In Ioh.* 33.5). Justice will not yield to mercy, but be elevated by it.

The intersection of secular and ecclesiastical leadership is best represented in the pastoral metaphor, which Augustine thought applicable to either role. His lengthy exposition of Ezekiel 34 (in defence of the coercion of the Donatists) announced the ideal of a Christian ministry that had taken on important aspects of community government (*Serm.* 46, 47). This model had some implications that alarm us and others that reassure us. It justified the official coercion of heretics as an act of adjunct pastoral care performed for the assistance of the church by the Christian emperor. It also allowed Augustine to express, in terms that only just stop short of outright condemnation, the church's great dislike of the death penalty, a form of punishment ill adjusted to the pastoral orientation of the merciful judgment introduced by Christ. Yet it is essential to recall that these assimilative moves at the level of leadership are founded upon the *Leitmotiv* of two cities. Though mingled and confused, these were distinct social entities, each with its principle, 'self-love excluding God [made] the earthly city, love of God excluding self the heavenly', and each its political expression, Roman empire and church respectively. The Christian emperor was in the end simply a penitent Nebuchadrezzar, the church a triumphant Shadrach, Meshach and Abednego (*Ep.* 93.3.9).

> For the definite identification of the two cities with Rome and the church, often denied, cf. *Ep.* 95.5 and *City of God* 16.2.3 respectively. On the misunderstanding of the two cities as purely ideal entities, and the corresponding interpretation of earthly political society as a morally neutral *tertium quid*, I refer to my discussion of *City of God* 19.17 in 'Augustine's *City of God* . . .', pp. 97–9.

3. Two rules. Half a century after Augustine's death, and from a Roman viewpoint, we see a very different picture. Gelasius' famous dictum transfers the duality from the level of *society* ('Two loves made two cities') to the level of *government* ('Two there are by whom this world is ruled as princes'). Sacred and secular rulers function within one universal society. This leads Gelasius a certain way towards assimilating their duality to the universal distinction between priest and king, a distinction valid not only for Christendom but for societies before and beyond the sphere of the Gospel. But his sense of salvation-history is too alert to permit him to go far down this road. What is distinctive about the Christian era, he tells us, is that the sacral and political *must* be separated; for Christ, combining in himself the two roles of priest and king, has made it impossible for anyone else to combine them. As the author to the Hebrews thought that Christ, as the great high priest, was also the last high priest, so Gelasius thinks of him as the great (and so the last) priest-king, and (following Hebrews) compares him to Melchizedek. The eschatological character of Christendom is seen in the distribution of the roles, ensuring that everyone is humble, knowing that the priestly–royal character of Christ's church is not for one individual alone to reflect but depends upon mutual service. Only the Devil could now propose an emperor who was also a figure of the religious cult. It is a curious anticipation of Hegel's view that history progresses by differentiation, this belief in the emergence of two 'trained and specially qualified professions', as Gelasius, with surprisingly modern sound, describes them.

In the Carolingian age Gelasius' famous saying was sometimes quoted with a single word altered: 'Two there are by whom the *church* is ruled.' From one point of view this simply made explicit something already implied in Gelasius' one-world-two-rules conception. How could the emperor not 'rule the church' if he inherited the kingly aspect of Christ's dual office? Yet with the change from 'world' to 'church' a fine but significant line was crossed. It meant the last consciousness of a notional distinction between the two societies had disappeared; one could no longer say that the ruler ruled Christians *qua* civil society but not *qua* heavenly city. Of course, Roman emperors from Constantine to Justinian had pursued definite ecclesiastical and theological policies, as had the pagan emperors *mutatis mutandis* before them. But the theological account of their service to the church was that they 'protected' or 'defended' it; and that they 'reinforced ecclesiastical discipline', so that 'what the priest does not achieve with the authority of his teaching, secular power may command with the terror of discipline' (Isidore, *Sententiae* 3.51). In the East an emphasis was laid upon the personal piety of the emperor, who, as a public person, demonstrated his zeal by concern for orthodox doctrine. By either standard it was a telling shift in *Gestalt* when in the ninth-century West it was said that 'the special ministry of kings is to govern the people of God' (Jonas of Orleans, *De institutione regia* 4). The king now exercised his office of ruling wholly within the church, as a kind of lay ministry or charism. Later, his governing role came to seem an essential safeguard for lay ministry against clerical domination.

The burden of distinction now fell wholly upon the two governing offices of priest and ruler. The high and late Middle Ages looked back to this conception of two differentiated and equally balanced offices as a benchmark, very often to protest that it was a lost ideal. The reason it was lost was that difference and balance proved very difficult to combine for any length of time. The history of the Christendom idea shows differentiation being sacrificed to equilibrium, the two offices turning into each others' shadows; and it shows us one establishing hegemony over the other as attention falls on the difference between 'temporal' authority and 'spiritual'.

A striking example of how the ideal of equilibrium could turn the two offices into look-alikes is provided by an anonymous document, written at the turn of the twelfth century to support Henry I of England against the new papal policy, upheld by Archbishop Anselm, prohibiting the royal investiture of bishops with their pastoral staffs. The author compares the consecration rites of kings and bishops, and finds them parallel in every way. Coronation with anointing and benediction is the 'sacrament' which 'consecrates' the king to the office of ruling the church. By the oil of consecration, kings, like bishops, are elevated to bear the *figura Christi*, and become the Lord's anointed. To be sure, the king is senior in dignity to the bishop, for he represents the divine nature of Christ and the eschatological reality to which we are called (an eternal *kingdom*, not an eternal priesthood!). Yet despite this and the diverse wording of the rituals of consecration, king and bishop receive a 'common grace', and their duties are in all significant respects indistinguishable, so that a bishop may properly be called 'king', and a king 'priest'. A king may not properly be called a layman (*York Tractates* 4).

4. The supremacy of spiritual authority. The remarkable political and administrative exertions of the papacy in the late eleventh century, the 'Gregorian' or 'Hildebrandine Reforms' as they are called, though 'revolution' has been suggested as a better name, are capable of being read in more than one way. At moments one can detect in them an echo of the sense of eschatological conflict with the principalities and powers, which marked the patristic two-societies Christendom. Gregory VII himself, in a dramatic text, describes kingship as an invention of violent men ignorant of God, and cites Satan's promise to Jesus (Matt. 4:9) as the genealogy of all secular authority. But it was both too late and too early to invoke the notion of an earthly city, doomed for damnation, lurking within the bosom of the church. The principal thrust, then, of Gregorian apologetic was to redefine the equilibrium within the church; the twin pinnacles of rule had to have twin structures of government supporting them. The 'soul' of Christendom had to be given a distinct social form over against its 'body'. Spiritual rule could not exercise equal authority with secular rule unless it had its administrative and judicial structure loyal solely to its head. As appears most clearly in the controversy over lay investiture, the line of spiritual authority had to run straight from pope to bishop without including the king. The effect was to pull the clergy out from their political and feudal loyalties and to make them juridically and fiscally a race apart.

But there was a new emphasis, breaking with the idea of equilibrium. Spiritual rule must have priority over secular. The reformers advanced new claims for the pope to exercise juridical supremacy, with the right to depose apostate rulers and to absolve Christian subjects from their oaths of allegiance. It had been a commonplace of the Gelasian idea that the responsibility of the clergy was more weighty than that of secular princes, since they would answer for the souls of princes before Christ's throne. But this was now transformed into a constitutional supremacy. And so the Reforms brought the ecclesiastical establishment into rivalry with civil rulers on their own turf.

This claim was developed, in the course of two centuries of papalist apologetic, into a subtle theory which combines a Natural Law basis for the supremacy of priesthood with a salvation-historical conception of civilisational progress. The basic material of political order, the thirteenth-century apologists argued, was sheer conquest and exertion of force; but that material on its own cannot constitute political right, but requires the 'form' of justice. But justice is 'a spiritual thing' (*res spiritualis*, Giles of Rome), and must be supplied by spiritual agents in society. Any society that has developed true political authority (as distinct from mere force) has done so only by involving priesthood in the legitimation and direction of its rulers. This natural concomitance of the material and the spiritual in the constitution of political order has now been transformed, in the era of grace, by the revelation of true priesthood in Christ, which can ensure true religion, true virtue and justice, and, consequently, true political legitimacy.

To read the papalist apologists at their most thoughtful and impassioned is to encounter arguments that are in some respects familiar to us from the internationalists of our own century, advocates of the League of Nations and of the UNO. They had the vision of a universal jurisdiction bringing order to the jungle of competing claims and interests. But the jurisdiction was not that of an empire. It was constituted by a court of last resort, a ruler of rulers. It would thus, they believed, be something better than the mastery by one potentate of others; it would be the rule of justice. Justice is the key requisite for any political order, and the pope's role would ensure it by providing two things that the disorderly struggle of kingdoms and princedoms could not of itself provide: 'virtue' and 'ratification' (James of Viterbo). Making this even more necessary, as they saw it, was a changing idea of what a ruler's position involved. The classical Christian idea of the ruler as judge had shaped the concepts of late Roman law throughout the first part of the Middle Ages. But now the rising kings, in struggling for position against their barons, drew from feudal theory an idea of themselves as owners or possessors; and the juridical rationale of political authority became increasingly submerged under competing claims for 'dominion' of estates. This loss of disinterestedness in the political system had to be made good by a competent authority. The pope, it was claimed, owned all property, not 'in particular' but 'universally'; we might say, all property rights that others exercised were grounded in his authority.

5. *The authority of word alone.* In this way spiritual authority was differentiated from, and elevated above, secular. The Aristotelian renaissance of the thirteenth century strengthened this development at first, encouraging theologians to extend the hierarchy of nature and supernature on the broadest metaphysical and epistemological front. The pre-eminence of

ecclesiastical jurisdiction corresponded to the pre-eminence of grace over nature and of God over world. But its longer-term effect was to undermine it. The study of Aristotle's *Politics* and *Nicomachean Ethics* could not help strengthening confidence in a 'natural' political society with a solid and independent structure of its own, a society for which much more in the way of social virtue could be claimed than might be suggested by those who liked to recall Augustine's aphorism about large-scale criminal gangs. Justice itself was a natural virtue. It did not require the presidency of the pope, whose business lay with the theological virtues of faith, hope and charity, to ensure the possibility of a just political society (John of Paris).

So the stage was set for a reversal. This, when it came, was precipitated by a non-intellectual factor, the quarrel between the Franciscan friars and the papacy over the possibility of absolute poverty. This provoked some intense questioning of what it meant to possess 'spiritual authority'. The threat which the Franciscans posed to current doctrines of the papacy was far more serious than that vague discomfort which poverty always poses to wealth. It lay in a chain of submerged equivalences: property meant power; power meant jurisdiction; jurisdiction meant authority; and authority meant a determinative role for the church in shaping society under the law of Christ. To tweak at this thread from one end risked unravelling the whole garment of Christian society. From the ideal of absolute poverty it seemed to follow that the church could play no role in society. Tracing this ideal to Christ and the apostles made it worse: it called in question whether Christ was, in any politically relevant sense, a king.

The valid element in the Franciscans' thesis, we may think, lay in its refusal of a notion of authority tied to property by that chain of equivalences. Out of the long controversy came an attempt to articulate a different concept of spiritual authority, one based on the authority of the word. This was the work of the imperialist theologians who took up the Franciscans' cause. Their role was, of course, ambiguous, serving at the same time the church's interest in recovering a truly spiritual authority and the secular rulers' interest in having an uncontested field. Their most important contribution lay in the principle that a word of Gospel truth has its own distinct authority, different from the authority of threat or command.

The *Defender of the Peace* of Marsilius of Padua (1324) is usually identified as the herald of this new conception. The scope of the work is extremely broad, weaving together an Aristotelian political theory of an Averroist type, Franciscan arguments about apostolic poverty, the imperial case against papal jurisdiction, and, as a unifying element, his own fateful doctrine of the genesis of government from the popular will. The publication of Marsilius in English, as an act of propaganda by the English Government in the 1530s, nicely unifies the period which spans two centuries from the Franciscan controversy to the Henrician Reformation, and shows how the Erastianism of the early Reformers reaped the fruits of the imperial theologians' arguments. But periodisation can be seductive. The intellectual currents of those two hundred years were complex; and less extreme voices, such as Ockham's, may give a better picture of the fourteenth-century challenge to papalism, as well as representing a more credibly theological concern with spiritual authority.

For Marsilius the heart of the matter is this: since Christ's judgment is still future, it is impossible to represent it totally now by any single icon of government. Earthly political authority represents Christ's judgment in one way, but it lacks the claim to finality and ultimacy; its concern is to ensure the sufficient life simply within the scope of this passing age. Ecclesiastical authority represents Christ's judgment in another way, by publishing the law which ensures the ultimate welfare of the community and of each soul, but it lacks the decisiveness of present coercion. The secular and spiritual law each has its judge and its coercive sanctions: the civil ruler on the one hand; Christ himself, in future judgment, on the other. But for the present there is no surrogate to represent Christ's future coercive powers. The priesthood only 'judges' in a very limited sense, for it has at its disposal no coercive sanctions, only *doctrina* and *disciplina* (understood as *intellectual* discipline). The authority of the priesthood is the authority of truth, revealed and natural, which must convict and persuade. It is not the same as the authority founded on human command and sanction; but it is a real authority, for all that.

This promised an interpretation of the two rules which would not end up by dividing the cake, whether into spheres of competence, levels of precedence, or however. The two authorities were of such different kinds that the elusive idea of total mutual compatibility without mutual infringement seemed to be within reach. The imperialists thus assigned to secular authority all administrative and governmental functions, not excepting the government of the church itself as an institution, right down to determining how large a staff of priests was needed; yet claiming to detract in no way from the sole and complete authority of the church to pronounce (in the light of revelation) on what was true. Obviously the secular power would depend upon the church, since its actions would presume upon certain truths which it was not in a position to establish for itself. But the church had no power to validate or invalidate any act of government.

With this conception of distinct kinds of authority we suddenly confront some familiar modern dilemmas. Does the authority of the Gospel word confer no social structure on the community which bears it? Does that community have no 'social space' determined by the truth? Does the secular order, too, not require truth of a kind as the foundation of its authority? Sometimes the imperialists could give the impression of returning to the sceptical notion, decried long before Christianity by Plato and Cicero, that 'right' is the interest of the ruling party. It is not clear what kind of justice can be intrinsic to political order, so conceived, other than the purely formal justice which requires it to appear legitimate in the eyes of its subjects.

Both Lutheran and Anglican Reformers founded their view of church–state relations on this distinction of authority into two disparate kinds. Luther combines this distinction with the reminiscence of the older, patristic distinction between two societies. His 'two kingdoms' (*zwei Reiche*) revives the Augustinian division between opposed, coexisting social realities whose interaction creates history. Under the sway of this conception he recalls the patristic doctrine that the just have no need of secular government, since they are governed by the Holy Spirit. But this division is quickly broken down by the important qualification that no Christian belongs exclusively to this category; each is at once righteous believer and sinner. Consequently, the distinction of the two kingdoms turns out to be an ideal one, needing to be complemented by the functional distinction of 'two governments' (*zwei Regimente*), which correspond to the two authorities of the Marsilian pattern (*Temporal Authority* 1.3f.). The authority of the church appears in the apostolic office, confessing Christ and guiding souls to eternal life. In the exercise of this role a caustic, confrontational dissidence may often be necessary; but in no other way can it be appropriate for the church to challenge public authority (*Sermon on the Mount* on 5:13f.).

The distinction of spiritual and secular was converted by Luther into an inner–outer distinction, between the realm of the mind and heart, on the one hand, and the realm of social relations, on the other. The sense of dynamic tension between the two is a hallmark of his anthropology. We find ourselves confronted for the first time with that characteristic figure of the modern West, the self-reflecting soul who, burdened with a sense of inward space, stands at a quizzical distance from the roles assigned him in society. Every Christian bears 'two persons'; that was Luther's characteristic metamorphosis of the doctrine of the Two, influenced, perhaps, by a reminiscence of the medieval lawyers' doctrine of the king's 'two bodies'. Some of his most memorable pages evoke the tension which the Christian ruler feels between the pomp and severity of the outward role and the inner abasement of the true self before Christ (*Sermon on the Mount* on 5:4f. e.g.).

6. Restoring the balance. The Marsilian pattern, having triumphed at the Reformation, steadily lost ground thereafter. To recover equilibrium, rather than to stress the differences, was the chief object of the later sixteenth century and shaped the final phase of Christendom.

On the one side the Salamanca school (Vitoria, Suarez etc.) disentangled Catholic opinion from the high doctrines of plentitude of power which had held sway in papalist circles since the thirteenth century. The secular power was deemed 'supreme in its own order' (Suarez, *Defensio* III.5.6). The pope could not challenge the act of any secular ruler for reasons lying within the ruler's sphere of civil justice. 'So long as a thing is not incompatible with the salvation of souls and religion, the pope's office is not involved' (Vitoria, *De potestate ecclesiae* 1.5.9). Only when the welfare of the universal church was at stake had the spiritual power any *locus standi* in directing the acts of Christian kings. Most remarkable in the Salamancan revisionism, and in the attitudes of the post-Tridentine church which were shaped by it, was the abandonment of an evangelical basis for civil rule and justice. Political order was founded solely on Natural Law, and existed with no less validity among pagans. Christ's kingship was exclusively spiritual. 'My kingdom is not of this world' came to assume its place as the proof-text for defining the limits of Christology. The nature–grace distinction of the Aristotelian schoolmen was put to new work in providing the basis for a secular–ecclesiastical duality.

The Calvinists, on the other side, were looking for an ecclesiastical authority to take the place of the papacy which the Erastian Reform had swept aside. They were disaffected with an authority to pronounce which conferred no social independence. They wished to claim back the church's social space. In Geneva, they believed, one could see secular and ecclesiastical structures corresponding as they ought, a municipal version of the way state and church authority had been supposed to correspond in the Gelasian model. Gelasius without the pope, we may call it – not forgetting that this Gelasius was conveniently without the emperor as well!

These city-state Reformers, for whom Calvin was the systematiser and apologist, did not renounce the idea of a church authority founded on the truth of the divine word. Church government should be 'exercised and administered solely by the word' (Calvin, *Institutes* IV.3.1). Calvin's formal statements about the 'twofold government in man' are quite compatible with the Marsilian model, urging that 'one has its seat in the soul', the other 'only regulates external conduct' (III.19.15). The theoretical task was to show that this authority could *extend into* a structured church authority which was subject to the exegesis of Scripture yet possessed sufficient social objectivity to provide effective institutional government. This was done by stressing two characteristic features of the Reformed churches. First, there was the claim for a scripturally ordained structure of ministry. This claim limited appeals to scriptural authority to a ministry which itself conformed to Scripture's requirements, so curbing the free-floating apostolate of the preacher armed with a Bible. Secondly, there was the 'jurisdiction', which maintained the 'discipline' (no longer in the intellectual sense!) over lay and ordained members of the church. This was supported by a modest element of church law. Like earlier Reformers Calvin execrated the pretensions of the canon-law tradition, and wished to stress the contingent character of 'godly ordinances' which had no power to bind the conscience. Yet the spiritual leaders of the church, when met in the consistory, were indeed judges.

> The remarkable affinity between Calvinism and its adversary, the revitalised Catholicism of the post-Tridentine period, has often been remarked – and not least by a frustrated Hugo Grotius when enmeshed in the Remonstrant controversy! If, as some recent historians have argued, the influential turn of second-generation Calvinists to constitutionalist ideals is borrowed clothing from the Salamanca school, then the appearance of affinity is remarkably reinforced. But in one respect the Calvinist influence was uniquely dependent on its city-state model. Church structures deprived of both universal papacy and bishopric were arranged in local units of a size that groups of ministers and lay elders could meet in consistory to exercise the church's authority. This created a powerful engine of shared lay–clerical decision-making at local level. The Calvinist Reforms provided a forum of local politics. Contending for the right of local churches to approve the appointment of their ministers, Calvinists under other regimes raised a standard around which all kinds of local grievances against central administration could rally.

Mission or coercion?

The doctrine of the Two was, before all else, a doctrine of two ages. The passing age of the principalities and powers has overlapped with the coming age of God's Kingdom. The confrontation of the two societies, the more attenuated balance of the two rules and the inner dynamism of the two persons are all generated by this eschatological fusion. The term 'secular' is defined by this *mise-en-scène*. Secular institutions have a role confined to this passing age (*saeculum*). They do not represent the arrival of the new age and the rule of God. They have to do with the perennial cycle of birth and death which makes tradition, not with the resurrection of the dead which supersedes all tradition. The corresponding term to 'secular' is not 'sacred', nor 'spiritual', but 'eternal'. Applied to political authorities, the term 'secular' should tell us that they are not agents of Christ, but are marked for displacement when the rule of God in Christ is finally disclosed. They are Christ's conquered enemies; yet they have an indirect testimony to give, bearing the marks of his sovereignty imposed upon them, negating their pretensions and evoking their acknowledgment. Like the surface of a planet pocked with craters by the bombardment it receives from space, the governments of the passing age show the impact of Christ's dawning glory. This witness of the secular is the central core of Christendom.

But any proposal that we should learn from it risks drawing fire from both of two opposing sides in a current debate. Recent natural-rights thinkers object to the idea of a political society in which a religious confession is built into its principles of government, making more than a 'thin' set of social values normative for the public conduct of affairs. Their communitarian opponents denounce the attempt to make the confession of the church look like a general rule of civilisation. They share the same objection, though with opposite agenda, to what looks like compelled belief: wrong to a natural-rights view because compelled unnecessarily; wrong to a communitarian view because, if compelled, then not an authentic witness of the community. But is the compulsion of religion a necessary part of the Christendom idea? Before attempting an answer, let us make two analytical observations about the idea we have briefly traced through its major historical phases.

1. The Christendom idea has to be located correctly as an aspect of the church's understanding of *mission*. The church is not at liberty to withdraw from mission; nor may it undertake its mission without confident hope of success. It was the missionary imperative that compelled the church to take the conversion of the empire seriously and to seize the opportunities it offered. These were not merely opportunities for 'power'. They were opportunities for preaching the Gospel, baptising believers, curbing the violence and cruelty of empire and, perhaps most important of all, forgiving their former persecutors. The same energy drove the church–state dialectic at subsequent moments of transition. What was required for mission in the eleventh century was a coordinated and free church-structure; but this had become an obstacle to mission by the fourteenth, when the Franciscans attempted to dissociate themselves from the worldly implications of that structure. But that same dissociation had itself become a liability to mission when the Calvinists attempted to reconstruct ecclesiastical jurisdiction. The ambiguities of Christendom, meanwhile, arose from a loss of focus on its missionary context. Once the two societies came to be seen as a single society, it was more difficult to frame the church–state partnership in terms of the eschatological Kingdom. It could seem, by a kind of optical illusion,

that there was no more mission to be done. The peril of the Christendom idea – precisely the same peril that attends upon the post-Christendom idea of the religiously neutral state – was that of negative collusion: the pretence that there was now no further challenge to be issued to the rulers in the name of the ruling Christ.

We can illustrate from the greatest of twentieth-century theologians how the missionary concern shaped and reshaped his political conceptions. As is well known, Barth's chief purpose in the early thirties was to help the church escape from what he saw as the quietist implications of Luther's doctrine of two governments, and to help it proclaim the revelation of Christ in direct challenge to the Nazi order. This was to recapitulate in the twentieth-century terms the Calvinist reversal of the Marsilian legacy of the early Reformation, and, naturally enough, Barth's early formulations look like the Calvinist reworking of the Gelasian parallel. In 1931 he wrote that the church 'contains the state in itself', and in 1938, more cautiously, that the state was 'a kind of annexe . . . included in the ecclesiastical order as such' (*Ethics*, p. 449; *Church and State*, p. 59). At this point, however, he seems to have become uncomfortable with the anachronistic Christendom-feel of these classic Calvinist assertions. In his most famous essay on the subject, 'The Christian Community and the Civil Community' of 1946, he took the decisive step of identifying the state as 'pagan' – a term which he had previously used quite specifically of the Nazis but which now comes to characterise 'the state as such' (p. 27). How, then, to maintain the principle of Christ's claim upon the state?

Here he advanced his well-known thesis of the 'analogy' of state and church to the Kingdom of Christ. 'The existence of the State [is] an allegory . . . a correspondence and an analogue to the Kingdom of God which the church preaches and believes in' (p. 32). The New Testament image for the final hope is 'not . . . an eternal church but . . . the *polis* built by God' (p. 19). In the witness to the Kingdom of God the state forms the 'outer circle', the church the 'inner circle', with the Kingdom at their centre. Although the state's 'presuppositions and tasks are different', it is 'capable of reflecting indirectly the truth and reality which constitute the Christian community'. So, without appealing to any notion of a Christian state or state-within-the-church, Barth makes the state as such a witness to Christ's rule. But how can it witness to what it has not heard? It is 'ignorant of the mystery of the Kingdom of God' and 'cannot remind itself of the true criterion of its own righteousness. It needs the activity which revolves directly around the common centre, the participation of the Christian community' (p. 33). The key to the state's fulfilling of its role, then, is the church's proclamation to it, 'reminding it' (p. 34). Mission, presupposing no prior commitment of the state to Christ or Gospel, now becomes the primary event which opens up the possibility of the state's discharging its function, which is to witness in its own appointed way to the Kingdom of God.

Yet there is something not quite in order about this formula, an inconsistency between the verb which describes the church's mission ('reminding', borrowed from the Barmen Declaration of 1934) and the new post-Christendom way in which the state is described. How is this constitutionally pagan state, by definition ignorant of its own righteousness, 'reminded' of what it never knew? And of what, if it knew it, would make it no longer ignorant, and so no longer 'the state as such'? Two ideas appear to have been combined, not entirely happily. On the one hand is the opposition of knowledge and ignorance, righteousness and paganism, which sets up the missionary tension; on the other there is the reminiscence derived from Christendom of the concept of a distinct secular function, which does not permit the state *qua* state to register concerns which lie beyond its sphere, the conception of the Gelasian parallel. When Barth in his last years returned to political questions in the uncompleted volume of *Church Dogmatics* iv/4, he approached it solely from the point of view of the church's mission. In place of a discussion of church and state we find a section on the church's struggle for righteousness (*The Christian Life* §78). How or whether he would have discussed the state from that starting-point we cannot tell; but we can appreciate the significance of the new point of departure. For the importance of mission in Barth's later ecclesiology, cf. *Church Dogmatics* iv/3 §72.2, where it is described as a forgotten *nota ecclesiae*.

Mission is not merely an urge to expand the scope and sway of the church's influence. It is to be at the disposal of the Holy Spirit in making Christ's victory known. It requires, therefore, a discernment of the working of the Spirit and of the Antichrist. These two discernments must accompany each other: to trace the outline of Christ's dawning reign on earth requires that one trace the false pretension too. One reason that the idealist language about the Kingdom of God in the late nineteenth century failed to avoid the trap of civilisational legitimation was that it never identified the false horizon, and could grasp social evil only as a regression from civilisation into barbarism. Recognition of the Antichrist is a recurrent theme in the doctrine of the Two. Gelasius observed it in the pretensions of imperial authority; Gregory VII in the involvement of kings in episcopal appointments; Wyclif and his successors paradoxically in the structure of papal administration which Gregory's successors created. Yet there is a single theme which connects the varied warnings of Antichrist in different ages: the convergence in one subject of claims to earthly political rule and heavenly soteriological mediation. John of Patmos found it present not in the Roman empire as such but quite specifically in the imperial cult. It was therefore not inappropriate to discern Antichrist even in the papacy, while it claimed universal juridical competence over political societies and wielded it in the name of mankind's salvation. The rejection of Antichrist is the rejection of a unified political and theological authority other than that which is vested in Christ's own person. That is to say, it is implied in the basic structure of the doctrine of the Two itself.

To reckon with the possibility of Antichrist is to reckon with the ultimate conflict between false and true Messianism. It is to reckon with the perennial possibility of faithful martyrdom for the Kingdom of Christ, which is never to be omitted from an account of the church's mission even if, in some generations, martyrdom is not demanded. Not all faithful martyrdom, of course, presupposes Antichrist. Much martyrdom is suffered simply at the hands of barbarians or civilisational revanchists, for whom the combination of irreligion and violence is more attractive than the rule of law. One can be martyred for refusing sexual demands, for opposing ruthless landlords, for asking embarrassing questions about forgotten prisoners, and for many other things. But these occasions of martyrdom are sporadic and unpredictable. The martyrdom to which the church must always be looking forward (from what distance, who can tell?) is the martyrdom exacted by civilisation itself when it lifts its arms against God. A church too determined to be at home in the world will be unprepared for this, and so unprepared for mission.

Yet readiness for martyrdom is not the only form the church's mission must take. Since true martyrdom is a powerful force and its resistance to Antichrist effective, the church must be prepared to welcome the homage of the kings when it is offered to the Lord of the martyrs. The growth of the church, its enablement to reconstruct civilisational practices and institutions, its effectiveness in communicating the Gospel: these follow from the courage of the martyrs, and the church honours them when it seizes the opportunities they have made available to it. No honour is paid to martyrs if they are presented as mere dissidents, whose sole glory was to refuse the cultural order that was on offer to them. Martyrdom is, as the word itself indicates, witness, pointing to an alternative offer. The witness is vindicated when it is carried through in a positive mode, saying yes as well as saying no, encouraging the acts of repentance and change by which the powers offer homage to Christ.

Here I must define an affectionate parting of the ways with my friend Stanley Hauerwas, whose insights into the imprisoning constraints of modern cliché have done so much to free us to envisage the church as a social presence. His attack on Christendom, which he often denominates as 'Constantinianism', seems to be founded on the premise: Christendom/Constantinianism is constituted by the improper acquisition of worldly power by the church. 'By taking up Rome's project', he tells us in a flagship article ('Why there is No Salvation

Outside the Church', in *After Christendom?*, p. 39), 'Christians were attempting to further the kingdom through the power of this world.' No historical justification is offered for this claim, and I am afraid I think it simply wrong. That is not what Christians were attempting to do. Their own account of what happened was that those who held power became subject to the rule of Christ. Of course, clear-sighted individuals could see the temptations this situation posed. Criticism of worldly churchmanship or papal pretension did not begin with the dawn of modernity. But they did not think this danger a reason to refuse the triumph Christ had won among the nations.

Hauerwas has a theological difficulty about this reading of Christendom. 'I do not believe', he once declared to me with customary irony, 'in justification by faith!' But the subjection of the angelic powers of government to the rule of Christ is one aspect of justification, the fruit of Christ's triumph over death and hell. Christians who believed in Christendom believed that they could discern this in world-historical developments. Yet they knew they could not count on it as a permanent right. So Augustine knew that the thesis he had to contest in his contemporaries' celebration of the Christian epoch was not that the empire had been converted to Christ, which was true, but that there would never be another persecution of Christians, which nobody could be sure of (*Ep.* 199).

This triumph of Christ among the nations Hauerwas is not prepared to see. His Christianity is marked by a kind of return to the catacombs. This is not 'sectarian'; I have the greatest sympathy with his scornful repudiation of that epithet. For was it not the *catholic* church that sheltered in the catacombs and which Augustine thought might be called on at any moment to return to them? The categories of 'church' and 'sect' to which this epithet appeals are a dishonest device, theologically speaking, to suggest that catholics may always, as a matter of their own decision, be respectable – as though martyrdom were a temperamental disposition or an ecclesiastical policy rather than a vocation thrust upon us terrifyingly from on high! Few modern theologians have been so conscientious in recalling the witness of the martyrs as has Hauerwas. His natural allegiance in the patristic age is not with Augustine's *City of God* but with Origen's *Exhortation to Martyrdom*. 'Genuine politics', he tells us in the same article, 'is about the art of dying'.

And yet – an observation offered in the spirit of his own remark that 'you can't learn to lay brick without learning to talk right' (p. 101) – Hauerwas does not talk about martyrdom in the way the master-builders did. 'The martyrs could go to their deaths confident that the story to which their killers were trying to subject them was not the true story of their death . . . "You can kill us"', he imagines them saying, '"but you cannot determine the meaning of our death!"' (p. 38). Is there not something missing here, something essential to the practice of dying constituted as a political and churchly, not simply as a philosophical, act? Where is the confidence in the resurrection? Has Hauerwas not suppressed it precisely because it means 'justification', the vindication of the martyrs' cause?

For someone who is striving to recover pre-Nicene innocence in these post-Constantinian times the very hope of vindication, which gave the martyrs their courage, has come to look like a temptation. Pre-Nicene Christians themselves, of course, always expected vindication, and when the moment came they embraced it – all too incautiously, perhaps. Lactantius' *Institutes*, composed for a martyr-church at the height of Diocletian's persecution, was easily repackaged in a second edition, with a dedicatory preface to . . . Constantine!

2. The Christendom idea describes a *mutual service* between the two authorities, predicated on the difference and the balance of their roles. Their authorities are different, because Christ's victory is, and appears, different from any secular exercise of power. Antichrist, with his healed wound, can parody but cannot replicate the victory of the resurrection. And since it is given to nobody but the risen Christ to raise the dead, the church's authority does not rest in exercising that power by delegation, but in pointing to its future exercise in an act of testimony. Yet there is evangelical truth in the distinctively Christian use of the word 'authority' to speak of the power of Gospel witness. The unhappy tension which tormented the classical world, between the philosopher with his truth and the ruler with his power, is overcome in the Word of God. The church does not philosophise about a future world; it demonstrates the working of the coming Kingdom within this one. Through the authorisation of the Holy Spirit it squares up to civil authority and confronts it. This may lead to martyrdom, or to mutual service.

The service rendered by the state to the church is to facilitate its mission. The state itself cannot pursue the mission of the church, for it is not consecrated to that task and its weapons of coercion are not fitted for it. But it may facilitate the mission of the church, or impede it. It may facilitate it, first, simply by performing its own business responsibly and with modest pretensions. In the Christian era there is no neutral performance on the part of rulers; either they accommodate to the energy of the divine mission, or they hurl themselves into defiance. The church's knowledge that its mission could be assisted by the Roman empire did not begin with the conversion of Constantine; nor was the early church unwilling to recognise a measure of 'anonymous Christianity' in such quarters, too.

Beyond that, however, there may be a conscious facilitation, based on the recognition of the church and acknowledgment of its mission. (We are not necessarily speaking here of legal 'establishment', a vague term at best, though this has sometimes been the way in which recognition was given.) Recognition implies some respect on the part of the rulers for the church's leaders, and a willingness to listen to them as they explain the church's tasks and seek assistance. But it by no means implies giving bishops whatever they would like. One of the advantages of 'deep Christendom', in which rulers could be counted on to have a lay Christian understanding, was that the state could be informed by other means about the church's mission and its needs. It was a mistake, however, to go beyond speaking of conscious facilitation of the church's mission and to speak, as the apologists of Christendom often did, of the ruler's duty to 'defend' the church, or 'reinforce church discipline'. These conceptions were among the false steps of Christendom, which helped to create ambiguity about the church's identity. Post-exilic Israel could look to the powers that ruled her land for defence, however unhappily, because she still awaited Yhwh's intervention. But the church does not await his intervention, but knows that that intervention has already come. Its security is guaranteed by the ascended Christ and needs no further underwriting. Still less does the church need its declarations of Christ's judgment to become a matter for civil prosecution. The character of the church as a community that 'judges not' is impugned if secular authorities follow up its declarations with coercive actions of their own.

> The mistake of introducing defensive action into the church's armoury naturally led to the mistake of locating the ruler's own role as an office in the church. It cannot be an office in the church, since it belongs to the old aeon that is passing away. For a Christian to be a secular ruler is a *vocation*, that is to say, a social situation 'within which' he was called by Christ (cf. 1 Cor. 7:20), and within which opportunities of service to the Kingdom are afforded him. It is not a *charism*, or a spiritual gift, 'for the equipment of the saints for the work of ministry' (Eph. 4:12), which, as such, is part of the Spirit's working in the church. The confusion of vocation and charism is strikingly apparent in that section of Hobbes's *Leviathan* devoted to the 'Christian Commonwealth'. 'The word of God delivered by prophets is the main principle of Christian politics', he tells us in the first sentence (32), an opening the theological vigour of which belies the common characterisation of Hobbes as a sceptical subverter of Christianity. The prophetic word is present in the Scriptures; but the canon of Holy Scripture is determined for us by no prophet, and must therefore be resolved on by the civil legislator himself, because, as canon, Scripture is law, and reason only allows one legislator (33). So the Christian commonwealth exists simultaneously as a contractual commonwealth, conferring authority upon its ruler and obeying him, and as a church believing and obedient to divine revelation. These two diverse characters of the commonwealth are held together by the ruler's single act of defining the canon, which has simultaneously the nature of a legislative act and that of a spiritual discernment of prophecy. The exercise of his vocation, in accordance with the contract, is at the same time the exercise of a gift of the Spirit.

The most truly Christian state understands itself most thoroughly as 'secular'. It makes the confession of Christ's victory and accepts the relegation of its own authority. It echoes the words of John the Baptist: 'He must increase, I must decrease' (John 3:30). Like the Baptist, it has a place on the threshold of the Kingdom, not within it. The only corresponding service that the church can render to this authority of the passing world is to help it make that act of self-denying recognition. It may urge this recognition upon it, and share with it the tasks of practical deliberation and policy which seek to embody and implement it. We may say that the church seeks the 'conversion' of the state, provided that we use that term analogously. In relation to the state its sense is different from that in which it can be used of individuals and societies. Not only individuals, but families, tribes and nations may repent and believe the Gospel. Whether families, tribes and nations have an eternal destiny we may debate (though Israel has one – is that not enough?); but there is no difficulty in saying that they belong within the church. The ruler may belong within the church, too, but not *qua* ruler. The essential element in the conversion of the ruling power is the change in its self-understanding and its manner of government to suit the dawning age of Christ's own rule. The church has to instruct it in the ways of the humble state.

What those ways are, how is the church to know? There was no revealed political doctrine in the New Testament, prescribing how the state was to be guided. The early church had simply to proclaim God's Kingdom come in Christ. The political doctrine of Christendom was discovered and elicited from the practical experience of Christian political discipleship, in which Christian rulers were accompanied and assisted by the wider church. But the existence of such a body of doctrine now poses a peculiar temptation: to offer the doctrine as a substitute for proclaiming Christ. The church may imagine that it discharges its responsibility if it repeats its lessons on the ways of the humble state *without* the proclamation that makes those lessons intelligible. For instance, think of Jacques Maritain's proposal of a 'democratic secular faith', which the church is to advocate in common with non-Christians in public, while each, in the semi-privacy of its own educational establishments, gives different reasons for it (*Man and the State*, ch. 5). What that means is that the democratic 'creed', not the Gospel, becomes the heart of the church's message to the state. Granted, the church may always make the best of any coincidence of political doctrine between Christians and non-Christians that it lights upon; but 'making the best' means making the evangelical content of the doctrine clear, not veiling it in embarrassment. Furthermore, even were the content of this democratic secular faith exclusively Christian, so that the question of coalitions did not arise, it would still not be enough to insist on the ideals of the state which this creed contained. To urge an ideal (which is best done remotely, at a distance from practical decisions) is not the same as to bring the ideal to bear upon practical decisions in concrete circumstances. Because the legacy of Christian political doctrine has to be proved afresh at every turn in engagement with political decision, it can only become useful in the context of an exploratory partnership between church and state in search of authentic political discipleship. Here, certainly, is the manna which when kept breeds worms.

We return, then, to the charge of religious compulsion. In the first place, such compulsion was undoubtedly attempted from time to time in the course of the Christian centuries (how consistently or how frequently does not affect the discussion); and the uniquely important testimony to that fact is borne by Jewry, still inextricably bound up with the church in a struggle for the fulfilment of God's promises. By their sufferings at Christian hands the Jews were appointed prophets to the church, through whom the Holy Spirit summoned it back to the service of the Kingdom of God; and when that prophecy was ignored, Christians fell logically into the next step, that of attempting to coerce each other. By realising that we cannot refuse to listen to the Jews' testimony at this point, we may, perhaps, discover that we were never authorised to stop listening to them at any point.

> Perhaps the whole problem lies with the structure of the doctrine of the Two: where is the third realm, the heir of the covenant? One would have expected to see a doctrine of the Three. At the base of the triangle, the two poles of Israel and the nations, linked by a line of hope in Yhwh's covenant-promises for the twofold gathering of Israel and the nations. At the apex the church's witness to the fulfilment of the promises, subduing the nations' lords on the one side for the sake of Israel on the other. But the patristic and medieval church thought it had so wholly taken over Israel's identity that no further engagement between church and synagogue was called for. The third realm became invisible. The church, it was thought, was Jacob confronting Esau (who represented the nations, or even, paradoxically, Israel itself, cf. Augustine *Serm.* 5). It would have made a better allegory to cast the church in the role of the wrestling angel, with whom Israel must strive for his blessing, and who must strive with Israel to equip him for his public role before the nations. The apostolic church's view of its double mission, to secure the identity of Israel on the one hand and the obedience of the Gentiles on the other, had been lost sight of. In its place was a one-sided mission to the Gentiles and a rather petty determination to triumph over Israel. The unashamed satisfaction with which the fourth-century church

greeted imperial decrees barring Jews from the Holy Land demonstrates how little the church thought it had to say to Jews about the Holy Land. And having little to say, it heard little. It was as though the angel left Jacob sleeping by the Jabbok and went off to wrestle Esau instead. The angel who does that had better beware that it does not learn from the Gentile lords to be a lordly angel, and so, in the end, a fallen angel!

The historical record of persecutions, however, and of a more usual repressive tolerance which permitted minorities to exist, but on pain of civil disadvantages, does not resolve the question whether it was a necessary entailment of the Christendom idea. It followed, evidently enough, from the thought that the state's duty was to defend the church, by coercive measures if necessary. If, as we have argued, this thought was a mistake, which, however deeply rooted it became, can be distinguished from the authentic stock of the Christendom idea, then the idea itself may be cut free from its parasite. Against this it will be asked, however: is there not something implicitly coercive in the very attempt to define a secular government as Christian? Does it not make some members of society 'outsiders', even if they are treated well as such? And is not the fundamental right of religious dissidents the right *not to have to be* religious dissidents? This suggestion, which certainly strikes to the heart of the Christendom idea, underlies a great deal of the discomfort that we now feel with the idea and its legacy.

We should understand its intellectual provenance, which is in the liberal tradition though it is not characteristic of what we might call 'classic' liberalism, i.e. the liberal doctrines of the early-modern period. Classic liberalism was hospitable to the project of resolving disputes on questions of truth by persuasion. The dialectical struggle of rational debate, in which each side marshals arguments to bring the other to agreement, seemed to early liberal theorists a healthy thing, the proper alternative to violent struggle. In an argument which had currency from Milton to Mill, they pleaded for the toleration of erroneous beliefs precisely on the ground that they stimulated rational discussion and so assisted the common quest for truth. But clearly one cannot approve the common quest for truth without approving the hope that common persuasions may emerge from it. They thought there was nothing to fear from shared convictions if they were rationally reached and rationally held.

Recent reworkings of the tradition, however, have lost confidence in the innocuousness of a search for shared convictions. It has come to seem perilous to allow persuasions of any kind, however reached, to shape the ordering of society. Doctrines that shape society are political doctrines, and all political doctrines are by their nature coercive. Even liberal doctrines of society are coercive, but since they define the *minimum* formal conditions for social existence (so the account runs) they have the indefeasible claim to make society as little coercive as it possibly can be; while any other shared doctrine is in excess of the necessary minimum and so imposes unwarranted coercion. Even societies that are actually in agreement on far more than minimal conditions *ought not* to express those agreements in political conventions, ceremonies or laws, lest they imperil the freedom of possible dissidents, present or future.

This impressionistic sketch will suffice for our limited purpose, which is not to engage self-conscious liberal theorists but to articulate the grounds for a common and largely implicit distrust of the Christendom idea. Those grounds seem to take us back behind alarm about governments to an alarm about *society*. For it is society that makes outsiders. Government may *wrong* dissidents by repression or persecution; but it does not *make them* dissidents by recognising and affirming things upon which its society agrees and they disagree. Deep social agreements unreflected in government would merely delegitimise the government. We are left with the suspicion that this liberal view springs from a radical suspicion of society as such and of the agreements that constitute it – to be traced back, perhaps, to the contractarian myth which bound individuals directly together into political societies without any acknowledgment of the mediating social reality.

However that may be, a theological discussion can take a short cut at this point: it is not Christendom but Christianity that is attacked, since by implication it makes the church inadmissible. If any social agreement is potentially coercive and to be justified only by the needs of civil order, then the agreements which constitute the church, with which many disagree, are coercive and unjustifiedly so. If there is no religious test on the right to vote, or to have access to education or medical care, why should there be one on attending Mass and receiving communion, which is, after all, a source of satisfaction to religious temperaments and an important means of social participation? This conclusion, that the church should not be defined by belief, seems to me to follow rather obviously from the general refusal of ideology, though I do not know of anyone who has yet drawn it, except for the incomparable Simone Weil, who proposed, in her wartime tract *The Need for Roots*, that it should be prohibited to publish any opinion on any subject in the name of a collective body. Any society defined by its belief was to be banned.

In particular the neo-liberal thesis is incompatible with a narrative theology which professes that agreement on a common 'story' is an essential element in social identity. Generally speaking this point is well taken by narrative theologians, who have understood themselves as fellow-travellers in the communitarian cause in the fight between communitarians and liberals. But they have not seen the implications for their customary repudiation of Christendom. Christendom ought to be precisely the kind of storied community they aim to celebrate. Of course, they criticise it not for having a story but for having the wrong story, a story made up of the praise of coercion; but that is precisely where they succumb to the liberal thesis. The story-tellers of Christendom do not celebrate coercion; they celebrate the power of God to humble the haughty ones of the earth and to harness them to the purposes of peace. In resolving to deconstruct the self-storying of Christendom the narrativists have simply followed the principle proposed by their adversaries: social doctrine of whatever kind is coercive; those who claim a social identity in terms of unnecessary belief do violence to those who do not share it.

In this context I notice the emphasis John Howard Yoder lays upon *voluntariety* in his characterisation of the church, at the expense of *belief.* If we study the rather carefully drawn-up charge-sheet which he lays against mainstream Reformation Christianity, we see that a variety of theological and practical issues are brought down to the single issue of individual liberty. They 'retained infant baptism, which identified an entire population with the church. They retained (or rather established more strongly than before) the control of the church by civil authority. They retained the compulsory membership in the church of all but Jews, and retained as well the approbation of the violence of civil government within the doctrine of the just war' (*The Priestly Kingdom*, pp. 106f.). My reaction to this list of charges is not to deny any of them, but to find it disconcerting that such a heterogenous collection of issues should be so drained of their theological distinctiveness as to serve the general cause of voluntariety. Is this what anyone ever thought the disagreement over infant baptism was about – that no one should make me join the church if I chose not to?

What is the relation, in Yoder's view, between this all-important act of will and Christian faith? And what role is played by divine grace in bringing faith to birth? And does divine grace not make use of the testimony of community faith in awakening individual faith? Certainly, a church defined by the faith it confesses will be free, for 'coerced faith' is a contradiction in terms. But does that make it appropriate to speak of a 'voluntary society', which usually connotes an association into which people contract *optionally*, i.e. not only without anyone forcing them to, but without any pressing need driving them to? A voluntary society is one that I could leave without incurring grave or irremediable loss, which might seem a strange thing for a Christian to think about the church. Finally, does the concept of the church as a voluntary society not commend itself chiefly because it fits late-modern expectations of how civil society will be organised? Is Yoder, in the name of non-conformity, not championing a great conformism, lining the church up with the sports clubs, friendly societies, colleges, symphony subscription-guilds, political parties and so on, just to prove that the church offers late-modern order no serious threat?

The idea of a Christian state, then, need not be the idea of a coercive state. Imagine a state that gave entrenched, constitutional encouragement to Christian mission not afforded to other religious beliefs, and expected of its office-holders deference to these arrangements as to constitutional law. Such a state would have no need to restrict the civil liberties of any non-Christian, even to the point of allowing the highest offices to be free of religious tests. What it could not do, of course, would be to protect its arrangements against constitutional reform, should that secure the necessary support. Which is merely to say that we should not expect of the Christian state the permanence of Byzantium. Like various aspects of the church's life, the Christian state may be disclosed from time to time as a sign of the Kingdom, disappearing at one moment to return at another. It cannot pretend (as Augustine understood) to be an irreversible datum of history.

Of the two perils identified by the fifth chapter of the Barmen Declaration, perhaps the church falls rather less into the temptation of assuming the state's authority, rather more into that of acquiescing with the state's assumption of its own. Political orders, whether or not they are professedly Christian, will tend to want to draw on the social strengths of the church for their support. The church need not always refuse such support; but it must be on guard against the danger that such a posture will distort its mission and message. 'Civil religion' poses a more serious objection to the co-operative church–state arrangements of Christendom than religious coercion does. Both, of course, offend against the Gospel, not merely against natural justice: coercion violates the openness of unbelief to come to belief freely while God's patience waits on it; civil religion violates the freedom of belief to believe truly. But civil religion wears the form of the Antichrist, drawing the faith and obedience due to the Lord's Anointed away to the political orders which should have only provisional authority under him.

For Stanley Hauerwas civil religion is so much the great danger in America that he finds it in him to congratulate his Australian hosts on 'the refreshing . . . absence of any abiding civil religion' in their purely utilitarian political society (*After Christendom*, p. 15). Elsewhere he and Will Willimon lavish indignation upon President Bush's 'idolatrous and pagan' Call for a National Day of Prayer before the Gulf War of 1991 ('Why *Resident Aliens . . .*', pp. 421f.). The extent to which civil religion is an immediate and pressing threat to the authenticity of the church must, of course, be a matter of judgment, which will vary from place to place and from time to time. Reading the essays collected by John Witte in *Christianity and Democracy*, I am open to persuasion that the American situation is distinctive in this respect. But I suppose that in Europe and Canada the problem of self-consciously anti-religious secularism is more acute, though even there it would be wrong to suppose that the peril of civil religion is absent. It may, indeed, grow greater with the pressure to accommodate religious pluralism as a permanent feature of civil society. But we need to be clear about what civil religion is. Not every gauche adventure into lay Christian leadership, such as US political leaders like to practise from time to time, will count. Could it not more often take the form of finding religious reasons to support the First Amendment?

Civil religion is a corruption to which the church is liable when it enjoys a close co-operation with the state. It is not a matter of serving the interests of *government* solely – civil religion can flourish in opposition, too – but the interests of the state at large, bolstering its legitimacy, supporting its political philosophy, inculcating virtues, both active and passive, which are useful to the political constitution of society. And not everything that the church may say or do along these lines is to be disapproved of. It is when this line of thought has become autonomous, cut loose from its evangelical authority, that it distorts the witness of the Gospel. 'Never mind how you vote, just make sure you go to the poll!' Messages like that delivered from the pulpit are the archetypal civil religion of modern democracy. They maintain the appearance of political neutrality, while actually suppressing important possibilities for Christian criticism: that the Gospel may raise serious difficulties for an order that conceives itself as democratic, that the Christian population may need to send a message of disapproval not to the governing party but to the political classes at large, and so on. Jacques Ellul waged periodic campaigns against voting; they deserve at least a respectful mention in the annals of Christian political witness.

However, civil religion is only one manifestation of a more general temptation: that of accommodating the demands of the Gospel to the expectations of society. Any successful mission will leave the church inculturated; any inculturated church is liable to lose its critical distance on society. Forms of prophetic criticism may persist, but they become increasingly intra-mural, taking up those causes which were controversial anyway rather than finding deeper grounds for evangelical challenge. Echoing political controversy, rather than calling its grounds in question, is the sign of a Babylonian captivity which cannot be avoided by purely constitutional precautions. The end of Christendom has not, in fact, resulted in a freer and more independent-minded church. Much Christian enthusiasm for 'pluralism' has less to do with a relation to the state than with the church's yearning to sound in harmony with the commonplaces of the stock exchange, the law-courts and the public schools. It is simply the modern Western version of 'Water-buffalo theology'. And the only precautions we can take are theological. To the extent that the Christian community is possessed by its Gospel, it will be protected against social conformity.

The legacy of Christendom

Notwithstanding the discontinuity of the West with its past in Christendom, there is a legacy still apparent in the institutions of Europe and America. Even if Christendom is not our tradition, we cannot forget that it was our great-grandfathers'. It lies in a fruitful constellation of social and political ideas which came together in a decisively influential way in the sixteenth and seventeenth centuries. Various inferences have been drawn from the dating: an over-confident Protestant apologetic has claimed it as the work of the radicalised Christian consciousness of the Reformation, while champions of secular political theory have seen it as the spring blossom that promised the fruit of the rationalist summer. What has become clear, however, from half a century of research in political history, is that the roots of this new organisation of political priorities run deep into the centuries that preceded it, not only through the late scholastics who are recognisably forebears of the Reformation, but through the earlier scholastics back into the Carolingian and patristic eras; and not only through theologians and their disputations but through the various concrete forms of life in the Christian community: corporations, monastic communities, canon law, penance and so on.

Almost any name we propose for this legacy is open to misunderstanding. The term 'early-modern liberalism', which we shall use, is no more proof against it than any other term would be; there are perfectly good arguments for confining the term 'liberal' to the era after the French Revolution. Its usefulness to us is that it highlights its relation to the dominant conceptions of our own late-modern age. But that relation, of course, is not one of identity. The 'democracy', based on the twin institutions of ballot-box and stock-market, in which the late-modern West takes such pride as to inflict economic misery and political disruption on the largest scale in order to export it, and even to threaten nuclear annihilation to avenge it, is not a simple prolongation of the principles enunciated in that crucial early-modern period. Still, behind the billboards set up by this brash ideology, certain habits and practices instilled by the formative traditions of the modern era can be discerned, at least in its traditional heartlands, and can provide, unacknowledged, much of the moral collateral that supports the giddy speculations of their offspring.

To what extent is Christian political thought tied to the liberal tradition? This question was posed at a fateful moment in the history of the twentieth century, in the course of the debates preceding the Barmen Declaration of 1934 which defined the resistance of the church to German National Socialism. We learn that Paul Althaus complained of the draft, which owed much to Barth's pen, that 'the concept of the state which is presumed here is that of the liberal constitutional state, as in all the writings of Barth' (quoted in E. Jüngel, *Christ, Justice and Peace*, p. 42). Setting aside the conventional resonances which terms such as 'traditionalist' and 'radical' assume *within* the liberal tradition (according to which Barth was the radical and Althaus the traditionalist), it is clear that what Althaus complained of was precisely Barth's refusal to think *outside* the terms set by the modern tradition of the West. Ought a Christian synod, especially when venturing a protest in a revolutionary political situation, to tie itself to a conception of political order which, though it had served Christ's people well in previous generations, had no direct warrant from Scripture? Or should it be open in principle to alternative answers? The same question has been posed from other points on the political spectrum. The Latin American theologians have often indicated that they saw in liberal preoccupations something of a bourgeois ideology which refused to respond to the problems of mass-pauperisation. And in a more philosophical context the critique of liberalism is now a standard element in the work of modernity-critics, who find in the meeting of liberal voluntarism and technological reasoning the nuclear fusion that energises the Leviathan of our age.

> Polemic against liberalism goes back a long way; but it is only in recent decades that it has been radicalised into a critique of the modern (i.e. post-medieval) tradition as such. Even such a figure as Reinhold Niebuhr directed his critiques of liberalism against a progressivist-rationalist strand of thought, whereas more recent writers take their complaint back to the fourteenth century, to Augustine, or to the meeting of Judaism and Hellenism. The precursors of the contemporary modernity-critics are those Catholic apologists such as Chesterton who, building on Leo XIII's *Libertas praestantissimum* (1888),

responded to the Protestant–modernist axis with an enthusiastic championing of what they saw as the medieval ideal of a humanistic, inculturated Christian faith, an antidote to the voluntarism of the modern era. This attempt to turn Protestant apologetic on its head, and lay blame where credit was asked for, has a special interest as an early indication of how the modern era could be conceived in its totality as oppressive. If there was at first something romantic about this conception, it began to attract a grimmer school of reflection between the World Wars (Guardini) and after the second (Ellul and Charbonneau), when reflection on the meaning of technological progress and the interpenetration of the liberal order with dizzying levels of violence demanded new attempts to think about modernity as a cultural whole. Heidegger and Leo Strauss gave serious philosophical resonances to the enterprise. But responsible history no longer allowed the partisan attribution of blame along the fissure-lines of the Reformation. The sources of modernity had to be confronted within Christendom as a whole – but now as a problem, not as a triumph for Christianity. The tradition derived from Christianity had led into a dangerous and inhumane *huis clos*, such as the human race had never encountered before.

What cannot be ignored in the modernity-critics is the demand for an explanation of the threatening aspect of the modern tradition. Clearly, no evaluation of the liberal legacy can get away without identifying the negative developments to which it was exposed. Yet this need not entail the repudiation of Christendom and its legacy. The wisest of the modernity-critics would warn us against any such reaction. We speak and think from within that cultural legacy. It is our 'fate', and its power is seen precisely in our own inability to transcend it in thought. To pretend to renounce it would be as ineffective as the wiggle of a tadpole's tail. Philosophy must invite us to recollect it, and to analyse our recollections. And so modernity-criticism has generally taken the form of sweeping intellectual and cultural history, which has it in view to notice the fateful turns, the points of departure, the path not taken, which have built modernity up into the 'necessity' that now surrounds us. As it has gained in sophistication, modernity-criticism has shown more clearly the multiplicity of threads from which the fabric is woven, and so has allowed us to think of other liberalisms, different possibilities of combination and development than those which have woven our contemporary bondage. By way of this closer view of the weaving of modernity, we are free to discern both the triumph of Christ in liberal institutions and the coming of the Antichrist.

The liberal tradition, however, has right of possession. There is no other model available to us of a political order derived from a millennium of close engagement between state and church. It ought, therefore, to have the first word in any discussion of what Christians can approve, even if it ought not to have the last word. To think through the demands of the Gospel in unfamiliar circumstances, we must have understood its demands in familiar ones; and nothing whatever is gained by a posture of studied distance from the legacy of Christian political reasoning. If the church has to formulate, not an abstract statement of what might *in principle* be conceded to political authority, but a challenge to an existing political situation, then let it begin from the challenge the state has already heard and already responded to. We cannot simply go behind it; it has the status of a church tradition, and demands to be treated with respect.

Two qualifications must be made, however. The first is that this, like all traditions, must be understood and interpreted, not merely perpetuated. The liberal tradition is not homogeneous or unchanging, and its central Christian witness does not always lie on its surface. Late-modern 'democracy' is, as we have said, a different thing from early-modern liberalism, a composite of rationalist, romantic and sceptical influences as well as Christian, some of them tending to subvert, some to strengthen the Christian contribution. The socialism contributed by the nineteenth century and still a most important element has had forms which have displayed both tendencies. The fact that something *is* done or said, and that it *has been* done or said, does not invest it with the authority of tradition in a theological sense; but only as it is shown to be organically derived from the guiding principles of Christian society.

Secondly, even if we can discern precisely the bearing of the Christian liberal tradition on our present concerns, its status is that of tradition, not of revelation; and therefore it cannot merely be posited or assumed. If we are to understand the point of anti-liberal protests from whatever source, we must see them as a warning against converting the fruit of historical experience into abstract statements of political right. To display the liberal achievement correctly, we have to show it as the victory won by Christ over the nations' rulers. It presupposes original political authority, on the one hand, and proclaims the transformation of it wrought by Christ's Spirit on the other. Apart from this salvation-historical background, liberal expectations lose their meaning, which is to point to a *bene esse* of political society which presumes an *esse*. They represent a (provisional) perfection and fulfilment of *political* order which derives its political character from the rule of divine providence. Were it not so, liberalism would be simply depoliticising, Utopian, as indeed it sometimes has appeared. For there are more ways than one in which the Utopian stalemate can be reached. If radical socialism has reached it by exaggerating the capacity of history for immanent transformation, so that social order is predicated on a human nature different from that with which we actually have to deal, liberalism can reach it by refusing to accommodate movement in history at all. There is no from–to in political history, only a posited moment in political experience, extracted from the original vocation of political authority and turned into a norm for all moments. This kind of liberal doctrine is brittle and unadaptable, unable to accommodate itself to the restless tide of history.

This observation has a special importance when we take into consideration societies outside the European sphere of influence, which do not have the historical experience of Christendom behind them. To demand that they conform to practices normative in the West deserves, perhaps, the over-used epithet 'cultural imperialism' as clearly as anything does, especially when those practices are expensive and the societies poor. To take an example of such well-meant but misplaced demands: when Amnesty International associates, as twin objects of its criticism, torture (which is contrary to natural right) and the death penalty (which is contrary to the best late-modern liberal practice), as though they were instances of the same kind of governmental evil, it merely shows it does not understand *why* torture is wrong! That is not to say that societies outside the Western tradition should be encouraged to respect only the most minimal natural-right principles, and never confront the challenge of Christ's triumph. It is simply that the church in those societies, which must be the best judge, has to articulate that challenge at the point at which it touches that society most nearly, not at the point which happens to offend the Western observer's sensibilities.

On this basis a Christian theologian can venture to characterise a *normative political culture* broadly in continuity with the Western liberal tradition. Such a sketch is necessarily general, and cannot foreclose discussion of any substantial question. There is no one political structure that can claim to have carried forward the traditions of Christendom in untainted lineage; there is only a family of political structures which may reflect them variously and with variable success. The arbitration of differences must be left to a later stage. Still, that does not make the general characterisation vacuous or unnecessary. In order to show the triumph of Christ over the kingdoms we must show broadly how their law has submitted to his. Yet if it is to avoid Utopian unreality on the one hand and the historicist illusion of necessary progress on the other, there are some precise disciplines to be observed: (i) We must show that the culture so described is genuinely political, not a Utopian post-political culture. That is to say, it must accommodate political authority, the conjunction of power, right and tradition mediating the divine rule. It must yield policies of government that are practicable in at least some recognisable social conditions. It does not have to be 'realist' to the point of demanding that all social conditions should be treated on the same basis as the least promising; but it must consider what is *practically* thinkable in the *right* social conditions. (ii) We must show that this culture responds to the proclamatory presence of the church in its midst. This requires ecclesiology. Yet it cannot *be* ecclesiology. Political order corresponds to the shape of the church, but may not be absorbed into it. (iii) We must differentiate, and maintain complementarity between, the conception of government, on the one hand ('political' doctrine in the proper sense), and the conception of society ('social' doctrine) on the other. These are the two missionary frontiers from which this chapter began. A set of expectations for government which did not correspond to a set of expectations for society would be abstractly ideal in the sense we have just condemned. Since our concern at this point is with the relation of the church to rulers, we deal with political doctrine here, reserving social doctrine for the next chapter.

The political doctrine that emerged from Christendom is characterised by a notion that government is responsible. Rulers, overcome by Christ's victory, exist provisionally and on sufferance for specific purposes. In the church they have to confront a society which witnesses to the Kingdom under which they stand and before which they must disappear. It is to that conception we refer when we describe political authority in terms of 'the state', a concept unknown to the ancient world because it describes something new, a form of political authority which has come to understand itself differently as a result of Christ's triumph. There are no words for 'state' in Hebrew, Greek or classical Latin. The nearest those ancient languages could come was the Greek *politeia* and the Latin *civitas* and *respublica*. But these terms refer to something concrete, what we properly call the 'political community', i.e. the unit of community defined by its political organisation as a primary (non-responsible) agent. Loosely, too, we use the word 'state' for this, as when we refer to the United Kingdom or the Republic of Ireland as 'states'. But when we speak of 'the church and the state' or of 'the university and the state', or of 'business and the state', we do not mean to oppose church, university and business to bodies like the United Kingdom and the Republic of Ireland. We mean to oppose the church *within* those political communities to that organisational structure within them which enables them to be governed. The state is neither, broadly, the community as a whole, nor, narrowly, the actual government. It is a structure of relations within the community that can perfectly well coexist with other structures that serve other purposes. And that has come to be conceivable only as people have learned not to think of themselves as defined by their political roles, as king, subject, slave, freeman or whatever. Without the self-understanding of Christendom as the meeting-point of two orders of authority, that conception of political relationships would not have come to be.

So when Stanley Hauerwas writes, 'It is not that the state has changed since the coming of Christ, but that now Christ has taken primacy over the old order', the very words he uses betray him ('A Pacifist Response . . .', p. 160). The word 'state' appears in Middle English as a derivate from the Latin expression *status regni*, the 'state of the kingdom'. The 'state of the kingdom' is a generalisation to other political communities of what is meant when we speak of 'the empire', as opposed to 'the emperor', i.e. it is the permanent structure that gives continuity from one reign to the next. The source, therefore, of the notion of the state is to be found in the idea of the Roman empire as a persisting political reality. But that notion depends on two intellectual forces of theological ancestry. The first is the notion of the empire as a factor in salvation-history, whether negative or positive, an instrument designed by God to further the effect of the Incarnation. The second is the concept that the empire had its true identity in a corpus of law which defined all relations, including that of the emperor to his subjects. By these means the empire was cast free of its ancient guarantee of continuity, the 'eternal city'. When this idea was transferred in the high Middle Ages to other kingdoms, it carried with it the implication that a kingdom could preserve its identity, its 'state', by being responsive to God's purposes in salvation and by being constituted as a law-structure derived from the eternal law of God.

Yet the word 'state' has been a constant seduction to theologians who believed they could use it of all political societies in history. To take an example from a generation or so back, Oscar Cullmann's *The State in the New Testament*, a book justifiably appreciated for its exegesis of New Testament texts, is dominated by a concern to say something about Jesus' and Paul's view of 'the state', with the result that its primary thesis is completely uninfluenced by that conception of salvation-history for which Cullmann's other writings became well known. 'The earthly state is God's servant so long as it remains in the order which is willed by God' (p. 89). Jesus and Paul apparently opposed two other views of the state, according to one of which ('the totalitarian claims of the Roman state') it was a divine or final institution, and according to the other, more fantastically, 'the religious community, the Jewish "congregation" (precursor of the Christian "ecclesia") coincided with the state' – this was 'the theocratic ideal of Judaism' (p. 8). It is enough to ask what Aramaic words the Jew used to express the view that 'the *qahal* coincides with the . . . X'. I think no word to fill the space will be found. But, if it can be, it will not mean the same as Cullmann means by the state, but will mean, like the Latin *civitas*, a 'political community'. Cullmann finds just two pages in his book for the victory of Christ over the angelic powers (pp. 69f.), pages largely unassimilated to the theses advanced elsewhere. Yet these pages contain the key to the change in political conceptions which is such a feature of the history of Western politics.

The responsible state is the *bene esse* which corresponds to the *esse* of political authority. The latter we described in chapter two as the union of power, the execution of right and the perpetuation of tradition in one centre of action. In chapter four we marked the transition from *esse* to *bene esse* in terms of the execution of right, which justified the persistence of secular authority until the full appearing of the Kingdom. But the *bene esse* cannot undo the *esse*. The subjection of all authorities to Christ's authority does not mean the dissolution of authority. The conjunction of power, judgment and tradition defines what political authority *is*. A judge has no authority apart from a constable to enforce his rulings and a community to bring pleas to his court. Power and community tradition are still essential to establish authority; the new development is that they are subordinated to just judgment as means to an end. The accumulation of power and the maintenance of community identity cease to be self-evident goods; they have to be justified at every point by their contribution to the judicial function. The responsible state is therefore minimally coercive and minimally representative. Not everything that it could cause to happen should it cause to happen; and not every energy within society that it could maintain should it maintain, but only what is necessary to its task of judging causes. This is not a restraint imposed by the nature of political authority as such, which can thrive on excesses of traditional legitimation and on splendid displays of force; it is imposed by the limits conceded to secular authority by Christ's Kingdom. The most striking instance of this reorientation of politics to the task of justice is provided by those sixteenth-century thinkers who developed the theory of war, interpreting it within the restrictive canons of a judicial act performed by judicial criteria.

The state exists in order to give judgment; but under the authority of Christ's rule it gives judgment *under law*, never as its own law. One might say that the only sense of political authority acknowledged within Christendom was the law of the ascended Christ, and that all political authority was the authority of that law. Those theologians who insisted, against Ambrosiaster, that the source of political authority was Christ, not God the Father alone, understood something important: however much political authority survives from the old aeon, it does so upon terms set by the new. Law as Israel had understood it was the law of Yhwh: the substance of the national self-possession, the form and guarantee of life lived as Yhwh's people. In the Christian proclamation this law divided, as it were, into two streams. Within the church it became more intimate. The substance of the community's self-possession was Christ's own presence. Yhwh's law was absorbed into the spontaneity of faith, written in the inner motivations of the heart, expressed in the workings of the Holy Spirit. It became, in Paul's phrase, 'the law of the Spirit of life in Christ Jesus' (Rom. 8:2). In this stream one might say that law had been converted into prophecy.

In the other stream Yhwh's law came to assume a commanding rule over the rulers that the church confronted. Subjection to the Christ was the 'decree of Yhwh' (Ps. 2:7–9). Certain key convictions about law became formalised in Christian Europe: all law derives from the will of God; all law is one; all secular rulers are subject to law. These shaped the creative remodelling of the existing traditions of Roman law, initially in the East by Justinian and his exponents, and later in the West by the canon and civil lawyers of the twelfth century and after. Independent traditions of legal conformity, which could establish independent foci of community, were suspect, not least that of English common law. In that great work of synthetic theological imagination, Thomas Aquinas' Treatise on Law (*Summa theologiae* II–I qq.90–106), what should attract our notice is not the much-discussed treatment of Natural Law, in itself a minor feature, but the architectonic conception of law as a unified structure finding its source in God's creative decrees for universal existence.

The legislative activity of princes, then, was not a beginning in itself; it was an answer to the prior lawmaking of God in Christ, under which it must be judged. Christendom in effect refused the classical commonplace that the ruler was a 'living law', his personal authority indistinguishable from the authority of the law he gave. Even those Christians who defended most determinedly the supremacy of the sovereign over earthly courts understood well enough that the sovereign's decree had no legal substance if it ran counter to divine law, natural or revealed. (So Grotius responded to Calvinists who demanded synods that could legislate on church affairs, that if a prince attempted to introduce idolatry, it needed no synod to invalidate the act since any civil lawyer would recognise that it was void.) In situating human legislation under the law of God in this fashion, the tradition stressed the juridical character of *all* governmental activity. Even making statutes was giving effect to law that already existed, acting like a court that makes law in the course of administering it.

Generically, government is legitimated by its judicial function. But how is any particular government legitimated? Constitutional reflection became one of the hallmarks of the Christian political tradition, following a course quite different from the classical reflection about what kind of government was best – democratic, oligarchic or monarchic. For Christian culture the question, rather, was how a government of any of these kinds can claim to be *the* government of a given people. In other words, how can a government be representative? For no people's identity as a people can be assumed; community identity is no longer self-evident. It is called in question by the existence of a new people, drawn from every nation, which by its catholic identity casts doubt on every other. If there is no longer Jew or Greek, how can there be a Jewish or Greek government? But, then, if there is no representative status, there is no authority of tradition, and no political authority either. Government appears like a fortress erected on an island which the sea is washing away. Significant of this was the relentless theological sniping directed against the principle of hereditary succession, especially, but not only, from papalist sources. It did not seem apparent to a Christian mind that continuity of regime ought to be maintained this way, which gave so little scope for the doctrine that every ruler held authority under the commission of the ascended Christ.

> John Wyclif, who was hardly unsupportive of the claims of temporal rulers, dismissed as 'insufficient' a claim to civil dominion based on hereditary succession. Virtue alone, he thought, was a sufficient title to rule, if it were recognised by the people. But virtue is charity; and charity is not transmitted naturally from father to son. Beyond any conventional forms of transmission, whether hereditary or electoral, a further title is needed, that of charity, which is conferred by baptism. Wyclif then develops a supporting argument of great interest. The meaning of 'sonship' is transformed in the Christian Gospel. It can arise not only by nature, but by law, adoption, imitation and instruction. Every true saint has a title to dominion by heredity, derived from Christ, who is the only and sole lord and who is our father and elder brother. By adoption, imitation and instruction the 'predestinate' is related to the three persons of the Holy Trinity. Spiritual generation, then, is what counts. Natural generation can count for little. If the claimant to the throne is spiritually regenerate, *then* the existing conventions for transmission, whether they be hereditary or electoral, may be followed (*De civili dominio* 1.30). Wyclif is, of course, a radical; but he always radicalises an existing tradition of thought, which is, in fact, the Augustinian tradition deployed by his papalist opponents.

We can trace several phases in the attempt to answer the question of representative legitimacy (though with the caution that the appearance of successive development is an illusion, since these theories overlapped and competed with each other for long periods). The first phase was marked by the belief that a world placed under God's universal rule by a universal church needed a universal secular government, a world-empire. A line of pre-Nicene apologetic had found it providential that the Roman empire appeared at the very moment it was needed as a setting for the Incarnation. Christ's rule could be reflected only by world-government. The idea found its most thoroughgoing exposition in Dante's *De monarchia*, when it was already a little old-fashioned. But, of course, the iconic appropriateness of empire made it also suspect. The presence of the Apocalypse within the canon did not allow Christians to forget that Antichrist, too, was perfectly expressed in world-rule. The age of the church surely needed a plural secular order, in which no prince, but only the church itself, could foreshadow Christ's universal Kingdom. A different and better way of conceiving the universal scope of Christ's present rule arose from the legal tradition. Law holds equal and independent subjects together without allowing one to master the other. The last and greatest of the legal accomplishments of Christendom was the conception that there exists, not merely as an ideal but in fact, an *international law*, dependent on no regime and no statute, but on the Natural Law implanted in human minds by God, and given effect by international custom and convention.

The second phase concerns the concept of kingship. 'Divine right' is a phrase largely associated with the late, seventeenth-century attempt to revive it in a baroque and autocratic form, but it focusses rather well upon an older theological principle: government, and with it every aspect of political organisation, is given from above. It is not grounded in any existing political form of nationhood, but imposed upon an essentially unformed social material by divine appointment of kings. The fragmented character of feudal society made it natural to envisage a complex and shifting relation between any local society organised around a baron and the monarchs who defined the political macrostructure. Large territories pass easily out of the control of one king into that of another. 'Kingdoms' are historical forms that rise and fall, expand or contract, by God's providential dispensation. They are not shaped in any necessary way by race or language. Still, human conduct is not left blind under divine providence. If right is not located in given identities, then it is located elsewhere – again, in law. *Lex facit regem*, the legal maxim declared. We witness the birth of constitutional law, at first hardly distinguishable from private law of various kinds to do with property or matrimony. Law not only proceeds from the ruler; it precedes him. His own legitimation must be a matter of appeal to law. What gives a regime its entitlement is a law-structure which defines rights of succession as well as rights and obligations of tenure, just like any other right and obligation. With this, political authority begins to be conceived as office.

In the third phase constitutional law, as it is separated out from other forms of law, becomes developed into constitutional principle. To mark out the distinctness of political dominion from other kinds of legal power, e.g. those of property or matrimonial state, the relation of the ruler to the people has to emerge more sharply. But still there is no appeal to a natural political form; the political community is defined in terms of a hypothetical act performed in common. A 'perfect society', one which is essentially self-sufficient, may decide on a type of government and elect to it; from this act derives the ruler's representative legitimacy. The 'perfect society', we may observe, is a purely formal unit, determined by the contingent fact of self-sufficiency, not a natural unit. What counts and does not count as a perfect society may change with history, so that the element of social plasticity under the providential sovereignty of God is still insisted on. The absence of a natural political form has thrown the weight of the theory back upon an act of collective will. This element of voluntarism, which was, of course, to become much more marked in later political theory, was due to the lack of any other social ground for saying that this, and not that, should be the unit of political society. However, in the constitutionalist stage of the theory, the act of will does not account for the nature of political authority as such. If later contractarians found the essence of political rule in the capacity of a community to will as one, the constitutionalists found only the occasion. The source of authority for them was the will of God. In appointing itself a head, society entered into a provision for political structure that God had decreed, and began to enjoy a power of political agency that it had not enjoyed while it was still acephalous. Society had no political authority otherwise.

In a critical and important paragraph of *De potestate civili*, Vitoria writes (according to the authoritative Palentine MS): 'Sed his relictis ad id quod dicebam antea reddeamus, scilicet regiam potestatem non esse a republica sed a Deo ipso ut catholici docti sentiunt. Item videtur quod regia potestas sit a Deo, dato quod reges a republica constituantur. Sicut namque summus pontifex ab ecclesia eligitur et creatur, potestas summi pontifex non est ab ecclesia sed a Deo ipso, ita videtur quod regia potestas sit a Deo, quamvis a republica reges creentur. Respublica namque in regem non potestatem sed propriam authoritatem transfert. Nec sunt due potestates, una regia altera communitatis, atque ideo sicut potestatem reipublicae esse a Deo et iure naturali constitutam asseruimus idem prorsus de potestate regia dicamus necesse est . . .' (8). Vitoria speaks of 'power' where we have spoken throughout of 'political authority'. The assertion, therefore, that the political community does not transfer *potestas* but *propria authoritas* is to be understood to mean that society authorises the particular ruler to occupy the seat of political authority, but in doing so does not alienate an authority of its own or bring into existence a second authority alongside its own. There is one authority which, simultaneously, he holds as appointed ruler and the state holds as politically organised society. The papal parallel controls the conception throughout.

An important development of the constitutional idea was the attempt to bring the act of deposing a ruler within the scope of lawful political action. Pope Gregory VII and his successors claimed the right to remove unworthy rulers as a central element in the duty of spiritual jurisdiction to judge secular. But the conviction that a ruler's office depended on the law of God made it important to envisage its lawful termination as a general possibility, apart from papal claims. John of Salisbury's famous argument about tyrannicide can be seen as a laicisation of the papalist principle. The tyrant is a figure hostile to the common good; he attacks law, and law is superior even to emperors. To slay the tyrant is to defend the law, an act on behalf of, rather than against, public order. But this depended on the notion that an absolute political vacuum was created by the tyranny. Subsequent discussion allowed that there would be an element of political order, however corrupt, in any actual tyranny. Yet this did not make the act of tyrannicide unthinkable, because one could make a distinction between the office of the ruler and the person who occupied it, so that to remove an unworthy occupant was not necessarily to resist the authority of the office. But if replacing a tyrannical ruler was an act in defence of law, there must be a lawful means of carrying this out; from the fourteenth century onwards there was a search for constitutional mechanisms which could effect a change of government at need. The radical Calvinist theories of the late sixteenth century, which identified a particular office, supposedly implicit in any constitutional order, which bore the responsibility for restraining or removing the supreme magistrate, were simply the conclusion of this search.

> At the end of the third book of John of Salisbury's *Policraticus* (*c*. 1155) the author remarks, curiously, that the tyrant is the only person to whom it is licit to offer flattery; for, as he formulates it in a strange rule, one may flatter whom one may slay. To slay the tyrant is not merely licit, it is equitable and right; for it is commanded by our Lord that whoever takes the sword shall die by the sword. The tyrant has taken the sword (rather than receiving it from God) and has subjected right and law to his own will. Tyranny is a 'more than public crime', since it attacks laws and laws are superior to emperors. To fail to prosecute the enemy

of the public realm is to sin against oneself and against the earthly republic. Formally John offers two criteria for discerning tyranny: usurpation and opposition to law. But the weight of his argument falls on the second of these, and in Thomas' discussion in the thirteenth century it is this criterion to which he attends, giving it greater precision with the aid of a definition from Aristotle's *Politics*: the tyrant is one who 'seeks his own advantage from rule, not the good of the multitude that is subject to him' (*De regno* I.II). Tyranny is thus the limiting case of the general principle which underlies all bad government, namely the substitution of partial and sectional interests for the good of the whole, but here the partial has become exclusively private, as the interests are not those of a dominant group but of a single person. From tyranny no law can be derived (*Summa theologiae* II–I q.95.4); for law is the structure of the public good and tyranny is the privatising of all public relations. Hence 'the overthrow of such a regime does not have the character of sedition' (II–2 q.42.2). Yet Thomas is not an unqualified enthusiast for the violent overthrow of tyranny. It is not for him, as for John, a duty. Since it involves shedding blood other than in just and authorised punishment, it requires at least proportionate reason. He warns that the civil disturbance of an insurrection may be an evil disproportionate to the civil good intended. For public order to be converted into a private feoff may not be the worst of all evils, especially if the lord appreciates that benevolence is in his own longer-term interest. Nevertheless, Thomas agrees with John on the rationale for resisting tyrants: the regime is so unqualifiedly private that it claims none of the privileges of true government.

The thought that crosses neither of their minds is that a ruler who possessed *public* authority might be resisted or overthrown. In the fourteenth century this thought commonly crossed theologians' minds. A new factor was the constitutional concept of how rule is conferred. Given that the highest office is received from God not immediately but through the hands of a collective body, there is within the structure of political order itself a principle that allows the correction of an abusive ruler. So Marsilius of Padua, not challenging the doctrine that all political order flows from the sovereign, makes a distinction between the sovereign's office and the person who, capable of false opinion and perverse desire, can be judged by the very law that flows from his office (*Defensor pacis* 18). There is, of course, a corollary to this conception: since the removal of a ruler is an act of law, not an act performed in a legal vacuum, it must be done lawfully. Here the case of the emperor provided a useful paradigm. Since he was constitutionally appointed by electors, he could, some civil lawyers argued, be deposed by the same electors. This provided a useful secular counter-proposal to the pope's claim to have that competence (e.g Ockham, *VIII quaestiones* II.9). In the fifteenth century conciliarists such as Nicholas of Cusa locate this civil-law principle within a general doctrine that government is illegitimate if not representative: 'all legitimate authority arises from elective concordance and free submission' (*Catholic Concordance* III.331).

Another element of discipline is now introduced. Since there is no political vacuum, there is no licence for anarchy. The ruler who may be deposed for his crimes remains, until removal, an authority who demands obedience. Wyclif argues that Christians ought to obey tyrannical powers (*De civili dominio* 1.28), on the ground that the subject must consent to just political order in principle, and in doing so is not consenting to occasional abuse. Responding to the argument that clergy need not pay taxes tyrannously imposed (i.e. from which clergy ought to be exempt!), he maintains that the goods of the realm are meant for the defence of the realm, and the goods of the church for the relief of the poor, so that from neither point of view have the clergy any business clinging to it; and that the consent they yield in paying taxes is consent to government as such, not to abuses. But after all that, Wyclif springs a surprise characteristic of this most disconcerting of political thinkers. He adds almost in passing that if the refusal to pay tax is actually likely to correct the abuse or overthrow the tyranny, then we ought to refuse with that intention. In other words: refusal of obedience is justified only as an element in a really serious strategy of revolution!

What we find in the sixteenth century is a variety of ways of developing the gains of the medieval thinkers. Differences arise from different conceptions of how the tyrant's removal is related to the structure of law. Calvin and his followers favour a constitutional answer derived by analogy from the empire. Private persons may not act alone. There are certain officials ('ephors' as they liked to call them) on whom rests the duty of correcting, restraining and if necessary removing the chief magistrate. Beza identified these with the parliamentary estates. An alternative pattern was favoured by radicals such as John Knox, who appealed directly to the relevance of divine law for civil government. John Ponet, a radical Anglican, invoked the authorisation of Natural Law. But for all of them the removal of a corrupt ruler is an expression of the operation of the rule of law. Only later, with the earliest contractarians, does the old opinion reassert itself that the deposition of a ruler is a reversion of society to a pre-political state of nature.

The legal-constitutional conception is the essence of Christendom's legacy. Why a quite different framework came to be superimposed upon that legacy in later centuries is not our concern here; but the concept of 'sovereignty' is often held to be pivotal to the transformation. Within the context of Christian constitutionalism, sovereignty (*suprema potestas*) had a clearly defined reference to that office of state which, by presiding over other offices, ensured the lawfulness and authority of the whole. Sovereignty within the state was compatible with, even depended on, the rule of divine law over the state. In the course of the seventeenth century, however, under the influence of contract-theory, an important shift of emphasis occurred in radical political thought: the ruler's primary responsibility ceased to be thought of as being to divine law, but rather to the people whose supposed act constituted him. This act of popular will came to be thought of as the source of all law and constitutional order. With this the meaning of the term 'sovereignty' expanded to encompass much more than had hitherto been meant. Even absolutist monarchs who, resisting the populist trend, claimed sovereignty for the Crown alone intended by that term something mythical and expansive. 'Sovereignty' became a corporate personality, or source of will, which gave the body politic its identity.

That change can be as well, perhaps better, described as a collapse of the idea of a universal Natural Law, and its replacement by a nationalist positivism. Either way, what has happened is that the immanent political form within society has reasserted itself. The 'nation' has made a reappearance, not constituted by blood now but by a common political will expressed in national history, the 'nation-state' characteristic of the modern era. With this change the young notion of international law withered into sceptical minimalism, not to be revived until the late nineteenth century. Revolution, on the other hand, casting off the limiting restraints of constitutionalist legitimacy, acquired a new foundation in the capacity of popular will to haemorrhage in episodes of precipitous destruction. Today, it is often thought, we stand at the end of this line of development. Internationalism has, in various forms, reasserted itself. Even the recovery of national identities in Eastern Europe from the experiment of Communism has done nothing to remove the general suspicion that nationalisms are reactionary. On all sides pundits proclaim that the nation-state is in trouble. The truth is, it has been in trouble ever since Christ rose from the dead. The challenge issued to given, a priori political identities has been a persistent *Leitmotiv* of Christian thought.

Yet the question still presses on us, as it always has, how we may qualify the claims of nations (or cities, or empires, or civilisations) without replacing them with abstract forms that lack sufficient representative authority. For the Christian political culture is also engaged on the side of social authenticity. The concept of divine law, as we have said, divides into two streams: secular government, on the one side, armed with the law of God under which it claims authority, encounters, on the other, the law of the Spirit of Christ, the law which has become prophecy, present wherever society has made a place for the church in its midst. And to that law, too, it must defer. Late-modern liberal freedom tends to describe this deference as offered solely to individual freedoms, and we will have occasion to note the element of truth in this. But as it stands it is too weak. A failure to see that *society* requires the state's deference underlies a great deal of 'liberal tyranny' in the late-modern age. The spontaneities which set bounds on the scope of human lawgiving are social before they are individual spontaneities. They have their authority because, and to the extent that, they too derive from the law of God.

7. The redemption of society

The end of Christendom

The Gentile mission had two frontiers, social and political. The church demanded the obedience of society, and it demanded the obedience of society's rulers. 'Nations shall come to your light, and kings to the brightness of your rising' (Isa. 60:3). The parallel in that text is complementary, not synonymous; the horizons of its two members are different. For while the nations gather to the rising light of Zion to bring gold and frankincense and to proclaim Yhwh's praise (6), their kings come only to be led in triumphal procession (11). Communities are incorporated into Yhwh's Kingdom; rulers merely resign their pretensions. Yet these are two aspects of one conquest; the submission of the rulers is not an end in itself, but a moment in the gathering of many societies into one. And so the first and last frontier of the Gentile mission is the social frontier. The conversion of Constantine, with all that followed from it, was only an intermediate frontier which developed from the effective mission of the church to society and led back to it. The drama of the Kingdom will end not with the rulers, but with the song of the innumerable multitude from every nation, tribe, people and language (Rev. 7:9f.).

In this sense at least, then, the goal of Christendom is 'After Christendom'. Since Christendom has, on our account, to do with the submission of rulers, it prepares the way for something beyond itself, the replacement of the rulers by the Christ. But the hope of such a fulfilment can lose its eschatological character, and be turned to support historicist ideologies which find the dawning of the Kingdom within late-modern secularism. Christendom has ended, we say – but in what sense of the word 'end'? Has it fulfilled itself in the transition from the rule of the kings to the rule of the Christ, or has it simply been eclipsed by the vicissitudes of mission, perhaps to return in another form or, if not to return, to provide a standing reminder of the political frontier which mission must always address? For the historicist conception directs the church to a social mission without a political aspect to it. The moment for the conversion of political agency is, in its view, past.

I take it as beyond dispute that Christendom has in fact ended, in the minimal sense of the verb at least. Our contemporaries no longer think that the rulers of the earth owe service to the rule of Christ. To say this much, of course, is not by any means to give an exhaustive description of the way things stand in Europe and America today. By written law or convention states continue to acknowledge the church's mission. The legal situation in England, Scotland and Sweden is well known; less well known are such arrangements as the triple establishment of Lutherans, Catholics and Orthodox in Finland, a model which could have been more widely imitated. Conventional acknowledgment such as is often found in traditionally Catholic lands may be no less significant. Perhaps there are few places in the world where the church never receives encouragement from government, though this may happen more usually on an occasional government-to-synod basis than on a constitutional state-to-church basis. Yet all this is, at best, a qualification to a prevailing ethos which demands that we accept the end of Christendom. The ethos is usually expressed in terms of a doctrine of 'separation of church and state', an uncommunicative formula, to be sure, since those words assert nothing that could have perturbed the most traditional apologist for dual jurisdiction in Christendom. The intent of this doctrine, however, in its modern context, is to deny at least one element in the Christendom idea: that the state should offer deliberate assistance to the church's mission. The development of the modern doctrine was associated with the sceptical conviction of the Enlightenment that religious questions were not open to public arbitration.

The First Amendment to the United States Constitution, prohibiting the 'establishment' and protecting the 'free exercise' of religion, is the paradigm assertion of this doctrine, and so can usefully be taken as the symbolic end of Christendom. There are, of course, many other events which could compete for that role. From the same period one might choose the French Revolution; from a much later one even the 1914–18 war suggests itself. But the American enactment is peculiarly suitable, since it propounds a doctrine meant to replace the church–state relations which Christendom had maintained, it was formulated largely by Christians who thought they had the interests of the church's mission at heart, and it was argued for, as it still is, on ostensibly theological grounds. But it also bears the marks of the Age of Revolution, reflecting a conception of society constituted from below by its own internal dynamics; government does not form society, but puts itself at its disposal. The evangelical Christians who helped shape the new doctrine wished to deny government the right to interfere. In the name of King Jesus they proposed to instruct princes that they were dispensable to the Holy Spirit's work, and to send them to the spectators' seats. But what might simply have been a radicalised announcement of Christ's triumph, though over-inclined to 'realised eschatology' perhaps, made common cause with anti-trinitarian heterodoxy which was permeated by rationalist conceptions of action and providence. So it ended up promoting a concept of the state's role from which Christology was excluded, that of a state freed from all responsibility to recognise God's self-disclosure in history.

The paradox of the First Amendment is that a measure first conceived as a liberation for authentic Christianity has become, in this century, a tool of anti-religious sentiment, weakening the participation of the church in society and depriving it of access to resources for its social role. The orthodox dissenters who framed it had, of course, no grounds to anticipate such an outcome. The situations they knew best, and expected to maintain, were those in which local religious hegemonies prevailed and shaped the communities they dominated. They had no idea of religious pluralism. They expected atheists, anti-trinitarians and even Roman Catholics to be legally excluded from public office. But they did not like their influence within their communities to be hamstrung by religious policies maintained by government, especially colonial government exercised from a great distance. They wished to overthrow the legal tie between the Crown and the church that existed in England. In this respect the First Amendment was no afterthought to the American Revolution; it simply articulated one of its dominant concerns. (On this see J. C. D. Clark, *The Language of Liberty*.)

The reasons for rejecting Anglican establishment begin with the brutal fact that Protestant Christianity was divided. This made any attempt on the part of government to promote Christian worship and mission appear arbitrary to those outside the hegemonic confession. *Cuius regio eius religio* was a policy nobody wanted in principle, generated as a necessary second-best by unnegotiably stubborn theological divisions. But there were other factors which made the general situation worse in this case. One was the positivist understanding of the role of the Crown which had developed in Stuart and Whig political theory. The Crown's privilege of determining the normative public form of Christianity was not defended in terms of its obligation to obey Christ and the apostolic testimony, but on the basis of divine providence which had set the crown mysteriously on this and not some other head. Positivism invites counter-positivism. It was understandable enough that dissenting groups, when in sufficient strength, should ask themselves what further mysterious twists divine providence might execute if put courageously to the test.

In the third place, there were features of the intellectual climate of the eighteenth century which weakened the Christian understanding of salvation-history, and replaced it with an open-ended concept of historical development, shaped by human action ventured, perhaps, in imitation of Christ but not in obedient faith directed back to his accomplished work. The shift from salvation-history to an unfolding providence undermined the intelligibility of Christian secular government, as it undermined the intelligibility of the doctrine of the Trinity itself, leaving it high and dry on the austere sands of the *Quicunque vult* without its necessary point of reference in the Paschal triumph. A Deist religion of divine fatherhood seemed sufficient to support the authority which government needed; while in evangelical religion worship of Christ could not unsuitably be seen as the prerogative of the converted few, the church within the church. Meanwhile the Puritan emphasis on the Holy Spirit had nourished a religion of private conscience. All these factors coincided to support the disestablishment thesis. Deists and evangelicals could agree that the state hardly knew enough about God to make a trinitarian Christianity normative. It suited them both to maintain revealed Christianity as a mystery for initiates.

But this convergence only amounted to a negative strategy of denial. Much damage was to be done in the later nineteenth and early twentieth centuries by anti-ecumenical strategies of this type: social institutions, notably schools, were lost to Christian influence as minority Christian communities, which could not control them, preferred anything to their falling under the control of the larger churches; while hegemonic churches disdained to give the smaller denominations any stake in them. And so it was in this case, too. By denying any church established status in principle, the framers of the First Amendment gave away more than they knew. They effectively declared that political authorities were incapable of evangelical obedience. And with this the damage was done. It did not need the anti-religious line of interpretation pursued by twentieth-century courts to make this formula, from a theological point of view, quite strictly heretical. The creed asserts: *cuius regni non erit finis;* and the apostle, that 'at the name of Jesus every knee shall bow' (Phil. 2:10). The First Amendment presumes to add: 'except . . .'

Excluding government from evangelical obedience has had repercussions for the way society itself is conceived. Since the political formation of society lies in its conscious self-ordering under God's government, a society conceived in abstraction is unformed by moral self-awareness, driven by internal dynamics rather than led by moral purposes. To deny political authority obedience to Christ is implicitly to deny that obedience to society, too. Precisely such a conception arose from the sociology which emerged in the eighteenth and came to maturity in the nineteenth century. Society was an acephalous organism, driven by unconscious forces from within, an object of study and, to the skilful, of manipulation, but in no sense a subject of responsible action. With this conception late-modernity, as we now experience it, stands on the threshold. This, after all, is society as it has been thought about in capitalist economic theory and in revolutionary socialism; it is liberal technological society, which functions like a computer constantly to extend the scope of its own operations in obedience to no rational purpose. The social sciences are the heartlands of this conception, but, to the extent that they have been methodologically self-critical and understood their own abstractions for what they are, thought-experiments designed to isolate and examine certain types of relation, they have also pointed to how it may be transcended.

Society so conceived presents itself as a 'secular' reality. Within the traditional meaning of the term, of course, society as a whole could never be secular. Secularity pertained only to certain functions within society which had their *raison d'être* in relation to this age (*saeculum*), not the next. The distinction of spiritual and secular was a distinction of two kinds of government within the one society. When in pre-modern Christianity two societies were distinguished as 'two realms' or 'two cities', they were polarised as moral and eschatological alternatives. There were not a spiritual society and a secular society, only a society of the saved and a society of the damned. (The use of the term 'secular' to mean non-monastic is confusing, but irrelevant.) The appearance of a social secularity could, however, be created by understanding society as a quasi-mechanical system, incapable of moral and spiritual acts. Such a social organism may, it has been urged, make no moral or religious decisions on its own part, but leave the whole range of such decisions open for its members to make. But this is an abstract conception, not a sustainable proposal. Imagine the questions that such a society would have to avoid deciding: Are sacred ancestral lands protected against plans for mining or other development? Is drug-taking, or sex with child prostitutes, a valid religious activity? Can racial discrimination be practised to preserve the elect people of God or to safeguard religious caste? May women be priests? Must those in quest of unemployment benefit be prepared to accept work on Sundays or Saturdays? Every actual society reaches answers to these questions which it treats as normative, and so makes definite religious judgments about the proper content of religious belief and practice. The false self-consciousness of the would-be secular society lies in its determination to conceal the religious judgments that it has made.

What effect does this nexus of ideas about society have upon the conception of justice? It dissolves its unity and coherence by replacing it with a plurality of 'rights'. The language of subjective rights (i.e. rights which adhere to a particular subject) has, of course, a perfectly appropriate and necessary place within a discourse founded on law. One's 'right' is the claim on which the law entitles one to demand performance. In such a sense *mishpāt* may sometimes be translated 'a right' in the text of the Hebrew Scriptures. What is distinctive about the modern conception of rights, however, is that subjective rights are taken to be original, not derived. The fundamental reality is a plurality of competing, unreconciled rights, and the task of law is to harmonise them. (This picture is not significantly improved when, cross-breeding natural rights with legal positivism, it is said that the law must first *create* these promiscuous rights, then harmonise them.) The right is a primitive endowment of power with which the subject first engages in society, not an enhancement which accrues to the subject from an ordered and politically formed society.

All this we can say without referring to 'individualism'. Individualism there certainly has been within the Western political culture, partly as a legacy of the contract-theory of the seventeenth century; and it has been especially imprinted upon the discussion of 'rights'. Yet not all appeals to original subjective rights have been concerned with individual rights, and there have been strong counter-currents to the individualist mainstream. Sociology itself developed as a reaction against individualism, insisting on the prior and inescapable reality of the 'social fact'.

> The idea of original subjective rights, though especially prominent in the modern era, has an instructive pre-history. It arose from the social conceptions of feudalism, which envisaged the construction of political order from below by the major landholding interests, whose 'right' was coextensive with their 'dominion'. These were by no means all individuals. Not only barons, but monastic secular chapters, city corporations and guilds, all with their estates, asserted their several rights and looked to royal and papal government to uphold them. To the Franciscans and their defenders belongs the doubtful credit of launching the concept of subjective right on a trajectory independent of property, though still parallel to it. Promoting a mendicant ideal of absolute poverty, and needing to explain how mendicants, though owning nothing, could eat and drink and command the necessities of life, they posited a 'right of natural necessity' (Bonaventure) or a 'right of use' (Ockham). Though dissociated from real property, this right still carried proprietary overtones. Gerson invoked the term 'dominion' to describe this right of self-preservation, and, indeed, initiated the tradition of conceiving freedom as a property in one's own body and its powers. All this explains why the concept of rights cannot be invoked without some care. It easily leads our imagination back to a pre-political conception of society composed of private powers rooted in wealth, a conception which the theory of law had to wrestle to overcome.

Our understanding of the role of sociology in the emergence of modernity has been much assisted by John Milbank's *Christianity and Social Theory*. On the material of this note see especially Joan Lockwood O'Donovan, 'Historical Prolegomena . . .'

The demoralised conception of society which follows from viewing it in abstraction from government makes it necessary for political theology, charged with proclaiming the victory of Christ over the ruling powers, to defend their provisional role against a premature enthusiasm for dismissing them. Still, it would be short-sighted to suppose that it was simply government, in the institutional sense, that demanded this defence. What is at stake here is the exercise of authority itself, under Christ's authority, whether by institutional government or by other informally constituted leadership. We wrote in chapter one of the 'political act', the act which is authorised and carries authority, which can give moral form to a community by defining its commitment to the good in a representative performance. Such acts are not confined to institutionalised governments, though governments are institutionalised to ensure that such acts may be performed as necessary. If they were, new institutional governments could never be brought into existence where they did not exist already. The scope and possibilities of the political act will have to be explored, should God grant it to be, in a sequel to this work that will carry its focus from political theology to political ethics.

In championing the authority of the political act, however, we champion society itself. For the concept of acephalous community is not a just or true one, and political theology is bound to replace it with a better. Here, too, the legacy of Christendom, the normative political culture which we introduced in the last chapter from the side of government, must be our guide. For the impact of Christ's victory shaped not only how rulers' tasks were thought about in Christendom, but how society itself, claimed for its own fulfilment by the rule of Christ, was understood. Early-modern liberalism (in the sense explained on pp. 226f.) implied not only lawful government but a community susceptible to it; it comprised a set of expectations about how human beings might live together.

What formed these expectations? In some measure, secular government itself did. As it was disciplined and restrained by the law of God, society had the opportunity to become law-governed. But such an opportunity would have come to nothing had society not also been influenced from the other side, by the missionary presence of the church within its midst. The other stream of divine law, the law of the Spirit of life in Christ Jesus, shaped civil society, too, and so helped change the forms of government from below into those which would accord with the presence of Christ's authority in society. We have had an opportunity to see such pressures exerted by the faithful witness of the church in the revolutions which, a few years ago, overthrew the Communist regimes of East-Central Europe. No event in our time, perhaps, is more striking than the Christmas Revolution of 1989 in Romania, where an internal struggle for purity of witness within the church (and that in an ethnic-minority church in an officially atheist country!) resulted in a few days in the downfall of a regime and the Communist system. Of course, such events offer multiple levels of explanation. There were many widows in Israel in the days of Elijah the prophet, we are told; and many pastors in the days of Nicolae Ceauşescu, not all of whom could exercise the role of Pastor Tokés. But for all the contingencies there is a telling theological significance in the role the church played in that event, which exemplifies the role the church has played, usually with less drama, in the history of Europe and America.

In tracing the characteristic features of liberal society, then, we need to show how it has been affected by the narrative structure of the church, which is itself a recapitulation of the narrative structure of the Christ-event. Once again, we shall deploy the structural device of the four moments, in order to maintain the full evangelical shape of this social order against a tendency to reduce it to a single principle, such as 'liberty'. A social order based on a single principle, however fine, becomes ideological; and a political theology which defends freedom without filling it out with the content of the divine command and the divine redemption of society in Christ is ideologically liberal.

This point has been well made by the Irish theologian Enda McDonagh, who has written (in *The Gracing of Society*) that political theology needs to be organised not around one but around four 'Kingdom values'. He lists these as: justice, freedom, peace and truth. Any one of them will become a mere slogan unless it is given content by the other three. The organising categories of social thought need to coexist (borrowing a term from trinitarian theology) in 'perichoresis', since the social order that God has willed is one, but is determined by more than one factor. I regret the choice of the word 'values', but otherwise find myself in strong agreement; and his list corresponds tolerably well with the four moments which I had arrived at independently. In place of his 'justice' I shall speak of 'merciful judgment', which is a qualification, not a suspension, of justice. For his 'peace' I have 'natural order'; and for his 'truth' I have used the term 'freedom of speech'. In each of these cases the compatibility of our trains of thought will emerge. What McDonagh does not offer is a reason for thinking this fourfold organisation necessary. My own reason for thinking it so is that society is shaped by the Christian proclamation of the Christ, who came, suffered, was restored and exalted.

But here an element of caution is in place. There is only one society which is incorporated into the Kingdom of God and which recapitulates the narrative of the Christ-event, and that is the church. Even in deep Christendom civil society was not identical with the church, but, at most, merged with it on the surface in a prosopic union. Society shaped by the presence of the church forms a kind of penumbra to the church, a radiation of it rather than a participation in it. Society in this form has constantly been challenged and invited by the proclamation of the church; it has been heedful, but not wholly obedient; it has been claimed for the Kingdom, but not sacramentally made part of it. It has respect for the community of Christ, even a profound sense of identification with it, to the point where it can lose the sense of the difference and conceives itself as being the church. Yet it is not the church. Pending the final disclosure of the Kingdom of God, the church and society are in a dialectical relation, distant from each other as well as identified. Though many members of a society have decided for the Gospel, society has not yet decided. It stands on the threshold, not within the door. It has before it the possibility of deciding either way, for the Kingdom or against it.

For that reason it would be disingenuous to describe a society formed in this way as a simple ideal, which may or may not be realised. In speaking of government we could describe a *bene esse*, forged by the traditions of Christendom, which might, however, coexist in any time and place with the simple *esse* of government or with government in various states of corruption and disintegration, depending on the circumstances that prevail from time to time and from place to place. Society as a whole, however, is too permeated by its memories and traditions to allow of simple relapse. Having taken on the narrative form of the Christ-event, it cannot become unformed. The possibilities open to society with history and memory of the Gospel proclamation do not include naïve malevolence, but only a formation that is demonic to the extent that it is not redeemed and redemptive. Here we must give substance to the exegesis of the Apocalypse on which we ventured in chapter four. The redemptive reality within history becomes the occasion for a disclosure of the historical possibilities of evil, an evil shaped in imitation and replication of the redemptive good. Personalised interpretations of the Antichrist theme, which lie buried like fossils in the palaeological deposit of religious thought, have tended to conceal the importance of the Antichrist conception precisely as an interpretation of the dynamic possibilities of society. For society has become a historical reality within the saving purposes of God. Social evil is not always regression, barbarism, a turning back to the primitive *esse* from the *bene esse*. It must, under historical conditions, become precisely misdirected progress, corrupt sophistication, the idolisation of historical evolution. Though political experience continues to be troubled by regressive movements, the worst, and the most characteristically twentieth-century, evils of political experience have been progressive. We must find room in our account, then, to display the turn from the *melius esse* to the *peius*, and so recognise the testimony of those modernity-critics who have claimed to see the worst menace and oppression precisely in the cultural totality of late-modern liberalism.

Liberal society

1. The narrative of liberal society begins to unfold, predictably enough, with its discovery of *freedom*. The epithet 'liberal' is wholly apt. For the voice of a prophetic church in its midst, which speaks with divine authority, loosens the hold of existing authorities and evokes the prospect of liberty. There is a moment of great drama touched on almost in passing in the course of one of St Paul's more prosaic passages about church order. An unbeliever or an outsider wanders into a church meeting, and hears the whole church prophesying. He is 'convicted by all, called to account by all, the secrets of his heart are disclosed; and so falling on his face he will worship God, and declare that God is really among you' (1 Cor. 14:24f.). It is a paradigm for the birth of free society, grounded in the recognition of a superior authority which renders all authorities beneath it relative and provisional. We discover we are free when we are commanded by that authority which commands us according to the law of our being, disclosing the secrets of the heart. There is no freedom except when what we are, and do, corresponds to what has been given to us to be and to do. 'Given to us', because the law of our being does not assert itself spontaneously merely by virtue of our existing. We must receive ourselves from outside ourselves, addressed by a summons which evokes that correspondence of existence to being. 'Where the Spirit of the Lord is, there is liberty' (2 Cor. 3:18). The church of Christ, which professes the authority of God's summons in the coming of Jesus, has the role of hearing it, repeating it, drawing attention to it. In heeding the church, society heeds a dangerous voice, a voice that is capable of challenging authority effectively, a voice which, when the oppressed have heard it (even in an echo or at a distance), they cannot remain still.

The Christian year reminds us of this liberating summons in the season of Advent. Churches with liturgical roots in the lectionary of the medieval West greet Advent with words from Paul's Epistle to the Romans: 'Owe no man anything, but to love one another!' Advent celebrates the dissolution of all obligations in the face of this one great obligation, the love which God commands us for himself and for our fellow human beings, both represented to us in the face of Christ. Of course, the direction of love to the fellow-human suggests and re-founds all kinds of obligation, political, social and personal: 'tax where tax is due, toll where toll is due, honour where honour is due'; but none of these obligations can be acknowledged unless they are first put in their place, authorised and sanctioned by that one commanding obligation. Even the Decalogue, the apostle tells us, finds its unitary centre of reference here (Rom. 13:7–10).

But why do Christians interpret this new command dangerously, as a *challenge* to authority? Why not simply say that the law of love revealed in Christ's coming *justifies* the claims of other authorities, provided they do not overstep their proper limits? That, too, is true; but it can only be a secondary truth. For history has shown us that the penultimate is displaced by the ultimate. Christ the awaited King has come; he has assumed every structure of law and authority under his own command. He *has come*, we say. The predominant tense in Advent is past-perfect, not future. Christians do speak of his coming in the future, of course, especially at Pentecost in receipt of the gift which turns their faces forward; but that future is founded on a prior past tense. Our assertions about freedom, then, have a historical aspect. God has done something which makes it impossible for us any more to treat the authority of human society as final and opaque. He has sent the anointed one to rule; and wherever he has appeared – to John the Baptist by the Jordan, to the sick in Capernaum, to the crowds in Jerusalem as he entered on an ass – he has loosened the claims of existing authority, humbling them under the control of his own law of love.

St Matthew's Gospel stresses one aspect of this almost to the exclusion of all others. Wherever Jesus appeared, the people gathered. Israel gathered; the Gentiles gathered. Luke, too, of course, has his 'crowds' – a centripetal motif which he contrasts with the centrifugal motif of mission. But in Matthew it is not mission that this gathering leads to, but conflict. The community gathering about Jesus unsettles the established centres of community. It does not, Matthew insists, overthrow them; but by disclosing the true source of their authority it disquiets them and attracts their hostility. The existing centres of community no longer have a prescriptive right now that they are confronted with this new and more authoritative one.

St Luke, for his part, focusses the conflict in his account of the early church. Peter defines the Sanhedrin's authority within new bounds when he declares it is incompetent to forbid the church to 'speak of what we have seen and heard' (Acts 4:20). This *de iure* claim quickly becomes *de facto*, as in answer to the young church's prayers God fills it with the Spirit and compels it to speak yet more boldly (4:31). The authorities, meanwhile, are represented in a cautious, defensive posture. They arrest the apostles but use no force (5:26); they heed Gamaliel's advice to wait and see (5:35ff.). Roman authorities, too, are taught to handle the church in a non-committal manner (16:35ff.; 18:12ff.). Civil society surrenders, with hardly a struggle, its notion of religion as a part of the unified fabric of society. When the old unities are defended by popular demonstrations, the authorities coolly warn the conservatives that they are liable to be charged with rioting (19:35ff.)!

Nor is it only civil order that is on the retreat. Family and ethnic religion, too, are threatened by the summons of the gathering church. In Jesus' own teaching the challenge to family solidarity was to the fore. The prophet Micah had mentioned the breakdown of family loyalties among the sorrows of the eschatological age; and in two distinct synoptic sayings Jesus refers to this warning (Mark 13:12ǁ; Matt. 10:35ǁ). In another saying he speaks of a clash between his claim and the claim of family, and in others again suggests that discipleship may involve desertion of the family and neglect of duties towards it (Matt. 10:37; Mark 10:29ǁ; Matt. 8:21ǁ; cf. Mark 1:20ǁ). Within the community of his followers the old family relations are superseded by new ones: the words 'brother', 'sister', 'mother' take on a new reference not given them in the family circle (Mark 3:31–5ǁ; Matt. 23:9).

Freedom, then, is not conceived primarily as an assertion of *individuality*, whether positively, in terms of individual creativity and impulse, or negatively, in terms of 'rights', which is to say immunities from harm. It is a social reality, a new disposition of society around its supreme Lord which sets it loose from its traditional lords. Yet individual liberty is not far away. For the implication of this new social reality is that the individual can no longer simply be carried within the social setting to which she or he was born; for that setting is under challenge from the new social centre. This requires she give herself to the service of the Lord within the new society, in defiance, if need be, of the old lords and societies that claim her. She emerges in differentiation from her family, tribe and nation, making decisions of discipleship which were not given her from within them. Between the old and new lordships, then, is a step she must take on her own, a responsibility for individual decision; and that, too, is a contribution to liberty, not because it creates a vacuum in which the individual is momentarily free from any society – *that* is not liberty! – but because it allows her to enrich society by the gift of her self-donation to it. Individual decision, the act of heart and mind, has now become fully and consciously engaged in and for society; so that society itself is free, being upheld by the free self-giving of each member. A society founded in conversion and baptism is a society unlike all others.

Modern liberalism is not yet ready to leap fully armed from the head that first conceived this thought. This is not yet 'freedom of conscience' in a generalised sense. It is 'evangelical liberty', which is to say, the freedom freely to obey Christ. Yet evangelical liberty has proved to be the foundation of a more generalised freedom, including a certain, not indefinite liberty for misguided and erroneous judgment. The logic which leads from the one to the other is that of St Paul, writing about the 'weaker brother': 'Who are you to pass judgment on the servant of another? It is before his own master that he stands or falls' (Rom. 14:4). Which is not to say that there is no such thing as evident and unarguable error; nor that each person's vocation is so hidden that the right and wrong of what he thinks and does is obscure. It is simply that he has (*has*, not *is*) his own master, and his master is not the ruler who governs him in the order of civil society. There are some judgments that may be evident enough, but which do not fall to the ruler to make. The ruler has to establish a prima-facie interest in the implications for civil order before intervening between any man or woman and the God who commands. That is the correct way of stating the liberal doctrine which is often put misleadingly as 'the separation of law and morality'. There can be no separation of law and morality; but what there can be, and is, is a sphere of individual responsibility before God in which the public good is not immediately at stake.

A perennial observation of political philosophy declares that there are two alternative concepts of freedom, a negative and a positive: freedom *from* control and freedom *for* self-realisation. For the sake of exposition one could characterise the two as the freedom-ideal of slaves and the freedom-ideal of aristocrats. The one consists in the abolition of oppressive constraints, the other in opportunities which are somehow given as a birthright; the one lacks an end beyond the goal of liberation itself, the other never needs liberation to bring its end within reach. If we situate the idea of freedom at the point where the church impacts upon society, we shall understand why neither conception will suffice. An adequate description of freedom has points of affinity with both. The truth in the negative conception is that freedom is a Gospel which, whether they know themselves to be in need of it or not, is addressed exclusively to those who are, in fact, unfree. But it is not a Gospel complete in itself, but only the first moment in the Gospel. The truth in the positive conception is that freedom is evoked and sustained by the command of God. That command does not merely say 'Be free!' and then fall silent; it puts before us a way of freedom, which is the way of Christ's victory.

2. To obey the command of freedom is to put ourselves into the way of opposition to the old authorities. This is made explicit in the baptismal promises themselves: the church is, from the moment of its calling, a suffering church. And the society which forms within the penumbra of evangelical freedom finds itself implicated also in the church's suffering. The form this implication takes is sympathy. It is forced to overcome the contempt which it would naturally feel for those who suffer, the unsuccessful in the world whose cause has been evidently disallowed by God. It sees them, on the contrary, as God's servants, representing in their sufferings both the innocence of God, whom the world judges, and the guilt of mankind, whom God judges. Its sympathies are claimed, then, not only for the pure victims of injustice but for the guilty perpetrators when they incur the recompense of their injustice. Society cannot live without judgment – it is precisely for this reason that political authority persists in its functions until Christ's coming – but it can qualify its judgment by taking the part also of those against whom it acts. Liberal society is marked by a *mercy in judgment*. It knows its own judgment to be under the judgment which God made upon the cross, a judgment that was at the same time a redemption. So it is forced to acknowledge the redemption that God has made in every act of judgment that it performs.

It might have seemed that the only conclusion to be drawn from the proclamation of the cross must be that all human judgment is suspended. We find this suggestion in the dominical teachings of the Sermons on the Mount and Plain ('Judge not, that ye be not judged', Matt. 7:1||Luke 6:37) and of the Parable of the Unforgiving Servant (Matt. 18:21ff.). Most strikingly of all it is expressed in the dislocated story of the woman taken in adultery (John 7:53–8:11), which was to be the subject of much medieval reflection in the mystery plays. 'Let the one without sin cast the first stone': that condemns us, we might think, to a complete abstention from judicial activity, and, inasmuch as governmental activity is judicial, from the work of government as well. It might at the very least have induced the church to develop a non-judicial paradigm for secular government. But that would be to proclaim the cross without the resurrection. In the light of the resurrection the cross is seen to be a judgment which is, at the same time and completely, an act of reconciliation: an act of judgment, because it effected a separation between right and wrong and made their opposition clear; an act of reconciliation, because by this judgment the way was opened for the condemned to be included in the vindication of the innocent. What appears, then, to deprive us of all confidence in judgment actually restores our confidence. Where this merciful judgment has been shown us, we are bound to show it. We too, to the limited extent that we are able, must point to the redemptive unity of judgment and reconciliation.

The sense of an intolerable tension between the demands of human justice and the requirements of divinity was, of course, well known to classical antiquity. We have only to think of the conflict between Creon and Antigone in Sophocles' *Antigone*, or of the Trojan War plays of Euripides, or, for a much more optimistic view, of Aeschylus' *Eumenides*. Yet it is focussed differently from the way in which it emerged in Christian thought later. It is only secondarily a question of the relation of mercy and justice. For justice is confined within the bounds of the polity, and the question is whether the polity can be so securely established as to allow of generosity towards religious claims that might undermine it. In the conflict between Creon and Antigone it is not quite justice that Creon stands for and not quite mercy that Antigone stands for; it is the claims of polity and domestic piety respectively. It needed, first, the philosophical tradition to raise the question of transcendent justice beyond the limits of the polity; and it needed, secondly, the Judaeo-Christian religious tradition to raise the question of forgiveness.

Seneca's *De clementia* allows us to observe the first transition, from a purely positive justice of the political order to a transcendent justice. For Seneca has two accounts of clemency, one directed to the classical political tradition, the other to the philosophical tradition. For the first he draws on Aristotle's 'moderation in respect to anger' (*Nicomachean Ethics* iv.ii), a purely private virtue which has to do with a person's attitude to his enemies. The emperor can and should be clement, Seneca declares, because he is too high-placed to be hurt by the injuries that others would like to inflict upon him. It is hard to see how anyone other than the emperor could be clement in this sense, since clemency consists in 'remission of punishment' which is 'contrary to law', and so requires a sovereign who is above the law to exercise it. We could read Seneca's first account of clemency as a criticism of the Greek city-state: what was a fault in that institution was its vulnerability, which could not allow at the public level the expression of those virtues of generosity and magnanimity which were recognised as fitting at the private level. A secure foundation like the empire permits its head to act with the same freedom and humane spontaneity as the most noble private person would. This was to answer the pre-philosophical Greeks on their own terms.

What happens in Seneca's second account, which introduces the idea of a transcendent justice, is that clemency once more becomes responsible and widely shared. It is now described as 'the inclination of the mind to mildness' in the administration of justice. It may *resemble* pardon or 'compassion' (for

Seneca, the name of a vice) but it is quite different in fact. It aims at a more comprehensive understanding of what justice demands in the situation. Here we find an antecedent of Renaissance 'equity', which complements Seneca's first account by providing another angle from which the immense discretionary powers of the emperor might be justified. Yet how could Senecan clemency encompass the simple fact of guilt? Making allowances can modify our view of another's guilt; but justice alone, however broad its view, cannot encompass forgiveness of the guilty. In making the emperor's discretion more responsible Seneca could not avoid narrowing it, and so by implication excluding the ultimate act of generosity which is the forgiveness of the offender.

Here the religious tradition makes its contribution. The Book of Wisdom (11:21–12:21) argued that God's treatment of Israel, punishing it in small ways rather than with total destruction, displays perfectly both the justice and the mercy of God. Human justice, correspondingly, is to be marked by the same 'humanitarianism' (*philanthrōpia*) as divine judgment. And then the author adds a thought of some weight: we consider God's goodness when we give judgment, and, when we are judged, we hope for his mercy (12:22). That is to say, the human judge dispenses judgment in the knowledge that he will in turn be the object of judgment at God's seat. To philosophical equity, then, is added religious humility, which includes an unwillingness on the judge's part to place himself above the offender whom he judges. But if this thought is treated radically – here is the challenge of Jesus' teaching – how can this allow us to judge at all? Once grasp the significance of divine judgment for Israel, and there will be no more space for human judgment. The search for a way in which mercy may *temper* justice, then, reaches an impasse.

This impasse is resolved only by Christological proclamation. St Paul, as he often seems to do in the Epistle to the Romans, corrects the Book of Wisdom when he finds the goodness of God displayed not in the gradualism of divine judgments in history but in an act of 'decisiveness' (*apotomia*), which has cut branches out from, and miraculously grafted branches into, the tree of his chosen people (Rom. 11:22). In the Christ-act mercy and judgment are united, but in their extremes, not by mutual qualification. Or consider the context which attracted the adulteress story to itself in John 8. 'You judge according to the flesh', Jesus says, 'while I judge nobody'; but then adds, 'Yet if I do judge, my judgment is true' (8:15f.). The judgment Jesus gives is his witness; and it is a famous Johannine paradox that witness and judgment are one and the same thing. This witness itself judges, by dividing mankind into those who accept it and those who reject it. So in Jesus' witness to the Father there is judgment and no judgment at the same time. And that is the meaning of the adulteress story, as it seemed to whoever first placed it in its present position. Jesus' refusal to condemn does pronounce judgment in a way, for her accusers leave the scene convicted. Again, in St Luke's Gospel the parable about making friends with your accuser on the road, which is a warning to show mercy while mercy may yet be shown to you, is prefaced with the question, 'Why do you not of your-selves judge what is right?' (12:57). That is to say, the reconciliation which the parable urges is itself a form of judgment. Those who avoid the lawcourt by set-tling their quarrel have in fact judged for themselves. They have confessed the justice of the cross, where God's mercy has condemned those who showed no mercy, and have made his judgment their own judgment.

The church did not proclaim, then, a posture of hesitant humility, waiting for the judgment of God, but a confident response to the fact of reconciling judgment already given. Out of this sprang a highly dialectical set of ideas about human judgment in which the judicial paradigm for secular government, so far from being displaced by the judgment of the cross, was strengthened. The intelligibility of the secular authorities in the resurrection age depended on their being seen to carry forward what God had set himself to do. The secular function in society was to witness to divine judgment by, as it were, holding the stage for it; the church, on the other hand, must witness to divine judgment by no judgment, avoiding lit-igation and swallowing conflict in forgiveness. Society, respecting the judi-cial function as the core of political authority, must shape its conception of justice in the light of God's reconciling work.

Of central importance in this unfolding dialectic was the church's for-malising of its penitential order into a practice of judgment formed towards the reconciliation of the sinner. The leading New Testament accounts of this practice (in St Matthew's Gospel (18:10–20) and the Corinthian corre-spondence of St Paul (1 Cor. 5:1–6:8)) point to a conception in which the act of exclusion from the eucharist was the sign that attempts to reconcile could go no further. To say that the *form* of this judgment was the search for reconciliation is not to say that the only *purpose* of it was that. It served the church's need to make a public distinction between right and wrong, to 'purge out the old leaven' (1 Cor. 5:6); but this was to be done by con-fronting the offender and inviting him in penitence to join the church in making this distinction. By drawing the line in this way between sin and holiness the church hoped to summon every sinner back to the com-munion table to confess with it Christ's death for sin as the only basis of its righteousness. Should it fail, and the sinner be excluded, the line drawn was a kind of standing invitation to think again and to return.

We cannot ignore the importance for European civilisation of an organ-ised system of moral judgment of this kind, parallel to the justice of the civil order, professing to serve the reconciliation of the wrongdoer. The penitential system could not, of course, replace the secular courts, but it could, and did, shape them. (The much more controversial elaboration of a complete legal system, 'canon law', was, perhaps, the sign of a corruption of the church's authentic institution by the secular; on the other hand, it was also one of the chief means by which the concerns of the church's jurisdiction were assimilated by the secular.) The church asserted its own evangelical justice in society's midst, and society, to a degree, had to defer to it. The tradition that bishops might intercede with magistrates for clemency in capital cases was established remarkably soon after the conversion of the empire. Officers of justice were expected to share the church's hope for conversion and amendment (cf. Augustine, *Ep.* 153). Augustine's commendation of the emperor Theodosius (*City of God* 5.24–6) focusses on his restraint in the face of wrongdoing, 'not to allow impunity, but in the hope of amendment'. And they were expected to bear with the church's pastoral interest in their own wrongdoing: Theodosius, again, was an ideal figure, having submitted to public penance after the massacre of Thessalonica.

Conceptualising the way in which justice could be merciful, however, was not easy. Secular justice could not itself effect what church justice set out to achieve, the repentance and regeneration of the sinner. The more it assumed the role of adjunct reinforcement to the church's pastoral discipline the more it risked concealing, in a mask of piety, the true limitations of its secular role. The clemency of human judgment cannot be like divine mercy, making all things new; it can only be a response to it, founded in humility, gratitude and fellow-feeling with sinners. It can only point, it cannot reach, to the place where justice and mercy are entirely one. When asked to say what that pointing might consist of, Christian thinkers could only reply that it involved the restraint of force to the minimum necessary. An imprecise answer, but one which has had some profound effects in Western civilisation, where the elimination of anything that looked like extravagance in sanctions or penalties has been a consistent theme. To this was added a second strand, which required the interpreter of secular law to bring to the task virtues of mercy and humility in order to discharge the office. There could be no autonomous self-sufficiency about the application of secular justice. If it were not drawn into the operations of the Spirit by the sanctification of the judge, then it would be an instrument in the hand of the devil.

These thoughts were given a more systematic exposition in the sixteenth century, which combined a number of rather heterogeneous elements in the service of Christian 'equity': the scholastic appropriation of Aristotle's *epikeia*, or 'reasonableness'; the Renaissance rediscovery of Seneca's *clementia*; the anti-authoritarian spirit of the medieval mystery plays; the criticism of common law and the attempt to mitigate its severity through Chancery; the Reformers' insistence on the centrality of the cross. We may refer to William Perkins's *Treatise on Equitie*, which is an extended meditation on Philippians 4:5, 'Let your moderation be known to all men. The Lord is at hand.' For Perkins the last part of that text is the clue to the whole. The nearness of divine judgment, final and immediate, demands of us a humble conduct in our justice as we hope to receive mercy from our judge. We who have to execute justice are 'flesh and blood and full of infirmities', and our society cannot endure if we judge one another with the rigour that an angel might use. This is not a reason to abandon justice. There are 'two reprovable kinds of men', Perkins tells us, those who always demand 'mercy, mercy' and those who demand 'the law, the law'. Justice must shake hands with her sister mercy in human judgment – the echo of Psalm 85:10 should not be missed, a text constantly treated in Christian tradition as a symbol of the cross. The prince's laws cannot be 'perfect and absolute' in their justice as God's laws are, and neither can the prince's mercy be perfect and absolute. But the prince, whose justice and mercy are both partial and incomplete, may witness to the union of them which God has accomplished to perfection. These ideas are common to the lawyers and theologians of the age.

Yet it is not from lawyers and theologians that we learn most memorably of this accomplishment of sixteenth-century thought, but from the two great plays of William Shakespeare which take up the same discussion, *Measure for Measure* and *The Merchant of Venice*. They share one theme: the justice which is appropriate to the human community must be 'merciful' – and that precisely for the reason which Jesus gave to the accusers of the adulteress: it must be administered by sinners on sinners. Strict rigour demands a different kind of agent, an angel who, unlike the pseudo-angelic Angelo, would have no infirmities of his own. But if that pure judgment were set loose among us, all would be destroyed, judge and judged alike. 'How would you be / If he which is the top of judgment should / But judge you as you are? O think on that! / And mercy then will breathe within your lips / Like man new made!' (*Measure* II.2). We should, therefore, not invoke it. But this does not mean there is no place for justice in the human community. Even a merciful judge recognises that at a certain point – say, the sin of the mercilessness itself – sanctions must be invoked, even the sanction of death: 'The very mercy of the law cries out / More audible even from his proper tongue: / An Angelo for Claudio, death for death. / Haste still pays haste, and leisure answers leisure. / Like doth quite like and measure still for measure' (v.1). Yet even that is not the final word, for the intercession of the victim Isabella saves Angelo. The reshaping of justice by mercy cannot reach a final settlement, but will always be an ongoing dialectic in which the forgiveness of the wronged has a dynamic effect. When the Duke marries Isabella, it is a sign that his moderate and humane justice cannot stand on its own. The liberal state is sustained by its partnership with the mercy of the church.

3. The possibility of forgiveness, and so of the tempered justice which takes form in the penumbra of forgiveness, rests on the assurance that God's mercy on the cross issued in vindication of created being. Confidence, not timidity, lay at the root of the church's reluctance to punish: a confidence in the security of the humane order, given back as a fit structure for social life in the resurrection of the second Adam. In his risen life the church could rejoice in the humane order that was opened to men and women. The structures of society were expected to defer to, and reflect, this evangelical humanity; it was not permitted to them to embody inhumanity, whether in the name of judgment (for absolute justice would be inhumane) or in the name of social order (for any order which did not conform to human needs would be an artifice) or in the name of transformation (for it would be a demonic transformation that excluded the humanity that God had brought back from the grave).

This is what was meant by the assertions of Christian jurisprudence that society must express and respect, *natural right.* (The use of the singular differentiates this concept from that of subjective *rights* which we discussed on pp. 247f. above.) Under this heading three elements may be singled out: first there is *natural equality*, by which each human being may encounter any other as a partner in humanity, neither slave nor lord. Secondly, there are structures of *affinity* by which homely communities are built; the intimate affinity of the family, the wider affinity of the local community, and the wider affinities still which create our national and cultural homes, affinities of language, tradition, culture and law. Thirdly, there is the *reciprocity* between homes and homelands which permits each community in its own integrity to interact in fellowship with other human beings, thus establishing the communication of a universal humanity, not as an integrated super-home but as a network of meetings and mutual acknowledgments. To these three we ought, of course, to add a fourth: the *creaturely cohabitation* of human and non-human species in a common world. But since this is a challenge which has hardly been faced in a radical way before our own time, I exclude it from consideration here, not because it lacks importance but because our concern is with the Christian political tradition as we have inherited it.

In addressing first the natural right of *equality* we must recognise the difficulty presented to the mind by any thought of equality which goes beyond the purely formal, and uninteresting, principle that people are equal except in respect of things that make them different. A substantial doctrine of equality must be capable of challenging some alleged distinctions which may be supposed to justify differences in the way in which we treat people.

But there is the difficulty: all the social structures of affinity, as we have called them, depend upon differentiated social roles which introduce or depend on inequalities between one person and another. Leadership, responsibility, initiative and authority are forms of differentiation without which a community cannot function or survive; and yet they imply differences not only of function but of power, which apparently frustrate the recognition of equality. It may seem, then, as if we have to choose between an idea of equality that is purely ideal and abstract, an equality before God without social implications, on the one hand, and a totalising egalitarianism that is destructive of all forms of society on the other. In fact what is required is neither of these choices, but a coordination of our understanding of equality with our understanding of the humane forms of community. To have any substance a claim for equality must reflect decisions about what differentiations are constructive and healthy for human existence and what are not. But those decisions in turn reflect a judgment about which differentiations help, and which hinder, the meeting of person with person on a basis of equality, with neither of them slave or lord.

We return at a later stage to the analysis of equality as an idea. Our concern here is with the way in which the presence of the church promoted the conception in Christendom, and we focus this by glancing again at one key test case, in which the church's record is usually held to be at best ambiguous, the ancient institution of slavery. As our account of this is somewhat revisionist, our glance will have to be a little longer than strict proportion would dictate.

A consensus going back to the Carlyle brothers at the beginning of the twentieth century (still far superior to their imitators) holds that the attitude of the patristic church to slavery was a twofold one of inner repudiation and outer acceptance. Troeltsch summarises: 'Inwardly, the nature of the slave-relationship was neutralized by the claims of the ideal. Outwardly, however, slavery was merely part of the general law of property . . . which Christians accepted and did not try to alter; indeed, by its moral guarantees it really strengthened it' (*The Social Teaching of the Christian Churches*, I, p. 132). From this agreed starting-point the debate really only turns on our moral evaluation of the church's performance, some writers adopting a sharply reproving tone, others pleading excuses. A development is made upon the latter position by some apologists, such as Helmut Thielicke, who argue that the church in effect subverted the institution by its attitude (*Theological Ethics*, II, pp. 643–6). This is true, as far as it goes, but, since Thielicke can give no account of how the subversion was effective, we are left wondering whether it really occurred at all. The Carlyle brothers read the Fathers as adding very little to the doctrines of the Stoic lawyers of the second century, who said that slavery was contrary to

Natural Law but yet had real legal standing. They thus projected upon the church a dilemma about the correspondence of society to nature with which it had nothing to do; and they then seemed to find this dilemma expressed in the Fathers' use of the soul–body distinction, which did enter the discussion of slavery from time to time but not in this way (*A History of Mediaeval Political Theory in the West*, 1, ch. 10). The interpretation is vitiated by the ideal–real distinction, expressed in Troeltsch's pair of terms 'inwardly . . . outwardly . . .' We need to be quite clear that Christians believed in an *outward*, social equality, as indeed did some Stoics.

Ancient slavery was an economic institution, or, more correctly, an aspect of an economic institution. The ancient household not only served as a unit of economic consumption, devoted to child-rearing, mutual protection and emotional satisfaction, but was also the most important unit of economic production. The presence of slaves in the household allowed it to expand its labour-power beyond its biological capacity, especially for tasks which required training or education, both of which had to be provided within the household if they were to be provided at all. The slave-market compensated for the absence of what, with unconscious irony, we call a 'labour-market'. The only labour-market the ancient world knew of was in unskilled day-labour. At the same time slavery absorbed into society floating and property-less populations and those dislocated by being captured in war, exploiting their capacities to better effect than if they were day-labourers.

We should note in passing how remote from conceivability in the ancient world was any thought of 'abolition' of slavery as a social reform. That would have required the elaboration of alternative economic structures, and these had yet to be dreamed of. Slavery was abolished in the end, of course – that is, it was replaced with the alternative institutions of the feudal system – but this required centuries of tentative evolution and the influence of the Germanic tribes. When it is casually suggested that the church might somehow have urged the cause of abolition on the ancient world, the assumption seems to be that the course of action followed in the eighteenth and nineteenth centuries against the colonial slave-trade and American slavery could have been anticipated nearly two millennia earlier. But, of course, colonial slavery, though devastating enough, was always a recidivist movement within later Christendom, thriving only on the colonial fringe of European society and never re-entering its mainstream economic organisation. Its abolition was a matter of adjusting the 'colonial system', and did not involve imagining new patterns of organising labour *de novo*, since such patterns were already in place and successful throughout Europe and in parts of North America.

The legal defencelessness of the slave in ancient society was a function of the autonomy of the household. The division between the private and the public realms was so sharply delineated that those whose roles confined them to the former had little or no standing in the latter. The analogy often drawn in the ancient world between slaves and children had a precise legal point as well as a moral one. The wise understood that within the family good relations of loyalty and affection could, and should, be cultivated. The philosophers inculcated the idea that a shared human nature was enough to ground duties of ordinary humanity and to provide a possible basis for friendship; the point was simply that these relations belonged within the domestic walls and had no reflection in legal or political relations outside.

Yet, at the time the Gospel began to conquer the Roman empire the institution was already evolving. The independence of the household was slowly being eroded by the encroachments of law, and restrictions began to be set around the freedom of the paterfamilias in respect of his dependants. Stoic philosophy, meanwhile, found it contrary to nature. In this it was like all political relations. Not only the dominion of master over slave, but that of ruler over people was included in this general critique of social structures; but its tendency was not to propose alternative structures so much as to encourage philosophic distance from them and to encourage the cultivation of truly humane relationships in private. With these evolutions the church was naturally associated. Christian thinkers echoed Stoic doctrines about the artificiality of 'owning' a human being (e.g. Gregory of Nyssa, *Hom. in Eccl.* 4), while Christian emperors strengthened existing protections, limited as they were, and permitted bishops to assume a role in legal emancipation proceedings

But the distinctive Christian contribution does not lie in these agreements with the evolving culture. It lies in the conviction that the church itself was a society without master or slave within it, and that this society of equals was so palpably real that the merely legal and economic relations of master and slave had only a shadowy reality beside it. Lactantius wrote: 'Somebody will ask, "Are there not among you differences between poor and rich, between slave and master? Do you not have social distinctions?" Not at all! Nor would we be able to use the term "brother" to one another if we did not believe that we were all equal' (*Inst. div.* 5.16). Allowing for a degree of apologetic flourish in this statement, we should still be struck by the confidence its author places in the empirical experience of life in the church. There is a man who believes he has demonstrable reality on his side! The church embodies the return of original righteousness to earth, displaying the equality conferred upon all members of the human race in their creation. Equality before God is no longer a hidden, metaphysical reality but a social one.

> For this reason the encroachments of Christianity upon the institution often concern the right of sacramental participation: the question of the freedom of a slave to be ordained without his master's consent was not resolved quickly; partly to prevent the priesthood from being abused as an easy escape-route, popes such as Leo the Great resisted this proposal, and in the high Middle Ages the matter was still being fought out with regard to serfs. But in the matter of admission to monastic communities both practice and law accommodated runaway slaves, while the freedom of slaves to marry without consent was consistently upheld.

Life in the church provided the bridgehead for God's rule over society, and social structures had to modify their demands before the experience and expectation of equality which life in the church fostered. The obverse of the church's witness to the natural right of equality was a witness to the natural right of *humane structures*, which could accommodate and complement the believer's knowledge of his or her own standing before God. For human beings cannot exist in bare, atomic dissociation from each other, or relate only in strictly reciprocal ways as equal to equal, but must group themselves in structures of community which provide them with 'homes' – that is to say, with settings which confer roles that give *penultimate* meaning to their lives. They have to venture upon non-reciprocal roles in order to sustain a context of sufficient cultural richness to nourish and develop them. It is not enough for three people to be together to have a home. Each must be to the other two something which they cannot be for themselves. The nuclear example of this is the family, where one cannot be parent, child and spouse to the same person, nor parent to the person who is parent to oneself.

The history of Christian teaching on the family is instructive. In Jesus' own message the primary note is one of criticism, challenging its claims to religious and social loyalty. In the apostolic age the attempt was made to re-envisage its demands in a manner appropriate to the Gospel. In our own time the family is usually mentioned in the church as in need of support and defence. If we are to justify this shift in perspective (as I believe we may), it has to be in the light of changing cultural circumstances, changing roles for the family in society at large, and, indeed, changes in the internal structure of the family unit. In late-modern Western civilisation families, like all communities of affinity, are threatened by erosion, a process which can only result in rootlessness and cultural impoverishment.

Still, we must not forget that the structures which now need defending have in the past required (and may still require elsewhere) to be challenged. Something similar may be said about other structures of affinity. It seems to me a true Christian instinct to defend small and imperilled cultural and linguistic communities liable to be overwhelmed by the homogenising pressures of Western technological culture. They are, inevitably, an offence to a radicalised concept of equality, since they exist by privileging members and excluding strangers (e.g. by limiting the right of land-purchase to those who speak the local language or were born there). To justify such measures we should reflect on the loss to everyone if all such communities should disappear from the face of the earth. Yet it is undoubtedly true that self-protective, xenophobic communities can be, and often have been, tyrannous to their members and threatening to their neighbours. The church has witnessed to their humane claims, allowing them neither to be overridden nor to be exaggerated.

> So, for example, Francisco di Vitoria's great treatise *On the American Indians* (1539), while strongly defending the autonomy of the native peoples against their European conquerors, also insisted upon the duty of cultural interaction with the Europeans. The form that this interaction was to take was trade; and it has proved irresistible to some modern critics to score cheap points off Vitoria, who was understandably unaware of how easily an unevenly balanced trading relationship could lead to exploitation and dependency. The point Vitoria wished to make, however, was entirely just: the Indians had the right to take their own place among the family of nations without, as was actually happening, being dismembered and engorged; but they did not have the right to immure themselves away from all contact.

This brings us to the third sphere of natural right, which is *universality*. It is the creator's will not only that human beings should live in communities and cultural homes, but that from their homes they should be able to engage peaceably with those of other communities. An ordered world peace is a part of the eschatological hope that Christians derived from Israel, and it has always been cherished. Less clear, however, has been the form which this peaceful order should take. A prominent strand in Christian thinking held that it would be embodied in a unified world-government or, to give it its traditional name, empire. The medieval legal tradition, on the other hand, opened up an alternative, a world order defined not as a universal government but as a unified law. The theological impulse behind the conception of international law is altogether superior to the theology of empire. It acknowledges the claim of Christ to be the sole ruler of the nations, and avoids erecting an icon of world-government in his place; yet his rule is not left as an empty ideal, but is given a clear institutional witness.

It also acknowledges that equality and reciprocity must have the last word in human relations. If human equality is qualified within the various levels of community to facilitate the non-reciprocal relations needed for affinity, it must, nevertheless, be reasserted at the universal level. The proper form that universal humanity should take is not that of a home but that of a meeting. The idea of world-government is inherently unfree, since it elevates non-reciprocity to be the ultimate form in which human beings confront one another. No community should ever be allowed to think of itself as universal. All communities, including the largest, should have to serve the end of equal, reciprocal relations between their own members and the members of other communities. One could put it this way: it is essential to our humanity that there should always be foreigners, human beings from another community who have an alternative way of organising the task and privilege of being human, so that our imaginations are refreshed and our sense of cultural possibilities renewed. The imperialist argument, that until foreigners are brought into relations of affinity within one cultural home they are enemies, is simply a creation of xenophobia. The act of recognition and welcome, which leaps across the divide between communities and finds on the other side another community which offers the distinctive friendship of hospitality, is a fundamental form of human relating. Xenophilia is commanded us: the neighbour whom we are to love is the foreigner whom we encounter on the road.

4. The fourth feature of liberal order, corresponding to the Exaltation of Christ and the presence of the articulate church, is an *openness to speech*. The church created by the act of God at Pentecost was characterised by freedom of address – to God in its prayer, and from God in its prophecy. The Greek noun *parrhēsia*, which the New Testament authors frequently employ to describe the approach of the church to God and the world, has a range of meanings which includes, from time to time, volubility, candour, publicity and confidence. The church's openness of mutual address and the assuming of mutual responsibility itself constituted an address to society, summoning society to admit the free passage of the word of God and to respond to it in its turn in speech.

We are accustomed to think of speech as a fragile plant within the political ecology, and to suppose that when somebody resorts to force the possibilities for speech are at an end. There is a measure of truth in this; force does indeed have the power to extinguish speech. But, confronted with the community empowered by God's speech, force could extinguish speech only at the cost of investing it with the dignity of martyrdom. It proved impossible in the event for Roman society to refuse an answer to the word that was addressed to it with this seriousness. The presence of the Spirit in the church shaped the form society took in the West and, especially between the fourteenth and seventeenth centuries, its relation to government. The conception of the church as a mutually responsive organism inspired the conciliar movement in church polity and the parliamentary movement in civil polity. The connexion between the two can be observed with great clarity in Nicholas of Cusa's *Catholic Concordance*.

Yet here, too, it would be wrong to think (as perhaps Nicholas was tempted to) that civil society could simply assume the character of church order. Just as civil judgments cannot be redemptive (though they can point beyond themselves to God's redemptive judgment), so civil speech cannot be prayer and prophecy. It can only respond to the church's prayer and prophecy in its midst. Western society could not take form in an order of pure speech and discourse such as the great idealists have sometimes projected for it. But it could be an order in which power, judgment and tradition, the staple elements of political authority, have to confront and accommodate the free discourse of a society which has learned to recognise authority also in the word spoken from God by manservants and maidservants (as the prophecy of Joel had said). Any voice within the public realm which could address the community about the common good had to be heard, lest the voice of true prophecy should go unheard. This is one element in what we have come to describe in the West as 'democracy': a civil society in which one person's voice may be heard to the same extent as another's, where responsibilities are not so structured and assigned that deliberation about the public good is confined to a particular class of deliberators. It rejects the classical thesis, common to Plato and Aristotle, that the rationality of a society belongs to a special ruling class within it.

The word 'democracy', of course, only ambiguously expresses this value set on openness to speech, and expresses much besides. Its original sense in the Greek city-states was the rule of the commons. The *dēmos* was a distinct class of society, and democracy was when they took control. The modern conception of democracy, on the other hand, understands the *dēmos* as the sum of all adult members of society and 'democracy' as that state in which everybody has a share in ruling. It is, of course, an impossible conception to interpret literally. The number of those who can participate in ruling is limited, and, in the end, democracy must always

amount to the creation of a special political class which differs from other
ruling classes in other forms of polity not by being representative (for they
too are representative) but by having its representative status clarified by
stringent electoral procedures. 'Democracy' as we use the term is strictly a
fiction, because the idea that we all govern by electing those who do govern
is a fiction. Governing and electing are not the same functions, though election may help secure a strong representative standing for the governing
class. Neither is electing those who govern the same thing as judging them.
Of course, an element of judgment enters into the electorate's decision as
to whether someone is fit to be trusted with further office; but electing is
one thing, judging another. The attempt to give substance to the notion of
universal rule by making elections look like acts of rule or acts of judgment
is not what is important about Western democracy.

The heart of the matter is a principle about access to public deliberations. Rulers, however they are chosen, have been required to be responsive
to a widely based context of public deliberation which is open to the community as a whole. For this reason the archetypal institution in the West is
not the general election but the representative parliament, which, without
itself governing, constitutes a forum of deliberation before which a government is expected to explain itself and expose itself to critical interrogation. There is a great difference between a parliament and a council. The
monarch's council was traditionally devoted to giving the monarch advice.
It made his or her own goals its own, and became a deliberative extension
of his or her own practical reason. The contemporary development of the
council appears to be the 'quango', an acronym correctly glossed (see *New
Shorter Oxford English Dictionary*) as 'quasi-non-governmental organisation' – which is to say that *only in a sense* is it outside government. The parliament, on the other hand, debated with the monarch and the council
about the common good. It was not oriented to the administrative accomplishment of the ruler's tasks, but to subjecting both the conception and
the performance of those tasks to critical discussion in the light of fundamental questions about the common good. But the essence of the parliament was its representativity. It deliberated not on its own behalf but in
response to a wider context of deliberation, open to all, to which it must
be attending carefully.

All four aspects of liberal society – freedom, mercy, natural right and
openness to free speech – have consistently proved more difficult to realise
in effect than to acknowledge in principle. We are especially conscious in
the Western democracies of the limited success of parliamentary institutions in bringing public concerns for the common good to bear on gov-

ernmental deliberations – a success which has, perhaps, become more limited since the late-modern adoption of universal franchise. This may not be the fault of the institutions as such (though they are not beyond improvement) so much as the difficulty of achieving any public concern for the common good at all. The private or sectional good is of more interest to most people most of the time. In Britain the issue that effectively roused public opinion in recent decades was not the dismal state of the prisons, the anarchy over abortion, the frightening growth of technologically induced unemployment, still less such major world issues as the unresolved crisis of Third-World debt or nuclear deterrence; it was the imposition of a new form of local government taxation. When such are the dominant pre-occupations of society, parliament is reduced from its role as a deliberative assembly to its primitive, pre-liberal function as a court of common pleas, defending the interests of particular sectors or persons against governmental impositions. Confronted with such evidence as this we may be inclined to agree with a point made constantly by Gregory the Great, the prime mover of the evangelisation of the English: a society gets the form of government from God that it deserves. Liberal order will presumably never thrive within these islands until the work which Gregory undertook fourteen hundred years ago is resumed!

Modernity and menace

Those thinkers who have converged upon a critique of 'modernity', though diverse in their intellectual provenance as well as in aspects of their diagnosis, have in common the conviction that it is possible to understand the social and cultural phenomena of our times as part of a greater historical totality – one which they date very variously, but always in centuries rather than in decades. What makes life in the late-modern period different – its high level of technologisation, its sexual permissiveness, its voluntarisation of birth and death, its concept of politics as economic management – can all be traced back to seed-thoughts that were present at the beginning of the modern era, and are aspects of a necessitating web of mutual implication.

The 'seed' metaphor helps us to grasp a rather important point about this kind of criticism. It is *late*-modernity, quite narrowly construed as life in the twentieth century, which demands accounting for. Modernity, as an era of several centuries past, comes into play as the explanation rather than as the problem. George Grant, who seems to me to have understood more clearly than other modernity-critics the distinctive character of the enterprise, thought it was the task of philosophy to 'enucleate' the structurally determinative ideas of our time, i.e. trace them from their seed to their flower. The flowering of an idea comes when it assumes a structural role that determines what else may be thought. Its origin is never contemporary with its flowering, nor are its organisational implications apparent to the minds that first conceived it. And so, as historians may point out with perfect justice, the eighteenth century was actually formed far less by the 'Enlightenment' ideas that we associate with it than by the older tradition of religious ideas common to Christendom. Modernity-criticism is less *history* of ideas than 'genealogy'. It is we who find the Enlightenment ideas particularly important, because it is we who have seen them grow to form a matrix within which everything that is to be thought must be thought.

Yet this does not abolish the concept of modernity as a 'totality'. Underlying this idea is an implicit theory of civilisational periods, which have their unselfconscious beginnings and development and attain at length to moments of self-disclosure and self-discovery. Just such an apocalyptic moment, the modernity-critics suppose, has been reached in the mid to late twentieth century, from which we are able to understand the earlier phases of modernity as they did not understand themselves. Modernity is 'our fate'. Its hold on us is ineluctable and denies the possibility of transcendence. Yet in thought the possibility of transcendence is not entirely lost; we can have the slightest intimations of what it might be, or might have been, to be pre- or post-modern, and it is the task of philosophy to garner these and formulate an understanding of the era from such celestial signals as may penetrate its atmosphere. Modernity-critics have been more or less marked by a note of resignation in the face of the all-embracing, all-permeating character of the modern culture. (In sharpest contrast, the self-styled 'postmodernists', finding modernity's root in an epistemological mistake of Descartes, seem all too confident that, once it is seen through, it can be shrugged off.)

It is an enterprise with glaring intellectual risks. The illumination that is shed upon our times may be paid for by a very high level of historical generalisation and selectivity. The interpretative decisions that are reached are unsusceptible of confirmation or rebuttal, and can only be, as it were, ventured. Like all treatments of contemporaneity, the problem of historical perspective may prove insurmountable. Theologians, moreover, will want to be on guard against that twilit owl-of-Minerva melancholy. However all-embracing the constraints of modern thought may be, God has ordained the Gospel of his Kingdom to redeem it and his Holy Spirit to interpret it.

Accepting these cautions, however, there are compelling reasons to proceed to a task at once impossible and inescapable. One is simply the founding moral principle of philosophy itself: *ho anexetastos bios abiōtos.* We cannot choose *not* to wonder at the characteristics of our era. If there are those who do not do so, let us by all means not awaken them. But when philosophical wonder, unbidden, uninvited, sets before us the culture of our time, we can no more suppress it than blaspheme against the Holy Spirit. There is plenty to show that those who do not make an effort to read their times in a disciplined way read them all the same, but with narrow and parochial prejudice. (Many a learned university pundit has become ridiculous attributing to Margaret Thatcher thoughts which belonged to the legacy of Thomas Hobbes!) The disciplines we need are those that good modernity-critics display: to see the marks of our time as the products of our past; to notice the danger civilisation poses to itself, not only the danger of barbarian reaction; to attend especially not to those features which strike our contemporaries as controversial, but to those which would have astonished an onlooker from the past but which seem to us too obvious to question.

There is another reason, strictly theological. To be alert to the signs of the times is a Gospel requirement, laid upon us as upon Jesus' first hearers. This is not an invitation to uncritical apocalyptic enthusiasm. Always the context of history is relevant to the discernment: 'the end is not yet . . . this is but the beginnings of the birthpangs' (Mark 13:7f.). But we are not excused the task of tracing the lineaments of the end-time through the transparency of our own. For each age, no doubt, this task is differently determined, though it will have formal features common to it in all ages. It will include discerning the signs of promise which alert us to the appearance of Christ's future coming; and it will include discerning the form of Antichrist, the warning of ultimate conflict.

We are tempted to think, perhaps, that the concept of Antichrist, capable of such shifting and contrasting applications from age to age, is useless for serious theological analysis; but it is not so. There is no one Antichrist; but in any period of history Antichrist may take shape as one thing, challenging the claims of God's Kingdom with its own. Every candidate nominated for the role of Antichrist has passed away. That does not of itself invalidate any attempt to identify it; for that identification is part of an age's secret knowledge about itself, its interpretation of its own 'today' from the point of view of its today. Of course, those who want never to be out of date will never interpret their today; they will wait until they can read about it in the newspapers. But those whose business lies with practical reason cannot take their place among what P. T. Forsyth called 'bystanders of history'. When believers find themselves confronted with an order that, implicitly or explicitly, offers itself as the sufficient and necessary condition of human welfare, they will recognise the beast. When a political structure makes this claim, we call it 'totalitarian'. More subtle and more pernicious is the same claim made by a society, or by a civilisation, in a series of self-interpreting doctrines which define metaphysical parameters for thought and action (even while innocently disavowing metaphysical intentions).

Behind the disparate appearance of the various critiques of modernity now current, we can detect a theme which recurs persistently. It centres on the notion of the abstract will, exercising choice prior to all reason and order, from whose *fiat lux* spring society, morality and rationality itself. Corresponding to the transcendent will is an inert nature, lacking any given order that could make it good prior to the imposition of human purposes upon it. To put it theologically: the paradigm for the human presence in the world is creation *ex nihilo*, the absolute summoning of reason, order and beauty out of chaos and emptiness. This does not, of course, honour God's creative deed, but competes with it. Faith in creation means accepting the world downstream of the Arbitrary Original, justified to us in being, goodness and order. Voluntarism, on the other hand, situates the agent at the source; it offers a mystical access to the moment of origination, and leads the spirit to the rapture of pure terror before the arbitrariness of its own choice.

With this reorientation the traditional subservience of practical to theoretical reason is reversed, and in the reversal both forms of reason are changed essentially. Those who have made 'technology' the centre of their account of modernity (often under the influence of Heidegger's famous essay 'Die Frage nach der Technik') have meant by the term not the technical *achievements* of the age, but the mutation of *practical reasoning* into 'technique'. Set free from obedience to comprehensible ends of action, confronting all reality as disposable material, its primary imperative is manipulation. Theory, too, is transformed. Instead of being ordered 'erotically', as Grant calls it, to the contemplation of the truth, it becomes a self-posited organising principle, which controls our experience of the world by defining illusion and reality for public purposes.

'Liberalism', too, has been a central theme of modernity-criticism. Here again what is in view is a false posture of transcendence, an illusion that society may be organised on formal principles from the perspective of a 'view from nowhere' (Nagel). This poses the question of how late-modern liberalism, conceived in these terms, may have sprung from early-modern liberalism and Christendom. Some critics assign a crucial role to Christianity in their genealogy of modern concepts. Augustine's use of the category of will; fourteenth-century speculations on God's *potentia absoluta* in creation; the Reformation challenge to the authority of tradition; the elevation of subjective conscience in the technique of the post-Tridentine confessional; all these have been identified as formative impulses which drove modern Western culture towards its present impasse. To explore the connexions further we shall arrange the key elements in a complementary narrative that parallels the narrative of liberal society that we sketched in the preceding section. This helps us understand at once how modernity is the child of Christianity, and at the same time how it has left its father's house and followed the way of the prodigal. Or, to paint the picture in more sombre colours, how modernity can be conceived as Antichrist, a parodic and corrupt development of Christian social order.

1. The point of departure is the moment of 'free' choice, indifferent and indeterminate. We may recall Rousseau's famous dictum, 'Man was born free, yet everywhere is in chains.' The chains he had in mind were the chains not of tyranny but of constitutional social order, and Rousseau announced it as his intention to 'legitimate' them (*Social Contract* 1.1). But what did he mean by 'free'? A state of pre-social and pre-moral individualism, which, for all the seriousness with which he takes society, is still surrounded with an aureole of nostalgia. The roots of this romantic conception lie, in the first place, with the concept of free choice as new beginning, developed by those heterodox Christians called 'Arminian' in the late seventeenth and eighteenth centuries (though the earliest bearers of that name, the Remonstrants of the church in Holland, had little idea of it). They lie also in the myth of the social contract, the tradition of political reflection which achieved ascendency in the two centuries before Kant: society derives from an original free compact of individuals, who have traded in their absolute freedoms for a system of mutual protection and government. So obviously is this myth unhistorical that it is easy to underestimate its hold on the modern mind. It means that society's demands are justified only in so far as they embody what any individual might be expected to will as his or her own good. It rejects the Christian paradox of freedom perfected in service.

Christian thinkers could, perhaps, allow a sense in which the individual must be the measure of the social good; but this would need to be balanced dialectically by the assertion that society is the measure of the individual good. Certainly Christians believe that community is good for individuals; but they do not believe society exists solely to serve individuals' private purposes. Social existence could never be accounted for as an instrument for private purposes, since private purposes have no intelligibility apart from social existence. But the detached pre-social individual becomes the basic unit out of which society is then constructed. Shorn of all prior contexts, natural or social, which could make him intelligible, he makes his appearance as a naked will, a pure originator.

Late-modern liberalism accordingly has followed the path of devaluing natural communities in favour of those created by acts of will. Communities formed by blood-ties or by local contiguities are thought to derogate from freedom, since they cannot be opted into from a position of indifference. It ceases to be a point in their favour that we can see something of ourselves in our natural communities and so embrace them as 'our own'. The very sense of being owned by some family or some neighbourhood is an embarrassment to modern freedom, putting in question the free choice of the will from which our ties and obligations are supposed to find their source. Voluntary societies, on the other hand, have become, as it were, the church, making sacred claims to override blood and neighbourhood. Constituted by agreement, their justice consists essentially in the one principle that what all parties have consented to, is fair. (From this principle derives free-market capitalism, on the one hand, and universal suffrage on the other.) Drained of substance and reduced to procedural standing orders, justice becomes no more than a refinement of decision-making processes, to ensure, and multiply occasions for, free choice. There follows the fissiparation, to which we have referred, of a singular notion of 'right' into a plurality of subjective 'rights'. For the founding element in the modern idea of right is 'that liberty which each man hath to use his own power as he will himself for the preservation of his own nature' (Hobbes, *Leviathan* 14).

2. The first consequence of this reorientation of society to individual wants is that suffering becomes unintelligible. The role society, on earth and in heaven, could play in justifying the individual's suffering is removed. The late-modern age, accordingly, is in perpetual rebellion against the 'pointlessness', the 'waste' of suffering. Compassion for suffering has become an all-important virtue. But our speech has learned to make a fine but important distinction: 'compassion' is not the same as 'sympathy'. Sympathy is the readiness to suffer with others and enter into the dark world of their griefs. Compassion is the determination to oppose suffering; it functions at arm's length, basing itself on the rejection of suffering rather than the acceptance of it. Armed with technical prowess, compassion has been a

world-transforming force in the reshaping of twentieth-century medicine. (On this I have written further in *Begotten or Made?*.)

Suffering has been a great preoccupation, too, with those who debate the issue between faith and unbelief. The link between late-modernity and atheism turns on the fact that suffering cannot be encompassed as a projection of our wills, but is, by definition, the defeat of the will in sheer imposed experiencing. Its order, in so far as we may discern it, is quite alien to any that we ourselves decree. But on the voluntarist hypothesis all order finds its source in our wills. This alien order is therefore unthinkable; the 'cruel' God, whose decrees, whatever they may or may not mean, run athwart of ours, cannot exist, for he lacks the basic ontological conditions of existence. In other contexts, of course, it had been possible to think the creator cruel and still believe in him. Many thoughtful pagans and Gnostics had done so, and had derived from such belief a kind of intelligibility for the torments of the sufferer. In principle a reversion from Christianity to a pagan fatalism was a serious possibility at the Renaissance; Grotius thought he saw it happening in the growth of right-wing Calvinism. But what closed that course to the modern age was a shift in the ground rules of rationality. A discerned universe could contain such a god; a constructed universe could not.

This difficulty was felt above all in understanding punishment. Whose will, after all, is supposed to be satisfied when an offender is sentenced? Not that of the authorities, who willed the threat of punishment only as an instrument of social order, and had no interest in penal right beyond its possible deterrent effect. Not that of the offender, who will be called upon to suffer. Not that of the victim, whose desire to see the offender suffer, if he has one, is something quite other than his will for self-protection, a merely atavistic fury. It was clear to Hobbes (*Leviathan* 28) that his contractual model of society could not support the traditional concept of punishment. No one could have the duty to suffer death, at any rate, without resistance, since no one could be understood to have contracted to forfeit his own life when the whole reason for the compact was, for each person, his own safety. If right derives from compact, and punishment does not, punishment is unsupported by right.

But this argument cannot be restricted to the death penalty. If one could not be supposed to have consented to the loss of one's life, is it any different with the loss of one's liberty or the loss of one's livelihood? Could anyone be supposed to have contracted to suffer, for no personal benefit, at all? What we call 'utilitarian' theories of punishment arising in the late eighteenth century were the philosophers' admission that the notion of

penal right in contractarian thought had collapsed. They came in two vari-
eties. One boldly tried to make suffering transparent *as a means*, by devising penal practices which would justify it by producing moral reform. Such
was the inspiration of the early 'penitentiaries', in which behaviour-
modification came for the first time to be posited as a social technique. The
other admitted that what could not be defended as the satisfaction of all
contracting wills had to be justified as the triumph of the will of the majority. The happiness of the greater number depended upon the suffering of
the few. The ominous significance of this is plain: civil society, supposedly
set apart from the war of all against each by the artifice of compact, breaks
down conceptually into a state of war again. Once society is thought of as
an agreement between competing wills, the cloud of competition never lifts
from it. Each new public endeavour serves as a further action in the war.
To be punished is simply to have lost.

Which is why late-moderns always suspect that a desire to see public
justice done is a subtle and hypocritical way of securing one's own interests. To understand why this suspicion is wrong we must understand the
part that Christian faith played in creating it. Christian liberalism taught
judges to look over their shoulders when they pronounced on fellow-
sinners' crimes. It taught them they were subject to the higher judgment of
God, who would judge mercifully those that judged mercifully. Ex-
Christian liberalism inherited all the hesitancy; but, no longer grounded in
religious humility, it became moral insecurity. From this springs the
haunted unease with which the West views its own agents of law, an unease
which cries out unmistakably from the incessant flow of police dramas that
flicker across our television screens. We have made the detection and punishment of major crime more efficient than any other society, yet we believe
in it less. When we punish we feel we have betrayed somebody. In effect we
betray the unspoken promise that everyone's will for life and freedom will
be satisfied.

3. Natural right was the point at which the transformation wrought by the
abstract will become most quickly apparent. Reconstructed from below, it
was given a new derivation in the interest of individuals in their own self-
preservation. Political association was interpreted correspondingly as a conventional construct to protect individual rights. The effect was to draw the
sharpest line between civil society and the 'state of nature' which was supposed to lie before it and outside it. This undermined the claim that international relations, not themselves part of any civil order, were already
mapped out by unwritten principles of law. By the end of the seventeenth

century Locke and Pufendorf had reduced the scope of natural international law to the general principles of mutual co-operativeness and the right of self-defence. In the next century we find Kant contemptuously dismissing this shadow. All international order, he claims, has to be constructed by treaty. Apart from the act of federation, nations are in a state of war irrespective of whether there are actual hostilities. Since our moral nature abhors a vacuum of principle, our duty is to invent legal and constitutional bonds between peoples, by voluntary federation if possible, though imposed relations may also be valid. The pursuit of 'perpetual peace' depends on constitutional construction (*Perpetual Peace*, AA VIII.354ff.).

Behind this view of international order lay a corresponding view of social order which had seriously embraced the contractarian myth. Order had to be posited. It was a project to be imagined and carried into execution, not a gift to be received and appreciated. It did not arise out of the natural and traditional structures of human community, but was created by political will or by arbitrary social self-determination. Early-modern absolute monarchies developed elaborate and artificial codes of etiquette to govern the relations between subjects and sovereign, conjuring up ersatz titles of nobility which had no real grounding in the communities of the realm and their representation. But the eighteenth-century reaction in the growth of the doctrine of popular sovereignty did not mean that the actual organic structures of society were restored to their place as the determinants of political order; it meant only that political order sought to legitimate itself by an abstract idea of collective will. Yet again, modern conservatism, asserting rights of tradition and continuity, failed in its turn to make contact with the idea of natural right, and, in effect, contented itself with putting revolutionary principles into slow motion. Conservative sentiments played a significant part in generating that belief in history which displaced the generic categories of moral order. Historicism, in turn, subverted the potential which undoubtedly lay within nineteenth-century socialism to recover a communal dynamic of equality, affinity and reciprocity.

Arbitrariness has been the nemesis of modern political order; and consciousness of this has produced a dialectic of construction and destruction, in which successive efforts to found order upon will are overwhelmed by resentment. The modern age invented the concept of 'revolution', a reversion to the state of nature which would begin the whole task of construction *de novo*. In this dialectic a special place has been held by the idea of equality, the only principle of order still held to be natural. Together with the idea of liberty, equality defines the pre-social state of nature, and that gives it a commanding critical role in relation to all other ordering principles. Instead of forming a constructive correspondence with the principle of differentiation within communities of affinity, equality has the role of pulling down whatever walls of differentiation the builders of social order have erected. It is not simply that modern equality is radical, refusing to be compromised with inequality at any point; it is a changed notion altogether, atomic in its vision of human individuals, suspicious of any form of non-reciprocal relation.

> The language of 'equality with inequality', by which social orders were traditionally defended, is unfortunate. It is not inequality that social order needs, but differentiation of role. A sheer poverty of vocabulary has sometimes concealed this distinction. Granted that insight, it could be possible even for radical egalitarians to read older descriptions of social structure sympathetically, understanding that not all talk of subordination (subjects to rulers, wives to husbands and so on) really intends to compromise equality. It can describe a functional precedence that is necessary for a given social purpose in a given social context (like the distinction between 'first' and 'second' violins in an orchestra). But such a sympathetic reading is precluded by a prior commitment to the concept of equality as pre-social. To invoke it is to introduce the state of nature and so precipitate a revolutionary situation, intolerant of all orders that find themselves in place.
>
> Consider, for example, the founding role of equality in relation to the feminism of our day. (Liberal feminists are correct, I think, to remind postmodernist feminists that feminism as a critical movement must be subverted by anti-foundationalism.) Confronted with the demand to recognise the 'full humanity' of women, one would be ill-advised to ask, 'But who ever denied it?' For a series of equivalences carry the argument irresistibly from the fact that women were assigned roles of subordination within various social structures to the conclusion that they were treated as unequal; and then, because equality is a state of nature constitutive for humanity, to the conclusion that their humanity was denied. But historically the important thing to grasp is that this logic, so ineluctable to the modern mind, would have been sheer *non sequitur* to a mind which understood equality in the traditional way. To trace the changes in the concept of equality; to show how the equal humanity of men and women was thought (or failed to be thought) in contexts which embraced a notion of subordination, must be an important task for feminist historiography.

To the disturbing threat of reversion to the state of nature, under which modern social structures have to live, there has been a defensive move: to put in play some form of mechanistic social necessity, which will act as surrogate for the lost objectivity of natural right. The social sciences have arisen to fill this need. Explicitly anti-revolutionary in tendency, appealing to a concept of nature, they have purported to find in social organisations laws that are capable of general enunciation and on which predictions can be built. Yet it is not *natural right* that is evoked, for the 'nature' of which social science speaks is non-teleological, but *natural necessity*, and for that reason social science has the tendency to sound a retreat from political tasks and responsibilities, which now appear too heavy to discharge. We have an example of this in the curious use the politicians make of economics to protect themselves from responsibility. The advice that 'you can't buck the market' has a comforting effect, assuring us that somewhere there exist natural forces which continue to limit our behaviour. It is the same advice, offering the same comfort, when we are urged to entrust the management of our affairs to 'independent bankers', i.e. those who will act according to strict scientific laws without reference to the benefits or harms which must be the concern of political discourse. The reassurance offered is like that of being tossed by Atlantic breakers after we have tied the pilot to the mast. The inhuman rationality of the elements inspires more confidence than the human irrationality of the unfettered will.

4. Modern society has striven to totalise speech. It is no accident of technological luck that late-modernity has become an era of mass communication, but the expression of a deep-rooted philosophical commitment. Those philosophers who have urged that speech is everything, that all social reality is a form of discourse, have, at least, articulated a powerful modern ideal, one which sets us at a far remove from ancient societies which valued the deed more than the word, and thought the warrior, whose deeds came closest to pure action, was the paradigm of human excellence. The warrior appears in our modern culture as, at best, a regrettable necessity, onto which we are driven back only when the sustained will to discourse falters. In all this we can see the continuing impact of a Christian civilisation. Yet there are features of our modern speech which set it apart from the prophetic speech of Pentecost. Our free speech has been drawn into the constellation of the 'state of nature', becoming both egalitarian and competitive.

Within the Pentecostal community prophecy both reinforced and qualified equality. Reinforced, because the prophet, who held no appointed office, could arise from any quarter and either sex. Qualified, because prophecy was a divine visitation, not given to everybody all the time but to be discerned, respected and attended to in silence by the rest of the community. An indiscriminate babel of prophetic speech, St Paul insisted, left no space for the divine speech to be heard, and so subverted true prophecy.

In this way the church modified, but did not discard, the ancient understanding, common to Greek and Hebrew, that wisdom was distributed rarely, its speech to be received by attendant, and therefore dependent, communities of learners. Once again, a different concept of equality came to prevail in modern Europe.

Those who pioneered broadcasting early in the closing century understood themselves to be contributing to 'education'. In this they aligned their aspirations with one of the great Whig ideas. 'Education' was a term which once belonged exclusively to child-rearing; but it expanded its scope to encompass all the activities of study, enquiry and instruction that are indispensable to adults in society. Implied in this reconception of the search for wisdom was the notion that large sections of society are like children, ignorant and in need of bringing up until they are ready to fulfil their calling to participate in the political discussions of their elders. Patronising in a Whiggish way, perhaps, but at the same time radically egalitarian and progressive. It conceived ignorance, like every other inequality, as a problem of social organisation, to be met by social technique. From this perspective it seemed possible to ignore the implications of the rarity of wisdom and of prophecy. Education concerned itself with the task of disseminating information. It was then for individuals to make what use of it their natural or supernatural endowment would allow. But since from a final point of view all were equally educable, from a formal point of view all educated voices counted for the same.

The mistake in this train of thought is one that postmodernism can claim to have identified. There is no 'information' that exists outside of any discourse. The idea of a purely formal task of education is a phantasm. To extract the dissemination of information from the goal of wisdom is to promote a thoughtless knowledgeableness, undercutting the ascetic and reflective disciplines which make wisdom possible. And so our modern organs of communication, which were intended to inform and clarify our speech, distort and corrupt it. The press, which has always advertised itself as the guarantor of free and informed discourse, has become a major obstacle to it – and not by printing photographs of naked princesses, but by amplifying to deafening level the dicta of an unreflective punditry.

Because the normal content of political communication, furthermore, has come to be the conflict of competing wills, speech has lost its orientation to deliberation on the common good and has come to serve the assertion of competing interests. Every form of political organisation, of course, has to be able to negotiate conflicts of interest; ours is remarkable (though perhaps reminiscent of the feudal organisation) in treating the assertion of sectional interests with great reverence. The language in which our ancestors used to speak with a shudder of 'sedition, privy conspiracy and rebellion' has fallen into disuse. 'Demonstrations' aimed at communicating anger or menace, rather than argument or reason, are viewed with complacency as proof of a liberal and open society.

Within the parliamentary system the failure of the deliberative ideal is represented by the institution of the political party, through which all debate is channelled into the service of a conflict between two or more competing constellations of interests. This has built into our expectations the idea that common deliberation is, in effect, no more than a condition of suppressed civil war, Kant's vision of the international system now turned back upon the body politic. When real debates about the common good occur, in which ideas and arguments prove influential and common understandings are formed, we are used to seeing the political machinery of democracy deployed to suppress them, since they threaten the predictability of the party conflict and so, by implication, the legitimacy of its outcome.

A hopeful doctrine still prevails within liberal self-understanding, that equal and opposite irrationalities will, somehow, produce rationality as their Aristotelian mean. There is, unhappily, every reason not to believe this. The competitive communities of discourse do not interact to construct a catholic vision of the common good. They conglobulate into would-be philosophies which are both sectarian in outlook and totalitarian in pretension. The term 'ideology' best expresses this meltdown of the democratic idea, an implosion of critical speech upon itself in which the very act of speaking is crushed beneath the ambitions speech is made to serve. Self-posited speech destroys its own point and collapses into silence. The silence in which Communist lands lived for half a century was born of a philosophy in which speech was taken captive to will. Those who have not had a Communist phase in their history cannot afford to ignore the fact that this fate arose from within the logic of the modern project itself. It was the fruit of a political culture habituated to speech but impatient of its disciplines, no longer believing in a Gospel word that could authorise and renew it.

We have sketched a pair of counter-interpretations of modernity, the one characterising Western society as a *bene esse* of political order which bears the narrative of the Christ-event stamped upon it, the other characterising it as a *pessimum esse*, displaying the emergence of the pseudo-Christ of the last times. What is achieved by this confrontation? We need to be clear that, although we have assigned certain trains of thought to 'early-modern' and 'late-modern' self-understandings, the point is not to identify a golden age of liberalism back in the sixteenth century and to set it in contrast with a current age of debased bronze. Not only is the practice of these two eras much more ambiguous than the constellations of ideas to which they have given birth; the ideas themselves in their historical contexts are more mixed up with other ideas, of other periods and provenances, than this attempt to schematise can allow for. The material of a civilisation's mind is so complex that our readings of it must be heuristic, provisional, subject to changes of perspective. The exercise, then, must be treated as an exploratory one, useful for bringing certain key features into view. Its function is to sharpen our understanding of the decisions we now face; to interpret the two loves which made two cities in a form appropriate to our historical situation, clothing the *amor Dei ad contemptum sui* and the *amor sui ad contemptum Dei* in the dress of those Euro-American truisms and aspirations which we drank in with our mothers' milk. So the counter-narratives are not alternative but complementary. To the extent that one does justice to key aspects of our civilisation, the other does too. To describe a crossroads, a moment of decision, is what all civilisational description must aspire to in the era between Ascension and Parousia, the era mapped out from its beginnings by the seer of Patmos. This is precisely the failure of the epoch-critical pretensions of postmodernism: resting complacently on the assumption that the postmodern era is *fait accompli*, it fails to bring us to decision. Inevitably this leads back to a secret celebration of the features of modernity it claims to have transcended, like a midnight feast on smuggled goodies hidden beneath the bedclothes.

Epilogue

Te decet hymnus in Sion, et tibi reddetur votum in Ierusalem . . . Ad te omnis caro veniet. The memorable opening of the Requiem Mass in the Tridentine tradition, drawn from Psalm 65, teaches us that the 'rest' to which Christ's faithful are called through death is no calm, philosophic contemplation, but a busy political affair. It is the rest of a city that has laid down its arms and turned to the tasks of cohabitation and to the celebration of worship. As the church performs its eucharist for the life now ended, it keeps before its eyes the civic character of its destiny. For no destiny can possibly be conceived in the world, or even out of it, other than that of a city. It is the last word of the Gospel, as it is of the New Testament: a city that is the heart of a world, a focus of international peace; a city that is itself a temple rather than possessing a temple, itself a natural environment rather than possessing a natural environment; a city that has overcome the antinomies of nature and culture, worship and politics, under an all-directing regime that needs no mediation; a city that has the universe within it, and yet has an 'outside' – not in the sense of an autonomous alternative, but of having all alternatives excluded, a city with a Valley of Hinnom, which does not, therefore, have to carry within it the cheapness and tawdriness that have made all other cities mean.

'The hope in which the Christian community has its eternal goal', remarked Barth in a famous aside, 'consists . . . not in an eternal church but in the *polis* built by God and coming down from heaven to earth' ('Christian Community . . .', p. 19). It is a true statement, but in need of some qualification, for it fails to acknowledge the political character of the church itself, veiled and hidden in the time of its pilgrimage, yet always present in its witness to the Kingdom of God. The church never was, in its true character, merely the temple of the city; it was the promise of the city itself. (Perhaps Barth's failure to develop this explains the character of his own political theology as a magnificent, but incomplete, beckoning movement.) If the Christian community has as its *eternal* goal, the goal of its pilgrimage, the disclosure of the church as city, it has as its *intermediate* goal, the goal of its mission, the discovery of the city's secret destiny through the prism of the church.

One last word about this intermediate goal will add to all that we have said so far some compass-bearings for what remains to be said within the scope of a Christian political ethics. Political ethics has to carry forward into detailed deliberation the principle established by political theology: authority is reordered towards the task of judgment. Judgment itself must be explored, and here is the occasion for a theological analysis of the notion of 'justice'. Here, too, arise questions of a constitutional kind about the relation of various governmental tasks to the judicial tasks, questions about the judicial, legislative and executive 'branches' of government, for example. Then the other elements of political authority have to be examined, in order to show how their claims may be brought to support the practice of judgment rather than to limit it. In the case of power, the broad lines for this task have been well laid down in theological tradition: the so-called 'just-war theory' of the sixteenth century was a sustained and exemplary attempt to reconceive, and in reconceiving to discipline, the most naked of all acts of governmental power as an ancillary to the task of jurisdiction. In the case of tradition, the architecture of a Christian doctrine of society has yet to be established, though, of course, many component parts have been discussed often and well. The task as I conceive it is to distinguish the various types of communication which frame communities: locality, economic intercourse, education, family affection. Each of these has its proper claims on the political order, and requires its own measure of deference; otherwise the governing authorities will be drained of their legitimacy. Yet none of them is autonomous; none dictates terms to the others or to government.

But, to conclude the present task, we let our thoughts rest on the eternal goal. What are the conditions, under God's sovereign disposition, for its realisation? In the first place we should notice the name of this city yet to be disclosed, with which the church claims hidden identity and which the state represents iconically. It is 'Jerusalem', 'Zion'. Neither church nor state can claim to inherit this name unless they have learned to recognise those who bear it originally and of right. The church's mission was, from the beginning, not only to the Gentiles – the *polis* – but to Israel. It was called to wrestle Israel, like the angel at the brook Jabbok, for the sake of Israel's own vocation. How can the church be clothed with Israel's name and vocation if the possessor of that vocation is remote from it? *Quam olim Abrahae promisisti et semini eius*: the hope of the Christian dead lies in the triumph of Abraham's seed.

> Whatever may be the symbolic significance of the events of 1949 and 1967, about which it is appropriate to remain open-minded, these events cannot possibly disclose any meaning for the salvation of the world if they yield only a defensive, exclusive and militarily oppressive nation-state. Those who love Israel and Jerusalem cannot be content with an empty prophecy-fulfilment motif at this point, but must wrestle for the soul of Jerusalem, which is the peace that flows from it to encompass all other nations. The angel struggling by the Jabbok must struggle still.

In the second place, the heavenly Jerusalem is disclosed through an act of judgment – so important an act, that John of Patmos described it twice under different aspects: as an act of war performed within history by the Christ and his martyrs against the Antichrist, his prophet and their legions (19:11–20:3); and as an act of judicial declaration performed by God the Father against his primal adversary (20:11ff.). It is an act of judgment that determines both history and ontology. It closes history, in the sense that history is composed of the witness of the faithful against infidelity, but it does not in any sense close time. It brings to clarity the unity of being and dissipates the appearance of ultimate difference. It is the founding act of a new creation, which is also a new political history, one which does not require repeated and continual acts of judgment but which unfolds out of that decisive one. Here, then, will be the community that 'judges not', because all judgment has been given. Here is the community for which power and possession are one and the same: power not *put forth* from time to time to defend or secure possession, but simply inhering in possession, so that possession is power and power is possession, the city existing in the throne and the throne in the city, with temple and wall alike swallowed up into one focus of perfect sovereignty.

Thirdly: we speak now of *possession* rather than *tradition*. In the fragmented cities of *this* history, possession of political identity arises only through the act of tradition, the transmission of the common goods of the society from one generation to the next. Yet even in this history tradition goes beyond mere diachronous transmission, and takes on the character of a synchronous sharing, a passing-round of goods among contemporaries rather than a handing-on. The final realisation of a civic identity can occur only as past generations, who have handed on their goods and identity to later generations, are restored to be full sharers again. The monstrous inequity of generational succession is that all our possession becomes a kind of robbery, something we have taken from those who shared it with us but with whom we cannot share in return. 'Abraham and the prophets are dead', said Jesus' opponents, rather snappishly (John 8:52), as though uncomfortably reminded that their status as Abraham's descendants meant being quite sure that he was dead and remained so. The secret guilt which infects every culture's thoughts about its ancestors, and which in ours has fuelled the famous 'quarrel' of the moderns with the ancients – and now (good Lord!) produces 'post'-modernity – must be overcome. The resurrection of the dead makes equal and reciprocal sharing. It is the condition of true politics.

And so, too, of political theology. The church will frame its political witness with authenticity, avoiding the characteristic evils of abstract idealism and colourless assimilation, when it stands self-consciously before that horizon and confesses that it looks for the resurrection of the dead and the life of the world to come.

Bibliography

The following standard abbreviations are used for series:

ANCF   The Ante-Nicene Christian Fathers, Grand Rapids, 1975.
CCSL   Corpus Christianorum, Series Latina, Turnhout, 1953.
CSEL   Corpus Scriptorum Ecclesiasticorum Latinorum, Vienna, 1866–.
FTC   Fathers of the Church, Washington, D.C., 1946–.
LTF   Library of the Fathers, Oxford, 1843–.
NPNF   The Nicene and Post-Nicene Fathers, Grand Rapids, 1975.
PL   Patrologia Latina, ed. J.-P. Migne, Paris, 1844–.

Aeschylus, *Eumenides* in *The Oresteia*, tr. R. Fagles, Harmondsworth, Penguin Books, 1977.
Ambrose, *Epistles*, tr. M. M. Beyenka, FTC 26.
   De officiis (*On the Duties of the Clergy*), NPNF ii.10.
Ambrosiaster, *Quaestiones veteris et novi testamenti*, ed. A. Souter, CSEL 50.
Arendt, H., *Between Past and Future*, London, Faber, 1961.
Aristotle, *Nicomachean Ethics*, tr. J. A. K. Thompson, Harmondsworth, Penguin Books, 1955.
   Politics, tr. T. A. Sinclair, Harmondsworth, Penguin Books, 1962.
Arquillère, H. X., *L'Augustinisme politique*, Paris, Vrin, 1955.
Augustine, *De baptismo* (*On Baptism*), NPNF 1.4.
   City of God (*De civitate Dei*), tr. H. Bettenson, Harmondsworth, Penguin Books, 1972.
   Contra Faustum (*Reply to Faustus the Manichæn*), NPNF 1.4.
   Enarrationes in Psalmos (*Expositions on the Book of Psalms*) Vols. 1–6, LTF.
   Epistulae 1–82 (*Letters*), tr. W. Parsons, FTC 12, 20, 30.
   In Iohannis evangelium tractatus (*Tractates on John*), NPNF 1.7.
   De perfectione iustitiae (*On Man's Perfection in Righteousness*), NPNF 1.5.
   De sermone Domini in monte (*Our Lord's Sermon on the Mount*), NPNF 1.6.
   Sermons, tr. E. Hill, ed. J. E. Rotelle, in *The Works of Saint Augustine*, Vol. iii, Parts 1–10, New York, New City Press, 1990.
   De spiritu et littera (*On the Letter and the Spirit*), NPNF 1.5.

Bibliography

Barker, E., *Social and Political Thought in Byzantium*, Oxford, Clarendon Press, 1957.

Barth, K., *Ethics*, tr. G. W. Bromiley, Edinburgh, T. & T. Clark, 1981.

'The Christian Community and the Civil Community' in *Against the Stream*, London, SCM, 1954.

The Christian Life, tr. G. W. Bromiley, Edinburgh, T. & T. Clark, 1969.

Church Dogmatics, tr. G. W. Bromiley and T. F. Torrance, Edinburgh, T. & T. Clark, 1956–62.

Church and State, tr. R. G. Howe, London, SCM, 1939.

Berman, H. J., *Law and Revolution*, Cambridge, Mass., Harvard University Press, 1983.

Bernard of Clairvaux, *De consideratione (On Consideration)*, tr. V. Anderson, E. Kennan, Kalamazoo, Cistercian Publications, 1976.

Boff, L., *Saint Francis: A Model for Human Liberation*, London, SCM, 1982.

Bonino, J. M., *Towards a Christian Political Ethics*, Philadelphia, Fortress Press, 1983.

Book of Common Prayer, Episcopal Church USA, 1979.

Brettler, M. Z., *God is King*, Sheffield, JSOT Press, 1989.

Brunner, E., *Justice and Social Order*, tr. M. Hottinger, London, Lutterworth Press, 1945.

Buber, M., *The Kingdom of God*, London, Allen and Unwin, 1967.

Calvin, J., *Institutes of the Christian Religion*, tr. F. L. Battles (Library of Christian Classics), London, SCM, 1961.

Carlyle, R. W. and Carlyle, A. J., *A History of Mediaeval Political Theory in the West*, London, W. Blackwood, 1909–28, reprinted 1962–70.

Chrysostom, John, *On the Statues*, ANCF 1.9.

Clark, J. C. D., *The Language of Liberty*, Cambridge, Cambridge University Press, 1994.

Clark, S. L. R., *Civil Peace and Sacred Order*, Oxford, Clarendon Press, 1989.

Cranz, F. H., 'Kingdom and Polity in Eusebius of Caesarea', *Harvard Theological Review*, 45 (1952), 47–66.

Cullman, O., *The State in the New Testament*, London, SCM, 1957.

Cyprian, *De ecclesiae catholicae unitate (On the Unity of Church)*, ANCF 5.

Dante Alighieri, *Monarchy and Three Political Letters*, tr. D. Nicoll and C. Hardie, London, Weidenfeld and Nicolson, 1954.

Davies, W. D., *The Gospel and the Land*, Berkeley, University of California Press, 1974.

Day, J., *Psalms*, Sheffield, JSOT Press, 1990.

Eliot, T. S., *The Idea of a Christian Society*, London, Faber and Faber, 1939, 1982.

Ellul, J., *Anarchy and Christianity*, tr. G. W. Bromiley, Grand Rapids, Eerdmans, 1991.

Les Nouveaux Possédés, Paris, Fayard, 1973. Eng. tr. *The New Demons*, The Seabury Press, London, Mowbray, 1975.

The Technological Society, tr. J. Wilkinson, London, Jonathan Cape, 1965.
Epistle to Diognetus in *Early Christian Writings*, tr. M. Stainforth and A. Louth, Harmondsworth, Penguin Books, 1987.
Eusebius of Caesarea, *Laus Constantini* (*Oration in Praise of Constantine*) and *Vita Constantini* (*Life of Constantine*), NPNF II.1.
Forrester, D., *Theology and Politics*, Oxford, Basil Blackwell, 1988.
Frost, R., *Complete Poems*, London, Jonathan Cape, 1951.
Gelasius I, *Epistula ad Anastasium Imperatorem* in ed. E. Schwartz, *Publizistische Sammlungen*, Paris, Garnier, 1963.
Gierke, O., *Natural Law and the Theory of the State*, tr. E. Barker, Cambridge, Cambridge University Press, 1958.
Giles of Rome, *De potestate ecclesiastica* (*On Ecclesiastical Power*), tr. A. Monehan, Lampeter, Mellen, 1990.
Grant, G., *English Speaking Justice*, Notre Dame, University of Notre Dame, 1974.
Technology and Empire, Toronto, House of Anansi, 1969.
Time as History, Toronto, Canadian Broadcasting Corporation, 1969.
Gregory the Great, *Moralia in Iob* (*Morals on the Book of Job*), Vols. 1–3, LTF.
Regula pastoralis (*The Pastoral Rule*), NPNF II.12.
Gregory of Nyssa, *Homiliae in Ecclesiasten* in *Opera* Vol. v, Leiden, Brill, 1962.
Gregory VII, *Correspondence of Pope Gregory VII*, tr. E. Emerton, New York, Columbia University Press, 1932, 1990.
Grotius, H., *De iure belli et pacis* (*On the Right of War and Peace*), tr. F. W. Kelsey, (Classics of International Law), Oxford, Clarendon Press, 1925.
Guardini, R., *Letters from Lake Como*, tr. G. W. Bromiley, Edinburgh, T. & T. Clark, 1994.
Gutiérrez, G., *The Power of the Poor in History*, tr. R. R. Barr, London, SCM, 1983.
Theology of Liberation, tr. C. Inda and J. Eagleson, London, SCM, 1988.
The Truth Shall Make You Free, tr. Matthew J. O'Connell, Maryknoll, NY, Orbis Books, 1990.
Hauerwas, S., *After Christendom*, Nashville, Abingdon Press, 1991.
Against the Nations, Minneapolis, Winston Press, 1985.
'A Pacifist Response to *In Defence of Creation*' in ed. P. Ramsey, *Speak up for Just War or Pacifism*, Pennsylvania, Pennsylvania State University Press, 1988.
Hauerwas, S. and Willimon, W. H., 'Why *Resident Aliens* Struck a Chord', *Missiology*, 19 (1991), 419–29.
Heidegger, M., *The Question Concerning Technology and Other Essays*, tr. W. Lovitt, New York, Harper and Row, 1977.
Hobbes, T., *Leviathan*, ed. R. Tuck (Cambridge Texts in the History of Political Thought), Cambridge, Cambridge University Press, 1991.
Honecker, M., *Einführung in die theologische Ethik*, Berlin, de Gruyter, 1990.
Honorius Augustudunensis, *Summa gloria*, PL 172.
Ignatius of Antioch, in *Early Christian Writings*, tr. M. Stainforth and A. Louth, Harmondsworth, Penguin Books, 1987.

Isidore of Seville, *Sententiae* (*Sentences*), PL 83.

James of Viterbo, *De regimine Christiano*, ed. H. X. Arquillere, Paris, Beauchesne, 1926.

Jeremias, J., *The Eucharistic Words of Jesus*, tr. N. Perrin, London, SCM, 1966.

John of Damascus, *Oratio de imaginibus* (*On Images*), tr. F. H. Chase, FTC 37.

John of Paris, *De potestate regia et papali* (*On Royal and Papal Power*), tr. J. A. Watt, Toronto, Pontifical Institute for Mediaeval Studies, 1971.

John of Salisbury, *Policraticus*, tr. C. J. Nederman (Cambridge Texts in the History of Political Thought), Cambridge, Cambridge University Press, 1990.

John Paul II, *Laborem exercens*, London, Catholic Truth Society, 1981.

Jonas of Orleans, *De institutione regia* in *Les Idées politico-religieuses d'un évêque du ixe siècle*, ed. J. Reviron, Paris, J. Vrin, 1930.

Jüngel, E., *Christ, Justice and Peace*, tr. D. Bruce Hamill and A. J. Torrance, Edinburgh, T. & T. Clark, 1992.

Justin Martyr, *Apology*, tr. T. B. Falls, FTC 6.

Justinian, *Novellae*, ed. R. Scholl and G. Kroll, 8th edn, Berlin 1963.

The Kairos Document: Challenge to the Church, Grand Rapids, Eerdmans, 1986.

Kant, I., *Perpetual Peace* in *Political Writings*, ed. H. Reiss, tr. H. B. Nisbet, (Cambridge Texts in the History of Political Thought), Cambridge, Cambridge University Press, 1991.

Lactantius, *The Divine Institutes*, tr. M. Francis McDonald, FTC 49.

Lampe, G. W. H., *A Patristic Greek Lexicon*, Oxford, Clarendon Press, 1961.

Leo XIII, *Libertas praestantissimum* in *The Papal Encyclicals*, ed. C. Carlen, McGrath Publishing, USA, 1981.

Luther, M., *On Secular Authority*, tr. J. J. Schindel and W. I. Brandt, in *Luther's Works*, Vol. XLV, Saint Louis, Concordia Publishing House, 1962.

Sermon on the Mount, tr. Jaroslav Pelikan, in *Luther's Works* Vol. XXI, Saint Louis, Concordia Publishing House, 1956.

McDonagh, E., *The Gracing of Society*, Dublin, Gill and Macmillan, 1989.

MacIntyre, A., *Whose Justice? Which Rationality?*, Notre Dame, University of Notre Dame Press, 1988.

Maritain, J., *Christianity and Democracy*, London, Bles, 1945.

Man and the State, Chicago, 1952.

Markus, R. A., *Saeculum*, Cambridge, Cambridge University Press, 1988.

Marsilius of Padua, *Defensor pacis* (*Defender of the Peace*), tr. A. Gewirth, University of Toronto Press, New York 1956, Toronto 1980.

Milbank, J., *Christianity and Social Theory*, Oxford, Basil Blackwell, 1990.

Mishnah, tr. H. Danby, Oxford, Clarendon Press, 1933.

Murray, J. Courtenay, *The Problem of Religious Freedom*, London, Geoffrey Chapman, 1965.

Nicholas of Cusa, *Catholic Concordance*, tr. P. E. Sigmund, (Cambridge Texts in the History of Political Thought), Cambridge, Cambridge University Press, 1991.

O'Donovan, J. L., 'Historical Prolegomena to a Theological View of Human Rights', *Studies in Christian Ethics*, 9 (1996).

Theology of Law and Authority in the English Reformation, Atlanta, Scholar's Press, 1991.

O'Donovan, O., 'Augustine's *City of God* xix and Western Political Thought', *Dionysius*, 11 (1987), 89–110.

Begotten or Made?, Oxford, Clarendon Press, 1984.

'Karl Barth and Ramsey's "Uses of Power"', *Journal of Religious Ethics*, 19 (1991), 1–30.

On the Thirty-Nine Articles, Exeter/Carlisle, Paternoster, 1986.

'The Political Thought of the Book of Revelation', *Tyndale Bulletin*, 37 (1986), 61–94.

Resurrection and Moral Order (2nd edn), Leicester, Apollos, 1994.

Origen, *Exhortation to Martyrdom* in ed. Koetschau, *Origenes Werke*, Vol. 1, Leipzig, Hinriches, 1899.

Homiliae in Numeros in ed. W. A. Baehrens, *Origenes Werke* (Die griechischen christlichen Schriftsteller der ersten drei Jahrhunderte), Leipzig, Hinriches, 1921.

Overall, John, *Convocation Book* (1606), Oxford, Library of Anglo-Catholic Theology, 1844.

Perkins, W., *Treatise on Equitie* in ed. I. Breward, *William Perkins* (Courtenay Library of Reformation Classics), Appleford, The Sutton Courtenay Press, 1970.

Rad, G. von, *The Problem of the Hexateuch*, tr. E. W. T. Dicken, Edinburgh, Oliver and Boyd, 1966.

Rashdall, H., *The Theory of Good and Evil*, London, Oxford University Press, 1924.

Rawls, J., *A Theory of Justice*, Oxford, Clarendon Press, 1972.

Raz, J., *The Morality of Freedom*, Oxford, Clarendon Press, 1986.

Rousseau, J., *Social Contract*, tr. M. Cranston, Harmondsworth, Penguin, 1968.

Sanders, E. P., *Jesus and Judaism*, London, SCM Press, 1987.

Schmitt, C., *Political Theology*, tr. G. Schwab, Cambridge, Mass., MIT Press, 1985.

Schweitzer, A., *The Quest for the Historical Jesus*, tr. W. Montgomery, London, A. & C. Black, 1954.

Seneca, *De clementia*, ed./tr. J. W. Basore, in *Moral Essays* (Loeb Classical Library), London, Heinemann, and Cambridge, Mass., Harvard University Press, 1928, 1985.

Shakespeare, W., *The Complete Oxford Shakespeare*, Oxford, Clarendon Press, 1986.

Simon, Y. R., *Philosophy of Democratic Government*, Notre Dame, University of Notre Dame Press, 1951.

Skinner, Q., *The Foundations of Modern Political Thought*, Vols. 1 and 11, Cambridge, Cambridge University Press, 1978.

Soelle, D., *Christ the Representative*, tr. D. Lewis, London, SCM, 1967.

Political Theology, tr. J. Shelly, Philadelphia, Fortress Press, 1974.

Sophocles, *Antigone*, tr. E. F. Watling, Harmondsworth, Penguin, 1947.

Strauss, L., *Natural Right and History*, Chicago, University of Chicago Press, 1953.

Suarez, *Defensio fidei catholicae adversus Anglicanae sectae errores*, ed. J. B. Scott (Classics of International Law), Oxford, Clarendon Press, 1944.

Thielicke, H., *Theological Ethics*, tr. W. Lazareth, London, A. & C. Black, 1968.

Thomas Aquinas, *On Kingship* (*De regno*), tr. G. B. Phelan, Toronto, Pontifical Institute of Mediaeval Studies, 1949.

    Summa theologiae, ed./tr. T. Gilby, London, Eyre and Spottiswoode, 1963–.

Tierney, B., *Religion, Law, and the Growth of Constitutional Thought 1150–1650*, Cambridge, Cambridge University Press, 1982.

Tolstoy, L., *War and Peace*, tr. L. Maude and A. Maude, Oxford, Oxford University Press, 1991.

Troeltsch, E., *The Social Teaching of the Christian Churches*, tr. O. Wyon, London, Allen and Unwin, 1931.

Ullmann, W., *Medieval Political Thought*, Harmondsworth, Penguin Books, 1965.

Vitoria, F., *De potestate ecclesiae, De potestate civilii* and *De Indis* in eds. A. Pagden and J. Lawrence *Vitoria: Political Writings*, tr. J. Lawrence (Cambridge Texts in the History of Political Thought), Cambridge, Cambridge University Press, 1991.

Weil, S., *The Need for Roots*, London, Routledge and Kegan Paul, 1949.

William of Ockham, *Breviloquium* (*A Short Discourse on Tyrannical Government*), ed. A. S. McGrade, tr. J. Kilcullen (Cambridge Texts in the History of Political Thought), Cambridge, Cambridge University Press, 1992.

    VIII quaestiones, tr. A. J. Freddoso and F. E. Kelley, in 2 Vols. (Yale Library of Medieval Philosophy), New Haven, Yale University Press, 1991.

Witte, J., *Christianity and Democracy*, Boulder, Col., Westview, 1993.

Wright, N. T., *The New Testament and the People of God*, London, SPCK, 1992.

Wyclif, J., *De civili dominio*, ed. R. L. Poole, London, Wyclif Society, 1885–1904.

Yoder, J. H., *The Christian Witness to the State*, Newton, Kan., Faith and Life Press, 1964.

    The Original Revolution, Scottdale, Pa., Herald Press, 1971.

    The Politics of Jesus, Grand Rapids, Eerdmans, 1972.

    The Priestly Kingdom, Notre Dame, University of Notre Dame Press, 1984.

York Tractates (*Tractatus Eboracenses*) in *Libelli de Lite* Vol. III, ed. E. Dümmler (Monumenta Germaniae Historica), Hanover, Hahn, 1897.

Index of scriptural references

16:10, 57
16:12f., 57
16:13, 76
20:8, 57
20:26, 57
22:9, 75
22:11, 76
25:2, 57
29:4, 57
29:14, 57
31:4–9, 57

Isaiah
1:17, 39
1:21, 59
1:26f., 39, 59
2:2–4, 66
2:3, 48
2:6–22, 68
2:15–17, 70
3:13, 38
5:22f., 39, 59
7:14, 118
9:1f., 175
10:5–19, 69
13:1–14:27, 71, 84
13:2–6, 68
14:1, 85
14:12–15, 70
18:1–7, 69
19:16–25, 71
20:1–6, 68
21, 154
21:1–10, 84
23, 154
23:15–18, 70, 71
24:21–3, 66
24:23, 34
27:12, 85, 178
28:11, 70
29:1–8, 43
32:1, 59
33:17–19, 85
33:22, 35
40:2, 43
40:27, 39
42:1–9, 84, 134
42:10f., 48
43:15, 34
43:21, 48
44:5, 85
44:2–45:8, 84
44:28, 55
45:8, 37
46:13, 37
49:6, 71
50:10, 80

51:1, 80
51:5ff., 37
51:7, 80
52:7, 34
52:13, 77
53:3, 77
53:4, 77
53:10, 77
53:11, 77
56:1, 37
56:1–8, 80, 186
56:2, 63
56:3, 85
56:4, 63
56:6, 63
57:19, 132
59:16, 55
60:3–11, 243
61:10, 37
62:1, 37
63:3, 127

Jeremiah
1:5, 68
1:8, 65
2:8, 60
2:9, 38
3:14, 178
4:19, 76
5:27f., 59
6:11, 76
7:3–15, 43
7:16, 77
7:22, 63
7:31, 63
8:8, 63
8:21, 76
9:1, 76
10:7, 34
10:10, 34
10:21, 60
10:25, 66
15:10–21, 77
17:14–18, 77
18:18, 60
20:7–10, 77
20:11, 36
21:2, 60
21:9, 78
22:3, 38
22:15, 38
22:24, 78
23:5f., 38, 124–5
24, 69, 78
25:9, 55, 69
25:12, 69
25:15–26, 69

26:1–24, 40, 65
26:20, 78
27:1–29:32, 83
27:6, 69
28:6–9, 65
29:1–23, 69, 83
29:7, 83
29:10, 69
29:19f., 78
30–3, 70
31:29f., 79, 124
31:33ff., 80
32, 70
33:15, 38
36, 78
36:11–19, 59
36:26, 79
38:2, 78
39:11f., 69
45:4f., 79
46:2–12, 68
46:26, 71
48:47, 71
49:6, 71
49:27, 71
49:39, 71
50, 84
50:4, 85
50:34, 66
51, 84
51:59–64, 69

Lamentations
3:24, 45

Ezekiel
7:26, 60
14:17, 60
18:1–20, 79
18:1–31, 124
20:11, 63
20:12, 63
20:25, 63
20:33, 34
26:1–28:19, 70
28:13–18, 70
29:1ff., 69
29:13–16, 69, 71
30:20–6,. 69
31:1–31, 69
34, 124–5, 202
34:23f., 85
36:23, 71
36:25–7, 80
37:15–23, 85
37:24–8, 85
45:9, 38

Index of scriptural references

Index of subjects

Arianism, 197, 199
Arminianism, 275
Ascension, 142–6, 161–2
atonement, 60, 125–30, 136–7
authority, 16–21, 30–2, 90, 128–9, 138–41, 146,
158, 167–8, 249, 252–4; of the church, 105–6,
123, 150, 159–62, 176, 179, 187, 189, 217;
divine, 32, 49, 81, 124, 142, 252 (see also
Kingdom of God/divine kingship);
epistemological, 30, 89; in Israel, 78, 117;
Jesus', 88–90, 103–4, 105–6, 137–8, 145; of
law 65; political, 20, 31–2, 46–7, 65, 94,
126–7, 147–9, 211–12, 233, 234–42, 286; of
Scripture, 15–16, 21–2, 45, 211

baptism, 172, 173, 177–8, 186, 190, 191, 223, 256

Calvinism, 170–1, 178, 187, 196, 210–11, 212, 213,
234, 238, 277
Christendom, 91, 165, 193–211, 211–26, 228,
230–2, 233–4, 236, 240, 243–4, 249, 251, 264,
272, 275
Christology, 115–18, 120–30, 133, 135–6, 161, 163,
197–8, 210, 258 (see also Jesus)
church, 158–92, 193–211, 244–6, 250–1, 252,
259–60, 261, 265–6, 268, 285–8; relation to
Israel, 23–7, 130–3, 162–3, 166, 178, 201,
220–1, 286–7 (see also Christendom;
ecclesiology; ecumenism)
church–state relations (see Two Kingdoms etc.)
civil religion, 2, 4, 7, 224–6
common good, 17, 238–9, 270–1, 282–3, 287
communitarianism, 223
conscience, 7, 80
covenant, 37, 45, 49, 60, 61, 63, 64, 68–9, 72, 79,
132, 180, 185, 220
creation, 14, 19, 26, 32, 181–2, 186, 274

David (King of Israel), 43, 53, 55, 57, 61
deliberation (practical reason), 13–14, 274
demons, 93–5, 114, 198

ecclesiology, 123, 150–1, 155, 158–92, 174, 231; in
the church's history, 170–1
ecumenism, 169, 172, 174, 176–7, 246
empire, 70–2, 86–8, 90, 154–5, 232, 236, 267–8
Enlightenment, 4–9, 14, 244, 272
equality, 262–6, 267, 268, 279–80, 281–2
Erastianism, 163–6, 187, 208, 210, 218
eschaton/eschatology, 52, 124, 128–9, 146, 147,
150, 152–3, 155, 165, 176, 178, 182, 198, 202,
203, 205, 211, 245, 247, 267, 273, 284–8
eucharist, 173, 180–1, 186, 191, 259, 285

faith, 113–18, 132, 223
force, 30, 233, 268–9
freedom, 18, 18, 30, 32, 126–7, 184–5, 250, 252–6,
268, 275–6, 279

government, 46, 52, 65, 72–3, 148–9, 156–7, 169,
222, 225, 231, 234–8, 246, 249 (see also
Christendom; authority, political)
grace, 128, 164, 210, 223

history, 9–12, 14, 19, 21, 27–9, 153–5, 203. 205–6,
229–30, 243–4, 246, 251–2, 272, 279, 287 (see
also eschatology); Israel's idea of, 39–40
Holy Spirit, 122, 161–2, 169–71, 176, 177, 178,
187–91, 214, 218, 234, 249, 268–9, 273

idealism, 9–10, 121, 214, 288
Incarnation, 82, 134–6, 164, 232, 236 (see also
Jesus)
individual, 73–80, 248, 254–5, 275–6, 278, 280
international order, 32–4, 66–73, 235–6, 267–8,
278–9

Jesus: crucifixion and resurrection of, 128–30,
136–46, 153, 178–83, 197, 256–7; infancy
narratives, 117–18; relation to John the
Baptist, 91, 113, 134, 137–8; relation to
Gentiles, 99–100; relation to zealots, 95 (see
also Kingdom of God)

Index of names and authors

Index of names and authors

Justin Martyr, 111

Kant, I., 6–7, 14, 101, 279, 283
Knox, J., 240

Lactantius, L. C. F., 217, 265
Leo the Great (Pope), 266
Leo XIII (Pope), 227
Locke, J., 279
Luther, M., 148, 165, 196, 209, 213

McDonagh, E., 250
MacIntyre, A., 18
Marcellus of Ancyra, 126
Maritain, J., 219–20
Markus, R. A., 7
Marsilius of Padua, 207–8, 239
Marx, K., 14
Milbank, J., 249
Moberly, R. C., 128

Nagel, T., 274
Nicholas of Cusa, 239, 269
Niebuhr, R., 121, 227

O'Donovan, J. L., 249
Origen, 126, 186, 216
Overall, J., 163–6

Palgrave, F. T., 160
Parker, M., 170
Perkins, W., 261
Plato, 148, 209, 269
Ponet, J., 240
Priscillian of Avila, 200
Pufendorf, S., 279

Rad, G. von, 41
Ramsey, P., 20–1
Rousseau, J. J., 275

Sanders, E. P., 97, 101, 113
Schmitt, C., 4
Schweitzer, A., 120
Seneca, L. A., 257–8, 260
Shakespeare, W., 261
Soelle, D., 17, 126
Sophocles, 257
Strauss, L., 18, 228
Suarez, F., 210

Tertullian, Q. S. F., 25
Theodosius I (Emperor), 160, 201, 260
Thielicke, H., 263
Thomas Aquinas, 234, 239
Tokés, L., 250
Tolstoy, L., 121
Troeltsch, E., 263–4

Valentinian I (Emperor), 199
Valentinian II (Emperor), 160, 199–200
Varro, M., 7
Vitoria, F., 26, 210, 237–8, 267

Weil, S., 222
Wilberforce, W., 185
William of Ockham, 46, 208, 239, 248
Witte, J., 225
Wright, N. T., 83, 104
Wyclif, J., 26, 41, 165, 214, 235, 240

Yoder, J. H., 151–2, 223–4